Richard Jaeckel,
Hollywood's Man
of Character

ALSO BY GENE FREESE

*Jock Mahoney: The Life and Films
of a Hollywood Stuntman* (McFarland, 2014)

*Hollywood Stunt Performers, 1910s–1970s:
A Biographical Dictionary*, 2d ed. (McFarland, 2014)

Richard Jaeckel, Hollywood's Man of Character

GENE FREESE

McFarland & Company, Inc., Publishers
Jefferson, North Carolina

ISBN (print) 978-1-4766-6210-7
ISBN (ebook) 978-1-4766-2249-1

LIBRARY OF CONGRESS CATALOGUING DATA ARE AVAILABLE

BRITISH LIBRARY CATALOGUING DATA ARE AVAILABLE

© 2016 Gene Scott Freese. All rights reserved

No part of this book may be reproduced or transmitted in any form or by any means, electronic or mechanical, including photocopying or recording, or by any information storage and retrieval system, without permission in writing from the publisher.

Front cover: Richard Jaeckel as Lt. Martin Quirk in *Spenser: For Hire* (Warner Bros. Television/ABC/Photofest)

Printed in the United States of America

*McFarland & Company, Inc., Publishers
Box 611, Jefferson, North Carolina 28640
www.mcfarlandpub.com*

Table of Contents

Preface   1

Introduction   3

1. Sunrise   5
2. Soldier Boy   15
3. The Actor   36
4. The Working Man   53
5. The TV Cowboy   70
6. Sailing Along   87
7. Riding the Wave   107
8. Choppy Surf   129
9. Back to the Beach   168
10. The Sun Sets   178

Filmography   185
Chapter Notes   189
Bibliography   191
Index   195

Preface

I have always had an interest in the unsung character actors of motion pictures and television. These are the legions of performers whose faces are instantly more recognizable than their names. I made it a point to learn these names and track the careers of many of those who so ably filled the ranks. As a youngster I was under the false impression that anyone appearing with regularity on TV must be rich and, if not famous, at least enjoying a financially sound Hollywood lifestyle. I couldn't have been more wrong, especially during the era of classic post–World War II films and television that brought these familiar faces into America's homes. The majority of these character types were blue collar workers living paycheck to paycheck and sometimes never knowing when that next check was coming.

No one epitomized a prolific hard-working character actor quite like Richard Jaeckel. This dependable craftsman worked seemingly non-stop for the better part of fifty years, gaining a solid reputation for his portrayals of heroes and villains, cowboys and soldiers, cops and robbers, and everything in between. Every time I saw his name mentioned in print by colleagues, there were positive words and memories. Many remarked on his agelessness and friendly nature, as well as the fact he was a dedicated family man with a tremendous sense of pride in his work. There was certainly something unique about Jaeckel, a positive energy that radiated off the screen. It's called charisma. The biggest stars have it. Yet Jaeckel was comfortable as a character man, perhaps even a little reluctant at playing make believe for the movie camera when his heart was really that of a seafaring sailor or a team-player athlete. He is perhaps best known for garnering a Best Supporting Actor Oscar nomination for the film *Sometimes a Great Notion* (1970), with his death scene in that picture arguably the most famous in Hollywood history. Digging into his background, I discovered he was in actuality a bit of a trailblazer on two fronts. He was one of the first actors to exercise regularly with weights and one of the earliest surfers on the West Coast. Due to his career longevity and bedrock presence, it's time he rose above the anonymous ranks to be singled out for his fine contributions to Hollywood history and popular culture.

In researching his life I accessed all the available books, newspaper, magazine, and Internet articles as well as the files on Jaeckel and his films at the Motion Picture Academy Library. I perused his Merchant Marine record that was provided by the United States Coast Guard and studied the golden days of Muscle Beach and West Coast surfing. Most importantly, I corresponded with nearly seventy individuals from Jaeckel's life who were willing to share their memories of their friend and co-worker. This is the first scholarly book on the life of character actor Richard Jaeckel.

Introduction

For several decades, popular character actor Richard Jaeckel was an ageless wonder. The well-muscled, baby-faced blond seemed to be the living embodiment of *The Picture of Dorian Gray* and a testament to the wonders of the California beach lifestyle. While everyone around him aged, the 5'7", 170-pound Jaeckel stayed eternally youthful and energetic.

Jaeckel made his film debut at age 16 in *Guadalcanal Diary* (1943) and played tough cowboys and macho military roles with authority for the next fifty years in familiar fare such as *Sands of Iwo Jima* (1949), *3:10 to Yuma* (1957), and *The Dirty Dozen* (1967). His résumé reads like a blueprint for classic tough guy cinema, as he regularly lent support along the way to legendary actors John Wayne, Glenn Ford, Burt Lancaster, and Lee Marvin. Jaeckel was a staple in the hard action films of directors Robert Aldrich and Don Siegel and received a Best Supporting Actor nomination for *Sometimes a Great Notion* (1970). He also earned critical accolades for memorable performances in *The Gunfighter* (1950), *Come Back, Little Sheba* (1952), and *Town Without Pity* (1961). He graced many a low-budget drive-in picture with his familiar presence and was a staple of TV cop dramas such as *Spenser: For Hire* playing stern but understanding police superiors. He finished his career as a regular cast member on the immensely popular TV series *Baywatch*. Fellow character player L.Q. Jones recalls him as "a good man" and "one hell of an actor,"[1] a recurring theme among those who knew and worked with him.

As a child of the 1970s, it was hard for me to watch television and not be aware of Jaeckel's gutsy presence and smiling visage.

Character actor Richard Jaeckel flashes a winning smile in a 1952 Paramount publicity picture.

He was everywhere on films and TV, and each time his perpetually tan, unlined face popped up on the screen, my dad would point him out and comment that the man never aged. It was uncanny how young he looked. Jaeckel had been playing battle-tested soldiers on screen since the early 1940s and it appeared he might be doing so for eternity with nary a gray hair on his head. Jaeckel apparently had secret access to the Fountain of Youth. I later learned that his high energy display, charismatic personality, and strong physical presence were the result of a lifelong devotion to physical fitness and outdoor exercise that enabled him to realistically charge the enemy long after others had hung up their combat helmets. It made sense.

What didn't make sense was when I found out in June of 1997 that Jaeckel had passed away at the relatively young age of 70. What happened? In my eyes this sparkplug tough guy with the thousand-watt smile was destined to reach a hundred years, just like exercise guru Jack LaLanne who was then approaching the age of 90 and still going strong. Coincidentally I was in the midst of traveling to California to meet actor William Smith for a series of gym workouts. My trip was briefly postponed because of the loss of Smith's close friend. Smith and I never did speak much about Jaeckel, but the affection for his pal was obvious and heartfelt. Smith said it was skin cancer that had metastasized into the bones, and I remember thinking how ironic given Jaeckel's love of the outdoors.

Any endeavor to dig deeper into Jaeckel involves the review of dozens of classic film and television shows from Hollywood's Golden Age. Thanks must be extended to the many generous people who answered my queries. Nancy Ellen Barr was especially helpful in getting me started while Robert Fuller's response and praise for my previous book on his friend Jock Mahoney opened the flood gates. Chris Poggiali contacted Robert Phillips, and surfing legend Walter Hoffman put me in touch with the invaluable Tim Lyon. It should be apparent that Jaeckel had several friends and touched countless lives. Following then is the story of Richard Jaeckel, one of Hollywood's greatest character actors.

1

Sunrise

R. Hanley Jaeckel was born in Long Beach, New York, on October 10, 1926. Initially, the letter "R" didn't stand for anything but lent a sense of prestige to the youngster whose family was a vital part of the Jaeckel fur dynasty. He was called Hanley around the home by his parents, Richard Jaeckel and Millicent Hanley. His Pennsylvania-born mother was a Broadway stage actress in popular fare such as *Tea for Three*. His New York City–born father had been a champion athlete on the wrestling mats at Williams College. There was an older half-sister, Dorothy (born 1904), from his father's first marriage. Hanley's grandfather was Hugo Jaeckel, a German immigrant who became an internationally known furrier. He founded his business in 1863, initially specializing in sables and chinchilla coats but expanding to include mounted rugs of African lions, Bengal tigers, and polar bears. Hugo brought his sons into the business, which became known as H. Jaeckel & Sons, Incorporated. Hugo's sons Richard, H. Francis, and Walter thrived in Manhattan's furrier district with their first shop located on Fifth Avenue.

In 1930 the Richard Jaeckel family resided in the city to be close to the Jaeckel Building located at 16–20 West 32nd Street. They had a summer home in Long Island, an estate which in all likelihood was the boy's actual birthplace. For his first movie studio publicity he would list the nearby area of Long Beach, New York, because of his fondness for the ocean and the images the name conveyed of California's own sunny and fun-filled Long Beach. The Long Island home is where the four-year-old Hanley showed his first interest in navigating water. On a day that the family's governess, Elly Kratzenstein, had off, Hanley's mom was shocked to see her son by himself heading a rowboat down a canal in back of the home. His action garnered a swift spanking as a warning. It wasn't enough. Hanley launched the boat twice more that day despite the resulting punishment for each infraction. The boy was fascinated by floating on the water and would be for the remainder of his life.

When it came to schooling, Hanley was raised in private institutions the likes of the Harvey School in White Plains, New York, a rural boys-only college prep program that prepared young students for the finest eastern universities. He spent a significant portion of his childhood travelling in Europe on business trips and family vacations to Paris, France, and Wiesbaden, Germany, where his grandfather Hugo retired. His dad Richard was known within the industry as "the Flying Dutchman" for his frequent air travel to Europe and was said to have popularized the white fox fashion craze. The boy's first language learned was French, and his first English sentences were formed with a French accent. Upon his return home he found himself in no less than a half dozen playground fights because of his hoity-toity verbiage. He was quick to lose the French and began to take on a tough Brooklyn accent around other kids for his own sense of survival and place. While much of America struggled through the Great Depression, the Jaeckel family continued to live somewhat comfortably even as they saw their business sales plummet. The rich continued to buy extravagantly while the middle class stopped buying furs completely. It's an interesting beginning for a boy who would later become known for his blue collar work ethic. "I'd rather be a spoiled child than a spoiled adult," he told the *Motion Picture and Television Magazine*.

In 1934 the family settled in Los Angeles, California, where the Jaeckel fur business attempted to flourish amongst the Hollywood elite with a new location on the Sunset Strip. The senior Richard Jaeckel routinely sold furs to the likes of Marion Davies, Mary Pickford, and Gloria Swanson. Hollywood columnist Louella Parsons became a friend of Millicent and the two families often celebrated Christmas together. Parsons once bought the boy a toy gun. The youngster did his best to fit in with the crowd at Bancroft Junior High, downplaying his background and partaking in every sport he could. From a very young age he was already playing football with boys ten years older than himself. He was extremely active with Boy Scouts of America and spent four years at YMCA summer camps getting dirt beneath his nails. He continued to have a great interest in the sea and began reading and collecting nautical books and ocean-related items. Dick Tracy and Superman comics also ranked high with him, as did the sports page of the daily newspaper. He grew to dislike the name Hanley and preferred to go by what his new school friends called him: "Jake." He never mentioned his family's background to his pals.

When he was ten years old, Jaeckel's mother Millicent fell off a horse and her back was badly injured. She spent a lengthy period of time in a body cast. The injury threw the Jaeckel house into a state of disarray. When Jaeckel asked the family servant Sam Wong about a fast-approaching Thanksgiving dinner, he was told there currently were no turkey plans. The youngster set about rectifying that situation, and less than a week later produced a bird for the cook to prepare. Jaeckel had entered a newspaper subscription–selling contest and won despite a late start. He did so well selling door to door that he was awarded over 55 pounds of turkey, so much that he was able to donate the other birds to four needy families. It's a fine example of his drive, focus, and determination; traits that would endear him in the future to filmmakers and casting directors.

Jaeckel could have been given anything within reason by his mother, but he requested that she reward him with a weekly allowance of only fifty cents. This was fine with Jaeckel, who didn't wish to flaunt his ability to buy things in front of his friends. He was more than willing to work for his own money, first helping out at a local drugstore. When he learned that some of his buddies were getting two dollars a week from their parents, he told his mother that she could bump his allowance up to that amount and he'd be okay with it. At the age of ten his mother did present him with a gift of a Springer Spaniel. Jaeckel was fond of the dog, but after a year the dog became ill and had to be destroyed. Jaeckel was stoic about the loss of his pet. His mom soon suggested they pick out another dog, but Jaeckel told her he wasn't interested. The loss had hit him hard but he learned to deal with it in his own low-key fashion. It wouldn't be his only loss of great significance in these formative years.

Jaeckel's grandfather Hugo Jaeckel died in March of 1939. His son Hugo, Jr., became the president of the business while Jaeckel's dad Richard, Sr., advanced from the head of sales to become the vice-president. The added responsibility began to weigh heavily on Jaeckel's father, who had been described by *The New Yorker* in 1932 as "remarkably youthful looking" and "vigorous" despite then being in his early 50s. The senior Richard Jaeckel was born in 1880 in New York and distinguished himself as a young man with his athletic accomplishments. Strong and robust at the time, he won the Stevens Cup Wrestling Trophy in 1905 while representing the New York Athletic Club. Although Jaeckel's father had been an amateur wrestling champion, by 1940 he was battling ill health as he approached the age of sixty and dealt with a decreasing list of fur clients and an increasing list of daily stressors.

The elder Richard Jaeckel suffered a number of heart attacks and was bothered by a nervous ailment. In February of 1940 he fell more than one hundred feet from his brother's 73rd Street New York City apartment and landed on an apartment's front canopy, suffering minor injuries to his head. It was a miracle he wasn't killed. Brother Walter Jaeckel told the press it was an accident and that the senior Jaeckel slipped while opening a window. Detective Thomas Neary reported nothing suspicious in his investigation of the accident, but events of the following year suggest that the fall was a premeditated suicide attempt. In July of 1941 Richard Jaeckel booked himself into the Stearns Hotel on Michigan Avenue in Chicago, Illinois, under the name Richard Jones. This time there was no canopy to stop him. He jumped to his death from the twenty-first floor, his body narrowly missing pedestrians on the sidewalk. He was wearing a suit jacket over his pajamas and had a black sleeping mask on his forehead. He had left a note in his room addressed to the hotel manager supplying his correct name.

At this late juncture it is difficult to pinpoint the exact reasons for Richard Jaeckel's suicide outside of a combination of mental strain and deteriorating physical health. It was later revealed he was in arrears on alimony payments and insurance premiums for his two previous wives. His 82-year-old uncle Adelbert Jaeckel had committed suicide by putting a gun to his head the previous year.

The loss of his father had to be a tremendous blow to the fourteen-year-old son. It was something Jaeckel never talked about publicly, and he became known for his extreme privacy with the press on family matters. By all indications the youngster put on a brave face in front of his valued friends, throwing his energies ever further into sports and a succession of odd jobs washing dishes, stocking shelves, or parking cars to prove he was his own independent man. There was the promise of an inheritance in waiting when he became of age, but Jaeckel was not one to sit around his new residence at the Beverly Hills Hotel waiting for that day to arrive.

In his early teens Jaeckel enrolled as a student at the famous Hollywood High, now calling himself Richard Hanley Jaeckel. He blended in nicely with the beautiful coeds and the handsome beach boys, many of them children of people working within the film industry in some capacity. Classmates among the approximately 2500 students included future actors Stuart Whitman, Larry Pennell, and Richard Long. The Hollywood High Sheiks offered a diversified program of intramural sports. An all-around athlete, Jaeckel was decent in football, basketball, swimming, diving, and track despite a relatively small stature (under 5'7" and about 145 pounds). He was undiscouraged going up against opponents with longer legs and greater arm reach, proving his worth by competing as a lightweight boxer where he matched up well pound for pound with other amateurs. Jaeckel and pals such as Zane W. De Arakel made sufficient use of the gym equipment at the Hollywood YMCA. Jaeckel also adopted a daily regimen utilizing an adjustable bar he could jam in any doorway for a succession of chin-ups.

Exercise became a passion. His favored nutritional sustenance during this period were steaks, green salad, and lots of milk in hopes that he would hit a growth spurt and stretch out his height.

When he wasn't in school he was a lifeguard at both Santa Monica Beach and the famed Hollywood Athletic Club on Sunset Boulevard where stars the likes of John Wayne, Errol Flynn, and Johnny Weissmuller took both workouts and libations. Being at the beach was all right with the easygoing Jaeckel, who enjoyed the warm sun on his skin and the crashing waves in his view. Jaeckel told the *Charleston Gazette*, "My mother kept me from being the world's oldest lifeguard. I worked at Santa Monica and was guard at the old Hollywood Athletic Club attempting to keep drunks out of the pool. These guys would tank up then sink like stones in the water."

With Jaeckel lacking a father figure, his mother became concerned about her only son, a young man who was dead set on joining up with the military to fight the Japanese after the bombing of Pearl Harbor in December of 1941. Jaeckel was only sixteen but hounded his mother to let him join the war effort as he graduated early from Hollywood High. She did her best to stall him with diversions as 1942 played out, seeking favors from her popular Hollywood columnist friend Louella Parsons to pull a few strings to get Jaeckel into the mail room at 20th Century–Fox. Jaeckel's mom promised to sign his military induction papers when he turned seventeen in the fall of 1943, and Jaeckel found that fair and agreeable. Besides, the movie studio job paid significantly better than the fifty cents an hour he had been earning as a soda jerk for a local drugstore.

Jaeckel was a bit intrigued by movies themselves, having been a fan of the scary films of Bela Lugosi and Lon Chaney. Columnist Parsons once dropped his name into her column in 1939 regarding his appreciation for the film *The Wizard of Oz*. The technical aspect of filmmaking fascinated him, even though acting held no interest. He had taken drama at Hollywood High only because it was one of his courses. For the next three months Jaeckel enjoyed riding a bicycle around the lot, visiting the various departments and chatting up the actresses who responded to the good-looking towheaded kid with the deep blue eyes and fantastic smile. His mom requested he take an extended trip with her to Mexico prior to enlisting in the military. He was prepared to give his notice at the studio when all his fortunes changed with a car that wouldn't start in February of 1943.

Jaeckel set out to hitchhike home from the studio after a day of work. He had a pickup basketball game scheduled for the evening and was looking forward to playing. Screenwriter Jerry Cady saw Jaeckel with his thumb out as he was leaving the studio and offered him a ride. Cady was currently putting the finishing touches on a World War II script entitled *Guadalcanal Diary*. The story was based on the popular Richard Tregaskis novel and featured a fresh-faced U.S. Marine named Johnny "Chicken" Anderson as one of the supporting characters. Producer Brian Foy had instructed Cady to keep an eye out for a young actor who could play the part. As Cady gave Jaeckel his ride, he realized that the fresh-faced Marine character was sitting in the seat next to him. Arriving at his destination, Jaeckel thanked Cady and shook his hand. The writer could hardly wait to tell Foy.

The next morning Jaeckel was called into Foy's office, thinking that he would be picking up a package to mail off. Upon entering the room he was met by Foy, casting director Lew Schreiber, and the familiar Cady. Foy laid his cards on the table: They were looking to cast the part of "Chicken" Anderson and Jaeckel looked perfect. So many actors had gone off to war already that they were having a hard time casting the film. They had Jaeckel read a little dialogue from the script and liked his delivery. Would Jaeckel take a screen test so that it could be determined if he was deemed ready for the movie camera? It was a lot for a sixteen-year-old kid to absorb.

"I don't know whether I can or whether I would even want to," he recalled saying in the fan publication *Motion Picture and Television Magazine*. "I've always figured actors were for the birds," Jaeckel later elaborated in the studio presskit for *Come Back, Little Sheba* (1952), cringing at the idea of a sportsman like himself having to apply greasepaint. "And besides, what would the guys I know say if they saw makeup all over me? I didn't want to appear ungrateful, but I didn't want to answer Mr. Foy."

A hesitant Jaeckel stalled enough on his answer that Foy suggested he go home and talk it over with his mother, knowing full well that he was underage and they would need parental permission anyway. He was counting on Jaeckel's mom to fill the youngster in on the break he was receiving. Here was the chance of a lifetime being presented and the kid seemingly wanted no part of it. When Jaeckel got home and casually mentioned the meeting to his mother, Foy's plan was set into motion. She told Jaeckel it was an incredible break and urged him to take the test. Even if he got the role, it wouldn't affect his future military plans. Jaeckel reluctantly agreed to be screen tested at the studio.

Jaeckel did his screen test with professional film actors William Bendix, Preston Foster, and Lloyd Nolan, three movie veterans already cast in important roles in the film. During the testing someone fired a shot from a pistol with a full load blank. The noise gave Jaeckel an honestly scared reaction, which he felt helped seal his getting the role of the frightened young Marine. Still, Jaeckel felt uncomfortable with the whole idea of theatricality. He told *The Washington Post*, "I was awful." In reality Jaeckel did have somewhat of a natural acting background, dating back to fantasy role-playing as a boy when he would pretend he was a cowboy or a sailor. The last few years of his adolescence had been spent covering up the fact that he was a child of privilege in front of his pals, then concealing his emotions when it came to his father's death. He was indeed a natural actor and it was only a matter of becoming comfortable in front of the camera.

Veteran assistant director Paul Wurtzel, the son of producer Sol Wurtzel and all of twenty-one years old at the time, was present for the screen test and recalled Jaeckel:

> They were testing all these young actors. He was one of them. His father had just committed suicide shortly before. He was underage and had to have schooling and a welfare worker there. That was a strike against him, but he had the looks and everything; a husky little guy. I don't even remember anyone else. They did two or three tests on him. It only took a couple of days. They signed him.
>
> We became friendly. I knew him over the years, right up to the end when he passed away. He was always down at the beach, always worked out, and stayed in good shape. We had some of the same friends. There was a lady that lived in Malibu on the beach that he was good friends with. Jaeckel would always come by to talk to her. I'd see him there. He had kind of an offbeat sense of humor, always kidding about something. I worked with him off and on over the years on different shows. He did a couple of cop series and did pretty well for himself.[1]

Brian Foy was impressed with the screen test and cast Jaeckel in *Guadalcanal Diary* (1943) as "Chicken" Anderson for $250 a week. The movie would film in Oceanside, California, north of San Diego at the Marine base Camp Pendleton. Some scenes were done at Santa Catalina Island. Jaeckel considered playing a fighting U.S. Marine to be a pre–boot camp experience that would have its own value to him in real life. There was little time for Jaeckel to learn to be a professional actor, but under the direction of Lewis Seiler and the guidance of co-stars Preston Foster, William Bendix, Lloyd Nolan, Richard Conte, Anthony Quinn, Roy Roberts, Ralph Byrd, John Archer, and Lionel Stander, he was in capable hands. A little on-screen nervousness worked well for the character, although Jaeckel instinctively knew that a true Marine would try to hide his fear in front of his buddies.

Sixteen-year-old Richard Jaeckel poses for one of his first publicity photographs for 20th Century–Fox in 1943.

One thing living in Hollywood had done was expose Jaeckel to any number of film actors. He personally despised the ones who hammed it up on screen and put on airs off. He decided he would try to act the exact opposite. When pressed by fan magazines for a favorite actor, he did admit an admiration for pint-sized tough guy James Cagney. Perhaps Jaeckel saw some of that actor's famous pugnaciousness in himself, although it was Cagney's versatility as a song-and-dance man that Jaeckel professed to liking. He told *Photoplay*: "I thought of all the muggers I have watched and I made up my mind that I might not be good, but by gosh I'd be natural. If I couldn't do something without feeling posey about it, I'd tell the director and ask him to let me do it another way. I did, several times, and Mr. Seiler was always swell about it—which helped a lot."

Jaeckel spent the summer pretending he hadn't been one of the stars of a major Hollywood movie. For a time he even returned to the Fox mail room and worked as an extra on the lot as a lark. The major films at the studio that summer had been *The Song of Bernadette*, *Jane Eyre* and *The Gang's All Here*, and it is possible Jaeckel was a nondescript background player on one or more of these. He would not remain anonymous for long. Studio executives who had seen early cuts of *Guadalcanal Diary* began dangling a seven-year acting contract in front of him. Jaeckel quit the mail room job and kept a low profile, not wanting to be tied down to a lengthy commitment. His mom had bought him a '41 Ford, which he promptly traded in for a '36 model that was more his style. He nicknamed the car the Cannonball and enjoyed working on the engine in his free time with his buddy Leo Ross. Jaeckel put the money he made off the auto sale into a savings account.

That summer was spent with his pals and girlfriend doing things a teenager does at the beach and the hamburger stand; cruising the glittering Pacific Coast Highway and the exquisite palm-lined streets. Due to his work ethic he took menial jobs at Bireley's orange juice bottling factory and as a soda jerk. He and a buddy even hitched a ride to Mexico with no more than a few dollars in their pockets. At the time Jaeckel held a curious disregard for his family's money. He was trying to get by on his own. A lawsuit materialized in the Los Angeles court system, filed by his dad's first wife Hazel, going after Jaeckel's insurance money. Studio execs were trying to corral him into an answer, and once again decided to utilize his mom's influence. His paperwork at Fox had listed his address as the Beverly Hills Hotel at 1220 Sunset Plaza and some of the people at Fox had wrongly assumed that his mom was a maid there. They couldn't have been more surprised to find she had her own suite.

Guadalcanal Diary was released in October 1943, days after Jaeckel's seventeenth birthday. It was a superior motion picture and Jaeckel came off as one of the most interesting faces in the film. He's a bit thinner than later audiences are used to seeing him, but his fit, fresh-faced look comes off well beside the established pros. Memorable moments include coughing on a cigarette, reading a letter from his mother, and discovering the first whisker on his chin. He registers as strongly as anyone in the cast and served notice that he was an up-and-coming talent (the fan magazine *Modern Screen* labeled him one of the top stars of 1944). His character Johnny "Chicken" Anderson is deathly scared of war at the beginning of the film but perseveres. Battle experience quickly grows into overconfidence to the point that he foolishly leaves himself open at one point and is shot going for a Japanese sword as a memento. If the film has a serious flaw, it's that Jaeckel not only survives a belly wound but is soon back in action with his unit.

Anthony Quinn (center) and William Bendix (center, right) are among those inspecting young U.S. Marine Richard Jaeckel's first whisker in 20th Century–Fox's *Guadalcanal Diary* (1943). Military roles became Jaeckel's forte in the film industry.

Through the course of the film he becomes a fighter, even utilizing craftiness to stay alive by the picture's close. Jaeckel's character was a testament to the fortitude of the American people and audiences responded to the All-American kid. So did critics and movie executives.

The New York Times noted in its review, "A youngster named Richard Jaeckel is fine as a beardless recruit," while the influential trade journal *Variety* said, "Richard Jaeckel scores as a downy-faced juvenile." *The Los Angeles Times* heralded, "The young lad Richard Jaeckel arrives with much distinction in the role of Private Johnny Anderson, who is sympathetic in his fears, his devotion to his mother, and his determination to be a good soldier." *The Boston Herald* wrote, "There are one or two newcomers, Richard Conte and Richard Jaeckel, who give a good account of themselves," while *The Dallas Morning News* added, "Young Jaeckel's performance is one of the most remarkable in several cinema weeks." *The Pittsburgh Press* called him "an attractive kid and a real find," while *The Lincoln Star* wrote, "Finest work in the film is done by William Bendix, Richard Jaeckel, and Anthony Quinn." *The Washington Post* acknowledged, "Chief interest centers in the characters so contrastingly played by Lloyd Nolan, Preston Foster, William Bendix, Richard Conte, and the unusually capable Richard Jaeckel." *The Spectator* crowed, "The best performance in the film is from an unknown newcomer named Richard Jaeckel." Such praise could swell a young kid's head but Jaeckel downplayed it all, embarrassed at the attention.

Jaeckel's ball-playing buddies such as Doug Stahl, Tom Smith, and Jay Richards actually began to brag about the sudden success of their pal, whom they had previously dubbed the Lotion King for the many skin and hair care products he applied daily. He could often be found at their family's homes, where the moms doted on him for his good looks and manners. He was the guest for many a dinner, which was okay with him. Jaeckel certainly saw the value in such a friendly gesture and would never turn down a free meal when it was offered. During this period he had become acutely aware of the need to put more meat on his bones. Jaeckel started to feel a bit more comfortable about the moviemaking experience after attending the film's premiere with his mom "Milly." Fox couldn't ignore the fact that Jaeckel was now second only to popular pin-up girl Betty Grable at the studio for fan photo requests. They once again dangled a long-term contract in front of him. In retrospect Jaeckel told the *Boston Herald* that *Guadalcanal Diary* was one of his favorite films simply because it was his first movie.

The stout little tough guy continued to impress people at Fox. At the studio gym, Jaeckel wowed the athletic trainers with his skill in the boxing ring, leading them to believe he could have success professionally in that endeavor. However, the only fight Jaeckel wanted was with the Japanese. Despite his sudden popularity he remained determined to join up with the military for real, either the Navy or the Merchant Marine. His mom didn't try to alter his choice but did implore him to delay it six months to make another film and weigh his options. Jaeckel wanted to be a career seaman, an athletic coach, or a Boy Scout counselor, not an actor, but he agreed with his mom's logic. "Very reasonable," he was fond of saying.

Jaeckel's Hollywood success served as an inspiration for aspiring actor Stuart Whitman, who would go on to have a long acting career that included co-starring opposite John Wayne in *The Comancheros* (1961) and being nominated for a Best Actor Oscar for *The Mark* (1961). Whitman also starred in the memorable television western *Cimarron Strip* (1967–1968) as stalwart Marshal Jim Crown. He says of Jaeckel: "I remember he had gone to Hollywood High, and I was going there. So, I got to know him a little. I always admired him. I certainly wanted to know more about how he made it. I remember on Sunset Boulevard there was a drug store and they had an ice cream shop. We'd all go there to get the newspaper to see what shows were going to be made. I ran into him there a lot. Later I got to work with him ... and he got to work with me. Nothing memorable. We did a couple of things together but never shared a scene. He did a lot of films and TV over the years."[2]

Jaeckel was up for a role as Van Johnson's co-pilot in Mervyn LeRoy's World War II film *Thirty Seconds Over Tokyo* (MGM, 1944) and was wanted to replace an ill Hurd Hatfield as the eldest Chinese son in MGM's *Dragon Seed* (MGM, 1944). Jaeckel couldn't see himself playing a Chinaman and turned it down. He felt at times this acting gig could be downright ridiculous. He did agree to appear in another ensemble military film, Fox's *Wing and a Prayer* (1944) (originally known as *Torpedo Squadron 8*), headlining Don Ameche, Dana Andrews, and Charles Bickford and shooting on a real flat top aircraft carrier, the U.S.S. *Yorktown*. No doubt the subject matter informed his decision and Jaeckel welcomed the opportunity to chat up the real seamen working on the film.

Jaeckel plays underage tail-gunner Beezy Bessemer in the Henry Hathaway film and again registers strongly in a story about an aircraft carrier in the South Pacific prior to the Battle of Midway. He has several scenes as a gung ho character eager to engage the enemy. Jaeckel seems so natural in the part because those were his own real-life feelings and it was easy for him to identify with his character. The bulk of the story is spent deceiving the opposition, with the ship's own pilots and gunners growing ever anxious over the Navy's failure to engage the Japanese. Jaeckel survives the battle in the final reel; in future war and western endeavors, he became known for his characters being killed on screen. Most reviews glossed over any direct mention of Jaeckel, although *The Washington Post* did make note of him among the large male cast, saying, "Richard Jaeckel, Murray Alper, Sir Cedric Hardwicke, Irving Bacon, Matt McHugh, Charles Trowbridge, and a long list of others comprise a supporting cast of unusual competence."

MGM was impressed with his performance and offered a deal similar to what Fox had proposed. Talking it over with his mom, Jaeckel realized that the structure of the contract didn't bind him to a full seven years of studio servitude. Several options arose during the ensuing years where the studio could let him go. He agreed to sign a studio contract but opted out of loyalty and familiarity to sign the contract 20th Century–Fox had first offered him. He entered a seven-year deal at Fox earning $500 a week in January of 1944 with the understanding that he would be allowed to join the war effort in the spring. Part of Jaeckel's contract stipulated that he must buy $1000 in war bonds by March 1, 1944. At the end of the seven years Jaeckel could be making as much as $2500 a week. Producer Bryan Foy wanted him to star in *Chips*, a Bill Girard project about a Doberman Pinscher Army dog. The prospective film, also known as *Rip Goes to War*, ultimately was never made.

In the meantime Jaeckel was kept busy fulfilling requests from fan magazines for interviews, feature stories, autographs, and photo ops. No less than sixteen magazines wanted his services. He began to be recognized when he was out in public. "It makes you nervous when people gawk," he told *Motion Picture Magazine*. "It's another part of being in pictures that I don't like." Still, he appreciated at least some of the attention and adoration. A Richard Jaeckel Fan Club sprang up in New York complete with a regular circular distributed to its members. "Imagine that," Jaeckel continued. "All typewritten, and it must take a lot of work. It's nice of them to do it."

The experience of making two films hadn't left Jaeckel any more impressed with the business of being in front of the camera. He would much rather be at the beach, the gym, or on a ball field. "Acting is all right," he told *Motion Picture Magazine*, "But it's just not for me. I like the money, and I'll do the best job I can. But I don't feel qualified. I feel silly, sitting around waiting for the director to tell me look happy, or angry, or sad."

He did repeat his "Chicken" Anderson character for a *Lux Radio Theatre* broadcast of *Guadalcanal Diary* on February 28, 1944, necessitating he sign an application for membership in the American Federation of Radio Artists. In reality Jaeckel felt the acting contract with 20th Century–Fox was all a laugh-out-loud joke and downplayed any great talent on his part. He later told *The Arizona Republic*, "Of course that was during the war. They were frankly scrounging for young fellows to play roles in all the war movies they were making." He told the *Daily Breeze*, "I did pretty well until the good actors came back from the war."

✦ 2 ✦

Soldier Boy

When it came time to decide between the U.S. Navy and the Merchant Marine, Jaeckel opted for the latter. The training period was slightly shorter and the assignments weren't confined to one naval station. Jaeckel hated the idea of being cooped up in an office doing paperwork. A Merchant Marine had the opportunity to travel the world, which is what Jaeckel wanted. He loved the idea of working on a ship's deck in the sunshine and the briny sea air. Members of the Merchant Marine typically work on civilian-owned ships transporting passengers and cargo around the globe. Off-duty they can even dress in casual clothing. However, in time of war the Merchant Marine becomes an auxiliary unit of the U.S. Navy and Coast Guard whose chief duty is to transport both military troops and supplies. It's anything but a safe occupation. According to the U.S. Merchant Marine website, the Merchant Marine suffered the highest rate of casualties of any branch of the service during World War II, losing mariners at a rate of one in 26. Nearly 1600 merchant marine vessels were sunk during the war with tons of freight lost at the bottom of the sea.

Jaeckel sold his car and entered the Merchant Marine with pal Leo Ross in the early summer of 1944. He was initially assigned to a training camp on Catalina Island, 26 miles off the coast of Los Angeles. Catalina was considered the first line of military defense for the western United States. Sailors were trained in the loading and unloading of cargo ships and even learned how to fire anti-aircraft guns and swim through oil fires after jumping from a 25-foot pier. However, most of Jaeckel's first boot camp duties were mundane, folding laundry for both the Merchant Marine and the U.S. Coast Guard at the expense of deepening his tan in the strong summer rays. He also had to endure taunts and the call of "Chicken" from another seaman who relentlessly kept after him trying to get a reaction from the reluctant actor. Interestingly, Jaeckel's military physical and subsequent records list his height at 5'8 1/2" and 5'9". Both measurements seem a little on the tall side for Jaeckel, who had a proclivity for innocent mischief and might very well have managed to surreptitiously boost his height.

After three months of training Jaeckel graduated from the Andrew Furuseth School of Seamanship and joined the Seaman's Union. Things quickly picked up as he was called into action, serving aboard vessels in both the Atlantic and Pacific Ocean over the next two and a half years. His first ship was the steamer *Mormactern*, which he sailed on from September 7, 1944, to December 21, 1944, as an ordinary seaman. Initially two weeks were spent as a stevedore loading the freight in San Francisco, with Jaeckel and training buddy John McCroskey of Hollywood High taking in the experience of the waterfront dives and bars in the evenings.

On one excursion Jaeckel got into a back alley fistfight with a member of the Marine Corps. It was the manly type of adventure he read about growing up and now he was living it and toughening himself in the process.

Jaeckel remained under contract to 20th Century-Fox while serving with the Merchant Marine during World War II.

One of his first voyages was to Alaska, a treat for a young man who wanted to see the world and was fond of writer Jack London. Ports of call in the South Seas included Hawaii, Guam, Saipan, and Leyte. Jaeckel fell in love with the beaches of Hawaii and had the opportunity to go to a luau and surf on a longboard at Waikiki. At one point in the Pacific his ship encountered rough seas and made it through a hurricane. In Saipan they were bombed by a Japanese air attack and Jaeckel got to see the island battlefields and dozens of piled-up dead bodies. The action and the experiences were what Jaeckel had long dreamed of.

During his time at sea on the *Mormactern* there was one incident involving Jaeckel that went before the 12th Naval District for review in San Francisco on December 23, 1944. The incident in question occurred on December 18 and involved a fistfight between Jaeckel and a wiper aboard ship. It echoed the taunts he had endured throughout his Catalina training. When interviewed about the incident, Jaeckel said the wiper had been verbally baiting him and the disagreement escalated to blows. As he had done when he was a child, Jaeckel stuck up for himself by silencing a bully's abuse with his fists. It was a tried and true method in dealing with blowhards but could have had repercussions. Veteran character actor William Phipps served with Jaeckel on the *Mormactern* and recalls,

> Dick Jaeckel and I were very good friends. He and I were in World War II together and served on the same ship. He was a deckhand and I was a U.S. Navy radio operator assigned to one of his ships—the *Mormactern*. It was one of six ships I served on in that capacity. We went all over the South Pacific and often swam and dived off of the ship together. We got to know each other very well. He had done a film prior to going in. I hadn't worked in the business yet. There was a story I'll tell you. There was a guy in what we called "the black gang"—the oil room below deck—who was taunting him and called him a "Hollywood faggot." Well, Jaeckel beat the hell out of him. He was very athletic and strong and beat the hell out of the guy who was calling him names.[1]

Since Jaeckel's record was clean, the board decided no disciplinary action would be forthcoming other than his admonition of guilt in the matter. His ship's captain did fine him $40 in pay, but that was okay with Jaeckel. A letter of apology from the first seaman who taunted him in Catalina found its way to Jaeckel in the Pacific, praising him for his toughness and telling him he was all right in that guy's book. Overcoming the Hollywood teenage idol fan magazine background that had literally been forced upon him, Jaeckel had been accepted by his swabbie peers. He was now a man's man earning his way in the wartime military at sea.

Jaeckel spent a short amount of his Christmas liberty back in Hollywood before shipping out of New Orleans for his next adventure. From January 28 to April 13, 1945, Jaeckel served as a seaman on the cargo vessel *Francis M. Smith*. Among his stops Rio de Janeiro rated high, even though some local girls tried to catch Jaeckel and a pal in a scam after meeting in a nightclub. In the spring of 1945 Jaeckel was off to England and then Italy for the German surrender. This was followed by a May–June assignment as an able-bodied seaman aboard the steam vessel *Wolf Creek*. By this time Jaeckel was a certified lifeboat man. From July 16 to August 15, 1945, he was aboard the *Notre Dame Victory*. His ship had engine trouble off Okinawa and had to stay back while the rest of the convoy sank the day before V-J Day. It was a lucky break for Jaeckel that he emerged from the war alive and well with five campaign ribbons. At the end of hostilities, he received an honorable discharge.

The family's financial situation had changed dramatically on the homefront. Jaeckel's mother Millicent married movie executive Watterson R. Rothacker in 1946, giving up her stake in the Jaeckel fur business. She continued to act with a Los Angeles stage company and set Jaeckel up with a small furnished house near the beach in Pacific Palisades and a new black Ford convertible. There was a closet full of nice clothes but Jaeckel found he now preferred t-shirts and khakis. Jaeckel continued taking maritime jobs through the early part of 1946, sailing up and down the California coast. In the back of his mind was accepting a job offer from Standard Oil in Rio de Janeiro. Upon his discharge from the Merchant Marine, Jaeckel initially wanted to enroll in college and become an athletic coach majoring in physical education. However, now in need of a regular paycheck, he went back to honor the acting contract he had signed in 1944. He told the *Los Angeles Herald Examiner*, "It was easy and it was outdoors, not like working for a living."

Twentieth Century–Fox had plans to pair Jaeckel and former juvenile actor Lon McCallister in an adaptation of George Agnew Chamberlain's *Scudda Hoo! Scudda Hay!*, about the training of a pair of mules, but the making of the film didn't happen for over a year. Bob Karnes ended up playing the antagonistic part originally envisioned for Jaeckel. Director Henry King wanted Jaeckel to play Jeanne Crain's boyfriend in the comedy *Margie* (1946). Having just returned from the war, Jaeckel was up for the action and adventure that had been offered by his debut films. He thought the *Margie* character Johnny Green was a sissy rah-rah college boy and turned it down. Conrad Janis ended up playing the part. Turning down the powerful King was a miscalculation with consequences, especially considering that upon his return home he married his longtime girlfriend and Palladium dancing partner Antoinette Helen Marches in Tijuana in May of 1947. To Jaeckel, the Philadelphia-born beauty was "Tony." Richard Anthony Jaeckel was born in 1947 and a second son christened Barry Louis Jaeckel would be born in 1949.

Jaeckel suddenly needed the movie money for his family's sake but ultimately ended up paying for the error of his ways. Although the fan magazines initially trumpeted his return from the war, the studio assigned him no new acting roles. In fact, Jaeckel didn't do any more immediate work at all for Fox despite a number of films in production at the studio. He now had a wealth of real-life experience to draw off of for his acting but no outlet for these personal emotions. Upon his next studio option in the fall of 1947, he was dropped and the fan magazines looked the other way. There was no money coming in at all, and it was an important life lesson. Jaeckel revealed in the *Come Back, Little Sheba* presskit, "I made a big mistake and I knew it. From that day on I tried to make up for my cocky attitude."

In an interview with columnist Erskine Johnson, Jaeckel elaborated: "That attitude of mine cost me a lot of potatoes. I've got a wife and kids to support now and I've got to straighten up. When they made all the fuss about me, I was going to high school and didn't know what a buck was. I said, 'Who wants to be one of those boob actors?' Now I'm wiser." He told *Motion Picture Magazine* that he did his first two films for his mother but now he was in pictures for himself. "I've got to eat, and I've seen enough of other jobs to realize they don't pay as well." He elaborated further to *The Washington Post* about this rude awakening, saying, "I found myself playing the twelth guy from the back in the westerns and the fifteenth guy from the left in the war movies."

The path to Hollywood success is seldom as easy as Jaeckel's had initially been. Lana Turner may have been discovered at Schwab's drugstore and Jaeckel in the Fox mail room, but those feel-good stories are extremely rare. Thousands of hopefuls have invaded Hollywood from all over the world looking for a big break with no measure of success at all. The Screen Actors Guild informs the public that of the members who lists their primary occupation as actor or actress, only a little over five percent of them are making a living above the poverty level in any given year. Side jobs and hustling for work are standard operating procedure. Success at any given time in a film or TV show is no guarantee of prolonged endurance in the industry. The fan magazine exposure and piles of letters of love and appreciation can stop as quickly as they started. In reality, Jaeckel had gotten his foot in the door, gained a small measure of recognition, and little more.

Columnist Bob Thomas wondered publicly whatever happened to the actor who had shown so much promise in *Guadalcanal Diary*. Jaeckel was suddenly in competition with all the other muscular young men who had returned from the service and were looking for work in Hollywood. And Jaeckel was indeed now a muscular young man, having added over thirty pounds of brawn onto his frame during his time in the service from dedicated weight workouts. He was stocky but not musclebound and he still looked normal when clad in street clothes. His compact frame and sturdy legs gave him a very symmetrical and even build. No one body part appeared overdeveloped in relation to another. He retained all his flexibility and natural athleticism. Had he not married and begun a family he would probably have been content for the time being to be a bicep-flexing beach boy. That lifestyle was now a luxury he couldn't afford, although he still made time where he could for his extracurricular passions.

Jaeckel was a dedicated member of Bruce Connors Gym on Santa Monica Boulevard and often exercised under the sun at Muscle Beach. At the time, weightlifting among this group of athletic gymnasts, circus performers, and stuntmen was seen as a useful method of fitness that aided in acrobatics and feats of strength they commonly displayed for impressed throngs of onlookers. Influential health and fitness experts Jack LaLanne and Vic Tanny got their starts at Muscle Beach. While iron weights were indeed being hoisted, these men and women were not muscle-heads. They were just as apt to be seen exercising on the parallel bars or the gymnastic rings as the bench press. They were well-conditioned and capable of walking on their hands or balancing their bodies at right angles from flagpoles. The stereotypic overly developed bodybuilder look was still a decade away. Steroids did not find their way to the California beaches until the late 1950s, and even then it was a gradual process before the bloated muscle builders lost all the athletic functionality of predecessors such as Jaeckel and his friends. Still, there was a crazy assortment of personalities at Muscle Beach ranging from circus performers to flamboyant professional wrestlers. "Jake fondly called it Gorilla Park," his friend Tim Lyon recalls. "He was hanging out down there a lot in the early days with all the grapplers and wrestlers—Gorgeous George and Baron Leone and all these characters. Jake was right in the middle of the whole thing."[2]

Bodybuilding actor Dick Tyler remembers Jaeckel fondly:

> Dick Jaeckel was an old and good friend. I remember meeting him for the first time when I began training at the Physical Services Gym in West Los Angeles. We developed a bond not only in weight training but in the acting profession. At the time I was a working actor. In fact I believe I began in the business even before Dick, so Billy Murphy and Dick and I got along pretty well. After a good workout we would often go into Westwood for something to eat and a show. If memory serves me we'd go to a place called Krumplers. It was famous for its thick milkshakes. The deal was that the shake was so thick that if so much as a drop fell from the glass when you turned it upside down you got another free.
>
> Every so often Dick and I would wander around Hollywood Boulevard looking for a show or we'd meet at the beach. Dick hated phonies and there were plenty around. He never seemed at all shy about expressing this belief. Years later, after I had become a chiropractor, he came in as a patient. That was years ago and I sadly lost track of him. I will always remember him as a strong man, a fine actor, and a loyal friend. And he was tough when he had to be. Anyone lucky enough to be his friend knew that he would back you up emotionally and if needed physically.[3]

For weekend recreation Jaeckel would pile his wife Tony and the young boys in a station wagon and head for the beach to indulge his love of surfing. The sport was still in its infancy at this point but Jaeckel's half-sister Dorothy Hamlin would tell the *South Florida Sun Sentinel*, "He was a champion surfer and he loved the water." One of his favorite surfing spots was south of Los Angeles at San Onofre, which at the time was a location inaccessible by today's speedy freeway system. After a leisurely drive down the coast, Jaeckel would hit the waves with the likes of surfers such as Burrhead, Hammerhead, and Donovan. The groups would sleep overnight in their cars near the jetty by the train tracks. Rubber tire bonfires provided light and warmth as they shared a collective surfer's stew. It was a great and simple time.

Actor James Arness, several years away from becoming a household name on TV's *Gunsmoke*, also surfed at San Onofre during the late 1940s. Like Jaeckel and the other board riders, Arness was a World War II veteran. He recalled in his autobiography: "I surfed with a small group of guys, using the heavy surfing boards of those days. Our mecca was San Onofre, and we named our fast-growing crowd the San Onofre Surf Club. We often traveled to other beaches like La Jolla, and even spent some time in

Jaeckel was a dedicated physical culturist and outdoorsman. He loved surfing, skin diving, and sailing in the California sun.

Tijuana, Mexico, below San Rosarito Beach. We just camped on the beach and spent a few days 'catching the big ones.' ... It was beautiful there, an unforgettable experience."

Barbara Bond, a young girl at the time, had a stepfather with a similar military background to men like Jaeckel and James Arness and he brought the family down from Burbank on the weekends. She recalls Jaeckel, saying, "We knew he was an actor. He was very handsome, blond, always smiling. Very friendly. On the beach, everyone was equal, so no one flaunted what they did for a living. There were a few of the guys that were rowdy and noisy and raising hell all the time, but Richard was not one of them. He didn't always go to San Onofre, not every weekend. Maybe he was away working."[4]

At the time there were only a little over a hundred active surfers on the whole West Coast, and Jaeckel had the uncluttered pick of surf spots from Rincon at the Santa Barbara County line to Windansea in La Jolla. Among closer wave locations, Santa Monica Canyon Beach became a popular spot with Jaeckel. Another wave destination where Jaeckel could be found was Malibu, which had yet to be popularized by the likes of Frederick Kohner's fictionalized characters Gidget and MoonDoggie. Jaeckel surfed there, as did Hawaiian big wave entrepreneur and Aloha shirt designer Walter Hoffman and actors Peter Lawford, Jackie Coogan, Billy Murphy, and Johnny Sheffield. Malibu surfer Les Williams ranked Jaeckel as top level among those who hit the waves there. Innovative foam and Fiberglas board maker Hobie Alter remembered him as "a good surfer" and, along with Hoffman, one of the earliest in the sport to begin using lighter-weight balsa redwood boards for their trimming. Jaeckel's lifeguarding days had made him an expert swimmer and he also enjoyed skin diving for abalone and water skiing. Hoffman recalls of Jaeckel,

> I introduced him to his first wave in Malibu. He was a good surfer. We never surfed big, big waves there but they were good. Six to eight feet. I don't think he surfed much in Hawaii. There were only fifteen to twenty surfers in Malibu at the time. A few other actors—Peter Lawford and Bomba the Jungle Boy Johnny Sheffield. His friend Red Gaines, who played his brother in *Sands of Iwo Jima*, surfed with us. Tim Lyon was another good friend of his. We hung out at the Sip 'n' Surf in Santa Monica Canyon. That's where the guys hung out from Malibu. We'd surf together at San Onofre, Windansea, Salt Break, and Doheny. My parents had a place in Laguna Beach and he'd stay with me in the summer and we'd surf and dive a lot.
>
> He was a good diver. We'd dive for lobster, abalone, and spear fish. We'd dive at a place called Harrison's Landing. That was a good spot. I never got a white sea bass and I remember one time we were diving and I said, "Let's get a white sea bass today." I was in the water diving around out there and when I came up he was on the rocks with a big sea bass he'd speared! It was huge. It must have been 35 pounds! He walked back down the beach and everybody was impressed at the size of it. I don't know how he did it. I never got one in my life. I said later I was only kidding about getting one that day![5]

Teenager Tim Lyon was part of the burgeoning West Coast surfing scene and would become a lifelong friend of Jaeckel. He came from a family that dealt in Malibu real estate and remembers, "Jake literally lived at our house for almost ten years. He was a big surf guy and we lived right on the surfing beach. We were good close pals. He had a big beach life and was a major player in the surf world. Walter Hoffman and his brother Flippy were really responsible for getting Jake into the surfing world. I met Jake in 1948 in San Onofre and over the years we became pals. As a surfer he was top-drawer. The surfing community thought of him as a surfer who acted and not vice versa."[6] Legendary Los Angeles County lifeguard Cal Porter remembers Jaeckel more as a beach volleyball player, saying:

> I only knew Richard slightly. I played volleyball with him, and he was a good player and a nice guy. There was a unique group of beachgoers in those days at Santa Monica Canyon Beach by the volleyball court, all connected with the film industry in some way. Actors, extras, stuntmen, technicians. There was a phone

booth right there on the beach, and when the bell rang a half dozen guys would rush to answer the phone hoping it was a call for an extra or a stuntman. All the studios had that number and knew there was any number of guys available. It was long before cell phones. Richard was a fairly established actor by then, but I think the studios knew he was there on the beach most of the time. There were lots of movie gals there also. Those were fun times.[7]

The waves offered both challenge and escape. It was intoxicating fun. Jaeckel enjoyed the laid-back beach existence but knew at some point he needed to get serious about a career. In the spring of 1948 he received a second chance at 20th Century–Fox, landing one of the leading roles as Lt. Dick Carter in the film adaptation of the William Bowers Air Corps play *West of Tomorrow*, about a USO entertainer visiting an uncommonly lucky group of flyers on a Pacific island. The $150,000 picture was directed by Joe Newman and produced by Frank Seltzer and was completed in only ten days during the summer of 1948. It also starred Kristine Miller, Arthur Franz, Gene Reynolds, Mickey Knox, Harry Lauter, Ross Ford, Tom Noonan, and Billy Murphy. Fox thought they had an efficiently made quickie on their hands and put it into general release at the end of the year under the more marketable action title *Jungle Patrol*. The film did modest business and put Jaeckel back in the good graces of the studio. Jaeckel was one of the cast members *Variety* praised for "giving his part a feeling of reality."

Twenty-one-year-old Jaeckel is natural and understated in his performance as a fresh-faced enlistee. He is one of the most fatalistic of the group, searching for a reason why they have shot down over a hundred Japanese planes without so much as losing one man. His character references the film *Death Takes a Holiday*. There is an on-screen occurrence that sets this apart from Jaeckel's other military roles and that's his use of cigarettes. It's somewhat odd to see him puffing away in a couple of scenes, though that trait was certainly common among men who served in World War II. It's only odd here because Jaeckel's future characters so seldom if ever lit up. As an actor Jaeckel didn't feel the need to fill his hands with the standard performer prop. In real life he was a non-smoker and a promoter of health and fitness. "Dick was definitely a non-smoker," says his long-time friend, gym owner Clark Hatch.[8]

Appearing in a supporting role in *Jungle Patrol* was Jaeckel's surfing pal and workout partner Billy Murphy. Originally from Sacramento, California, the muscular Murphy had played football at USC and served with the Navy during World War II until he suffered a knee injury. When once asked if it was true he had been a football All-American, Murphy answered cryptically, "Yeah, but somebody else got credit for it." He later joined the U.S. Marine Reserves while pursuing an acting career with small

A husky Jaeckel as he appeared in Fox's *Jungle Patrol* (aka *West of Tomorrow*) (1948).

parts in a number of films such as *The Story of G.I. Joe* (1945) and *Till the End of Time* (1946). Legend has it that Murphy was the model for the Hasbro G.I. Joe action figure. William "Red" Murphy and Jaeckel would appear in a number of films together and at this stage of their careers it was hard to tell who showed more promise. In *Jungle Patrol* Murphy is allowed to display his talent playing the piano. In addition to the name Billy Murphy he was sometimes known as Red Gaines and Hal Mohr, among other monikers. "He had more names than he had toes," Tim Lyon recalls. "He was quite a guy."[9]

In November of 1948 Jaeckel and his wife were in San Francisco when their oldest son Richard, Jr., nearly drowned in the backyard pool at home. The one-year-old was saved by his uncle John Marches. The loss of a child could have been catastrophic to the young Jaeckel family, especially coming on the heels of Jaeckel's father's suicide. Jaeckel became more concerned with the present and future welfare of his family, determined to provide them with a safe and steady lifestyle. Still not sure if acting was to be his life's work, Jaeckel began formally studying motion picture technique in the classroom with an eye toward one day becoming a director. He was particularly interested in photography and the composition of images. As a result, he gained a great deal of respect for film directors.

Jaeckel's acting career picked up steam with a major role in Universal-International's *City Across the River* (1949), an adaptation of Irving Shulman's book *The Amboy Dukes* about the brawling Brooklyn street gang. In his biggest screen departure thus far, Jaeckel plays the violent character Bull, sporting a thick neck, crewcut, and clipped tough-guy speech. It's a physically intimidating performance with Jaeckel's every move calculated to be deliberate and threatening. When it came time to film a fight scene, Jaeckel didn't need to be doubled by a stuntman. He could handle all the action demands of the script himself. A young Tony Curtis was also in the cast, which featured Peter Fernandez, Joshua Shelley, Al Ramsen, and Mickey Knox in support of Stephen McNally, Thelma Ritter, Richard Benedict, and Jeff Corey. Director Maxwell Shane handled the young cast, who got to travel to New York City for brief location work in the Bowery.

The Washington Post gave the film a near rave, stating, "The cast, made up chiefly of newcomers, is very good. No one in the cast is famous, so they all have to stand up and deliver good performances." *Stars and Stripes* wrote, "Curtis, Knox, and Jaeckel turn in excellent performances." The *Morning Star* found that the same three "superb [actors] turn in rousing performances," while the *Syracuse Post Standard* praised their "remarkably vivid and credible performances." The *Oakland Tribune* pointed out Jaeckel's "worthwhile character presentation," and *Variety* mentioned "performances by all members of the cast are marked by Shane's accent on naturalness." *The Los Angeles Times* remarked that the film "gains by the presence of players who have not been typed—at least yet." *The New Republic* reviewed the young actors collectively: "Any of these six, perhaps all of them, might develop into a first-rate dramatic actor; as a group they show a remarkable sense of interplay, conflict and clear individuality." It was an important turning point for Jaeckel as it showed he was fully capable of handling antagonistic roles. In fact, he went on to excel at them.

City Across the River with its $120,000 budget is an interesting film but a minor one. Despite its literary background, Universal-International gave it the quickie treatment. Behind the scenes there was an interesting contrast of egos among the young members of the cast. Jaeckel was grateful for the job and worked hard at presenting an authentic Brooklyn accent. Tony Curtis was a few years away from getting his big build-up at the studio, but thought he

Young Brooklyn hoods Tony Curtis, Peter Fernandez, Al Ramsen, Joshua Shelley, Richard Jaeckel, and Mickey Knox make a deal with shady Richard Benedict in Universal's *City Across the River* (1949). The role helped establish Jaeckel as a big screen tough guy.

was already star material. Curtis had a natural Brooklyn accent from his upbringing and was bitter at not being given the lead. He remembered in his autobiography, "I was the only one out of that group of guys that made it. Dick Jaeckel worked again, but the rest of them went down the Toilet of No Return."

MGM's *Battleground* (1949) from director William Wellman and writer Robert Pirosh was another ensemble World War II film that pushed Jaeckel's acting career in the right direction. It told the story of the Battle of the Bulge's 101st Airborne Division, nicknamed the "Battered Bastards of Bastogne." Heading the cast were Van Johnson, James Whitmore, John Hodiak, Douglas Fowley, George Murphy, Marshall Thompson, Don Taylor, and Ricardo Montalban among other up-and-comers such as James Arness and Jerome Courtland. Jaeckel is far down the cast list as a shell-shocked combat coward named Bettis who prefers digging foxholes to engaging the enemy. He pulls KP duty in Bastogne after running away from the film's first bombing. Ironically, he is killed in a shelling of the city while the soldiers in his platoon fight it out in the snowy Ardennes Forest on the front lines. Dickie Jones, Tommy Noonan, Dewey Martin, and Jaeckel's good friend Billy Murphy have small unbilled parts in the film, which was shot almost entirely on Hollywood soundstages.

Critics heaped praise on *Battleground*, with *Variety* calling it "extraordinary" and *Boxoffice* terming it "a masterpiece." However, Jaeckel's role was too small to be singled out in reviews. *The New York Times* summed it up appropriately, saying of the cast, "It is difficult to make a selection of those who merit special praise." That was okay with Jaeckel. He was building his résumé and learning. There was also a bit of fun to be had as the main cast endured two weeks of Army boot camp on the MGM lot prior to cameras rolling. They crawled around

Jaeckel as the shell-shocked soldier Bettis in MGM's World War II film *Battleground* (1949). Jaeckel was effective as part of a large ensemble cast in the Oscar-nominated film.

on their bellies, fired guns, tossed grenades, and endlessly marched in cadence to "Jody's Call." It was the type of physical action Jaeckel got a kick out of being paid for. The Academy Award–nominated film was also valuable as a high quality credit that allowed him to see how other actors worked and prepared. Jaeckel talked about his acting process to the *Charleston Gazette*, saying: "I stole here and there. I learned that you must keep doing something while the camera is running. Once you stop, the others know you've had it and take over.... I'm not going to hurt anyone out there. I'm not a great actor, but I'm a professional one."

Sands of Iwo Jima (1949) from director Allan Dwan and Republic Pictures starred John Wayne in an Oscar-nominated performance as battle-hardened U.S. Marine Sergeant John M. Stryker. Forrest Tucker and John Agar lend support as the top men in his unit. In a large cast, Jaeckel is given a running role as Pfc. Frank Flynn and is memorably paired with Billy Murphy as his brother Eddie. Hailing from the City of Brotherly Love, they're called the Fighting Flynns due to their penchant for fisticuffs. They constantly fight each other over trivial matters but are intensely loyal. Both show off their muscular physiques throughout the film, which was made with Marine Corps support at Camp Pendleton during the summer of 1949.

Sands of Iwo Jima is remembered as the movie that put Jaeckel back on the map in Hollywood and solidified his reputation as a pugnacious soldier on film. He is seen here at arguably his toughest and most virile, ready to engage in fisticuffs at the slightest provocation. In a motion picture in which much of the cast is dropping right and left from explosions and enemy fire, Jaeckel manages to survive until the end with no more than a bullet in his leg, carried out of the line of fire by his brother. Jaeckel's light blond hair helps him to stand out from the M-1 rifle–carrying crowd in several scenes as does the generosity of John Wayne himself. In several instances Jaeckel is positioned to advantage on camera near Wayne, something the film-savvy Wayne was well aware of. "John Wayne really liked him," Jaeckel's close friend Tim Lyon recalls.[10]

To John Wayne, Jaeckel was still "The Kid," the sturdy little lifeguard by the pool at the Hollywood Athletic Club who had inexplicably defied odds and become a well-known actor overnight with *Guadalcanal Diary*. Wayne had scored an early starring role with *The Big Trail* (1930) before languishing in B-westerns for nearly a decade until John Ford's *Stagecoach* (1939) solidified his stardom. Jaeckel could now relate to the in-betweens. To Jaeckel and everyone else on the film, John Wayne was the biggest man in Hollywood. At 6'4" and well over 200 pounds, Wayne carried clout and wielded it. He lobbied Republic for Forrest Tucker and John Agar to co-star and got his way. Jaeckel had no doubt received approval from the Duke before he was cast. Jaeckel watched how the macho Wayne interacted with the cast and crew. The star lived hard but he knew his lines and was always the first on the set in the morning. He also knew everyone else's job on the film, from the director down to the grip. If they did their job, he praised and respected them. If they didn't, he showed them the door. Jaeckel learned a great deal about professionalism working with Wayne on *Sands of Iwo Jima*. As a result Jaeckel always made it a point to treat everyone on a movie set with respect. Jaeckel could just as easily be seen chatting with an extra as he could a star of the film.

Wayne put the young actors at ease and often played chess with them while waiting for the camera set-ups. He even threw a football around with Jaeckel and Forrest Tucker. It was eye-opening behavior for a star of his magnitude. Jaeckel recalled his enjoyment working with Wayne in the book *John Wayne: The Life and Legend*, saying: "You're pretty feisty at 22, but you weren't feisty around this guy, really. He just set the tone for everything. And yet when

Billy Murphy (left) and Richard Jaeckel mix it up as "The Fighting Flynns" in Republic's *Sands of Iwo Jima* (1949). The classic World War II film's popularity gave Jaeckel a small foothold in the industry.

it came time to zig and zag, he'd horse around with the best of them, but when he declared, 'This is the time,' you'd better decide along with him because otherwise, it'd be hard; it'd be tough.... I knew each day was going to be better than the preceding one because we were having such a great time, all of us—it was more than a job."

Others in the large cast include Richard Webb, James Brown, Wally Cassell, Martin Milner, Arthur Franz, Hal Baylor, Dickie Jones, and Leonard Gumley. Dwan had a Camp Pendleton drill instructor put many members of the young cast through a strenuous boot camp to whip them into fighting shape. In a short 1993 Leonard Maltin documentary entitled *The Making of* Sands of Iwo Jima, Jaeckel recalled the sense of brotherhood a director could develop amongst the cast on such a film: "I think that's the prime ingredient, other than special effects, in a war film.... Take *All Quiet on the Western Front*, which is one of the great examples of camaraderie. Sometimes it actually brings tears to your eyes. You can get in there and have that affection for somebody, and you see them take the bullet, take the special effects, and go down, and it's done so realistically. Again, the director's in charge, just for the moment you well up. It's quite a treat when that happens. Of course somebody's doing something right to bring that emotion out of you."

Although he was very much still an acting rookie himself in relation to an old pro like Wayne, Jaeckel was able to relate to other film newcomers in the cast and pass along his own growing knowledge of the camera. Such was the case with Leonard Gumley, who played Pfc. Sid Stein in his lone film appearance. "I'm 94 years old, and to my knowledge I think the only living cast member from the *Sands of Iwo Jima*," says the World War II veteran Gumley in 2014. "As to my memory of Richard Jaeckel, he and I didn't get to know each other well during the making of the film, but he was very helpful to me on a personal level. It was the first film I was in and he gave me all kinds of tips and pointers on how to stand, how to move, and where to be when it came to being in front of the camera. He was very helpful to me in that regard, and I owe him for that."[11]

Variety mentioned Jaeckel among the cast members who "indelibly imprint their individual performances." *The Hollywood Reporter* chimed in with, "Others who impress particularly are James Holden, Peter Coe, and Richard Jaeckel." *The Los Angeles Times* wrote, "The audience may naturally have its problems keeping track of individuals in uniform while watching the action. They make an interesting group, pretty well identified in the performances of Cassell, Brown, Franz, and Webb, as well as James Holden, Peter Coe, Richard Jaeckel, Bill Murphy, and various others." *The Washington Post* thought likewise: "While the supporting roles are stockily written, they are ably played by a solid bunch of young fellows, including Forrest Tucker, Wally Cassell, James Brown, Richard Webb, Peter Coe, Richard Jaeckel, and Bill Murphy, the last two eternally scrapping twins." In his book *Leonard Maltin's Movie Encyclopedia* the popular film historian wrote of Jaeckel: "He belongs to the legions of competent, sometimes exemplary actors who've peopled motion pictures in secondary roles for decades."

Veteran movie military advisor Captain Dale Dye spoke of Jaeckel's lasting contribution to the World War II combat film genre on the DVD commentary for *The Dirty Dozen*, saying: "Jaeckel was always the baby-faced kid in every movie I ever saw. Even before I was in the Marine Corps I was watching Dick Jaeckel play the baby-faced kid in every war movie there ever was. I was in awe of him…. He had a legendary career. Never became a huge star. Always a supporting star. Always that kind of guy and always a team player. He understood how movies are made. It's a synergistic effort. He brings something to the plate, and he doesn't ever care how much face time he's got and so forth…. He was an extraordinary guy, and I was blessed to have met him and be able to work with him."

In October 1949 Jaeckel signed with the Rosalie Stewart Agency for representation. At this point Jaeckel had appeared in a half-dozen films, all but one which placed him in a soldier's uniform. *Battleground* and *Sands of Iwo Jima* were surprising successes as the studios weren't sure the public wanted to see combat films now that the war was over.

Fox had Jaeckel on a short list for those under consideration to portray the comic relief character Sgt. McIllhenny in Henry King's B-17 drama *Twelve O'Clock High* (1949) opposite Gregory Peck. Fresh-faced Fox contract player Robert Arthur ultimately ended up playing the part, but it was a positive sign that King and the studio even considered Jaeckel for this World War II film.

In contrast, the western was a tried-and-true genre and that's where Jaeckel moved next. In King's *The Gunfighter* (1950) he was cast as a cocky young upstart who tests the fast-draw reputation of a mustached Gregory Peck in the classic opening scene. Jaeckel keeps pushing Peck's Jimmie Ringo, calling him Mr. Frazzle Bottom as his own itchy trigger finger hovers over his sidearm. Peck reluctantly guns the annoying braggart down and the rest of the film concerns Jaeckel's family seeking revenge. Jaeckel told the *Oregonian*, "I had a pivotal role in that, and I liked the picture, but for me there was very little of what you would call acting."

Director King was giving Jaeckel a second chance after their *Margie* differences, and although it's a small role in *The Gunfighter* it's an important one that sets the entire film in motion. The role of the egotistical punk would become a signature one for Jaeckel that saw him cast in a similar vein on many films and TV shows. The critics were kind to *The Gunfighter*, with a few making mention of Jaeckel in their reviews. *Variety* noted, "Without exception, the performances are strong," praising Jaeckel among others in the cast (Karl Malden, Helen Westcott, Jean Parker, Alan Hale, Jr., and Millard Mitchell). *The Los Angeles Times* called Jaeckel "excellent" in "an important role." *The Chicago Tribune* said, "Skip Homeier and Richard Jaeckel are expertly irritating as brash kids." The book *Great Western Pictures* noted that the film "contained a fine performance by Richard Jaeckel as a young gunfighter itching to challenge the feared Jimmie Ringo." Leonard Maltin wrote of Jaeckel in his *Movie Encyclopedia*, "He's hard to forget as the youthful hotshot who tries to draw on Gregory Peck."

Gregory Peck was another consummate professional Jaeckel learned a great deal from. Tall, dark, and handsome, Peck also happened to be a highly cerebral actor who was much respected in Hollywood circles. He'd only been making movies for a little over five years and had already received four Oscar nominations as Best Actor. The former member of Berkeley's college rowing team remained a star of high standing throughout his long and illustrious career. Although they shared only this one scene together on film, Peck would play an important role later in Jaeckel's life.

Jaeckel is seen in support in the formula Universal-Inter-

Jaeckel as the cocky young gunman Eddie with the itchy trigger finger in Fox's *The Gunfighter* (1950). Westerns became the actor's favorite genre to work in.

national western *Wyoming Mail* (1950). As an outlaw named Nate, he's a tough-talking member of a gang of train robbers infiltrated by undercover agent Stephen McNally in order to prevent a mail heist. The trades originally announced that Jaeckel would be playing Billy the Kid in the film, but no mention of William Bonney is made in the finished product. Jaeckel acquits himself well and looks comfortable on horseback. Short action clips of Jaeckel and this film's co-stars James Arness and Gene Evans in pursuit of a train are recycled and seen in the Universal-International film *Cave of Outlaws* (1951). In the film's climax Jaeckel is shot in the leg and blown up atop a luggage car, one of the few cowboy flicks in which he didn't eat lead in the belly as his comeuppance. *Wyoming Mail* is a decently realized B-plus western from a studio that mass produced such second feature films during this era.

Poverty Row favorite Reginald LeBorg directed and cameraman Russell Metty provided effective Technicolor photography on location in Tuolumne, California. The legendary stuntman Dave Sharpe contributed to the excellent action scenes. Alexis Smith was the female lead with veteran character players Howard Da Silva, Ed Begley, Whit Bissell, and Roy Roberts lending support. Upcoming actors Richard Egan and Armando Silvestre had small parts alongside Jaeckel. The book *The Films of Reginald LeBorg* called it an "excellent cast" and "perhaps the finest group of performers LeBorg ever directed in one film." Noteworthy to Jaeckel was the small nondescript role played by former 1930s youth star Frankie Darro, who by various accounts was exhibiting an alcohol problem on the set. Jaeckel watched and learned. He would never be unprofessional on a movie set. His career depended on it.

Felipe Turich, Stephen McNally, and Richard Jaeckel do their own horseback riding in the Universal western *Wyoming Mail* (1950). Actors who could ride got more work.

Despite his long list of war film credits, westerns became Jaeckel's favorite genre, and in the ensuing years he worked steadily amongst the sagebrush and sun-baked rocks. Jaeckel was a fine horseman and did the majority of his own riding for the camera. He realized an actor who could ride believably on screen got hired for more jobs, especially in this era when westerns dominated the box office. When he wasn't pumping iron or riding a surfboard in his free time he could be found astride a horse at one of the local stables. He got along well with the stuntmen on his pictures and often associated with them between scenes. Men such as Paul Stader, Allen Pinson, Fred Zendar, and Ted Grossman became some of his closest pals. They were a physical bunch, and many of them had armed services backgrounds Jaeckel could identify with. He fit right in. If not for his multitude of military roles, Jaeckel would probably be best known as a cowboy actor.

Jaeckel would have seemed ideal casting for the leading part of the scared young Union soldier in John Huston's screen adaptation of Stephen Crane's Civil War tale *The Red Badge of Courage* (1951). It was a part he was no doubt up for. However, director Huston was firmly behind the casting of World War II hero Audie Murphy in the lead despite the young soldier's inexperience in front of the camera. MGM subsequently cut Huston's film by more than twenty-five minutes and released it as a 69-minute second feature to little fanfare. Given Huston's resulting career, scholars now consider it somewhat of a classic and pine to see the footage that was edited out. Jaeckel would also seem to have been a perfect choice to play Audie Murphy in the actor's autobiography *To Hell and Back* (1955), but Universal-International convinced Murphy to play himself on screen despite Murphy's strong and obvious reservations at revisiting his war experiences so vividly.

Despite the new experience in westerns, Jaeckel still welcomed aquatic adventure. *Fighting Coast Guard* (1951) from veteran action director Joseph Kane was made at Republic Pictures and starred Forrest Tucker and John Russell as likable rivals. The macho story is built around the new Coast Guard cadet training program at New London, Connecticut, and features scenes on ships and at sea as the film concludes with World War II Pacific island action. An in-his-element Jaeckel is cast as Coast Guardsman Tony Jessup, one of the second leads among a strong and interesting cast that features Brian Donlevy, Hugh O'Brian, Martin Milner, and Steve Brodie. Jaeckel's pal Billy Murphy plays his brother Richard Jessup, in a brawling extension of their entertaining *Sands of Iwo Jima* characters. A highlight involves Murphy climbing into a wrestling ring to take on former Mr. America bodybuilder Eric Pedersen with judo moves. Jaeckel spends much of the film with a cigar in his mouth playing the wild, girl-crazy recruit with a delightfully mischievous gleam in his eye. In the film's bullet-riddled climax Jaeckel is shot up and trapped on a boat by inclement weather, only to be rescued too late by Tucker.

Many reviewers began to make note of Jaeckel and his screen presence. *The Hollywood Reporter* said, "Richard Jaeckel is a standout as the cocky, cigar-smoking young officer with a winning personality." *Variety* noted, "Richard Jaeckel and William Murphy show up best among featured players." *The Los Angeles Times* added, "Richard Jaeckel and William Murphy are prominent in support." *The Los Angeles Herald Examiner*, said, "Tops in support are Richard Jaeckel and William Murphy as the two brothers who are always razzing each other." *The Motion Picture Herald* wrote, "Effective in supporting roles are Richard Jaeckel and William Murphy as brothers." *The L.A. Daily News* said, "Richard Jaeckel and William Murphy, playing twin brothers, liven things up considerably." *The Boston Herald* commented, "Richard Jaeckel and William Murphy are engaging as a pair of spunky gamecock twins." *The*

Washington Post noted that "the players are perfectly adequate to their stereotyped chores" and that Jaeckel in particular "makes much of a cigar-chewing young fellow who dies for his country."

Fighting Coast Guard was the first film that involved Jaeckel going on a meet-the-public tour. Jaeckel, Murphy, Tucker, and co-star Brian Donlevy appeared in person for an armed forces premiere of the film in San Diego. Republic quickly hired Jaeckel for a follow-up film *The Sea Hornet* (1951), another seafaring adventure starring Rod Cameron, Jim Davis, Chill Wills, Lorna Gray, Grant Withers, Ellen Corby, James Brown, and William Haade. Jaeckel is cast as earnest young Navy man Johnny Radford, brother to the film's leading lady Adele Mara. He doesn't show up until more than midway through the film when it's revealed that their dad died on the ship *The Sea Hornet* due to Davis' interest in the gold aboard. The climax of the film is a race between hero Cameron and a timed explosive with Jaeckel monitoring Cameron's dive equipment from topside.

The Sea Hornet is a quickly made B-picture that is efficiently entertaining thanks most in part to the cast and director Joseph Kane's experience in such matters. Cast as a waterman, Jaeckel was no doubt firmly entrenched in his area of expertise. Few reviewers thought it merited much newspaper space and mention of Jaeckel's presence is usually glossed over due to

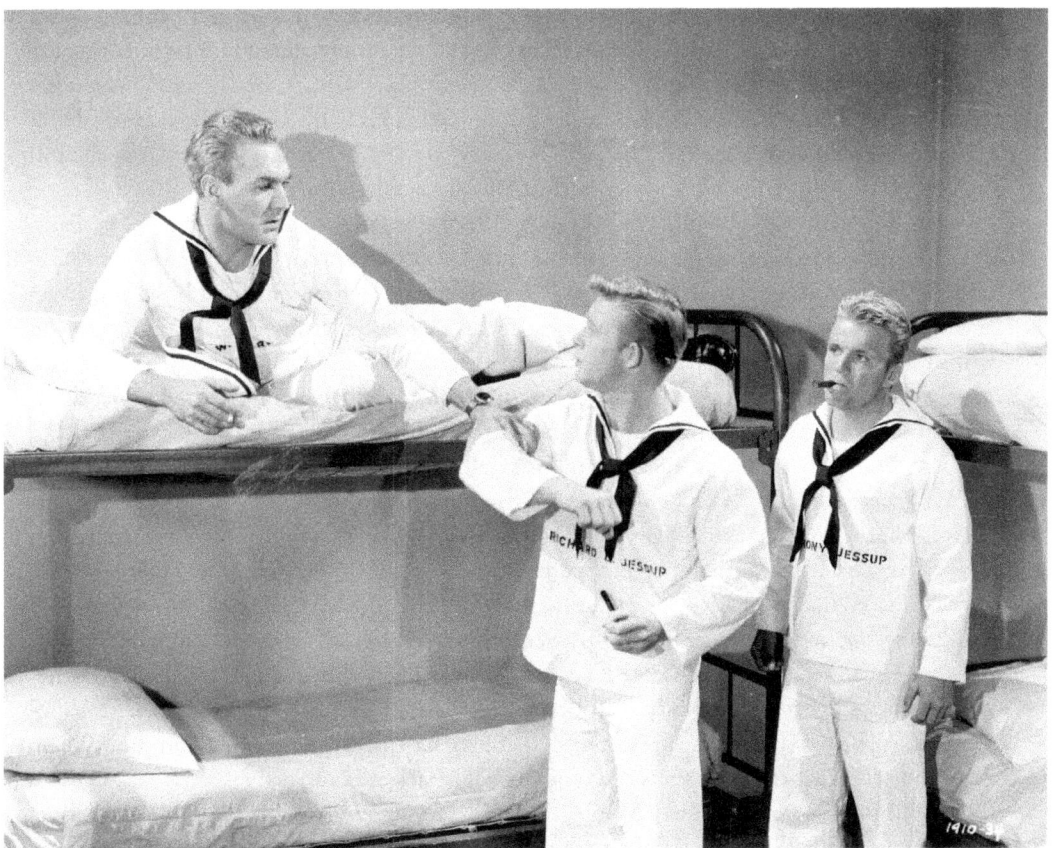

Forrest Tucker, Billy Murphy, and Richard Jaeckel in Republic's *Fighting Coast Guard* (1951). Murphy and Jaeckel, again playing brothers, were often cast alongside one another during this period.

the second banana nature of his part. He does what he is called upon to do by the director and performs admirably; there's one nice moment where he stops along the coast to salute his drowned father. *The Los Angeles Times* praised Jaeckel's "excellent work."

The outgoing and affable Jaeckel had apparently found himself a professional admirer in Republic Pictures boss Herbert Yates, who kept him on the lot with another assignment. However, the cost-conscious Yates didn't spend a great deal on either production or talent. The Joseph Kane crime drama *Hoodlum Empire* (1952) was released in April of 1952 and features a reunion of the *Fighting Coast Guard* cast. A melodramatic film about a Senate investigation into criminal activities, it headlined John Russell, Forrest Tucker, Brian Donlevy, Claire Trevor, Vera Ralston, Grant Withers, Roy Barcroft, and Luther Adler. Jaeckel is far down the cast list as Ted Dawson, a former G.I. buddy of Russell who has gone to work with him in a garage alongside their pal Billy Murphy. At one point Jaeckel and Murphy help Russell in a fistfight against some syndicate thugs.

The *Hoodlum Empire* part is minor, although it was work and kept Jaeckel in the public eye. So did early TV appearances on the Jerry Fairbanks–produced *Bigelow Theatre* and *Front Page Detective* for the DuMont Network. The latter was a crime drama starring Edmund Lowe. The former was an anthology with Jaeckel appearing as a boxer opposite Martin Milner in the 1951 episode "TKO." James Dean also has an early part. Columnist Hedda Hopper suggested Jaeckel should star in a big screen adaptation of the Milton Caniff cartoon strip *Terry and the Pirates* after Audie Murphy's Universal contract prevented him from taking the role of the adventurous young pilot. Nothing came of the suggestion, but it was obvious that the charisma and good looks that had made Jaeckel such a hit in his *Guadalcanal Diary* debut still had pull with audiences and critics alike. *Terry and the Pirates* actually surfaced the following year as a short-lived TV series with John Baer playing the title role.

The dated propaganda film *My Son John* (1952) was released in April of 1952 by Paramount Pictures. Jaeckel appears in support as Chuck Jefferson, one of the blond All-American football star brothers of disconnected lead Robert Walker. Parents Helen Hayes and Dean Jagger are suspicious of Walker's behavior as Jaeckel and fellow brother James Young leave to fight in Korea. FBI agent Van Heflin shows up and it is revealed that Walker has become a communist spy. Director Leo McCarey plays up the McCarthyism and Red Scare paranoia in a film that was thrown into turmoil by the death of Robert Walker during filming. Politics aside, Jaeckel is believable and engaging in his small part. *The San Diego Union* said, "Richard Jaeckel, James Young, and Minor Watson are good in brief roles" while *The New York Times* was less impressed, remarking, "James Young and Richard Jaeckel are studiously standard and colorless as the dutiful football-playing brothers who go away to war." The book *The Versatiles*, dedicated to character players like Jaeckel, called this one of his "small but impressive roles."

Doing a solid job for Paramount proved important. Jaeckel won a top supporting part in the studio's critically praised *Come Back, Little Sheba* (1952), beating out nearly eighty other young actors such as Scott Brady, Tab Hunter, Robert Horton, Dewey Martin, and Vince Edwards. All were vying for the part Lonny Chapman had played on Broadway in the William Inge play. Jaeckel is perfectly cast as egotistical college track athlete Turk Fisher, a bare-chested wolf on the prowl for pretty Terry Moore. She rents a room in the home of middle-aged Burt Lancaster and his wife Shirley Booth, a couple whose distant tolerance of one another stands in stark contrast to the youngsters and their amorous pawing. Former alcoholic Lancaster becomes extremely unhinged every time Jaeckel shows up at the door to flex his muscles. Booth won an Academy Award as Best Actress and Moore was nominated for Best Supporting Actress. Jaeckel's exceptional one-on-one work with Moore contributed greatly to her nomination.

To physically prepare for the role, Jaeckel had daily two-hour weight workouts. At around 180 pounds, he's the most heavily muscled he ever appeared on screen, a physical appearance he was quick to back away from for the sake of future roles. International fitness ambassador Clark Hatch, a future friend, writes of Jaeckel : "He had a sportsman's body and a youthful face which made him well suited to play soldiers and athletes in many movies. Dick was very involved in exercise long before it became in vogue amongst Hollywood celebrities. When I would visit Los Angeles we would work out in a number of gyms there. He was popular in the weight training circles."[12]

According to Terry Moore's biography, the film's stage-trained director Daniel Mann initially made Jaeckel his whipping boy on the set until Jaeckel became so unglued that Mann backed off. It became a Mann ritual to pick out someone to unleash his own frustrations on, and the unfair treatment made the dedicated and hard-working Jaeckel extremely angry. If making a tactical error in turning down a Henry King–offered part on *Margie* could dry up all work opportunities, punching out director Mann would no doubt put an immediate end to his career. The moment eventually passed and was one of the few instances of Jaeckel ever having a problem on the set with a director. To Jaeckel, the director was the man with the

A muscular Jaeckel strikes an athletic pose as an admiring Shirley Booth and Terry Moore observe in Paramount's *Come Back, Little Sheba* (1952). Jaeckel spent a lot of time at the gym training for the role.

ultimate vision for a film, and his words ruled the day. Many actors and actresses would be labeled as troublemakers and difficult on the set, earning reputations for arguing with directors and fighting studio heads. Not Jaeckel. He never rocked the boat.

Jaeckel and young Terry Moore had notoriously hot love scenes in the film that the press hyped. There were also publicity shots of the fit pair working out together at the gym, and they briefly became the talk of the town in Hollywood. The extensively rehearsed romantic scenes proved especially difficult for Moore. She was going through a divorce with Army football player Glenn Davis as she saw billionaire RKO studio head Howard Hughes on the side. During filming, the athletic Jaeckel reminded Moore of her Heisman Trophy–winning husband. Because of this, she forced herself to imagine Jaeckel was Howard Hughes every time they clinched for a passionate kissing scene. Due to the complexity of the camera angles, they had to do these intense kisses again and again to make it look natural and non-staged. Moore told columnist Erskine Johnson their sizzling hot scenes were "very exciting but innocent as two puppy dogs."

The critics were quick to laud Jaeckel's contribution to the film. Reviews came back strong, with *The New Yorker* praising Jaeckel as "staggeringly convincing" and even singling out his "incredible biceps." *Variety* noted, "Jaeckel mirrors his character excellently," while *The New York Times* wrote, "As the pretty and hot-blooded boarder, Terry Moore strikes precisely the right note of timeless and endless animalism and Richard Jaeckel is good as the boy who carnally pursues her." *The Kingsport Times* wrote, "Lending more than capable assistance to Burt Lancaster and Shirley Booth are Terry Moore and Richard Jaeckel, who round out the remaining important roles in handsome fashion." The *Plain-Dealer* noted, "Terry Moore and Richard Jaeckel are good as the younger generation trying to get a taste of life." *The Morning Star* claimed Jaeckel and Moore were "a talented pair of young players" while the *Pittsburgh Press* labeled them "beyond exceptional." The *Ellensburg Daily Record* said that the couple "bring vibrant youth to the screen," while the *Richmond Times Dispatch* commented, "Terry Moore's freshness and vitality and Richard Jaeckel's lusty animalism have the advantage of excellent writing and canny direction." *The Omaha World Herald* wrote, "I have nothing but praise for both these youngsters, who are remarkably convincing and natural in their roles." The *Springfield Union* added, "Terry Moore is a blithe and colorful personality as the college girl, and Richard Jaeckel as her impetuous and persistent boyfriend whom she sensibly pulls away from, is somewhat electrifying."

The film provided Jaeckel with the most press coverage he'd had since his debut in *Guadalcanal Diary* nearly a decade prior. Jaeckel downplayed winning the role, telling the *Los Angeles Daily News*, "Of course once an aspiring actor passes his screen test, the studio is on his side. Screen tests cost between $4000 and $5000, and that's an awful lot to throw away on a bum investment. I was chosen for the role out of seventy other possibilities, so I'm over the first hurdle." Regarding his character Turk Fisher, Jaeckel told syndicated writer Ben Cook, "I knew a lot of 'Turks' in school. They were not bad guys, really. They were just used to getting their own way, particularly with the girls. They swaggered. They strutted. They wore their college letters everywhere. They were idolized…. It's the best part I've had. I want to be such a heel that the audience will want to throw me out of the theater."

Veteran actor Robert Fuller, star of television's *Laramie*, *Wagon Train*, and *Emergency*, worked on *Come Back, Little Sheba* and vividly recalls watching Jaeckel on the set. "It must have been early 1952, the first year I entered the business. I was just an extra and worked three or

Jaeckel pulls Terry Moore close as Burt Lancaster looks on in Paramount's *Come Back, Little Sheba* (1952). The love scenes between Jaeckel and Moore were the talk of Hollywood.

four days. I never talked with him. Of course I knew who he was from all the war films and westerns like *Guadalcanal Diary* and *The Gunfighter* with Gregory Peck. I'd grown up watching him, even though he was only seven years older than me. He always had that baby face."[13]

The film proved to be a crucial turning point in Jaeckel's acting career. Up to this time he was still considering a career as a lifeguard. In fact, he was already an honorary member of the Los Angeles County Lifeguard Association and considered *Sheba* his sink-or-swim film role. In reflecting on the film, Jaeckel told the *Oregonian*: "The picture that really opened my eyes to the fact that there was more to it than carrying a rifle in the jungle or getting shot in the belly off a horse was *Come Back, Little Sheba*.... I never saw the play, but I think they built my role up a little for the movie. I played the young athlete, and here was my first glimmer that there was such a thing as concentration or characterization. It was the first time that I really had to create a character. My whole approach to acting has been different since then."

Interviewed for the Burt Lancaster bio *Against Type*, Jaeckel recalled Daniel Mann's directorial approach: "At the first rehearsal he told the actors not to come with ideas etched in stone, but to be prepared to change and experiment. I looked around and everyone was paying strict attention, including the stars Shirley and Burt." Regarding swashbuckling leading man Lancaster, Jaeckel continued, "I began to realize that this wasn't just a physical guy. This guy was a very cerebral gentleman, and boy, was I wrong in thinking that he could only swing from one tree to another."

· 3 ·

The Actor

Jaeckel developed a natural, believable style of performance in which the viewer is seldom aware he is acting. He inhabits his characters with a realism that rings true while avoiding the sometimes mannered pitfalls of the emerging Method process. Jaeckel instinctively plays it cool, understanding the varying emotional arcs of his character and capturing that appropriately by doing his homework. Preparation was key to achieve this clarity. When the camera rolled, Jaeckel internalized with total concentration and brought forth the necessary facets of his own personality that were true to the character. He didn't mumble, rant and rave, or go over the top, but often chose to underplay and utilize his own coiled-up toughness to create tension when called upon to enact villainy. He realized he was capable of a great deal of range; sensitive, studious, funny, loyal, romantic, hard, heroic, cocky, larcenous, vicious, evil. He could play them all without overreaching. There would be no Richard Jaeckel impersonators as there were no identifiable manners exhibited to imitate.

Jaeckel began to read scripts and see how his character factored into the narrative flow and interacted with others. Even when a role was small, he looked at ways he could make the overall story better with his performance. This didn't always result in more dialogue for his character. Jaeckel realized that silent bits of business could sometimes say more than any number of lines. He perfected the ability to act without words; his eyes following the action and suggesting volumes. By living in the moment and being actively engaged in a scene, Jaeckel learned to listen to his fellow actors and respond accordingly. He was often there to make them look good. It was his job. Despite no formal acting training, Jaeckel possessed an intuitive adaptability for scenes and situations. Each new role was approached from a slightly different angle, offering new shades of gray for the audience to absorb. Technically he always knew his lines and hit his marks. When his name was called, he was ready for action.

Jaeckel could be a pleasant presence on the set and simply turn his performance on or off for the camera when needed. He was always approachable and didn't need to psyche himself up beforehand to get into his bad guy characters. He would arrive early and ready to go, harkening back to his days in the military as a sailor and his observance of pros like John Wayne on *Sands of Iwo Jima*. In the commissary and studio gyms he was always smiling and full of laughs. Jaeckel toed the line and didn't make waves. Casting directors and co-workers began to praise his fine work and enjoyable off-screen demeanor. Paramount was so pleased with Jaeckel's acting progress and future that they signed him to a long-term contract before *Come Back, Little Sheba* had finished filming. Jaeckel put the ink to the contract in March of 1952.

Jaeckel was pumped full of praise by new agent Milton Grossman and the Paramount suits who told him he would be the studio's next Alan Ladd, a popular leading man in action and adventure films. The way it turned out, Jaeckel became an insurance policy for the studio in negotiations with their short-statured leading man Ladd. If Ladd or his agents balked at the language in a film contract, the studio could point to Jaeckel as his logical replacement, even during the course of a studio production such as *Thunder in the East* (1952) or *Botany Bay* (1953). Although he was collecting a regular studio check, Jaeckel filmed nothing for Paramount over the next year and received scant fan magazine coverage with nothing new to hype. With the release of *Sheba* in the fall of 1952 Jaeckel received critical kudos and audience recognition. He had hoped to have a couple of starring roles in the can to unleash upon audiences in 1953 and take that next step to stardom. Because of the Paramount–Alan Ladd situation, he had nothing. Jaeckel became neither cynical nor jaded from the experience, but he did grow to temper his expectations and expect promises made within the business to go largely unfulfilled.

Jaeckel's boyish handsomeness, bulging muscles, and short height may have worked against him, although highly successful actors such as James Cagney, Humphrey Bogart, Kirk Douglas, and the aforementioned Ladd were hardly any taller than Jaeckel. War hero Audie Murphy and Tony Curtis were both getting a push at Universal, even though Murphy was near Jaeckel's size and Curtis was only an inch or two taller. The 1950s, however, were leaning toward tall leading men with stalwart presences such as Charlton Heston, Sterling Hayden, Rock Hudson, and Jeff Chandler. In addition, Kirk Douglas and Tony Curtis had flamboyant acting styles that drew attention in contrast to an understated performer like Jaeckel, who was more apt to comfortably blend into the scenery than stand astride it. Jaeckel could carry a lead with his natural charm and energy when given the opportunity, but he was clearly more in his element as a vital cog in the machinery rather than the center of attention.

There were also serious changes afoot in Jaeckel's private life as Antoinette filed for divorce. The couple began living apart in November of 1952. The boys stayed with Antoinette while Jaeckel lived with friends. He was especially close with his bodybuilding and beach pals such as Billy Murphy and Tim Lyon. As the divorce proceeded into early 1953, Antoinette claimed "extreme cruelty" as the grounds through lawyer Milton Linder. She told Superior Court Judge Clarence L. Kincaid, "His conduct made me extremely nervous and continually upset," explaining that Jaeckel would come home from the studio, change clothes, and go out without having dinner. He would often not return until early in the morning. Although

Jaeckel was poised for serious leading man stardom at Paramount in the early 1950s.

he wasn't filming anything, Jaeckel was making $350 a week at the studio. He was ordered by the court to pay his wife $100 a week with an additional $50 a week support for the kids. Antoinette would also receive $5700 in government bonds that were put in a trust for the children.

The popular bar and restaurant Tail of the Cock was a familiar hangout for Jaeckel during this period, as were his beach haunts such as the Sip 'n' Surf. Jaeckel denied to the press there were other women, later stating that he had merely gone "Hollywood" and was buying into the career buzz *Sheba* was generating. Jaeckel told reporter Aline Mosby that he felt guilty about the paycheck he was receiving for doing nothing at the studio. "I loafed at the beach, and not having some work to do didn't help my marriage any. After sitting around for a year, I knew I had to decide whether to be an actor or a bum."

Jaeckel asked out of his Paramount contract and was granted his wish. Ironically, Alan Ladd left Paramount around this same time; this might have opened the door for Jaeckel at the studio as a leading man.

Jaeckel immediately landed work as a supporting player on a minor MGM baseball picture titled *Big Leaguer* that would shoot for fourteen days at the New York Giants facilities in Melbourne, Florida, in the spring of 1953. Jaeckel and the other cast members were put through two weeks of baseball training prior to the first camera rolling, a field day for a wannabe athlete like Jaeckel. In the film he plays a confident young pitcher named Bobby Bronson who religiously squeezes a rubber ball to improve his hand and grip strength. The likable young man runs afoul of manager Edward G. Robinson for throwing a brush back pitch during warm-ups. Despite his talent and work ethic, he is cut from the team of major league hopefuls that include William Campbell and Jeff Richards (the latter a real ex–minor league player and a friend of Jaeckel's from the beach). Robinson realizes he might have made an error in judgment, and Jaeckel's character ends up signing with another team to pitch against the Giants in the film's climax.

Despite it being a relatively low-budget second feature, *Big Leaguer* was an important film for Jaeckel for a couple of reasons. He especially valued the chance to act opposite Robinson, the former tough guy star of gangster pictures such as *Little Caesar* (1930) who was known for his consummate professionalism and cultured sensibilities. Jaeckel learned from Robinson the same way he learned from veteran actors such as Helen Hayes and Shirley Booth. *Big Leaguer* was also the debut film of director Robert Aldrich, who proved his mettle here and quickly became a rising talent in the industry. Aldrich shot fast and applied television techniques for his first film, also insisting that all his principals wear no makeup. This was fine with Jaeckel, who always photographed well with his perpetually sun-bronzed skin.

Former University of Virginia football player Aldrich was impressed by Jaeckel's acting and adopted him as a stock player in many of his future endeavors. Jaeckel was equally impressed with the speed at which Aldrich worked and the cohesiveness he was able to create among the cast and crew. The two became lifelong friends, enjoying a rapport with one another that centered on their mutual love of sports. In *The Films and Career of Robert Aldrich*, Jaeckel recalled his first encounter with the director: "Aldrich couldn't emphasize quality. He had to do as many set-ups as possible. You could be the star or have one line; even then he showed a great respect for you. I really learned my professionalism from him. You soon began to feel that you were making a contribution to the film."

Big Leaguer didn't receive a ton of notice upon its release, but it's a fine little film that has accumulated interest over the years based upon its detailed and informative handling of the subject matter. Jaeckel's height and build saw him much better suited to playing a catcher or a second baseman rather than an imposing mound presence, but that perhaps fits the character of a young man who can be dropped by one team's scouts but possess enough talent to quickly be picked up by another. In early scenes Robinson gives him a catcher's glove, but Jaeckel is adamant that his fastball and pinpoint control belong on the mound. Upon cutting Jaeckel from the team, Robinson makes a passing reference that Jaeckel might keep growing and is welcome back the next spring. If there was a way to play a heel underdog, Jaeckel managed it here with the audience alternatively rooting for and against his friendly but headstrong character during the climax. According to *The Boston Herald*, "[T]he assorted aspirants for the Big League are nicely played by Jeff Richards, Richard Jaeckel, and a half dozen more."

Jaeckel next went into a co-lead opposite John Derek at Republic Pictures on *Sea of Lost Ships* (originally *American Eagle*) (1953). Jaeckel is cast as Coast Guard Ensign H.G. "Hap" O'Malley. His father was played by veteran character actor and three-time Academy Award–winning Best Supporting Actor Walter Brennan. Jaeckel and Derek are raised like brothers in the storyline but end up both vying for Jaeckel's on-screen girlfriend Wanda Hendrix. Brennan is forced to mediate their conflict between seafaring adventures. The uneven film suffers from its episodic narrative and the lack of a sufficient payoff. Considering the director is action pro Joseph Kane, the audience expects a big fistfight between the young men, but they merely go their separate ways. Finally, so much time passes that so has Jaeckel's bitterness at having his girl stolen. Derek and Hendrix wind up with one another and Jaeckel is finally okay with that outcome. Although it doesn't add up to very good drama, Jaeckel is able to display his appealing persona throughout the film and looks sharp in his uniform.

In real life Jaeckel struck up a long-lasting friendship and professional association with Derek that would see them work together numerous times over the next decade. Horse lover Derek had been a U.S. Army paratrooper before becoming a swashbuckling star at Columbia Pictures in the early 1950s. Today he is best known for being married to blond beauties Ursula Andress, Linda Evans, and Bo Derek. Behind-the-scenes publicity photos from *Sea of Lost Ships* show Derek and Jaeckel laughing and cutting up for the camera. Filming on the ocean and climbing ship's rigging was also good for Jaeckel's peace of mind. While on the set Jaeckel hinted at a possible reconciliation with Antoinette, telling columnist Erskine Johnson, "I love my wife, my children, and my home. I'm doing everything possible to set things right."

Others in the cast include Barton MacLane, Roy Roberts, Tom Tully, Douglas Kennedy, James Brown, and Steve Brodie. Jaeckel and Wanda Hendrix, recently divorced from the volatile war hero Audie Murphy, traveled to Washington, D.C., for the film's premiere in October 1953. According to *The Washington Post*, "Jaeckel is able to do very nicely as the boy who loses her." *Sea of Lost Ships* was given a general release that winter but none of the major trades bothered to review it. The by-the-numbers film did little to elevate Jaeckel to stardom.

Neither did his next leading role in a picture for Republic, a studio that was on its last legs. Jaeckel was cast as Knuckles Greer, a seafaring American adventurer in the Orient who may or may not be a spy sought by the Communist Chinese in *The Shanghai Story* (1954). The film co-starred veteran actor Edmond O'Brien and Ruth Roman and featured solid character players Barry Kelley, Whit Bissell, Philip Ahn, Paul Picerni, and James Griffith. It was directed by Frank Lloyd, a former Academy Award winner. An appealing Jaeckel spends most of the movie sharing drinks and playing cards on screen with fellow detainee O'Brien, biding time until their climactic escape from the communists.

It's an improvement on *Sea of Lost Ships*, but still no great shakes. Critics were generally kind to Jaeckel's steely presence in the film. *The Los Angeles Times* applauded Jaeckel's acting talents, calling this assignment "an odd characterization as a grizzled little fighting bantam cock of an American ex-sailor." *Variety* wrote, "Jaeckel has a salty look befitting those who follow the sea." *The Hollywood Reporter* praised Jaeckel for his "excellent support" while the *Springfield Union* wrote that he delivered a "competent performance." The reviews were feathers in Jaeckel's cap, but he was aware of the presence of stronger material needed in the wake of his work on *Come Back, Little Sheba*.

Television was still in its beginning stages and was initially considered by both the motion picture studios and the actors employed within to be an inferior product. Many actors were reluctant to work in TV and be pigeon-holed in that medium—and perhaps lose out on potential film assignments. However, the long-standing B-western was dying out, replaced by popular TV shows such as *The Lone Ranger*, *The Cisco Kid*, and *The Range Rider* that brought the action into the viewer's homes. Cowboy stalwarts William Boyd of Hopalong Cassidy fame, Gene Autry, and Roy Rogers all ventured into small screen projects. The talent that had been employed on their films had no choice but to work in television for their livelihood. With the passage of time, television began to be accepted by the studios.

Jaeckel saw television as an opportunity to play leading roles and jumped at the chance to appear in the right projects. In 1954 he filmed an episode of the western series *Stories of the Century* at Republic Pictures for veteran director William Witney of serial fame. Jaeckel played the famous real-life outlaw Billy the Kid opposite rugged series star Jim Davis. The William Bonney character, purported killer of twenty-one men, was perfect casting for Jaeckel and a role he would revisit through the years even as the date of Jaeckel's real-life birth certificate indicated he should be beyond the proper age to portray a man who was shot down by Pat Garrett in his early twenties. Jaeckel does a fine job portraying Bonney as a jumpy young tough wary of strangers. *Billboard Magazine* said, "Richard Jaeckel is a standout as the brash, conceited young hoodlum who dies by the same means he lived—by the gun."

On the TV series *Public Defender* Jaeckel plays a good-hearted boxer who won't take a dive on 1954's "The Prizefighter Story." Jaeckel's character Davey Davis starts off with a promising 14–0 record and ten knockouts before crooks try to get their hooks in him. Jaeckel appeared in a second episode of the series that same year, "The Last Appeal," playing Jimmy Morse, a young man awaiting execution and still proclaiming innocence. Both episodes were directed by noted western helmsman Budd Boetticher and showcased Jaeckel's versatility. *California* was a dramatic TV special that aired in October of 1954 on the West Coast only, detailing the history of the state's development. In addition to Jaeckel, actors Doris Day, Jack Benny, Paul Kelly, and John Carradine appeared. Outside of the *Public Defender* boxing role, Jaeckel began to make an effort to keep his shirt on before the camera to cut down on the beefcake label generated by his appearance in *Come Back, Little Sheba*. Jaeckel was quoted in the Erskine Johnson column as saying, "I'd like to keep my shirt on and prove that I'm a serious actor."

Still seeking to capitalize on the good will generated by his performance in *Sheba*, Jaeckel decided that he was going to dedicate himself to being the best actor he could be. It was time to step away from the beach and the gym and become serious about his profession. He had grown comfortable on the small surf of his career thus far and needed to seek out bigger waves to challenge himself. This meant he needed to be exposed to styles of acting and variations of character other than his customarily rugged athlete, soldier, and cowboy film roles.

Jaeckel opted to head to the East Coast to act on both the stage and live TV to better hone his acting instrument and prevent himself from falling into bad habits.

Initially Jaeckel stayed in a small single room at the YMCA on West 63rd Street in New York City, an arrangement the fan magazines found unusual for someone who seemed to be knocking so hard on the door of movie stardom. He literally had to make and take all his phone calls on a community phone in the hallway by the showers. The "Y" did give him the opportunity to work out and swim in the pool as much as he liked. He also spent time exercising at the New York Athletic Club where his father had been wrestling champ. All the activity helped him shed nearly fifteen pounds of extra muscle he had put on for *Sheba*. In Central Park, Jaeckel could be seen horseback riding, ice skating, and engaging in pickup ballgames with total strangers. No one asked for his autograph. Jaeckel decided he liked the change of scenery and would make his New York stay at least semi-permanent.

The move was the stuff of legend as Jaeckel literally took much of the West Coast beach scene with him. His good friend Tim Lyon traveled to New York to stay with him, as did Billy Murphy and other Malibu surfers trying to break into TV. The group shared a $40-a-month cold water flat apartment off Broadway in Hell's Kitchen that became their base of operations. Jaeckel's actor friend Robert Fortier had originally secured the apartment while working on Broadway. Other actor pals such as Lee Marvin, Jack Warden, Robert Webber, and James Garner crashed there when they were in the city and needed a place to stay. "It was a crazy time," Lyon recalls. "We were having so much fun, and Jake was the ringleader of it all."[1]

In late 1953 Jaeckel traveled back to the West Coast in a cross-country drive worthy of one of the episodes in Jack Kerouac's bohemian beatnik adventure *On the Road*, with Jaeckel possessing at least some resemblance to that novel's driving force character Dean Moriarty. Jaeckel had answered an auto delivery ad in a New Jersey newspaper and arranged to transport an old Pontiac to Los Angeles. He and Lyon set out on a southern route to avoid the snowy winter roads of the north while trading turns at the wheel. On Christmas Eve they found themselves in a saloon in Maud, Texas, with Jaeckel nearly coming to blows with a drunken local, a problem that has long plagued actors who play tough guys. There was another brief layover in Phoenix, Arizona, for Jaeckel to secure the deal that would see him cast in the play *Suds in Your Eye*. Taking a plane might have been quicker and easier, but it wouldn't have been an adventure and might have cost a few more bucks for the convenience. "Jake was always so cheap he never wanted to spend the money to fly," Lyon laughs.[2]

After time in California it was back to Arizona for play rehearsals. In February of 1954 Jaeckel made his stage debut at the Sombrero Playhouse in Phoenix for a week-long engagement in the Jack Kirkland play *Suds in Your Eye* with Academy Award winner Jane Darwell, Cora Witherspoon, and Nancy Hale as his co-stars. Jaeckel played matchmaker Darwell's nephew in the comedy adapted from the popular Mary Lasswell novel. Ads proclaimed it "a play the whole family will enjoy." *Suds in Your Eye* gave him the opportunity to learn a part from beginning to end and perform in a way far different from the segmented style of film. There was also a sense of fun to the proceedings. At one point in the play Jaeckel had to pick up a suitcase, and Lyon recalled a fellow cast member would fill the bag with all kinds of things in an effort to throw Jaeckel's performance off. Sometimes the suitcase even contained live animals that Jaeckel had to deal with in front of an audience. From Arizona it was back to Hollywood and New York City for more TV work.

On television he made the rounds of filmed plays on *Four Star Playhouse*, *Goodyear Play-*

house, *The Elgin Hour, The Ford Television Theatre, Kraft Theatre, Producer's Showcase, Matinee Theatre, Jane Wyman Presents the Fireside Theatre, Front Row Center, The 20th Century–Fox Hour, Schlitz Playhouse, Studio 57,* and *Playhouse 90.* Playing so many different characters in such a short amount of time proved to be great experience. Jaeckel was constantly learning lines and preparing for the camera. Live TV also turned out to be quite an adventure. Jaeckel remembered this unintentionally hilarious period of live television for *The Washington Post*: "You never knew if a prop would be in the right place if you needed it, or if an actor in the same scene would be in the right place when you needed him. After each telecast I used to think, well, that's the last they'll ever see of me. Then I'd go home, have a few drinks and sleep it off. A day or two later I'd be back on the phone to the agency, asking if they had anything down my alley.... Whenever I'm asked if I've done comedy, I say no, but I've done a lot of things that came out funny." Jaeckel told *The TV Collector*, "People used to watch those live shows, unfortunately, just to see what would happen."

There was one live TV show where everything came together perfectly, and Jaeckel was front and center in it. In 1954 *The U.S. Steel Hour* presented an ambitious western episode entitled "The Last Notch" with Jaeckel playing Vinnie Harrold, a deadly gunfighter ready to draw on storekeeper Jeff Morrow, himself a fast gun trying to live a peaceful life. The taut suspense story from director Alex Segal featured a complete western town built on ABC's New York stage. The show had fast draws, gunshots, and even horses on the stage and the whole thing went off without a hitch for the performers. Jaeckel was in top form as the story's taunting villain, a performance that would put him into consideration for top bad guys on both film and TV. The *Boston American* praised his ruthless acting as "especially fine" while the *San Mateo Times* crowed, "Jaeckel did just as sinister a job as Jack Palance did in *Shane* or many another western bad man." Syndicated columnist Eve Starr wrote,

> His portrayal of a cold killer beat anything I've seen to date. As a lead-throwing bad man, he portrayed everything he's not in real, off-stage life. It's amazing that this arrogant and grim fellow (on the screen) becomes a very likable, happily married family man when the cameras stop grinding and he heads home to play with his two young kids. That means but one thing—he's a talented, accomplished actor, who puts himself into a role and plays it for all it's worth.

Two years later, "The Last Notch" was adapted into the MGM western *The Fastest Gun Alive* with Glenn Ford as the storekeeper and Broderick Crawford as Vinnie.

Another notable TV show was the *Four Star Playhouse* episode "The Squeeze," as it was directed by Robert Aldrich and written by Blake Edwards, the future acclaimed director. The half-hour episode showcases Jaeckel as Stanley Warren. The cocky son of the district attorney, he insists on playing dice in the back room of Dick Powell's nightclub. There are a couple of well-acted scenes as the egotistical Jaeckel faces off against the crafty Powell. This type of smug character was becoming a Jaeckel specialty, and casting directors liked the fact that Jaeckel could play off his sharp good looks. He was the antithesis of the usual plug-ugly heavy. Ultimately Jaeckel is punched out and leaves the establishment with only cab fare provided by Powell. This episode was filmed in Hollywood.

Having established himself as a premier TV villain, Jaeckel was cast opposite Glenn Ford, Barbara Stanwyck, Edward G. Robinson, and Brian Keith in the Rudolph Maté western *The Violent Men* (1955). Jaeckel plays black-clad Wade Matlock, a sadistic young gunman who kills in cold blood as much for his own amusement as to enforce boss Robinson's wishes. He shoots sheriff James Westerfield in the back and guns down Ford's ranch hand William

Phipps. It is Jaeckel at his most magnetic and volatile. He projects great energy and confidence into his part as the sinister gunslinger with the crooked smile. Much of the Columbia release was filmed in the Alabama Hills of Lone Pine, California, and it's another superior credit. The film was released in January of 1955 to generally positive reviews.

Supporting player Phipps, renowned as being the voice and the physical likeness of Prince Charming in Disney's *Cinderella* (1950), recalls his old Navy buddy Jaeckel and the making of the film:

> We knew each other as seagoing guys on the same ship the *Mormactern* better than we did as actors. I hadn't been in the business yet at that point. As fate would have it, we ended up getting to work together on *The Violent Men*. It was amazing that happened. A great coincidence as we were very good friends on the *Mormactern*. We had got together a few times over the years and of course we contacted each other socially during the making of the movie. We were both friends with the stuntmen. There's not much else to say about *The Violent Men* except that he killed me on screen on that, the dirty son of a bitch. He was a good guy.[3]

The Los Angeles Times remarked, "Miss Stanwyck, Robinson, and Ford could play their parts in their sleep, to be sure, but they are wide awake as Benzedrine. So are the rest of them, notably Keith and Jaeckel." *The Dallas Morning News* wrote of the film, "One's favorite character could be Wade Matlock as played by Richard Jaeckel. He is the best-integrated sadist of recent film carnage. He shoots the sheriff in the back which is pure inspiration of common sense. Matlock wants to kill the sheriff and takes the minimum risk for himself. He leads a gang of Lew Wilkison's men up to an unoffending cowhand. He beats him with a rain of lariats, then he drags him around like a mere steer. Finally getting bored, Matlock shoots him to end the sport. He wastes only a few words and these are arrogant and threatening. There is no explanation why this fascinating character should have been so fatally slow on the draw when he faces Glenn Ford in the saloon except that the scriptwriter had to be on Ford's side." *Variety* called Ford's gunning down of Jaeckel "among the stronger sequences" in the film.

The showdown with Ford is one of Jaeckel's most memorable screen moments, on a par with his comeuppance at the hands of Gregory Peck in *The Gunfighter*. Jaeckel taunts the quiet, mild-mannered Ford, unaware he's dealing with a fast draw in self-imposed hibernation. He calls Ford "Mister" with not a trace of respect in his tone or manner. When Jaeckel pushes too hard, Ford slaps him in the face and Jaeckel instinctively goes for his gun. Ford deflects Jaeckel's draw with his left hand and shoots him in the belly with his right. A shocked

Jaeckel as the black-clad gunman Wade Matlock in Columbia's *The Violent Men* (1955). This part led to many jobs for Jaeckel as a western bad guy.

Jaeckel stumbles backward and falls dead on the saloon floor. The scene required multiple takes as Jaeckel's deflected bullet smashes a whiskey glass on the saloon counter, taken out at the precise moment by an off-screen rifle shot from sharpshooter Rodd Redwing. On each take, former U.S. Marine Glenn Ford actually slapped Jaeckel for real. The inside of Jaeckel's mouth was full of real blood, but he never complained. His professionalism in this case won him prime parts on future Ford projects.

Character actors compliment the stars they are working with. They don't detract from the top-of-the-line talent by drawing attention to themselves. It's not about competition. It's about collaboration. There is no hammy overacting or scene-stealing tricks that might enhance their own performance. The character actor is expected to be prompt and know his lines, delivering them in a manner that allows the story to move forward as efficiently as possible. Sometimes, depending on the lead, a character actor may be forced to exchange lines with the script girl as some egotistical stars feel it is beneath them to feed lines to a lesser player for their close-ups. That's the nature of the business, and it's a point Jaeckel understood. He took each Glenn Ford slap with the understanding that he was earning the star's respect and it would pay off further down the road. It did.

Jaeckel developed a long and sustainable career because he didn't rock the boat and minded his own business. He was there when called upon, said his lines, and always carried himself well in the presence of the cast and crew. He rarely complained and always worked to get what his director wanted. Because of this, Jaeckel became a valued player as much as for what he did behind the scenes as for what he delivered on camera. Reliable presences like Jaeckel were in demand and worked often. They couldn't command life-altering salaries but they knew their next job was always somewhere in the near future. As a result, Jaeckel began to feel more comfortable in his profession.

"I think stars need good supporting players and I'm pleased to be in that particular league," he told *Daredevils* magazine in 1985. "I'm truly happy in the niche that I'm in. People often ask me, 'Don't you ever wish you were somebody bigger like Paul Newman or Redford?' My answer is always the same. 'No, thank you very much. I'm very happy with what I do and who I am. I'm a character actor. I have no qualms about it. What do I care? As long as the telephone rings once in a while.'"

Tim Lyon reveals that Jaeckel had a great appreciation for character actors and classic old movies. Utilizing old Academy Players Directories that displayed photos and talent representation info for leading men, women, character players, and atmos-

Jaeckel's engaging personality made him extremely popular with his co-workers in Hollywood.

phere extras, the two would have a contest where they'd turn to a page and try to be the first to put a name to a face. Jaeckel almost always beat Lyon when it came to naming the character players. "You could go to any page in the character actor book and Jake knew all the old-timers," Lyon says. "He could name any actor in the book by looking at their picture."[4]

A few TV shows from this period stand out on Jaeckel's résumé. He worked with other top talent on the *20th Century–Fox Hour* episode "Smoke Jumpers," a tale of forest fire fighters that co-starred Dan Duryea and Dean Jagger. The episode was a cost-cutting remake of the film *Red Skies of Montana* (1952) with Jaeckel cast as Duryea's foil. He portrayed Janet Blair's criminally inclined brother opposite Bob Cummings and Dorothy Gish on the *Elgin Hour* segment "Floodtide." A *Ford Television Theater* episode, "Daughter of Mine," had no-good gas station attendant Jaeckel man-handling Margaret O'Brien and acting with movie vets Maureen O'Sullivan and Pat O'Brien. *Jane Wyman Presents the Fireside Theatre* saw Jaeckel playing the character of "The Kid" opposite big-screen veteran Victor McLaglen in the Blake Edwards–directed episode "Big Joe's Comin' Home." The *Front Row Center* episode "Dinner Date" saw Jaeckel appearing alongside Lee Marvin.

There was so much quickly filmed activity that it no doubt all blended together in Jaeckel's brain. But he was establishing contacts, building rapport with screen veterans and other up-and-coming talent both in front of and behind the camera. Actor Brett Halsey, just starting his career at the time, had a role in the *20th Century–Fox Hour* episode. He says, "I have very little memory of 'Smoke Jumpers.' It was a long time ago. I don't have any specific memories of Richard Jaeckel during the shoot, but I do remember him through the years as always being cheerful, friendly, and quick with a smile."[5]

The glut of live and taped TV opportunities were putting Jaeckel in solid company, none more so than a 1955 *Producer's Showcase* version of "The Petrified Forest" with Humphrey Bogart, Henry Fonda, Lauren Bacall, Jack Klugman, and Jack Warden. It was quite simply the finest cast ever put together for a small-screen project. Major film star Bogart was paid $50,000 for his lone television appearance as criminal Duke Mantee, the character that launched his career in the 1936 film version of the story. Playing Ruby, a member of Bogart's tommygun-toting crew, Jaeckel experienced a memorable moment of his own when he was able to get Bogart started on a line after the star missed his cue. Lauren Bacall donated the only know kinescope of the episode to the Museum of Television and Radio, and it's an interesting piece of history with Jaeckel playing a small but important part. *The San Diego Union* noted, "The rest of the cast was fine, including Jack Warden, Paul Hartman, Richard Jaeckel, Natalie Schafer, and Joe Sweeney."

Jaeckel's best role was yet to come. He landed a starring role as a manipulative bad guy holding a suburban family hostage in a touring version of the Joseph Hayes play *The Desperate Hours*. Jaeckel's role of Glenn Griffin was played that same year on film by none other than Bogart. For ten weeks during the summer of 1955 Jaeckel and co-stars William Gargan and Nancy Coleman played to capacity houses on the West Coast. When the show landed at the Carthay Circle Theater in San Francisco, the *Oakland Tribune* wrote, "Not in a couple of blue moons have we seen three performances to equal those of Gargan, Coleman, and Jaeckel as the psychopathic killer. They do three terrific jobs." Portland's *Oregonian* wrote, "Richard Jaeckel is appropriately vicious as the killer out for revenge."

The play ended its exciting run in Los Angeles in October 1955 even as sets were shipped from Seattle and built at the last moment while the audience waited outside the theater. Bogart's film was being released concurrently to great Hollywood expectations. Among those in attendance to see Jaeckel's performance was a promising young leading man named Paul Newman, who had originated the role played by both Jaeckel and Bogart on Broadway. Newman would meet Jaeckel backstage that night and file away the memory of his acting ability for a later date. *The Los Angeles Times* gave the play a rave review, singling out Jaeckel in particular: "Most demanding is the assignment Richard Jaeckel undertakes as the convict leader. Much of the early portion of the play depends on the force and resourcefulness which he brings to his portrayal."

As a result of the buzz surrounding the play, Jaeckel received a flood of new film offers. He also permanently reconciled with his wife and they shelved plans for a divorce. Things were good for the happy family residing in an apartment complex at 156 Beverly Court near UCLA. Jaeckel's rollercoaster career had once again reached one of its highest points. He told columnist Aline Mosby,

> Actors who leave home blame their homes for their career problems. But it's their own problem of insecurity. I went Hollywood to a certain extent. I didn't play around but the fields looked greener on the other side of the fence. I can only speak for myself, but when you've got a good wife and home you don't pass it up for something that's different.... She's a great source of encouragement. Having a good wife at home gives a person security and solidarity. Sometimes when actors start working, they get carried away by things they think are important on the surface, but they're really not. You finally learn to hold to the solid, important things.

Feeling he had cemented a foothold in the industry, Jaeckel bought a new three-bedroom, two-bath ranch style house in Brentwood near Pacific Palisades where he and his family lived for over twenty-five years. He and Antoinette decorated the modest 2000-square-foot home at 475 Avondale Avenue with antiques, fine silver, and paintings. There was a garden with fruit trees in the backyard where Jaeckel enjoyed relaxing. Jaeckel still liked going to nearby Santa Monica Beach, with swimming, sailing, skin diving, water skiing, and jogging on the sand rating high. He also valued his quiet time at home where he tried to read at least one book a week and sometimes enjoyed watching old films on television. Attending ballgames and participating in sports remained a favorite pastime and he belonged to various athletic clubs.

When it came to any other hobbies, Jaeckel liked to joke that the only thing he collected were bills. Although he was now a highly visible character actor, finances would remain a concern for him throughout the remainder of his life. Being a valued husband, father, and head of the household became of utmost importance. The history of his own fractured family unit no doubt weighed heavily on his subconscious. He may not have voluntarily talked about the loss of his father, but that void in his life was undeniably there. One of his treasured keepsakes was a photo of his dad in his wrestling prime.

Jaeckel made it a point to be an integral part of his own boys' lives. He encouraged his sons to go out for every sport that they could. Baseball and basketball were favorite endeavors. As his boys grew, he became active in Little League baseball as a coach from April to July of each year and partook in social functions at St. Martin of Tours Catholic School in Brentwood. Jaeckel's neighbor, UCLA basketball coach John Wooden, gladly gave the boys pointers. Jaeckel's son Barry even worked for a time as the university's ball boy. Barry was quite good at basketball until he broke his hand roughhousing with his brother. While his hand was in the healing process, he picked up a set of golf clubs and discovered a talent for that sport. Jaeckel was not the country club type but encouraged his son's obvious ability to drive a golf ball. Barry would play all the sports at Palisades High, setting a school basketball scoring record as a sophomore (35 points). Richard, Jr., continued to excel at baseball and later batted leadoff for the Loyola High team. "I wouldn't change anything about the way it was when I grew up," Barry told the *Hartford Courant*. "Sports was our number one outlet. We had a damn good time."

Jaeckel's follow-up film to *The Violent Men* was of far lesser quality and impact. *Apache Ambush* (1955) is a minor black and white western from director Fred F. Sears and Columbia Pictures filmed at Iverson Ranch and released in the late summer of 1955. TV cowboy Bill Williams of *Adventures of Kit Carson* fame has the main lead with Jaeckel playing second fiddle as one-armed Confederate soldier Lee Parker. The action-packed movie was shot under the title *Renegade Roundup* and concerns a cattle drive through hostile Indian country endangered by marauding Apaches and Mexicans. Jaeckel's sympathetic young character is

Jaeckel gets into character as the one-armed Confederate soldier Lee Parker in the Columbia western *Apache Ambush* (1955).

mixed up in illegal rifles and ends up belly-shot by Alex Montoya at the film's climax. He dies in his sister Adelle August's arms. Don Harvey, Ray Teal, James Griffith, George Keymas, and former cowboy stars Tex Ritter and Ray "Crash" Corrigan show up in supporting roles.

Jaeckel approached the part the same as if it was a top-of-the-line production and brought added nuance to the film as the conflicted young man. A posed publicity photograph for the movie is especially revealing and shows Jaeckel in character for the picture. He could have smiled and sold himself for the camera but instead presents a man haunted by his war experience and clutching the shirt sleeve where his arm used to be. *Variety* opined, "Williams, Harvey, Teal, and Jaeckel carry the acting burden in acceptable fashion." *The San Diego Union* wrote that star Williams is "aided capably by Richard Jaeckel and Alex Montoya."

In 1955 Jaeckel served as a celebrity judge for the Mr. Muscle Beach contest won that year by competitor Dennis Nelson. Jaeckel no doubt was approached by popular physique publications such as *Strength and Health* wanting to run articles on his workout but that type of publicity was something he chose to avoid. He didn't want beefcake photos in circulation when he had worked so hard to be seen as a serious actor. He also avoided parading around his physique in the costume gladiator epics popular for the time. In retrospect it was a wise choice, although he remained popular in bodybuilding circles. Professionally Jaeckel was now represented by sub-agent Jay Richards, his boyhood sports chum. (It's not uncommon for actors to frequently switch representation throughout their careers, and Jaeckel was no exception. There is always the hope that a new agent will be able to broker better deals and land bigger roles for their client.)

For the most part Jaeckel worked as often as he could, finding a nice balance between films and television assignments as he realized one medium's check cashed as well as another. On TV he played champion boxer Joey Saxon whose contract is bought by schoolteacher Ellen Corby on the 1955 episode of *The Millionaire* entitled "The Nancy Marlborough Story." Corby enlists Jaeckel to teach her schoolchildren how to defend themselves against a bully. It's a nice change-of-pace part for Jaeckel coming on the heels of the impact he had made in his villainous assignments. So too was an appearance as a smiling college jock competing with Dwayne Hickman for a girl in the half-hour comedy *The Bob Cummings Show* (aka *Love That Bob*).

The unsold TV pilot *The Mighty O* starred Craig Stevens and Alan Hale as good-natured chief petty officers aboard a creaky Coast Guard ship known as the *Ortega*. Jaeckel appeared in comedic support as one of the ship's sailors, a gum-smacker dubbed Lover Boy for his prowess with the ladies. He's perfectly cast, but there's no telling if he would have continued in such an undemanding part had the CBS series sold. Lola Albright, Jamie Farr, Don Garner, Whit Bissell, Tom Monroe, and Dick Wessel also appeared. The light comedy, filmed at Hal Roach Studios with an accompanying laugh track, eventually aired in August of 1962 as network filler. In a sense, typecasting meant continued work at that form of character, but it was always beneficial to remind casting directors one was capable of something different. Jaeckel kept reinventing himself by jumping genres and always approached life and his career from a logical point of view.

Jaeckel returned to familiar war film territory playing Pvt. Snowden in Robert Aldrich's classic action drama *Attack!* (1956). Based on the Norman Brooks play *Fragile Fox*, the film featured an Oscar-caliber performance from Jack Palance with fine support from Eddie Albert, Lee Marvin, Buddy Ebsen, Robert Strauss, and William Smithers. Albert is an ineffectual commanding officer who sends Palance's platoon into harm's way in hopes it will garner him political standing. When they're cut to ribbons, a near-death Palance returns to settle the score with Albert. Jaeckel has a running part and makes it to the last reel among a handful of survivors. Ironically, he is scouting the perimeter of the building for Germans when his unit takes turns putting a bullet into the already dead body of Albert to protect Smithers. Although he didn't pull the trigger himself, in the film's conclusion Jaeckel acts as if he did before in-the-know Colonel Lee Marvin. Aldrich received no cooperation from the Army during the making of the $750,000 black and white film. It was filmed on the RKO and Universal lots and at Albertson Ranch.

After his experience on *Big Leaguer*, Jaeckel was once again the ultimate team player for Robert Aldrich. With Jaeckel on board, there was one less headache for the director to deal with as he butted heads with studio and military bureaucracy and the eccentricities of his leading man Jack Palance. There might not have been a showy scene for Jaeckel this time around, but Aldrich would remember him and take care of his friend further down the line. Jaeckel was simply pleased to be working with Aldrich again. Paired with the wisecracking and heavyset Robert Strauss throughout, Jaeckel perfectly conveys the sense of cold and battle fatigue this soldier feels. Publicity played up the nearly 30-year-old Jaeckel's "bobbysoxer appeal" as the young private. "If you call me an actor, I say thanks," Jaeckel said in the film's presskit. "Me, I think I'm lucky."

Reviews for the film were uniformly strong. *Variety* wrote, "Robert Strauss, Richard Jaeckel, and Buddy Ebsen command attention with exceptional work." *The Los Angeles Times* found, "Robert Strauss, Richard Jaeckel, and Buddy Ebsen stand out as soldiers," while the

Plain Dealer remarked that Jaeckel "stands out" among the supporting players. *Stars and Stripes* noted that Jaeckel and the supporting cast were "excellent." *The Motion Picture Guide* again praised the supporting players: "Palance's men Ebsen, Strauss, Jaeckel, and others are particularly effective as mud-slogging GIs." In his book *The Films of Lee Marvin*, Robert J. Lentz wrote, "Smaller roles are played with aplomb by film veterans Buddy Ebsen, Robert Strauss, and Richard Jaeckel." It was a top-of-the-line film that is now considered a World War II classic.

One of the secrets to Aldrich's filmmaking success was a great deal of preparation. Aldrich liked to undertake extensive cast rehearsals prior to the start of filming. Jaeckel said in *The Films and Career of Robert Aldrich*, "If a line was changed, it had to be then. He didn't like surprises on the set. 'Don't change it without me,' he'd say. He was special. He did give you the time. He did give you the allowance. It was more or less like a stock company. It was an easy set if you paid attention. If you didn't pay attention, then you were off."

Former U.S. Marine Lee Marvin was a friend of Jaeckel's. As for 6'3", 210-pound former professional boxer Jack Palance, a legendary method actor and physical presence who could work himself into a frenzy for the cameras, Jaeckel remembered: "Palance was quite a scary guy. You never knew where he was coming from. He could stand there one minute and then he could jump thirty feet in the air. There was just a very scary side. There were scenes of incredible tension—Palance coming down the stairs to get Albert—we were all impressed, even in rehearsals. It was a heavy project."

In early 1956 Jaeckel appeared in the Vitaphone film *They Seek Adventure* with Marshall Thompson, about a former football player turned doctor in a small town. It had the markings of a TV pilot. May 1956 saw him headlining a *Matinee Theatre* version of "Night Must Fall" with Jaeckel playing the charming psychopath Danny that had garnered Robert Montgomery an Oscar nomination in the 1937 film version. In June of that year he was cast as a phantom prowler opposite Diana Lynn and Dewey Martin in the "To

Armed and ready for action, Jaeckel fights Germans for director Robert Aldrich in United Artists' *Attack!* (1956).

Scream at Midnight" episode of the anthology show *Climax!* The story, which ends with a fight scene between Jaeckel and Martin, was directed by an on-the-rise John Frankenheimer. Ohio's *Chronicle Telegram* wrote, "Richard Jaeckel, the bank robber, had a role with little dialogue, but he's a powerful young performer, an apprentice Dick Widmark sort of."

At this time Jaeckel auditioned for the part of Bret Maverick's brother Bart on the long-running Warner Bros. TV series *Maverick* starring James Garner. Although Jaeckel was in the mix along with Rod Taylor and Stuart Whitman, Jack Kelly ended up with the part. No doubt Jaeckel's physical appearance played more of a factor in him losing out on the role than his talent. It would be hard for anyone to believe that the short and blond Jaeckel and the tall

Jaeckel has a light moment on location for the classic Columbia western *3:10 to Yuma* (1957). His villainous character Charlie Prince remains one of his signature roles.

and dark Garner came from the same loins. There were other missed opportunities that no doubt changed the trajectory of Jaeckel's acting career. The underwater adventure series *Sea Hunt* would have been an ideal match for Jaeckel's aquatic talents, but six-foot Lloyd Bridges ended up making the scuba diver character Mike Nelson his signature role for four years beginning in 1958. Although he couldn't catch a break as a leading man, Jaeckel did continue to excel in meaty character parts.

3:10 to Yuma (1957) from director Delmer Daves was another classic big-screen western with Jaeckel memorably cast as outlaw Charlie Prince, right hand man to Glenn Ford. Taken from an Elmore Leonard story about a simple family man (Van Heflin) escorting a prisoner for much-needed cash, the stark black and white film shot on rugged locations around Old Tucson and Dragoon, Arizona. It was very much an offbeat psychological western with Jaeckel given a chance to shine as the loyal and lethal gunman who fondly remembers a long gone love by saying, "I never hit her too hard." It's one of his top performances. Jaeckel's take on Prince was subtle in comparison to the entertainingly over-the-top scene-stealing performance Ben Foster gave in the 2007 remake. Jaeckel's job was to provide realistic support to the stars, not attempt to upstage them. He does not disappoint.

Ford is superb as heavy Ben Wade, generating audience sympathy throughout the course of the film as he presents himself as a fair criminal willing to negotiate his release with Heflin before turning Jaeckel and the boys loose. During the course of the story Jaeckel also builds up a fair degree of audience empathy, flashing a winning smile when he discovers Ford's whereabouts and gallops off to bring back the rest of the men. This feeling is immediately jettisoned the moment Jaeckel shoots town drunk Henry Jones in the back at close range, then drags his wounded body to hang him in the hotel lobby of the town of Contention. It's one of those shocking moments that stick with an audience and often follow an actor throughout the remainder of his career. It was quite a one-two punch coming on the heels of his outright villainy in *The Violent Men*.

In the film's climax Jaeckel attempts to stop Heflin from putting Ford on the train to the Yuma Territorial Prison. Ford himself offers up a surprise for Heflin as Jaeckel runs alongside the departing train firing his Colt. Jaeckel is shot down in the belly in mid-stride as he empties his gun and tumbles into the dirt. Jaeckel enjoyed performing many of his own stunts for the camera and this impressive death scene is a fine example. His pride in performing in this capacity is one of the few times Jaeckel would ever make an egotistical and slightly disingenuous boast. "I love action in my movies," Jaeckel told the *Los Angeles Herald Examiner*. "I love movement. I want to be all over the place. I do all my own stunt work."

Jaeckel's contemporary L.Q. Jones enjoyed doing many of his own stunts as well. He worked closely with his stuntmen to find what he could do safely for the screen to enhance the film. "It's something else working with that group of people," Jones says. "They are a force onto themselves. I was lucky to get in with the best of them. You learn or you move along, and I was lucky enough to learn the pieces that allowed me to do it and learn it. Hell, I've done horse falls, draws, drags, hops, drags under wagons, trains. Everything. You get tired of sitting on your ass letting them have the fun. All you had to do was say all the crappy words. It works out and it's fun. Richard was part of that group too. It's not a large group that got to work with the stuntmen and do your own stunts."[6]

Jaeckel attended the world premiere of *3:10 to Yuma* in Denver, Colorado, alongside Glenn Ford and Van Heflin; then travelled to Dallas, Texas, for another showing. He received some of his best critical notices, with *The New York Times* stating, "Richard Jaeckel is harsh as [Ford's] top henchman." *The Hollywood Reporter* noted, "Richard Jaeckel makes a good henchman," while *The Los Angeles Times* found Jaeckel to be "menacing." *Variety* said, "Richard Jaeckel is hampered by a role a shade too simple-minded for complete acceptance but registers well nonetheless." *The Hollywood Citizen News* agreed, writing, "Richard Jaeckel is somewhat less satisfactory as Ford's lieutenant. His acting is sharp, but the way the role has been written is too young, pleasant, and shallow." *The San Diego Union* wrote, "Richard Jaeckel makes a good henchman for Ford." The part set him well on his way into the next phase of his career.

4

The Working Man

As Jaeckel gained more stability in his acting career and family life, his good friend Billy Murphy seemed to lose his. Murphy (aka Red Gaines) became known within the industry as an eccentric hipster, prone to dressing in gunfighter black and roaming Hollywood Boulevard with a script for a Billy the Kid film in his hand. It's not known if Jaeckel or Murphy himself was meant to star in the prospective story. It seems that Murphy had adopted Jaeckel's *Violent Men* character Wade Matlock as his own persona. In addition to Jaeckel, Murphy had some heavyweight Hollywood friends the likes of John Wayne, Robert Mitchum, and Rory Calhoun who thought highly of him as a fun guy to have around even if producers and casting agents were turning their heads the other way due to his sometimes erratic nature and threatening aura. No doubt some in the industry confused the *Sands of Iwo Jima* siblings, which couldn't have been beneficial to Jaeckel's own employment opportunities.

Jaeckel's friend Nick Adams told wild, worshipful stories about Murphy to anyone who would listen, and this extended to no less than rock 'n' roll idol Elvis Presley. Murphy would drag his weights to the end of the pier and work out in front of the ocean. He'd find a perfect lone wave to surf in otherwise calm seas. He'd toke on weed with the legendary iconoclast Mitchum. Elvis was briefly fascinated with Murphy after Jaeckel's buddy Vince Edwards introduced them. Presley and his friends thought Murphy was a colorful character who impressed them with his toughness and fondness for pet phrases such as, "You bet your life, mister, and you may have to." Presley liked that Murphy referred to everyone as "mister" and began to interject Murphy-isms into his own speech. Presley also adopted Murphy's walk as his own stride for the movie cameras. For a brief period of time, until Presley was inducted into the Army, he kept Murphy around as one of his pals. Murphy even sailed to Hawaii for a vacation with Presley and his friends. He wasn't, however, landing any significant acting work.

Actor Stuart Whitman remembers Presley making *Jailhouse Rock* (1957) at MGM during this period and Murphy hanging around for the girls. Whitman says,

> Elvis Presley invited him to go over to Hawaii with him. There were so many women around Elvis, and he was catching the overload. Elvis was a magnet for it. Elvis had nine or ten guys hanging around him all the time at MGM who were his pals and he bought every single one of them a Cadillac! Elvis was something. When [Murphy] came back from Hawaii he was wearing a black jacket and outfit. A black hat. Everything was black like a gunfighter. Every time I saw him after that, he was wearing it. He kind of lost it and must have got a crack in his cookie. He was a funny dude, but I guess he lost his mind a little.[1]

Jaeckel maintained the straight and narrow. He continued to hit the gym for regular workouts, although he toned down the intensity of his weightlifting so as not to appear overly muscled on-screen. He was still sufficiently muscular that when it came time for him to be stunt doubled, calls went out to the local gyms or college football fields. During this period Jaeckel was doubled by Brad Harris, a popular muscleman who had played collegiate football and would go on to be a star of European adventure films in the 1960s. Acrobat Russ Saunders, who posed for Salvador Dali's "Christ of St. John" thanks to his perfect physique, was another stuntman who worked with Jaeckel. Jaeckel's double and stand-in for many years was bodybuilder Irvin "Zabo" Kozsewski, a former Mr. Los Angeles and Mr. California who was well-known among the Muscle Beach crowd for his incredible abdominal development. Harris remembers:

> There was a television series called *Navy Log* and they were looking for two fellows to double two actors for a collegiate wrestling scene. I was chosen to double Richard Jaeckel, and the other guy, he was a UCLA football player also, was chosen to double Dick Davalos. We doubled those two actors, Dick and Dick. That's when I met Richard Jaeckel, when we were shooting this wrestling scene. In the process Richard and I had a conversation. He worked out, and I worked out. So we worked out a few times together. He was a California beach guy; so we sort of hung out.
>
> In the business he was very well respected and very well liked. I remember being on a couple of the big lots; on the MGM and the Paramount lot. Everybody knew him. Everybody liked him. They'd say, "Hey, Richard, how you doing?" And he was very kind to everybody. He was just a gentleman. So that's my relationship with Richard Jaeckel. I went on to be inducted into the Stuntman's Hall of Fame, and I had a big career in Europe. Even over there Richard Jaeckel was very popular among the film buffs. I'm sure other people will back up what I said, that he was always a gentleman and a good guy.[2]

In the late 1950s, Hollywood fitness enthusiasts Jaeckel, Harris, Billy Murphy, Vince Edwards, Chuck Pendleton (aka Gordon Mitchell), Dan Vadis, Read Morgan, and William Smith would often work out with weights near Santa Monica's Muscle Beach in a hideaway basement gym called The Dungeon alongside such competitive bodybuilders as Zabo Kozsewski, Armand Tanny, and Joe Gold. The macho group would tan their bodies a golden bronze and end up playing football and volleyball in the sand as the waves crashed on the beach nearby. They were good times, and the fun the men had under the clear blue skies laid the foundation for the massive influx of bodybuilders who moved to California in the 1960s from such faraway places as Europe. No less than Arnold Schwarzenegger was inspired by the European films of Brad Harris and took his earliest California workouts with the actor.

Jaeckel has an especially fine acting showcase in the October 1956 *West Point* episode "The Honor Code" portraying a conflicted cadet torn between friendship and honor when he catches a pal cheating on an exam. There is a scene with Jaeckel working out with the Army gymnastic team and he shows off a little on the high bar, though he is doubled by a real gymnast for the long shots. The episode was rebroadcast and syndicated under the title "The Harder Right." The episode of *West Point* entitled "The Command" (February 1957) was actually the job that stuntman Brad Harris doubled Jaeckel in. The episode concerns Jaeckel and fellow guest star Dick Davalos trying to best one another athletically. Jaeckel plays the studious, appealingly dedicated character of Leo Tanner in both *West Point* episodes. Jaeckel also did a *Navy Log* titled "War of the Whaleboats" about a whaling vessel fighting in North Korea. Brad Harris worked on several *Navy Log* episodes, leading to the minor confusion of credits. Jaeckel's *Navy Log* segment aired in March of 1957. Jaeckel also filmed two episodes of the submarine drama *The Silent Service*, ensuring that the image of Jaeckel in uniform would remain fresh in audience's minds.

The June 1957 *Playhouse 90* episode "Ain't No Time for Glory" presented a solid World War II drama about a suicide raid on a formidable underground German fortress. Barry Sullivan, Gene Barry, Bruce Bennett, John Drew Barrymore, and Hal Baylor co-starred with Jaeckel, who was cast as Sgt. Luke Mertz. He's one of the happy-go-lucky G.I.s at the beginning, thinking that he's on his way to Paris. Instead his captain, Sullivan, is given an order of certain death for the outfit. Sullivan and the German-speaking Jaeckel devise a scheme to enter the fortress to talk German officer Barrymore into surrendering. The story was directed by Oscar Rudolph and is a nice opportunity to see Jaeckel in a heroic light after so much recent skullduggery. For rebroadcasts and foreign showings, the talky 90-minute drama was promoted by Columbia's Screen Gems as a film under the title *Ain't No Time for Glory*. The syndicated *TV Key* announced that it was "[b]etter than most film shows in this series thanks to plenty of action and a strong cast."

The half-hour anthology *Panic!* gave Jaeckel a choice assignment in the June 1957 episode "Mayday." He plays Steve Bridges, a paraplegic Korean War veteran who spends his days as a ham radio aficionado. The simple but effective plot has an overzealous family dog knocking Jaeckel out of his wheelchair and upending a space heater. Jaeckel finds himself alone and pinned between a desk and a sofa with a small fire burning only a few feet away. The suspenseful story concerns his resourcefulness in contacting his radio buddies in Alaska and Honolulu to send for help. It's interesting to see the physically superior actor incapacitated and vulnerable. Jaeckel is quite believable in his desperation, and it's a nice showcase for his talent at portraying a likable everyday Joe.

As good as he could be playing an audience favorite, there was no denying that he excelled at portraying villains. Jaeckel was given a top bad guy assignment as the bank-robbing character Rogers in the November 1957 premiere episode of the syndicated half-hour western *Man Without a Gun*. The 20th Century–Fox series starred Rex Reason as a newspaperman for *The Yellowstone Sentinel* with character actor Mort Mills portraying a stalwart lawman in the 1870s Dakota Territory. Familiar heavy Mickey Simpson was also one of the villains in the episode entitled "The Seven Killers" from director Douglas Heyes. The book *Syndicated Television* remarked that the episode "featured a bravura performance by Richard Jaeckel as a sneering villain.... Compared to colorful guest stars like Jaeckel, Rex Reason looked a little over-starched."

On the big screen Jaeckel teamed up again with director Delmer Daves and star Glenn Ford for the trail drive drama *Cowboy* (1958), based on the Frank Harris book *My Reminiscences as a Cowboy*. This time Jaeckel's supporting role was nowhere near as showy as *3:10 to Yuma*'s Charlie Prince, but extended location shoots paid extremely well if a featured character player was kept on salary and per diem for the duration of filming. In *Cowboy* he is high-spirited Paul Curtis, a veteran drover herding cattle with Ford and cowboy wannabe Jack Lemmon. One of the more rambunctious of the cowpokes, Jaeckel catches a rattlesnake and maliciously teases the less sturdy of the group. Unfortunately the rattler ends up biting Strother Martin, who dies as a result. Jaeckel lives with his remorse as merely one of the things that happens amongst cowmen on a drive; he later gets into a fistfight with fellow cowboy Dick York due to his juvenile action. During this fight Jaeckel threateningly brandishes a knife and memorably intones, "Let's see what you had for breakfast!" before Lemmon breaks it up. Not a nice or admirable guy, but Jaeckel plays him like he thinks he is. The film was shot on location in El Paso, Texas, and Santa Fe, New Mexico, for the better part of two months during the summer of 1957.

Critical praise was generally strong for *Cowboy* although once again Jaeckel was far enough down the cast list to receive only brief mention. *The Los Angeles Times* wrote, "Richard Jaeckel and others provide strong support." The *Times-Picayune* praised Jaeckel as one of "the rough silent men who do their jobs well" while the *Toledo Blade* noted his role was "handled in rough and ready fashion." *The New York Times* remarked, "Performances are average. Mr. Ford, his usual sardonic self, while Brian Donlevy, Dick York, and Richard Jaeckel affect the cow-puncher roll." It was Jaeckel's third film with Glenn Ford, who told the publication *Wildest Westerns*, "Richard Jaeckel was a pro. We had worked together before on a few westerns. I remember Richard very fondly as a fine actor and friend." High praise coming from a major star of the day.

After the completion of *Cowboy*, Jaeckel did the half-hour TV show *Alcoa Theatre* with co-star Jack Lemmon. Their segment, the Korean War drama "Days of November," was about a Marine whose assignment is so dangerous his men draw up a lottery for which day of the month he'll be killed. The well-received action-packed episode aired in February of 1958. A tense and authentic military drama headlining Jaeckel as the lieutenant of a paratroop training squad came on the June 1958 "Flight" segment of

A late 1950s publicity photograph of a smiling Richard Jaeckel—perhaps an attempt to remind casting agents that he could play nice guys as well as his assortment of evildoers.

the anthology show *No Warning* (aka *Panic*), with the *Miami News* noting, "Richard Jaeckel does a fine job as jumpmaster." Jaeckel also appeared as a guest star on episodes of *Crossroads* (as another paratrooper) and the Civil War drama *The Gray Ghost*. On the latter he portrayed a disillusioned medical student considering desertion from the Confederate Army.

The Lineup (1958), Jaeckel's first film with acclaimed director Don Siegel, offered him a chance to sink his teeth into one of his more memorable characters, the bow-tie wearing getaway driver Sandy McLain. The barely hinged Jaeckel is hired to drive for unstable killer Eli Wallach and rational crook Robert Keith. It is revealed that Jaeckel's character has a drinking problem, but he is a great driver with ice water in his veins behind the wheel. There is an outstanding six-minute chase scene at the climax from stunt coordinator Guy Way where Jaeckel literally runs out of freeway with the police in hot pursuit. Nut-job Wallach clobbers him over the head with a pistol as he faces down the cops. The process shots of the actors in the car are done as well as possible for the time, with Jaeckel realistically handling the car's wild maneuvering. The film was loosely based on the popular TV series of the same name and shot on location in San Francisco and the then uncompleted Embarcadero Freeway. Jaeckel's stuntman friend Chuck Courtney has a small role.

Reviews for Jaeckel and Siegel's B-film were strong, with *Variety* noting, "[T]he cast go about chores with intelligence." *The Los Angeles Times* and *Mirror News* both found Jaeckel to be "excellent" in his part. *The Hollywood Reporter* concurred: "Richard Jaeckel is excellent as the youthful alcoholic." *The Hollywood Citizen News* crowed, "Richard Jaeckel plays the driver of the car impressively," while *Film Daily* praised the overall "convincing performances." The *Boston American* found him to be "thoroughly competent." On the film's DVD release, film noir historian Eddie Muller claimed Jaeckel "always gave a good performance." The positive reviews were nice, but Jaeckel wasn't the type who needed his ego stroked. He was more apt to praise his director than take credit for his own acting skill. (Jaeckel had signed for a lead in Siegel's *An Annapolis Story* (1955) but another film schedule conflicted.)

The Naked and the Dead (1958) was a highly anticipated Raoul Walsh film from the acclaimed Norman Mailer World War II novel of the same name. Landing the part of the character Gallagher was a ten-year dream-come-true for Jaeckel. According to a press release, Jaeckel said, "I read the book when it was published in 1948 and vividly saw myself as Gallagher, the soldier who doesn't like to kill. I followed the film plans ever since. When I read Paul Gregory was to produce the picture for RKO, I arranged to see him. After he learned how long I had thought about the character, he was impressed and let me take a test. I was lucky enough to pass it and win out over other applicants."

Jaeckel and fellow ensemble cast members Aldo Ray, Cliff Robertson, Raymond Massey, L.Q. Jones, James Best, William Campbell, Jerry Paris, Robert Gist, and Joey Bishop spent nearly three months in the jungles of Panama making the challenging South Pacific combat picture. Unfortunately, the screenplay adaptation of Mailer's novel ran 600 pages and was deemed un-filmable. Walsh and his cast arrived in Panama without a workable script and time to kill. In the early going, a local drill instructor put the cast through "boot camp" while they got a feel for their characters. It was a tough shoot with Walsh insisting the cast and crew stay on location throughout the holidays of Thanksgiving and Christmas. Although it ultimately did good business at the box office, the film proved to be a disappointment for most concerned, including Jaeckel. The profane, temperamental Gallagher that came off the page became lost in the shuffle of a large cast and plodding cinematic narrative. Jaeckel was, however, given a greater range of emotion to play than the other actors when his character's wife died during childbirth in the States. He also survives through the final reel after successfully relaying the enemy's strength and position.

At this point Jaeckel had become well-conditioned to charging off a LST craft after his previous cinematic invasions of Guadalcanal and Iwo Jima, remarking to *Films and Filming*, "I've made an awful lot of landings in practically every uniform there is." Raoul Walsh favorite L.Q. Jones, a veteran of *Battle Cry* (1955), was in the same grueling boat as Jaeckel, noting, "For Dick and me, westerns and war films were our bread and butter."[3] *The Naked and the Dead* was indeed a tough, physical film. The Panama jungle was full of deadly snakes, spiders, and scorpions. The actors had to learn a great deal of taxing choreography to evade dangerous potted special effects explosions. For one scene Walsh set a large section of the jungle ablaze. Jaeckel remembered the making of the movie for newspaper reporter Ray Bennett, commenting on the legendarily masculine director Walsh by saying, "He was always yelling. Bullets, guns, blood, action. Go, go, go! As a result the movie did little justice to Mailer's book."

Jaeckel is very good at showing the emotional devastation his character feels when he's told he has lost his wife. He conveys it all without dialogue. It's arguably the best moment in the entire uneven film, although it seemed to be overlooked by most critics, who offered little mention of the cast outside of Aldo Ray as the sadistic Sgt. Croft. Early on Jaeckel clashes with Ray after the latter kills a Japanese captive, but that plot thread is not explored further. A no-holds-barred bare-knuckle brawl between the two movie tough guys might have given the film a much-needed spark. Instead, Jaeckel's character turns into a grieving widower who is silently relegated to the background during the latter half of the picture. The film's opening featuring then popular stripper Lili St. Cyr and later flashbacks with Barbara Nichols as Ray's unfaithful wife do not benefit the main story, which pitted the underdeveloped grunts against uncaring, self-serving military brass. Mailer hated it. Walsh blamed censors for cutting the film apart. Critics had a field day.

The Los Angeles Times listed Jaeckel first among "the A-1 male company," while *The Boston Herald* wrote, "There are numerous small roles, capably enough played by William Campbell, Richard Jaeckel, James Best, Jerry Paris, and Robert Gist." *The New York Times* termed Jaeckel as merely "competent" while Pauline Kael of *The New Yorker* blasted the "lackluster casting" of "the assorted types." *Variety* called it "just another war picture" with characters who "go through the motions." Coming on the heels of his fine notices on *Attack!*, *3:10 to Yuma*, and *The Lineup*, the film was a minor setback for Jaeckel's forward momentum with the critics. As a supporting actor he merely moved on to the next offer. It became increasingly apparent that Jaeckel did not have the luxury to weigh his film and TV jobs for their potential

Richard Jaeckel and Aldo Ray clash in Warner Bros.' World War II film *The Naked and the Dead* (1958). Both actors were known for their military roles.

career advancement. He took what came his way, and in rare cases aggressively pursued roles he coveted such as the part of Gallagher.

The husky, perpetually crew-cut Aldo Ray was a real-life Navy frogman and small town football hero who was signed up for movie stardom by Harry Cohn and Columbia Pictures in the early 1950s due to his unique and forceful presence. Like Jaeckel, the gravel-voiced Ray was most at home in military pictures such as *Men in War* (1957). *Unlike* Jaeckel, the outspoken Ray drank himself out of big studio jobs and fell out of favor with drinking buddy John Wayne during the making of *The Green Berets* (1968). Cleaned out financially after three divorces, Ray slid into a succession of mostly lousy B-films by the 1970s. He was a friend of Jaeckel's. Ray recalled the type of actor director Raoul Walsh favored for *Movieline* magazine in 1991: "Raoul Walsh directed me in *Battle Cry* and *The Naked and the Dead*, my two best roles. Raoul and I got along because we drank together a lot, and he liked my kind of character.... He didn't like actors who weren't *men*."

Co-star L.Q. Jones remembers Jaeckel during the making of *The Naked and the Dead*:

> Richard is an unusual person. Weird, I don't mean. Just unusual. If you look at the part he was doing in *Naked* you realize he was the only contact with the reality of the outside world in the piece. The rest of us were nutty, more or less standard Army. You had to stand in awe of him because he had a hell of a bunch of people working—just a wild group of people—and right in the middle of that was where you got the information that his wife died. To take a man who is going along with this bunch of nitwits. I mean, look at me. Here I am madly in love with a stripper with her portrait inside the raincoat poncho, which I'm trying to make out with every day. The whole thing was a nut. And you take Richard out of that and slam him right across the face with a personal tragedy and nobody to help him. He's trying to swing at it by himself. It was a hell of a tough transition; one minute you're one way, the next you're the other. And he did a marvelous job with it. Richard always does. He was a good actor. He caught the little inferences of that, both sides, and made them work. Other than Cliff; the only human in the whole piece when you really get down to it. So you have to take your hat off and admire him for that, for goodness sakes.
>
> We were on the picture for damn near three months down in Panama. So you get to where you're in a family, and when you leave you miss everybody for a month or so because everybody else feels like a stranger. You do make good friends. Richard was a little different than most of us, thank God. A good actor and a good person, fun to be around, but no BS. He was there to work. If you could have fun at the same time, that was great. Of course almost everybody in the group was that way or you wouldn't have been working with Raoul. He really enjoyed a good time but, boy, when you had your hours and your marching time, that's what you did. No piddling around. You got it done. Richard fit right into that, or Richard was that way and the rest of us fit in. It's hard to say. He was a good friend, as I recall, on the shoot—you become professional friends—with Cliff and with Raymond Massey. We got along fine and had a good time, and I think we made as good a picture of it as you could do.[4]

The Gun Runners (1958) had Jaeckel cast in an even smaller role as a violent hired gun man named Buzurki, although his contract with Seven Arts did guarantee him a minimum of three weeks work at $1000 compensation per week. Director Don Siegel was hired to film this version of Ernest Hemingway's *To Have and Have Not* with Audie Murphy in the lead as a boat skipper. The short story was previously filmed with Humphrey Bogart in the 1944 version and in 1950 as *The Breaking Point* with John Garfield. Siegel was unimpressed with the quickly shot film that had Balboa, California, and Newport Bay subbing for Cuba and Key West. He considered it an assignment he would honor for the studio and little else. There are none of the little touches of *The Lineup* that made that film so interesting. As a result, Siegel brought on board actors he was familiar with such as Jack Elam and Jaeckel to make the process easier. Jaeckel and Robert Phillips play a pair of tough thugs in the employ of gun smuggler Eddie Albert. They don't appear until the last ten minutes of the eighty-minute black and white film for a shootout aboard Murphy's fishing boat.

Six-foot, 185-pound real-life tough guy Robert Phillips became a good friend of Jaeckel's. Phillips had played professional football for the Chicago Bears and served as a self-defense and swimming instructor in the Marines. He became a law officer and was the personal bodyguard for Governor Adlai Stevenson. Phillips was injured in an undercover assignment in Los Angeles and entered the film business in the late 1950s when his life became the basis for the Mike Connors TV series *Tightrope*. He quickly earned a reputation as one of the toughest men in Hollywood and was often hired by the studios as a minder for Lee Marvin. If the hard-drinking Marvin were to get into a bar fight, Phillips would be there to end it. Jaeckel and Phillips would work together again in Europe on *The Dirty Dozen* (1967). Phillips remembers of *The Gun Runners*,

> That was one of my first things. The producer was Clarence Greene and Greene-Rouse were putting together *Tightrope* based on my life as an undercover cop in L.A. They thought they had discovered me, this undercover Sunset Strip cop. I tested for that but the sponsor General Foods didn't think I was the General Foods type, but Mike Connors was. So that's how I got the part on *Gun Runners* and got in with Siegel. Jaeckel came in on that. Jaeckel and Siegel were very tight. He used Jaeckel on everything, practically. Dick was an old pro by that time. We had a lot of fun on that. Dick and I were friends from practically the first time we met. He was a good friend and a good co-worker. I never had a bad show with him. We were friends until he died."
>
> I liked The Jake. He was built like a little brick shithouse. Good legs, good upper body. He was very even. He looked good in clothes. He worked with weights but not too much. He wasn't out of proportion. He had that great natural blond hair, blue eyes. He was one good-looking little dude. He was quite a package. Even though he was in good shape, he was not an athlete like I was. I never touched a weight. Never went to a gym. I never worked out with anybody. I used to carry a chin-up bar with me everywhere I'd go that I'd put in the doorway of the dressing room or the hotel wherever I was staying so I could do my chins every single day. I had a professional skip rope, and I'd run, run, run, run. Fast, fast, fast. That's how you build good legs—by exploding. Climbing stairs. So that was part of the thing that Jaeckel liked—that I was in such good shape. He was in great shape and he respected anyone who kept in great shape. I had all kinds of short cuts and secrets as far as he was concerned for staying in shape. So Jake, whatever he did, he kept himself in very good shape.[5]

When Hell Broke Loose (1958), a very minor black and white independent film from director Kenneth G. Crane, is notable now only as an early starring vehicle for Charles Bronson as an American soldier in World War II. Jaeckel is cast as Karl, the suspicious brother of female love interest Violet Rensing. He is given second billing although he is only in the last third of the film playing a German soldier posing as an American G.I. in Allied territory at the close of the war. The film is loosely based on factual material as the Nazi "werewolves" led by Jaeckel are on a mission to kill General Eisenhower until Bronson foils their plans. The film closes with a brief, disappointing fight scene between the two tough guy actors. The low-budget, barely passable time-waster could have benefitted from a more substantial role for Jaeckel and a lengthier battle with Bronson. *Variety* said, "The cast try to give some vitality to their shapeless characterizations," finding Jaeckel to be the "most successful" at that task. The *Monthly Film Bulletin* wrote, "A capable cast can do little with the feeble script."

By most accounts, quiet tough guy Bronson kept to himself on film sets and rarely attempted to broker friendships among cast or crew. The former coal miner with the intimidating presence was more apt to do pushups in the corner than make small talk over trivial matters. There were a few notable exceptions who became lifelong acquaintances either through repeated work assignments or the proximity of his Bel Air and Malibu homesteads after Bronson made the unlikely climb from character actor to film superstar in the early 1970s. Among those relationships of mutual respect for Bronson were such strong, manly personas as Lee

Marvin, Ernest Borgnine, and Richard Jaeckel, who worked with Bronson again on *4 for Texas* (1963), *The Dirty Dozen* (1967), and the TV show *Luke and the Tenderfoot*. Jaeckel's friend Tim Lyon recalls, "Charlie Bronson was a class act. He was a Malibu guy and good friends with Jake off and on over the years."[6]

As Jaeckel appeared to be open to taking whatever film role was offered, he continued to rack up a number of episodic TV appearances. On some of them he had graduated to the guest lead and enjoyed the coveted "single card credit." The TV show *The Millionaire* was one of the more notable from this period. "The Betty Hawley Story" aired in September of 1958 and cast Jaeckel as a truck driver transporting a dangerous load of nitro so he can return his wife and unborn child to the States from Mexico. His wife Lisa Daniels receives word she has become a millionaire as her husband transports the deadly cargo for $1000. She hops in the car to try to overtake him and save his life. New York's *Times Record* wrote: "Richard Jaeckel as the truckie gave an earnest performance and in one short scene there was a mildly effective moment in which Jaeckel had a fight with his wife."

Luke and the Tenderfoot is an early 1959 western TV pilot that headlined Edgar Buchanan and Carleton Carpenter as a wily itinerant peddler and his naïve East Coast charge. There were in actuality two pilots for the show, as the network wasn't convinced the first 1958 effort would make a worthy series. Fond of Buchanan's lightly comic characterization, Ziv Productions was willing to retool it for a second chance. The second pilot is entitled "John Wesley Hardin" with Charles Bronson playing the title outlaw, a legendary gunman whom Buchanan boasts of knowing. When Bronson actually appears, Buchanan is caught in his lie and tries to save face in front of Carpenter. Jaeckel is cast as Bronson's equally deadly partner Sandy Burke.

The initial appearance of the two gunmen is quite memorable as they clear out an entire saloon so that they may drink alone. The duo is so serious and fascinatingly threatening in their portrayals that it throws off the tone of the entire show. Director Herman Hoffman must be faulted. The show was intended to be a comedy but there are dead bodies falling right and left courtesy of the dynamic guest star duo. After a shootout with a gang of bounty hunters, Buchanan offers up an escape plan for Bronson. When Jaeckel balks at being left for the bounty seekers, Bronson shoots him in the belly. Jaeckel is as shocked as the audience as he falls to the saloon floor, dead. Not surprisingly the second pilot did not sell either. Both segments eventually aired on the 1965 CBS summer show *Vacation Playhouse*.

More TV followed as Jaeckel played the character Von Kellwitz in the obscure *Behind Closed Doors* episode "The Germany Story" (aka "Message from Hardenburg") that aired in January 1959. The plot concerned a fencing society that operated as a front for illicit activity. Corey Allen also appeared. An April 1959 segment of *Alcoa Theatre* titled "Ten Miles to Doomsday" saw him portraying a cocky pilot who nearly creates an atomic war with his foolhardy actions. The cast includes Keith Andes and Jeff Richards. More visible and lasting were his appearances on the many western series that dominated the airwaves. Jaeckel guest starred on the George Montgomery series *Cimarron City* in the December 1958 episode "The Blood Line." Jaeckel is the character Webb Martin, son of supposedly reformed gunfighter J. Carrol Naish. When honest cowboy Jaeckel realizes that his father is actually planning to rob Montgomery's town, he joins with Deputy John Smith to foil the heist. It's a nice twist on Jaeckel's usual fast-gun duties. The episode filmed on the old Republic Pictures lot.

A February 1959 episode of *The Texan*, "The Man Behind the Star," saw Jaeckel play hotheaded young cowboy Clint Gleason, who makes off with a cattle drive payroll after being teased by the other drovers. In the process he inadvertently kills a female friend of series star Rory Calhoun. A desperate Jaeckel retreats to his homestead where his father Brian Donlevy presides as a lawman. Donlevy is conflicted between family and official duty as Calhoun arrives on the scene to see that justice is meted out. By playing the character as slightly vulnerable, Jaeckel manages to elicit some sympathy from the audience for this impulsive young man. Thirty-two-year-old Jaeckel is appropriately shifty and scared as the teenage cowpoke. Despite his advancing age, he still looks the part of a misguided youth.

On the April 1959 *Trackdown* episode "The Protector," Jaeckel plays rotten Frank Wilson, another in his string of gunslingers with ice in their veins. It's a fine bad guy portrayal that sees him romancing Sheriff Russell Thorson's daughter Grace Raynor as Texas Ranger Robert Culp tries apprehending him in a town that offers sanctuary to the criminal. Jaeckel is in full strutting peacock mode for this assignment, making no attempt to engender sympathy for his heavy. In the conclusion he is belly-shot by Culp during a gunfight. Thanks to the care and creativity of star Culp, the somewhat claustrophobic show is remembered as being of superior quality. The episode was directed by western vet R.G. Springsteen on Desilu sound stages for Four Star Television. Jaeckel's killers seemed to stick in everyone's minds, and casting directors kept hiring him for those assignments. "I was making a living killing people," he told the *Toledo Blade*.

Jaeckel was also a guest star on an April 1959 episode of *Naked City*, "Baker's Dozen." A legendary mob hit man (Joseph Ruskin) comes out of retirement for one last kill. Much of the show was shot on location in New York City, differentiating it from the other cop series on the air. Jaeckel portrays Lance, a brash young mob gunman whose pride is damaged when Ruskin talks down to him. Jaeckel nicely conveys his character's hurt at being made an underling with silent facial expressions and body language. Because so few lines were often thrown his way, Jaeckel became exceptional at creating inner dialogue for his characters. In this case he mulls over his response and when he does choose to answer, it only leads to another verbal beat-down from Ruskin and more silent Jaeckel angst. The thirty-minute episode ends in a shootout with the police, with Jaeckel as doomed as ever.

Due to his prolific rotation of TV guest assignments, Jaeckel had no new films released in 1959, although he was in the running to be cast in a pair of classics. His name was brought up for the starring part of Lt. Joseph Clemons in Lewis Milestone's Korean War drama *Pork Chop Hill* (1959) until Gregory Peck agreed to take on that role. Jaeckel was still in the running for an important part in the grim action film until casting director Helen Moore opted to use new faces such as George Peppard and Robert Blake in key supporting roles. Jaeckel was also one of the actors under consideration to play the part of Colorado in Howard Hawks' western *Rio Bravo* (1959) opposite heavy hitters John Wayne and Dean Martin. Rising actors Stuart Whitman, Michael Landon, and Rod Taylor were also vying for the role, which ended up going to singer Ricky Nelson from the *Ozzie and Harriet* TV show. It was a blatant attempt by the studio and the producers to draw young rock 'n' roll fans to the box office to see the teenage idol. Nelson does his best, but the part would have benefitted tremendously by the presence of an established film actor.

The role of the heroic young fast draw would have been a boon to Jaeckel's career, but his increasing identification as a touchy screen villain probably worked against him. Despite his skill at getting audiences to hate him, being cast as a bad guy opposite Wayne was out of the question for Jaeckel due to his short height. The 6'4" Duke needed imposing mountains the likes of Leo Gordon, Lee Marvin, Claude Akins, and Mike Mazurki as his heavies so it wouldn't look like he was picking on a little guy. The same went for tall TV heroes such as Chuck Connors on *The Rifleman* and Clint Walker on *Cheyenne*, explaining why Jaeckel never appeared on those shows.

The TV series *Tightrope* starring Mike Connors offered Jaeckel one of his most forceful portrayals: a cruel psychopath nicknamed Cruncher who delights in shooting a defenseless man four times at close range when one bullet would suffice. Undercover agent Connors infiltrates a confidence racket that uses Jaeckel as their muscle. The two are at odds from the beginning and the climax is yet another shootout that sees Jaeckel gunned down. He plays the part with a sadistic edge, and it's another testament to his versatility. Connors' character was based on Jaeckel's real-life *Gun Runners* co-star and friend Robert Phillips. The episode, entitled "The Cracking Point," aired in October of 1959.

In February 1960 Jaeckel guest starred on the Dick Powell-produced and -hosted western anthology series *Zane Grey Theater*. The episode "The Man in the Middle" starred Michael Rennie as an Indian agent attempting to bring in the killer of an Indian boy but meeting indifference and opposition from the townsfolk. Jaeckel is cast as Tod Mulvey, the antagonistic young townsman who shot the Indian and is resistant to Rennie's pursuit of justice. The thirty-minute episode was helmed by veteran director Rudolph Maté and is top-quality even if it treads into very familiar territory. Jaeckel had the market cornered on this type of character who believes he is in the right for all the wrong reasons. The climax finds Rennie daring Jaeckel to gun him down. The young man who has come on so tough throughout the episode ultimately hands his gun over, trying to ascertain the reason he could gun down an Indian but not a white man with a clear conscience.

One of Jaeckel's best TV western guest shots came on the March 1960 episode of *The Rebel* entitled "The Rattler." Snake-bit star Nick Adams rides into all kinds of trouble when Deputy Roader (Jaeckel) sets him up as the fall guy for the murder of the town marshal. Killer Jaeckel is as charming as he is conniving, setting himself up as the new husband and father for the marshal's family even as he intends to collect a thousand dollar out-of-state bounty on the marshal's head. Painting Adams as a hired killer, Jaeckel intends to whip the town into a hanging party to perform his final dirty work. There's a tense fight over a gun between Jaeckel and Adams, with Jaeckel once again winding up belly-shot and dead. By this point Jaeckel was becoming an expert at dying on screen. "Psychologically, much can be done in the villain roles if you can avoid the traps," he told the *Toledo Blade*.

The film *Platinum High School* (1960), another black and white low-budgeter, gained some measure of notoriety for its oddball casting in a murder mystery set amongst rich delinquents on the exclusive Sabre Island. Director Charles Haas filmed on Catalina Island and MGM sound stages with former child star Mickey Rooney headlining alongside Dan Duryea, Terry Moore, Yvette Mimieux, Elisha Cook, Jr., Warren Berlinger, Christopher Dark, Harold Lloyd, Jr., and country singer Conway Twitty. The entire cast, including Jaeckel, towers over the 5'2" Rooney, who is solid in his role of a grieving father trying to get to the bottom of the mystery of his son's death.

Jaeckel is surprisingly far down the cast list as an antagonistic military academy's ex–Marine physical education instructor. Jaeckel's character Hack Marlow and Rooney engage in a fight scene using rifle butts to parry and thrust, before lead heavy Duryea throws an errant knife that sticks in Jaeckel's shoulder. Marine combat instructor turned stuntman Charles Horvath choreographed the fight. Jaeckel's scenes with Rooney have pep but the film was another in a growing line of big screen misfires and disappointments. The bare-bones production is a far cry from *Come Back, Little Sheba* for both Jaeckel and Terry Moore, here cast as camp commander Duryea's secretary. Buried at the bottom of double-bills, the unassuming little film was barely reviewed by critics. In 1964 *Platinum High School* was re-released as drive-in fodder under the sensational title *Trouble at Sixteen*.

Director Robert Montgomery's *The Gallant Hours* (1960) offers Jaeckel one nicely acted moment opposite screen legend James Cagney as Admiral Bull Halsey. The well-mounted war biography was filmed in San Diego and sees Jaeckel as Lt. Commander Roy Webb, attempting to relinquish his position after losing too many men in battle. Despite Jaeckel's command fatigue, Cagney manages to convince him to stay on his ship for the good of the men still serving under him. In the final cut of the film, Jaeckel has only one other brief scene, this one opposite Dennis Weaver. It's a small role in the big picture, but gave Jaeckel the chance to go toe to toe with Cagney in a dramatic scene. It was an opportunity he relished. "Actors were better in the old days," he told Dick Kleiner. "I worked with Cagney and Bogart and all of them, and they had flair, they had class, they had style."

Despite the brevity of the assignment, *Variety* singled Jaeckel out, noting he "commands most favorable attention," while the *San Diego Union* found he strengthened the picture with "good supporting work." The *Boston American* praised his "interesting characterization" and the *Motion Picture Herald* claimed, "Dennis Weaver, Ward Costello, Richard Jaeckel, and Les Tremayne adequately portrays Halsey's staff." The extended cameo proved Jaeckel could hang with the Hollywood heavyweights, but the small part had little immediate impact on his career despite it being a solid credit. He kept chipping away, hoping that his best role was on the horizon. A good role could snowball into more quality offers. Too many small or bad parts strung together could kill a career or lower one's asking price.

In the spring of 1960 the Screen Actors Guild went on strike against the major studios, halting film and television production. During the winter a few films had rushed into production to beat the looming strike. One of these was director John Sturges' *The Magnificent Seven* (1960), a western version of Akira Kurosawa's *Seven Samurai* (1954). Sturges had a star in place in the form of Yul Brynner and quickly cast the rest of the anti-heroic seven with soon-to-be stars such as Steve McQueen, Charles Bronson, and James Coburn. For the part of the gunman character Lee, Sturges cast then-hot actor Robert Vaughn, who was currently being nominated for a Best Supporting Actor Oscar for *The Young Philadelphians* (1959). Vaughn is interesting as the psychologically haunted gunslinger, but he seems perhaps less comfortable in a western saddle than the others. Although *The Magnificent Seven* helped Vaughn's career, the western was a genre for which he is not known outside of this film. In retrospect, the part of Lee would seem to have been tailor-made for a screen cowboy like Jaeckel based on his previous fast gun killers in *The Violent Men* and *3:10 to Yuma*. Perhaps had Sturges not been rushing against a strike deadline, Jaeckel might have found himself cast in this star-making film.

Flaming Star (originally *Flaming Lance* and *Black Star*) (1960) is a Don Siegel project that turned out to be superior western entertainment. It was originally conceived as a Marlon Brando film; instead Siegel found himself directing popular rock 'n' roll singer Elvis Presley as a half-breed Kiowa torn between his white family upbringing and his warring heritage.

Siegel was concerned that he would have problems with Presley and cast the remainder of the 20th Century–Fox western with trusted veterans. Jaeckel is found far down the cast list as Angus Pierce, brother of female lead Barbara Eden. The beginning of the film sees Jaeckel dancing and singing along with Presley's rendition of "Cane and a High Starched Collar," even picking up a wooden chair as his partner in an in-joke nod to lyrics from Presley's famous hit song "Jailhouse Rock." However, after friends are killed he is ready to shoot any Indian he sees, including Presley. His emotion is raw, his anguished tears believable. He is only stopped from violence by Presley's full-white brother Steve Forrest. There is fine work by Dolores Del Rio, John McIntire, Karl Swenson, and Ford Rainey, and in smaller roles such favorites as L.Q. Jones, Tom Reese, and Roy Jenson.

Character men like Jaeckel and L.Q. Jones were on hand to offer Presley help where and when he needed it at director Siegel's request. Siegel ended up having little difficulty with the earnest and hard-working Presley and the film is fondly remembered by the singer's fans as one of his very best. It garnered Presley some of his best critical reviews. It's a shame that he abandoned further attempts at serious drama for his silly formula musicals; *Flaming Star* demonstrated his obvious potential. *Variety*'s reviewer made mention of Jaeckel and Jones and their "vigorous supporting work." Jones says:

> Elvis really wanted to act. But nobody would give him the chance. Elvis would come around to us and say, "do you think this will work, maybe this, how about that?" But mainly Don Siegel gave him John McIntire. John was certainly one of the best character men in our business. And Dolores Del Rio, even at that age, was a shockingly beautiful woman, and just as sweet and nice as she was pretty. They would work things out with him so that he could exercise his acting muscle. He really wanted to do that. All the people worked together, having a good time. Elvis was getting a chance to act for a change. A happy company.
>
> When you have people who are so superior, you can't work around them and not pick up the things you have to do. Richard fit right in with that when we made *Flaming Star*. You can't turn your back on how good an actor he really is. You can because of his looks and because of his parts dismiss him if you're not careful. If you watched him in that thing he did with Lee Marvin, *The Dirty Dozen*, which is probably his best part as the sergeant, you realize just how good he was doing his part. Which comes to do with all that talent and all that stuff going on. I take my hat off to Richard. He was a good man.[7]

The actors' strike extended through the spring of 1960. The Screen Actors Guild was negotiating for residual rights regarding television broadcasts of films and TV. The eventual settlement declared that anything made from 1960 on would be eligible for residual payments up to a certain number of television broadcasts. So, all of the films Jaeckel had made prior to 1960 would not be eligible for any further compensation to the actor. However, all of his new product would continue to generate him a decreasing percentage of pay as long as the project's producers were still seeing money. The major advantage to this settlement was the first network repeat showing of a television episode would pay Jaeckel an equal amount to his original negotiated pay for the job. This meant a busy character actor could go from show to show and make a fairly comfortable living. Jaeckel went right to work.

On episodic television Jaeckel appeared on the September 1960 episode of the Dale Robertson western *Tales of Wells Fargo*, "The Kinfolk." He played the antagonistic character Len Lassiter. English stuntman Raymond Austin was working in the States at the time and recalls:

> I was introduced to the young Richard Jaeckel by Robert Hoy, stunt actor, on a back lot of a Hollywood set in the TV show *Tales of Wells Fargo*. I was a very new member to the stuntman industry and Hollywood's Stuntmen's Association. Richard was young, good-looking and a nice, fun guy to be around. We were never great friends but our paths crossed over the years and we always picked up where we left off at our last encounter. When I was doing a car chase on the TV show *77 Sunset Strip* with Carey Loftin; he

reintroduced me to Richard. We worked together again on *Naked City* and again on *Tightrope*. I then returned to England to work as a stuntman and was on the stunt team of *The Dirty Dozen*, in which Richard played Sgt. Bowren. It was great to see him. He had not aged a day.

All of us friends and colleagues of Richard Jaeckel knew he had the picture in the attic, i.e., Oscar Wilde's classic story about a mysterious young man.... Richard never seemed to age, no matter what. Soon after *The Dirty Dozen* I graduated to being a writer, then director, and later returned to America as such. I met Richard again as a director on *Salvage One* in 1979; you guessed it, he had not aged one bit. In 1985 we worked on *Spenser: For Hire*. He was as young as ever. That was Richard, with his picture in the attic.... I have very good and happy memories of you, Richard. Rest well, my friend from across the years.[8]

Jaeckel was once again a guest star on *The Rebel* for the October 1960 episode "Run, Killer, Run," directed by Bernard McEveety. Sporting dark hair, a beard, and cut-off sleeves, Jaeckel is Traskell, a haunted man on the run who becomes chained to Nick Adams for the duration of the show. Traskell gives indications of being psychologically damaged, claiming he's running to avoid killing his twin brother. Bounty hunter Ed Nelson is hot on his trail, and Adams is forced to outwit the dangerous Jaeckel before he goes completely off the deep end. As was becoming customary in these westerns, Jaeckel winds up gut-shot before the climax. The dark hair is a different look for Jaeckel, whose edgy performance is a creative triumph. As a side note, his arms are as muscular as they've ever appeared on screen.

Producer-writer Andrew J. Fenady created *The Rebel* and became friends with Jaeckel at Paramount. He recalls:

> I was first aware of Richard Jaeckel when I was at Woodward High School during the war in 1943 to 1944 when he made his first picture *Guadalcanal Diary*. I think that he was going to Hollywood High School at the time. He was 16 or 17 when he made that picture. I used to see him every once in a while when I worked out at a gymnasium here but I didn't make so bold as to talk to him. He was kind of a private guy. Always affable, but not the kind of a guy that would come up and start shooting the breeze. He was serious about his working out and it showed.
>
> I used him on *The Rebel* not once but very often, especially after the first time. He was so damn good and Nick Adams was great. Nick was not worried how tall any of the other actors were. Some of the actors that I worked with were. Jake was a very good match for Nick. They were about the same size. He was a very good match except when he took his shirt off; then there was a discernible difference between them. Though Nick was built pretty good and he worked out too. I used Jake as much as I could. He played good guys sometimes or crazy people sometimes. He was very effective either way. We'd go so far as to put dark coloring on his hair, so you wouldn't say, "There's the same guy doing the same part again." He was very good that way.
>
> There was a café or a saloon place called Oblath's across from Paramount on Bronson Avenue. Quite often Jake would come in and we'd have breakfast together. I got to love him despite the fact that he was a thief. Richard Jaeckel was a thief. I'll give you some evidence. He would never ever leave without stealing something. He told me this, "I never leave here or practically any other place without stealing something." He would either steal a *Variety*, a *Hollywood Reporter*, some kind of a magazine, or some other kind of a newspaper. He was proud of it. He looked so damn innocent as he was walking away. He would always manage to grab something. But the best thing he was good at stealing was any scene that he was in. He didn't have to do much with those eyes; and that expression could convey an awful lot. Besides stealing that, he would steal the hearts of those of us that knew him.[9]

One of Jaeckel's silliest assignments came in October 1960 on an extremely light episode of the popular Warner Bros. detective series *77 Sunset Strip* entitled "The Office Caper." Jaeckel is the beer-loving character Bob Bent, who with his wife Sherry Jackson is somehow considered to be the top trigger team in the city. Mobster Bruce Gordon hires the hit artists to murder star Efrem Zimbalist, Jr. However, hotheaded Jaeckel's drunken bumbling sees him get into a fistfight with carhop Edd "Kookie" Byrnes and then shot in the belly after he telegraphs his whereabouts within the detective agency's offices. It's hard to take anything about this episode seriously, although Jaeckel and Jackson make an attractive couple.

Jaeckel had a notable guest shot on the classic Desilu crime drama *The Untouchables* in December of 1960. "The Otto Frick Story" concerns gangster Jack Warden being recruited by members of the Nazi party to pressure Jewish store owners into paying protection money. Warden's Frick has in his employ young muscle Hans Eberhardt, played by Jaeckel. The Nazis play up gullible Jaeckel's German ancestry and attraction to blonde Erika Peters to turn him against Warden by the episode's end. Jaeckel does an excellent job as the conflicted gunman, especially when Warden reveals that Jaeckel has been duped by the Nazis and it's too late to take back a bullet. By episode's end Robert Stack's Eliot Ness arrives to take a remorseful Jaeckel into custody. John Peyser helmed the excellent episode, a high-water mark for Jaeckel.

In the January 1961 episode of Revue's *The Tall Man*, "Grudge Fight," Jaeckel plays a gunslinger named Denver who heads up into the mountains with Billy the Kid (Clu Gulager) to settle their personal score with a shootout. As they take rifle shots at one another among the rocks, Jaeckel gets hit in the leg. Although the two have seemingly been trying to kill one another, their shots have been mysteriously off, suggesting it is more sport than shared hatred. Now that Jaeckel is injured, Gulager spends the remaining portion of the episode desperately trying to save him.

In a particularly gruesome and unsettling scene, Gulager is forced to amputate Jaeckel's leg. In many of Jaeckel's western assignments it was inevitable that he would be dead by the episode's end. On *The Tall Man* he spends twenty-five agonizing minutes reaching that conclusion. His final scene, being held in Gulager's arms as he unblinkingly reminisces about family, is *tour de force* acting. It's the kind of performance that rates Emmy awards. Director Richard Irving focuses his camera on Jaeckel's expressive eyes. On many of these TV guest shots Jaeckel played the line-snapping bad guy but consistently sought to bring extra depth to these characters. He liked to think they were compassionate people with feelings and a sense of humor and tried to bring that across on screen. He does that and more here.

Clu Gulager remembers:

> We did seventy-nine episodes of *The Tall Man* and I think Dick's episode was by far the best. I was playing opposite Dick, and he and I carry the show. I shot Dick, he gets gangrene in his leg, and I held him in my arms as he died. I thought that was pretty heavy shit. I like it. That episode was very well-written. In my mind it's the best we did by far. Dick was excellent as always. He was a great actor. Of course, we all knew that. I was impressed very much by the episode and by Dick. I'll always remember Dick because he was very well respected and liked in my town of Hollywood.[10]

The March 1961 *Lawman* "Blue Boss and Willie Shay" guest stars Jaeckel as Al Janaker with Sammy Davis, Jr., as the singing cowpoke Willie Shay. Davis rides into town with his special trail-herding cow Blue Boss. When whiskered cowboy Jaeckel is embarrassed by the Sarsaparilla-sipping steer, he empties his gun into the animal in a shocking display of senseless cruelty. Davis vows vengeance and turns out to be deadly with a firearm. Shifty troublemaker Jaeckel tries to get the upper hand and draw first on Davis, only to be belly-shot, running backward into a river. It's a solid episode of the Warner Bros. western, made memorable by the appearance of Davis and the villainy of Jaeckel.

Jaeckel and his current agents at the Frank Cooper Association would attempt to land the highest quality, the most popular, and the best-paying shows to maximize respectability, visibility, and profit. In the March 1961 *Alfred Hitchcock Presents* episode "Incident in a Small Jail," Jaeckel is cast as an accused murderer who switches clothes with jaywalking cellmate John Fiedler and escapes as a lynch mob descends upon the jail. There's a nice contrast on screen between the meek Fiedler and the dangerous Jaeckel as they interact between the bars. As was typical of the Hitchcock stories, the finale throws the audience a curve. The half-hour show was directed by Norman Lloyd and introduced by Hitchcock. It is widely regarded as one of the best episodes of the entire series. When the show was rebooted in 1985, "Incident in a Small Jail" was the first episode to be re-filmed. Ned Beatty played the John Fiedler role with Lee Ving cast in Jaeckel's part.

The May 1961 *Wagon Train* episode "The Chalice" features one of Jaeckel's most finely delineated performances to this date: Barker, the young sidekick to fellow guest star Lon Chaney, Jr., an aging, unlucky dreamer whose life has been a series of empty schemes. Joining up with the wagon train, Chaney befriends an immigrant couple and convinces Jaeckel that their kindness will be repaid with good luck. To push his luck along, Chaney has Jaeckel sneak into the couple's wagon to make off with a family heirloom. However, in the process of stealing a gold chalice, Jaeckel accidentally strikes and kills the woman. Chaney now sees the chalice as bad fortune, but Jaeckel sees it as his chance to become something more than Chaney. The two squabble in their escape and, befitting a tragedy, gun one another down. Jaeckel is given a chance to register several emotions throughout the course of the episode and is believable in his portrayal of a young man whose mistake leads to desperation. Virgil W. Vogel directed for Revue.

Off-duty soldiers Mal Sondock, Frank Sutton, Richard Jaeckel, and Robert Blake take a drunken walk that leads to trouble in United Artists' controversial *Town Without Pity* (1961).

Jaeckel's film career had been stumbling along for three years; Gottfried Reinhardt's controversial *Town Without Pity* (1961) put him back on the map. Jaeckel does solid work as Cpl. Birdwell Scott, an American soldier on leave who gets drunk and rapes bikini-clad German teenager Christine Kaufman with three of his buddies. Filmed in Bavaria, Germany, the motion picture top-lined Kirk Douglas as the defense counsel representing Jaeckel, Frank Sutton, Mal Sondock, and Robert Blake. To reduce the sentence facing his soldiers, Douglas is forced to put the girl on the stand and tear apart her character. E.G. Marshall co-starred as the prosecuting attorney. Jaeckel's Cpl. Scott is a professional soldier, honored with a Bronze Star and a Silver Star for heroism but facing the death penalty for his sexual transgression. He is stoic throughout much of the trial as he awaits his punishment, callously explaining the rape to Douglas by saying, "It was hot, I was in the mood, and the dame was there." One of the more interesting aspects of his performance is his protectiveness of the young and troubled soldier Blake. Although he appears in several scenes, Jaeckel has a minimal amount of dialogue. Still, it's a performance he is well remembered for. Early on there's a downward glance as he's seated in the tavern that speaks volumes about Jaeckel's character's state of mind.

As a character actor, Jaeckel occasionally had to deal with inflated star egos. It says something of the admiration that powerful producer-star Kirk Douglas had for Jaeckel that he was even hired for the part, although the studio pressbook indicates director Reinhardt was fond of Jaeckel's performance in *Come Back, Little Sheba*. Muscular young blond actors were rarely given the chance to share the screen with Kirk Douglas, lest they draw attention away from the film's intended central figure. The viewer will notice that the camera seldom dwells on Jaeckel, and in early scenes he's seen wearing a fedora. As always, Jaeckel was merely grateful for the work, although one can't help but feel that some of his best close-ups and camera coverage ended up on the cutting room floor. (Douglas' next film was the 1961 western *The Last Sunset* with director Robert Aldrich. Jaeckel would have been perfect as an outlaw named the Julesburg Kid opposite fellow heavies Jack Elam and Neville Brand, but dark-haired Rad Fulton was cast instead. Producer Douglas likely had pull over Aldrich in that regard.)

The Los Angeles Times thought Jaeckel was "well-cast" in *Town Without Pity* while *Variety* found his performance "skillfully delineated." The *San Diego Union* commented, "Blake and Jaeckel stand out among the GIs," while the *Toledo Blade* praised Jaeckel for his "competent" performance. The Turner Classic Movies website notes, "Richard Jaeckel and Frank Sutton are convincingly creepy as two of the accused." In his *Movie Encyclopedia* Leonard Maltin wrote that Jaeckel was a "standout" in the film. Most critics of the day understandably chose not to heap a lot of praise on the portrayal of an unremorseful rapist.

Town Without Pity served as a reminder of his talent and skill in front of the camera, guaranteeing continued offers for employment. Unfortunately, it didn't elevate him to a higher level of prestige or billing. The TV guest shots remained extremely varied, as was their impact. Good-looking Jaeckel still had potential as a leading man, but the majority of work came as a supporting player and evildoer. If he were ever to achieve leading man status, now was the time. He was at a prime age, but he couldn't quite compete with the dramatic heights achieved by contemporaries Marlon Brando and Paul Newman. New leading talent such as George Peppard, Robert Redford, and Steve McQueen were on the upswing, and Jaeckel didn't push it. He was happy being a character player as long as the phone kept ringing.

✦ 5 ✦

The TV Cowboy

As Jaeckel guest-starred on one television show after another, he kept his options open for a regular TV gig, something that might make him a household name and guarantee his family's financial future. Personal appearances in support of such a show often proved more rewarding to the pocket book than the actual work itself, which for someone of Jaeckel's caliber would likely yield several hundred dollars an episode. For comparison's sake, James Garner and Michael Landon earned $500 a week at the outset of *Maverick* and *Bonanza*, Clint Eastwood earned $600 a week during the first season of *Rawhide*, and Steve McQueen made $750 a week as the star of *Wanted—Dead or Alive* in its debut season. Those salaries were bumped up significantly when the shows proved to be hits. A successful series that ran three seasons or one hundred episodes could be profitable in the short *and* long term when syndication came into play. Work that kept money rolling in later years was a sound investment in Jaeckel's mind. Unfortunately, an unsuccessful series could also prove to be the death knell to a promising career. It could kill the ability to work in any film as well as future TV. As a result, Jaeckel tried to be choosy when it came to the extended television projects offered him.

He liked what he saw in *Frontier Circus* (1961–1962), a western that featured a traveling caravan of specialized performers roaming the Old West and encountering weekly adventures. It was *Wagon Train* with pizzazz and would be coming out of the same studio through Universal's TV division Revue. Jaeckel would also be co-starring alongside veteran character actor Chill Wills and his *Sea of Lost Ships* pal John Derek. Jaeckel signed on as the T&T circus group's advance scout Tony Gentry, a Civil War veteran who could handle himself in a fight. Jaeckel would be the one who rode into various towns to set up the deal and survey the prospects of danger for the troupe. If there was trouble, tough guy Jaeckel dealt with it. The storyline of some episodes would be carried by Jaeckel alone; others he would share with Derek and Wills. Jaeckel could also involve himself in plenty of interesting action. He'd get to ride elephants, hang under a hot air balloon, and participate in a cross-country horse race.

The pilot and opening episodes were high in production value. The cast and crew traveled to locations such as Reno, Nevada, for filming and presented a three-ring circus for the cameras with a variety of real-life circus performers. The episodes guest starred such accomplished actors as Mickey Rooney, Sammy Davis, Jr., Brian Keith, Aldo Ray, Claude Akins, Eddie Albert, J. Pat O'Malley, Rip Torn, John Anderson, Vera Miles, Barbara Rush, Stella Stevens, Cloris Leachman, and Red Buttons. Quality character players such as Harry Carey, Jr., R.G. Armstrong, Bob Wilke, Alan Hale, Jr., Lane Bradford, Jack Lambert, and Chris Alcaide also

Jaeckel as the heroic trail scout Tony Gentry on Universal-Revue's TV western *Frontier Circus* (1961). It took Jaeckel's career a long time to overcome the cancelation of this series.

appeared. Veteran directors Tay Garnett and William Witney helmed the action. Other directors included Alan Crosland, Jr., and an emerging Sydney Pollack. In an article in *The Saturday Evening Post* Crosland spoke of Jaeckel: "He's a very nice boy. Very nice. No temperament, no problems." *Variety* commented on the debut episode's stars: "They stack up as a reasonably interesting threesome and should have strong appeal with the younger viewers."

Jaeckel's charismatic character Tony Gentry was two-fisted, an expert horseman, and a great shot with a rifle. He was loyal and dependable to the circus, considering Chill Wills' Casey Thompson a father-figure (Wills took him in after he served with the Confederate Army under General John Bell Hood). He also had a sense of humor and enjoyed a good time, wearing his cowboy hat flipped up at the brim and often flashing the trademark Jaeckel smile. Sly, funny, and appealing, Tony was as close a character to the real Jaeckel as ever made it to the screen. *Frontier Circus* displayed Jaeckel to advantage in many of the stories, and he was more than happy to carry the action load. With dark and handsome John Derek as co-star, Jaeckel more often than not didn't get the romantic storylines, but he entertained a few during the course of the season—most notably with Elizabeth Montgomery in the episode "Karina." Tony Gentry is Jaeckel's best, most well-rounded leading role. He tried to make it last. "After ten years of being hated on the street, I'm ready to go straight," he told the *Toledo Blade*.

Jaeckel was featured on a television interview segment on *Here's Hollywood* and posed with a chimpanzee in his lap for a *TV Guide* photo feature. He did plenty of initial publicity for the series, describing it to *Plain-Dealer* columnist George E. Condon as being "sort of like *Wagon Train*, with lions, tigers, and elephants.... I'm opposed to revelation of inside stuff about TV pictures. It's a pet peeve of mine. All it does is destroy the illusion we're trying to build in a picture. It all has to do with the way the public has become so sharp today. A man could be fleeced by an illusion many times in the old days and he didn't mind it as long as he didn't know it was a trick."

"I wish I could say honestly that I always wanted to run away and join the circus," Jaeckel told Hollywood writer Isobel Ashe, "But I didn't. I didn't even want to run away from home. For that matter, I didn't even plan to be an actor as a kid. I didn't even know how to act. It wasn't until ten years ago that I began studying seriously because I realized what a great business this is, and how lucky I am to be in it." As for his sons visiting the circus set, Jaeckel said, "They'd have given anything if we'd given them permission to cut school that day to come out and see Dad work."

Jaeckel was more than happy to have a regular paying job, especially one that presented him in a more heroic light to his own children. He told Joe Finnigan of UPI: "The main thing is to be working, and it's much nicer to be working as a villain than not at all. This series represents a certain amount of financial consistency, and I'm sure everybody is interested in financial consistency." He followed this up by telling *The Salt Lake Tribune*, "When you play tough guy roles all day, you can't help taking a little bit of the character home with you. It's a little hard on the wife and kids. It will be a relief to play a part in which I smile my way through instead of shooting my way through."

Despite having arrived as a TV lead, Jaeckel still felt like he was merely part of a team. He didn't let his new "star" status go to his head. There would be no sudden change in ego or perceived treatment. He was still the same simple, undemanding Jaeckel. Actor James McMullan had just signed a studio contract and appeared opposite Jaeckel in the episode "The Race." He says:

> It's hard to remember much from my early days under contract to Universal. *Frontier Circus* was my very first TV show. What I do remember about Richard Jaeckel is his kindness and graciousness. It's always difficult to go to work on a new TV show, especially working with an established cast. You are the newcomer who has to prove himself. I remember Richard making the transition easy and painless. He knew I was green and went out of his way to make me feel comfortable. He was also a very talented actor.[1]

Unfortunately the series aired opposite popular favorites *The Adventures of Ozzie and Harriet* and *The Donna Reed* Show, leading to poor ratings. Despite quality acting and storylines, it quickly became lost amidst all the other westerns on the tube. Audiences were hesitant to commit to new characters on a black and white series when so many cowboy shows were taking the route of *Bonanza* and going color. The high production value for *Frontier Circus* dwindled into bare bones wallet-crunching as the CBS series played out its twenty-six sixty-minute episodes from the fall of 1961 through the summer of 1962. The three-ring circus became one ring, and the contingent of exotic animals provided by Ralph Helfer eventually disappeared. The large cast of extras scattered as the series stayed on the cost-controlled Universal back lot for its latter episodes.

Despite the disappointment of the series not lasting more than a single season, Jaeckel had a great time doing it. He reflected on the series over twenty years later in an interview for *The TV Collector*: "The most fun of all about those western things is you could really lose yourself. You were totally different people. You were on a horse all day, sometimes you were chasing rustlers. You were doing something that you never would do if it were not in the motion picture or television business."

He also became friends with a number of cowboys and stuntmen on the Universal lot, in particular Chuck Courtney and Robert Fuller who was starring on *Laramie* at the time. Fuller recalls of Jaeckel,

> We were very good friends and remained so for the rest of our lives. Chuck knew him well too. I think he may even have doubled for him some. Jake was super, super nice. Always laughing and smiling. Very gregarious. He had one of the all-time great smiles. He was quite a character and loved life.
>
> We met at Universal when I was doing *Laramie* and he was doing *Frontier Circus*. Every night after work a bunch of us would end up in my dressing room having a drink and raising hell. There would be Lee Marvin, and Terry Wilson and Frank McGrath from *Wagon Train*. One night Jake came over and saw us and that fit right in with Jake's idea of having a good time. We saw quite a bit of one another over the years. He and Jocko Mahoney would come over to my house in Toluca Lake and swim in the pool. Jock was friends with Jake too. Talk about two super-fit guys. Jake was a lifter. He pumped iron a little bit.[2]

Frontier Circus was cancelled and Jaeckel moved on, hoping he'd be able to overcome this failure in the eyes of the studios and casting directors. The stigma of the failed series proved difficult to shake. As an itinerate actor, there was always the fear that any job could be the last. There might have been a few trips to the unemployment office, but Jaeckel was soon back in the saddle filming a succession of TV guest shots. However, a return to A-list films would be far off in the future. Making the series likely kept him out of a supporting part in Don Siegel's World War II film *Hell Is for Heroes* (1962) starring Steve McQueen, though that solid credit may not have changed the trajectory of his career.

Jaeckel's son Barry commented on the up-and-down nature of his dad's business in *Golf Week*: "Everybody thought there was $100 on the table every morning. The difference between a character actor and a Ronald Reagan is like Tiger Woods and Joe Ogilvie. I remember my dad being down at the unemployment office several months a year between acting jobs. I thought that was his office. I was dumb." Watching his dad struggle financially convinced the young man that acting was not in the cards for him. Barry told the *Hartford Courant*, "I never wanted to be an actor. I saw too many strange things happen. It looked too much like a dog-eat-dog life. I never wanted it."

The fall of 1962 saw Jaeckel given a nice lead guest shot on the popular western series *Have Gun—Will Travel*. The episode "The Predators" cast Jaeckel as prisoner John Tyree, who teams up with Richard Boone's Paladin to save an isolated woman and her boy. Throughout much of the episode, anti-hero Jaeckel is attempting to escape from his captor, and the two actors work well together as opposing forces. Early in the episode they draw on one another, with Jaeckel ending up nearly shot dead. The saddlebag over his shoulder absorbed Boone's bullet, leading Jaeckel to a reassessment of his escape tactics. There's also a fight scene near Vasquez Rocks in Agua Dulce where the leads are doubled in the long shot by top stuntmen Hal Needham and Ronnie Rondell. The cat-and-mouse foot trek through the desert was directed by Andrew V. McLaglen, who had been an assistant to Allan Dwan on *Sands of Iwo Jima*. It's classic TV and superior western entertainment with a satisfying twist at the end. *The Bridgeport Post* said, "There's enough action here and actor Jaeckel, given a decent role, comes through quite well."

Stuntman Rondell, a former gymnast and U.S. Navy vet, began doubling for Jaeckel at Universal Studios on *Frontier Circus*. "That's where I met him," Rondell says.

He continued,

> We got to talking. He was so nice. Just unbelievable. He was such a great guy, and not a mean bone in his body. He was tough though, a real jock. He kept himself in fantastic shape and looked like a kid for about a million years. He was really something as a beach guy. We used to surf together. I'd meet him down at the beach at one of his surfing spots and try to hustle work, find out what he had coming up. I had a ton of dark hair, so they'd stick a blond wig on me depending on what they were doing. He could have done all the fights, but he'd step aside and let me set them up and do them.[3]

More TV westerns and dramas followed in the form of *Wagon Train*, *Gunsmoke*, *The Dakotas*, *Perry Mason*, and *Suspense* opposite veteran actor Basil Rathbone, with Jaeckel portraying a scuba diving criminal. There was even a TV pilot entitled *King Surf* in development in late 1963 and early 1964. Jaeckel would have had a starring role as the surfing lead had the show sold. For obvious reasons, that's a series Jaeckel hoped would come to fruition. However, the logistics of shooting on the surf proved too difficult for a weekly series. One film that Jaeckel did not make during this period that would have been interesting was Don Siegel's *The Killers* (1964). Jaeckel would have been most intriguing paired up with Lee Marvin as the title hit men. Clu Gulager played the idiosyncratic role and made it perhaps his most memorable performance. Jaeckel never did work with Siegel again.

In February 1963 Jaeckel guest starred on the *Wagon Train* episode "The Lily Legend Story" as Piper, a greedy, conniving, contemptible cowpoke described by another character as "hopelessly villainous." Jaeckel casts a leering eye at female guest Susan Oliver as they are sequestered with regulars Denny Miller and Frank McGrath in a storm-ridden cabin. Jaeckel tries to make off with Oliver and a satchel full of money, but his fear of her tuberculosis sees his fortune cast to the wind. It was his second and last appearance on the classic western. Six-foot, four-inch former UCLA basketball player Denny Miller, no stranger to the gym, recalled that Jaeckel was a friendly guy and kept himself in great shape.[4]

Later that month, Jaeckel guest starred on the stark Warner Bros. western *The Dakotas* in the episode "Fargo." Jaeckel plays the character Cal Storm in support of fellow guest star David Brian, cast here as a legendary lawman who returns to Deadwood with a chip on his shoulder and an apparent death wish as he bullies the town into action. Jaeckel is once again seen as a local braggart with an itchy trigger finger who turns into a remorseful coward when facing faster guns like Brian and Jack Elam. Fortified by liquid courage, a drunken Jaeckel shoots down Brian in the climax only to meet his maker at the hands of Chad Everett in a well-staged gunfight in the street. Outside of main guest star Brian, series regular Elam is the focus of this episode as Brian attempts to goad him into a gunfight in an effort to go out in a blaze of glory before going completely blind. Elam was one of the best character actors in the business and Jaeckel had a great affinity for him.

Gunsmoke was the longest running dramatic TV series of its day, occasionally sprinkling in a change-of-pace comedic episode throughout its 20-year run (1955 to 1975). The March 1963 episode "Two of a Kind" was a lighter show with Jaeckel playing Sean O'Ryan, one of a pair of feuding Irishmen caught in a squabble over a woman and a salt mine. Despite continuous warnings from series star James Arness, Jaeckel and fellow guest Michael Higgins think nothing of pulling their rifles out to take a shot at one another, or smashing up the Long Branch Saloon in a fistfight when their Irish tempers get the better of them. The show is played largely for laughs and sees the pair joining forces by episode's end to take on nefarious interests. Jaeckel sports an effective Irish brogue and delivers a colorful portrayal. It's one of his most enjoyable performances. This grand entertainment was directed by Andrew V. McLaglen.

Jaeckel does some of his own stunts in the bar fight with Higgins' double Hal Needham, including diving off the top of the bar. Stuntman Ronnie Rondell doubles Jaeckel for the longer shots. "I don't specifically remember doing that fight," Rondell says. "There were so many dailies back then. We'd work on five or six different shows a week and they all blend together. I worked mainly at Universal, but I'd do a lot of stuff on other shows with Hal.... Dick could do a good fight scene, but we can't let our actors get carried away. An actor gets hurt and then everybody's out of a job. He could have done the fights though. There were a few actors who could do great fight scenes like Bobby Fuller. He was as good as any stunt guy in the business. And Charles Bronson was incredible the way he moved."[5]

Jaeckel was a guest on back-to-back episodes of *The Alfred Hitchcock Hour* in early 1963. The first, January's "Forecast—Low Clouds and Coastal Fog," cast Jaeckel as a fun-loving surfer with pals Chris Robinson and Peter Brown. Thirty-five-year-old Jaeckel wears a college letter on his sweater in one scene as the trio comes to the aid of a frightened Inger Stevens when her husband is out of town. However, as the Hitchcock formula proved, things aren't always the way they seem. The May *Hitchcock* episode "Death of a Cop" featured Victor Jory and Peter Brown as father-and-son cops. Jaeckel is a gum-chewing, heroin-dealing thug named Boxer who beats up and kills Brown, shooting him four times. The rest of the episode sees Jory seeking vengeance on the cocky Jaeckel and his fellow hoods Rex Holman and Read Morgan. At the conclusion, Jaeckel is shot to death by Jory. Louisiana's *State Times* found Jaeckel to be "properly nasty" in a rare review of a television episode.

Six-foot, four-inch, 200-pound character actor Read Morgan, a former collegiate basketball player at the University of Kentucky, was a casual friend of Jaeckel's from the gym and the beach.

He recalled, "I first met Richard at a gym in New York City back in 1954. He had come east for a TV show. Then we knew each other out in California from the gym and the beach. Richard was very familiar with the Muscle Beach guys. They all liked him. He was one of the first bodybuilders to have success in the movies. He was quite a surfer and water man. I remember he had a catamaran and was a very accomplished sailor. He and Armand Tanny used to sail to Catalina Island and dive for abalone. He had a terrific career and body of work and was very well thought of in the industry. Very professional and always ready for the camera. When you cast him in something, you didn't have to worry. He was ready to go to work. A very practical guy with a lot of common sense. I remember on that *Alfred Hitchcock* he liked to have his shoes shined for the character. I said, "Why are you doing all that, Richard? Nobody is going to see your shoes on this," and he looked at me and said, "I'll know."[6]

The April 1963 *Perry Mason* episode "The Case of the Lover's Leap" featured Jaeckel as the seafaring Willie, paramour of recently widowed Julie Adams, whose husband may or may not have committed suicide in the ocean. Intrepid defense attorney Perry Mason (Raymond Burr) investigates, taking note of Jaeckel's oceanic abilities. As an egotistical cad with an eye on the big financial prize, Jaeckel has a peripheral part in the proceedings until the closing of the case. As he did so often during this itinerary period, he does what is asked of him in his part and does it well. He is perfectly cast as the opportunistic scoundrel. The producers of *Perry Mason* would call on him again.

In terms of career, the repetitive cycle of television guest shots is a routine many character actors with "leading man looks" and aspirations are never able to break away from. Jaeckel is a shining example. The important thing was to be working, but even then there was the risk of overexposure. Despite consistently good work, parts could suddenly dry up because an actor might be deemed by the studios or networks to be working too much. It was an intriguing paradox and a Catch-22 that concerned Jaeckel enough to mix in any film work offered as a change of pace. Jaeckel was versatile enough to make multiple guest shots on the same TV show, although it was extremely rare for that to occur during a single television season.

As a result, Jaeckel was always on the lookout for a role that could put him over the top with a large financial windfall in the manner of a Cagney or Bogart. Admittedly, the odds were not in his favor. Worse, Jaeckel was never quite certain when the demand for his talents might suddenly evaporate—a common refrain from actors. Instead of "Get me Richard Jaeckel," producers might suddenly begin saying, "Get me a Richard Jaeckel type," or "Get me a young Richard Jaeckel." Ultimately, that often turns into the question, "Whatever became of Richard Jaeckel?" Unlike some of his contemporaries, Jaeckel was not harboring personal screenplays or creating his own production outfit to make better roles for his own gain. Drawing that kind of attention to himself wasn't his style. "I just love the work," Jaeckel told the *Daily Breeze*.

Nevertheless, Jaeckel was determined to continue to build a solid name for himself with his preparation, on-set punctuality, friendliness, and willingness to meet a director's needs and goals. He would show up knowing his lines and hitting his marks. If a producer or director chose to work with him again, so be it. Jaeckel felt if they were willing to hire him for a job, it was his duty to be on time and perform to the best of his capability. This strong work ethic won him many admirers in an industry rife with egocentric personalities. "I realized long ago that this is a cynical business of numbers," Jaeckel told the *Daily Breeze*. "Once you realize that, you understand that it will go happily on without you. I also realized that I would rather work than not."

During the 1960s producer A.C. Lyles made a number of modestly budgeted westerns featuring casts filled with Hollywood old-timers. *The Young and the Brave* (1963) is distinguished amongst Lyles' films because it was a war picture set in Korea (but filmed over ten days in Ventura County, California). Outside of that, there's not a lot going for it. This was certainly one Jaeckel did out of loyalty to long-time Paramount employee Lyles when nothing else was on the horizon. He even accepted less than his established price. His main competition for acting parts during this period came from talented tough blond character actors Jeremy Slate, Jan Merlin, Paul Carr, and Rayford Barnes. Jaeckel was always concerned they'd land something he could have done and reap the rewards. "It's always been the thing of taking every part that was offered to me," Jaeckel explained to writer Dick Kleiner. "Because that was all there was. If I didn't take it, somebody else was going to grab it."

Jaeckel, as Cpl. John Estway, is third-billed in the film behind solid actors Rory Calhoun and William Bendix. However, Calhoun and Bendix are woefully miscast, far beyond the age of plausibility for their characters. Richard Arlen and John Agar are also in the black and white Francis D. Lyon–directed film about a group of escaped P.O.W.s behind enemy lines trying to avoid a North Korean foot patrol. After making his own escape, Jaeckel becomes the liaison trying to bring them back to safety. Few critics bothered saying much about the little film, with *Variety* remarking, "Some fairly respectable cast names have been assembled by Lyles for the enterprise, but these experienced actors have very little dramatic meat to sink their veteran teeth into. The three leading roles are dispatched mechanically by Rory Calhoun, William Bendix, and Richard Jaeckel." Even when a low-budget production was obviously beneath Jaeckel's talents, he still approached it as professionally and was as upbeat as possible. To be around Jaeckel was to be around a near constant flow of positive energy.

4 for Texas (1963) is an entertaining big-budget Robert Aldrich mess pitting Frank Sinatra and Dean Martin against one another in the Galveston, Texas, of the 1870s. Jaeckel is credited far down the large comic-western cast as Pete Mancini, the scarred, red-headed muscle for Sinatra. Jaeckel is paired up with the 6'5" professional wrestler Mike Mazurki to menace Martin and his men as they try to set up a riverboat for gambling. He has a fistfight with Martin and is involved in a wild climactic brawl where Sinatra and Martin's minions join forces to take on Charles Bronson and his bad guys. In theory Jaeckel's bad guy becomes good, but there's not a lot of character depth found anywhere in the film. Outside of Jaeckel's solid presence, a consistently surly Bronson probably fares best in the film's acting department menacing banker Victor Buono. Between fights, Sinatra and Martin lounge around with scantily clad Anita Ekberg and Ursula Andress.

Aldrich was glad to have pros like Jaeckel on board as he became exasperated by Sinatra and his refusal to offer more than a single take for many scenes. Aldrich estimated that over the course of 37 days on the picture, Sinatra worked a total of only 80 hours. Robert Mitchum had originally been offered the Sinatra part, but then Sinatra and his production company joined in to co-star with fellow Rat Pack member Martin. In response, Aldrich uncharacteristically threw everything but the kitchen sink onto the screen, including Jack Elam, Jack Lambert, Arthur Godfrey, and the Three Stooges. Only some of it sticks. In the book *Robert Aldrich: Interviews*, the director specifically addresses why he cast actors like Wesley Addy and Jaeckel in his films: "I like to use these actors because I know exactly what to expect from them. Just tell them what you want to do, they do it. You don't have to waste time explaining the whole history of the characters to them."

Given his varied screen history, one would think that Jaeckel was wholly capable of playing the colorful main heavy that was essayed by tough guy Bronson. Instead, Jaeckel found himself in a near-nothing supporting part. But it did at least run the course of the film and kept him on salary for the duration of the shoot during the summer of 1963. Jaeckel's character actor contemporary Bronson had recently received a boost in recognition from the success of *The Magnificent Seven* (1960) and *The Great Escape* (1963), and the powerful talent agency MCA negotiated a $50,000 salary for him. Jaeckel wasn't earning anywhere near that wage for this film, but he was more than appreciative of Aldrich offering him a job.

4 for Texas is widely regarded as one of Aldrich's most disappointing films. Critics generally lambasted the picture and its star-fed excesses, although *Variety* did mention Jaeckel in its review as one of the actors "of note." The climactic brawl alone had over 400 extras and was captured by no less than five cameras. Jaeckel can be seen having some fun during the fight donning Frank Sinatra's top hat as he urges on the action. The muscular Jaeckel is an effective combat presence throughout the picture, perhaps swinging more punches here than in any other film role. He did all of his own fight stunts although he is naturally doubled for a dangerous fall off a balcony and what appears to be a relatively simple toss off a pier. The latter stunt is done by professional wrestler-judo champion Gene LeBell, and the poor editing in this sequence does not disguise that fact. It is doubtful that Aldrich cared much about the film at all by that point.

Jaeckel was quoted in the book *The Films and Career of Robert Aldrich*: "It was an entertainment, nothing serious. In fact, people came from all over Hollywood to watch the filming of the final fight scene. You could see that at some point, Aldrich just wanted to cut his losses—just wanted to get in and get out." Aldrich did appear to favor Jaeckel during some of his screen moments, letting him tower over the diminutive character actor Nick Dennis and even stand significantly above the 5'5" Ursula Andress when he comes on to her with the line, "My daddy was an alcoholic who loved the dollies…. And I can't say I blame him." Jaeckel's groping of Andress and attempt to kiss her prompts the balcony fight with Dean Martin.

Tim Lyon recalled Jaeckel inviting him onto the *4 for Texas* set with a day pass to see the craziness going on. When Lyon arrived, he was approached by Jaeckel, Dean Martin, and Mike Mazurki who were unsuccessfully attempting to suppress big grins. When they reached Lyon, the guest quickly realized that Jaeckel was standing at eye level with him. The three men broke into hysterics, revealing that Jaeckel had stuffed his cowboy boots with toilet paper and crushed beer cans to give him an extra three inches in height so that he wouldn't be dwarfed on screen by the towering Mazurki. It was not uncommon for Jaeckel to wear the popular Adler Elevator shoes of the day when he had to be taller than a leading lady for a specific scene. His short stature was often the topic of gentle ribbing from his friends and castmates. "We used to say he was always the last guy to know when it rained," Lyon laughs.[7]

One interesting association did come out of the film for the Jaeckel family. During production, Jaeckel became friendly with singer turned actor Dean Martin, a dedicated golfer and nothing like the inebriated playboy that his public image evoked. The likable Martin switched from playing the golf course in Bel Air to the Riviera course near the Jaeckel home. Through their behind-the-scenes camaraderie, Jaeckel's son Barry would begin working for Martin as his caddy, earning $20 a day. Eventually Martin became the one to stake Barry to his professional golf career on the European circuit in the early 1970s. So even out of something as seemingly pointless as *4 for Texas* came something worthwhile for Jaeckel and his son.

With *King Surf* kicking around in development, Jaeckel had no new films released in 1964. Jaeckel did stay active on television appearing on episodes of *Combat*, *The Virginian*, *Temple Houston*, *The Outer Limits*, and *The New Phil Silvers Show*. The airwaves weren't all westerns, with the World War II series *Combat* proving extremely popular. It was considered a prestigious credit amongst rising young actors. On the December 1963 episode "Gideon's Army," Jaeckel was cast as a German sergeant captured after a firefight with the U.S. soldiers led by Vic Morrow. Held in a concentration camp, he does not hide his scorn for its other occupants (Jews). Jaeckel does his entire part speaking German, refusing to divulge the whereabouts of the rest of the German soldiers. At the episode's conclusion Jaeckel attempts to escape and is clobbered over the head with a rock. Vic Morrow's blond-haired stuntman Earl Parker doubles Jaeckel in the long shot. Due to having the Holocaust as subject matter, the episode is one of the most controversial of the MGM show's extended five season run. As for Jaeckel, it's a solid part on a much beloved action series that shows the extent of his versatility.

February 1964 saw Jaeckel appear on two western series. The long-running *The Virginian* is solid entertainment from Universal Studios and provided another notch in Jaeckel's gunfighter belt. In the well-acted ninety-minute color episode "A Matter of Destiny" he appears as Pat Wade, an old cowhand friend of Trampas (Doug McClure). He drifts into town and hires on at the Shiloh Ranch to work beside Trampas. Meanwhile ranch foreman James Drury is dealing with a new rancher in the area, a Chicago businessman played by Peter Graves. McClure is concerned with the presence of Graves because the man has swept his lady friend Jean Hale off her feet and is proposing marriage. Jaeckel is around to console his pal, telling him with confidence that he will end up with the girl. As the story unfolds, Jaeckel's own presence begins to weigh on McClure's mind. McClure learns Jaeckel has become a gun for hire and is really in town to kill Graves (rival Chicago interests have hired him for $1,000). Jaeckel tries to talk McClure into letting him go through with the killing for the benefit of both men, but they ultimately draw upon one another. Jaeckel ends up shot in the belly and dead by the story's close.

It's a good performance by Jaeckel. He is pleasant and engaging throughout, except the audience is made aware of who he is early on. The nuances he brings to the role are subtle and his character's motivation persuasive. In real life, California surfer McClure was a friend of Jaeckel's, and James Drury would become his good friend and future co-star on the TV series *Firehouse*. According to Drury,

> I'm afraid I don't really remember that episode or working with Jake on *The Virginian*. I think Doug McClure was involved with him a lot more than I was on the show. They would have me sometimes working on as many as five different episodes of *The Virginian* in a single day. I'd go in and do a little scene here and then go over and do something someplace else; then go to another set and do three pages, and sometimes to another set for two or three words, and come back to another place and do fifteen pages. I don't remember any particular involvement with Jake on that. I'm sure he was great in whatever he did. He was an amazing guy. He did some fantastic performances. Everywhere he went he created a character out of whole cloth and it would be memorable.[8]

Warners' *Temple Houston* was a one-hour Jeffrey Hunter western about the famous Texan Sam Houston's lawyer son. It lasted only a single season after chaotically being rushed into production. Veteran character actor Jack Elam co-starred in the series, which introduced humor into the episodes midway through its run in an effort to attract an audience. It didn't help. Jaeckel guest stars in "The Case for William Gotch" as the card sharp character Coley. Actors James Best, Denver Pyle, and Ray Danton were also featured in the episode from director Leslie H. Martinson. In real life U.S. Navy veteran Hunter was another of Jaeckel's many friends from the beach. Hunter died tragically in 1969 at the age of only 42 following a stroke.

On the classic one-hour sci-fi series *The Outer Limits*, Jaeckel appears as astronaut Captain Mike Dowling in the episode "Specimen: Unknown." During the course of the story his spaceship is overrun by alien spores that make it back to Earth and begin proliferating until the inevitable twist ending. The quality of the episode varies wildly and David J. Schow recalls in his book *The Outer Limits Companion* that producers Leslie Stevens and Joseph Stefano were in a panic that it was an embarrassing failure due to its short running time and budgetary limitations. The spores were puffed wheat cereal and many of the background flowers were merely Kleenex.

Ironically, "Specimen: Unknown" would prove to be *The Outer Limits*' highest rated episode, although fans of the series recall it being one of the lesser entries. In regard to the performances, Schow writes, "Since the players are all interchangeable Air Force Joes, the performances, while competent, are all trapped inside their uniforms." An interesting bit early in the show sees Jaeckel using a sunlamp meant for a flower bed to tan himself. Stephen McNally, Russell Johnson, Peter Baldwin, Arthur Batanides, and Dabney Coleman co-starred in the Gerd Oswald–directed episode, which aired in late February of 1964. Coleman's scenes were shot as an add-on after all the other actors were done with principal photography.

Jaeckel guest starred on *The New Phil Silvers Show* in the April 1964 episode "Keep Cool." Silvers and Jaeckel, as the character Danny, are among those locked into the factory's walk-in freezer in the situation comedy. Professional boxer Roland La Starza also appeared. In contrast to the popular *Sgt. Bilko*, this Silvers show lasted only a single season and is generally forgotten. For Jaeckel it was a chance to work with a classic comedian and introduce a little levity to his own screen image, mixing it up from the usual array of gunmen and screen toughs.

Although he was doing fine work as a television guest star, there had not been a good film role for Jaeckel since *Town Without Pity*. Former benefactors such as Raoul Walsh and Delmer Daves were winding down their directing careers at this point. Jaeckel was in danger of being considered a television actor only, with the recent failure of *Frontier Circus* continuing to cast a shadow over any other leading parts or more lucrative paying film assignments. Producer Gene Roddenberry's personal papers reveal that Jaeckel was under consideration to portray starship navigator Jose Tyler on the pilot for the TV series *Star Trek*, a role eventually filled by Dan Duryea's blond-haired son Peter. Rising actors Bruce Dern and Christopher Connelly were also discussed for the part. Ultimately, the Tyler character did not make it into the weekly series. Becoming a regular member of the *Starship Enterprise* would have no doubt drastically altered Jaeckel's career.

On a non-professional level, Jaeckel remained a steady part of the Malibu oceanfront scene, although the waves were becoming increasingly crowded with the popularity of *Gidget*, Beach Boys-Dick Dale surf music, and Frankie Avalon-Annette Funicello movies. Well-known surfers Buzzy Trent, Charlie Riemers, and Ricky Grigg were some of his pals. Jaeckel often stayed with Tim Lyon's family and had many good friends from Malibu including studio executives Albert Kaufman and Arthur Loew and actors Doug McClure, Robert Webber, Peter Lawford, and Van Williams, whose wife Vicki Flaxman was a professional surfer. When Jaeckel was done hitting the waves, he could sometimes be found at a Malibu beer bar called The Cottage downing cold ones with power guzzlers Lee Marvin, Neville Brand, Jack Warden, and Jack Palance. It was a colorful group of vibrant personalities Jaeckel hung around with.

Bonanza was a classic western about the Cartwright family and their ranch, the Ponderosa. The series ran fourteen seasons and featured two strong guest appearances from Jaeckel. In the November 1964 episode "Between Heaven and Earth," he is cast as Mitch Devlin, arm-wrestling champion friend of Michael Landon's character Little Joe. While trying to corner a puma at Vasquez Rocks, Landon finds himself stuck on the side of a cliff in desperate fear of the height. He develops an insecurity that manifests itself throughout the rest of the episode, leading to friction with Jaeckel and an especially poignant moment when

Jaeckel loses an arm-wrestling contest to Landon. Jaeckel's sense of pride is shattered in the defeat. At the episode's conclusion Landon conquers his fear of heights, but curiously there is no scene where he loses the arm-wrestling championship back to Jaeckel to restore that character's lost dignity. In real life Landon knew Jaeckel from the Paramount Studio gym. Jaeckel's biceps measured near 16," and he was well known amongst his friends for his arm-wrestling skill. His workout partner Clark Hatch remembers, "His arm-wrestling strength was well above average."9

The indie *Nightmare in the Sun* (1965) is an odd little melodrama starring Jaeckel's friend John Derek. The story concerns a desert hitchhiker who becomes the object of a small-town manhunt after alluring married woman Ursula Andress turns up dead. Aldo Ray, Jack Albertson, Sammy Davis, Jr., and Keenan Wynn appear in support, as do Jaeckel and Robert Duvall as a pair of antagonistic sweater-wearing motorcyclists hunting down Derek for a perceived reward. Jaeckel and Duvall play up their characters' close friendship, and the gay subtext makes for a somewhat daring and interesting subplot. However, as soon as Duvall's violent tendencies are revealed, the characters are abandoned as inconsequential to what there is of a plot. Actor Marc Lawrence is the film's screenwriter and credited director although future auteur Derek had a hand behind the camera as well.

Shooting from a rough draft script, the film was done on location in Calabasas, California, in fifteen days. In his autobiography Lawrence recalls the cast was comprised of "friends and people I liked" who agreed to work for far less than their established rates. Derek became a co-producer because a deal was struck to film a then-groundbreaking nude scene of his wife Andress that would have guaranteed a much needed pre-sell of the low-budget film. However, Derek waffled on the deal and Lawrence was further hindered in his directorial efforts by producer Ricky DuPont, who insisted that filming should be dictated by astrology and the position of the stars on a given day. Lawrence managed to finish the film within budget, but had the negative bought out from him for $50,000 by DuPont after assembling a rough cut. Lawrence was forced to go into litigation after DuPont defaulted on the payments. The case dragged on for years as Lawrence attempted to get his money or ownership of the barely released film. Burdened by the unfinished editing and a poor score, *Nightmare in the Sun* is considered a curio and little else.

Town Tamer (1965) is another oddity, a nearly geriatric, routine western from producer A.C. Lyles and veteran director Lesley Selander that is best known today for *Bonanza* star Michael Landon stunt-doubling character actor DeForest Kelley during a short fight scene. The tried-and-true Frank Gruber story is fine, but a generic and intrusive Jimmie Haskell score sets Lyles' penny-pinching film back significantly. Shot on the Paramount lot on existing *Bonanza* sets, it's one of Jaeckel's lesser films. He's one of the few actors in the movie (along with fellow bad guys Kelley, Roger Torrey, and Phil Carey) whose actual age realistically fits their parts. Dana Andrews, Bruce Cabot, Lyle Bettger, Richard Arlen, Pat O'Brien, Barton MacLane, and Lon Chaney, Jr., were all years past their prime but are cast by Lyles in the main roles. Terry Moore is the female lead, while former B-western stars Bob Steele and Don "Red" Barry show up in bits. It's a rather blatant nostalgia show that gives these aged actors needed work and their fans a chance to see them on screen once again.

Jaeckel has a showy running role as crooked deputy Johnny Honsinger, one of the main antagonists to honest gunman Andrews. He's full of venom and gives probably the best performance in the quickly shot film. An energetic Jaeckel delights in calling Andrews "old man" and recommends a noose when Andrews is put on trial. Jaeckel's tough-talking fast-draw confronts Andrews in the conclusion, hoping to nab a $2,500 bounty offered by town boss Cabot. Jaeckel manages to shoot Andrews first, but is shot in the belly himself. He hits Andrews a second time before conflicted town marshal Bettger finally guns Jaeckel down. Jaeckel hangs dramatically on a stairwell for a prolonged second before crumpling to the bar floor.

There might not be an official tally, but Jaeckel has to rank among the actors who have suffered the most on-screen deaths in Hollywood history. Of course, *The Gunfighter*, *The Violent Men*, and *3:10 to Yuma* contain the most memorable screen fatalities for Jaeckel up to this point. In each of these instances he clutched his belly and staggered backward or tumbled forward with a minimal showcasing of blood or the bullet's entry point. It should be noted that these screen deaths pre-dated the exaggerated squib shots that became so popular on screen by the end of the 1960s. A squib shot is a small special effects charge that simulates a bullet hitting flesh. There is usually a packet of fake blood attached that is graphically released with the mini-explosion. Jaeckel's death scenes seem decidedly old-fashioned in comparison. "There's a great deal of difference between action on the screen and pure violence on the screen," Jaeckel told the *Fort Lauderdale News*.

Jaeckel received only ninth billing in the cast of old-timers but managed to garner some positive reviews in overcoming the film's obvious limitations with his robust portrayal. *Variety* wrote, "The hates-himself marshal has an alter-ego sadist-aide played with convincing nastiness by Richard Jaeckel, whose fortune in films is his cocky strut and cold physiognomy." *Town Tamer* did next to nothing for Jaeckel's career and the abbreviated shooting schedule at A.C. Lyles—friendly rates hardly filled his pockets.

Jaeckel spent several months in the Philippines in 1964 making *Once Before I Die* (1965) for his *Frontier Circus* co-star John Derek, who handled the directorial reins. Filmed under the title *No Toys for Christmas*, the movie was about the 26th Cavalry during the beginning of World War II and a young soldier's desire to make love to the beautiful widow Ursula Andress before he dies in combat. Unfortunately, there are other soldiers around in the form of a dynamically unhinged Jaeckel and the towering Ron Ely who have designs on Andress as well. To play the gung-ho, kill-crazy Lt. Custer, Jaeckel shaved his head and showcases his muscular arms with cut-off sleeves. It's a fiery *tour de force* performance that sees Jaeckel command the screen. Surprisingly, he even shows off his naked backside while bathing in a river in front of Andress. Once seen, the rugged image of a baldheaded Jaeckel grinning maniacally as he guns down the enemy with a .50 caliber machine gun is hard to forget. He is shot in the back by a Japanese soldier in the final action-packed combat reel.

The best individual scene in the film has Jaeckel return from a machine gun outpost and enter a watering hole where he boasts to officer Jock Mahoney (in a cameo) that he has just killed a squad of Japanese soldiers single-handedly. Mahoney doubts Jaeckel's story and explains to others present that there are no Japanese soldiers reported in that area. The others have a laugh at Jaeckel's expense, writing him off as a liar until a minute later when Jaeckel returns with a dead Japanese soldier and tosses the corpse onto Mahoney's table. Jaeckel's Custer is as deadly as he is psychopathic, a dangerous and fascinating combination.

Shaving his head in the sun-drenched tropical conditions had serious repercussions for Jaeckel, both temporary and perhaps long-term. His actor friend James Drury says, "I remember him telling me about that thing he did for John Derek where he shaved his head. They were out in the sun all day long and he got a terrible sunburn on his scalp. His head swelled

Jaeckel, with shaved head, as combat-loving Lt. Custer in the Filipino-made World War II film *Once Before I Die* (1965).

up and he looked like somebody from outer space. He had a real bad sunburn. I remember him talking about that experience and working with John Derek's wife, which he enjoyed."[10]

There were many problems with the film involving funding and location difficulties. Despite the lengthy stay in the Philippines, Jaeckel wasn't paid for all of his work. However, he believed strongly in Derek's vision and the footage they were capturing. He also got to work closely with friends Ely, Mahoney, and stunt coordinator Allen Pinson and that camaraderie went a long way. Ironically, it was one of Jaeckel's favorite pictures. The scenery is green and lush and Derek captures several excellent compositions. Jaeckel told the *Oregonian*: "All I can say is, you should have seen it. It was really beautiful. But the released version was completely re-cut, and in fact just cut to pieces."

The film and Jaeckel's strong performance were barely reviewed at the time. Some who saw the disjointed film tore it apart, although there are passages that display the talent on board. *Films and Filming* wrote, "Richard Jaeckel is more than compensation for the weaker performances. It's the toughest role I've seen him play and one that I would associate usually with Aldo Ray's military characters." The *Oregonian* noted, "The other character who might be construed as a central one is a bald-pated lieutenant played by Richard Jaeckel. His role is well played, but again the script shows no insight into his character, other than that he loves war. He is interesting enough that one wants to know more." Danny Peary writes in his book

Guide for the Film Fanatic, "Richard Jaeckel is perfectly cast as a bald, psychopathic soldier," while the Turner Classic Movies website notes Jaeckel is "a chrome-domed action hero decades ahead of Vin Diesel."

The extended time in the Philippines likely kept Jaeckel from pursuing a role in the western *Major Dundee* (1965), a film directed in Mexico by Sam Peckinpah that featured parts for many of Jaeckel's contemporaries such as Ben Johnson, Slim Pickens, L.Q. Jones, Warren Oates, R.G. Armstrong, and John Davis Chandler. Back in the States, Jaeckel appeared in the final episode of *The Alfred Hitchcock Hour*, "Off Season," for young director William Friedkin and screenwriter Robert Bloch. Jaeckel is cast as former small town deputy Milt Woodman who holds a grudge against new deputy John Gavin, an impulsive man who has earned a reputation from the big city as being trigger happy. Gavin senses that the ego-challenging Jaeckel is having an affair with his girlfriend Indus Arthur and itches for a show-down. After a climactic fistfight with Gavin, Jaeckel is shot in the belly and killed. The twist to the story is that it is not Miss Arthur that Jaeckel has been having his affair with, but the wife of Gavin's boss, the town sheriff. The episode aired in May of 1965 and is primarily of interest due to being the first directorial assignment for Friedkin.

In 1966 Jaeckel joined Lloyd Nolan, Pat O'Brien, Jeffrey Hunter, and Rod Serling on the advisory committee for a non-profit community theater, the Brentwood Playhouse. Stage work wasn't something that greatly interested Jaeckel at this point, but he saw it as a chance to give back to his community. Jaeckel was also known to accept invitations to speak to the students of local schools about careers in the motion picture industry. It was, however, a bit of a down point in his career. *Once Before I Die* had taken him out of circulation in Hollywood, and upon his return he was quick to have his agent begin submitting him for more work.

He did stay active on television. Rugged character player Read Morgan went from show to show as well, appearing on *Gunsmoke* alone more than ten times. Morgan remembers, "It was a wonderful time to be around. I was fortunate to be there because you'll never see the quality of those shows again. I was never a guy who turned down work unless I was working someplace else. I worked as often as I could. I thought the residuals contract from 1960 would pay off later. So I'd be working for residuals. Richard was the same way. I remember on *Alfred Hitchcock* there was a guy complaining and Richard just looked at him and said, 'You're working, aren't you?'"[11]

In early January of 1966 Jaeckel appeared in his second segment of the long-running courtroom drama *Perry Mason*. In "The Case of the Bogus Buccaneers" Jaeckel plays out-of-work actor Mike Woods, a combative, surly suspect in a murder case involving a popular TV show. When the cagey Jaeckel realizes he is wanted for questioning, he disappears as a tactical career move. Series star Raymond Burr ropes Jaeckel in under the pretense of a casting request. When Jaeckel realizes he's been had, he explains the foibles of being an actor chasing work in a town where having a name goes further than having talent. He was well aware that his disappearance in a murder case would put his name in the paper and perhaps lead to future work. It's a very well-conceived moment and one Jaeckel pulls off superbly. He had plenty of real-life feelings to draw from, tapping into his own history of prepared auditions and cold readings.

The two-part *Gunsmoke* episode "The Raid" (January 1966) was one of the last of the series' black and white episodes. It features a powerhouse guest cast including John Anderson, Gary Lockwood, Jeremy Slate, Jim Davis, and Michael Conrad. Jaeckel is cast as Pence Fraley, one of the members of a bank-robbing gang besieged by in-fighting. At first he's barely distinguishable from the rest of the large gang of outlaws, but by the end of the first part he begins to emerge. Jaeckel and his on-screen brother Slate clash with head outlaw Lockwood after their younger brother is shot robbing the bank. Marshal James Arness and his posse are hot on their trail. Lockwood gives a standout performance as Jimmy Stark, the gang leader who loses his cool. As was the usual fate of his bad guys, Jaeckel doesn't survive the end of the second part. The book *Gunsmoke Chronicles* called it "one of the very best" episodes of the series and praised the "excellent guest cast."

Actor Gary Lockwood recalled an amusing anecdote from the making of this episode in his autobiography:

> We filmed part of it on location out in the middle of nowhere, somewhere in the desert halfway between L.A. and Las Vegas. It was 7:00 in the morning, I'm playing the head of a gang of outlaws, and we're still on horseback. I had a lot of good actors working with me. We were doing chases in this thing and all that, and about 11:00 we hear this "whup-whup-whup" sound and here comes a helicopter, kicking up dirt for a hundred yards. The helicopter lands, and out steps Jim Arness, the star of the series: Marshal Matt Dillon. With his arrival, all of us heavies—when you play a bad guy you're called a "heavy"—got down and rested our horses. Jim works till about 2:00—then gets back in his helicopter and disappears. Then we heavies mounted up and got back to work.

The director of the episode, Vincent McEveety, worked well with Lockwood and cast him in a strong villain role in the western *Firecreek* (1967) opposite Henry Fonda and James Stewart. It was Jaeckel, however, who won over McEveety on the location of that *Gunsmoke*. "He's a very good actor," McEveety says of Jaeckel, "But he personally impressed everybody on the set. We became friends. I was impressed with Richard because of his background in the service and where he came from. I must say I can't think of another actor I was more impressed with personally. Richard was a fine young man. He wasn't cocky at all because of his service or because of his acting. People would come up to me and say, 'Who is that guy?' And that guy was Richard Jaeckel."[12]

Jaeckel guest starred on a pair of *Wild Wild West* episodes during this period. The popular show was as non-traditional as a western could get, often mixing in elements of science fiction and martial arts fighting. In January of 1966 Jaeckel was in "Night of the Grand Emir." This was followed in March of 1967 by "The Night of the Cadre." On the black and white first season episode he plays Christopher Cable, an assassin in league with beautiful female dancer Yvonne Craig. She eventually falls to the charms of star Robert Conrad and cracks Jaeckel over the head with a high-heeled shoe. Jaeckel's pal Chuck Courtney can be spied as one of the stunt thugs. In "Cadre," a second season color episode, he is the scarred Sgt. Stryker who controls his robotic soldiers with a hypnotic whistle and trades punches with the well-matched Conrad on location at Vasquez Rocks. In the finale Jaeckel succumbs to poisonous gas. Unfortunately, Jaeckel is not seen to his full potential in either of these underdeveloped subservient parts, taking orders from Don Francks and Don Gordon respectively.

After being introduced by mutual friend Robert Phillips, Jaeckel got on well with fellow tough guy Conrad during filming. He joined the cast after work for a drink at the Back Stage bar across from the studio. Jaeckel fit right in with Conrad's regular stunt crew headed by Whitey Hughes. In his book *Inside* The Wild Wild West, stuntman Dick Cangey wrote, "Richard Jaeckel is a pleasure to work with, but if you're normal and age like normal people, Richard Jaeckel is someone you can easily dislike. He's as young and handsome looking as he was when he was doing those war movies in the 1940s. He's also as friendly and unpretentious as a star of his caliber can possibly be."

Jaeckel had an especially strong part on the *Bonanza* episode "Night of Reckoning" playing a charismatic crew-cut villain named Dibbs. The shrewd bad guy has the Ponderosa Ranch under siege, demanding from hostages Hoss and Little Joe $60,000 in loot hidden by injured ranch cowboy Ron Hays. Jaeckel backhands Dan Blocker's Hoss, slaps female cook Eve McVeigh, repeatedly taunts Hoss as a "fat mouth," and holds a knife at a woman's throat. It's a great bad guy role and a tense, well-acted episode. Jaeckel ratchets up the intensity of the part until he is scalded by boiling water at the show's conclusion, letting out a scream as he crumples to the floor. It's a classic episode and a showcase for Jaeckel's talents. It was also a nice payday for Jaeckel, as *Bonanza* was known for paying its guest stars $6,000 for a "top of show" appearance.

The Irwin Allen sci-fi series *The Time Tunnel* had Jaeckel as a guest star in the January 1967 episode "The Ghost of Nero." In a story set in an Italian villa during World War I, Jaeckel plays German sergeant Mueller, who at one point has the ghost of the emperor enter his body. It's not much of a role—subordinate in nature to his superior officer—although Jaeckel does get to turn maniacal and strangle other cast members when invaded by the ghost. Unlike his appearance on *Combat*, his character here speaks English for the cameras with a German accent. The one-year-only series has its admirers, but it's toward the bottom of Jaeckel's canon of television work. Taken into context with Jaeckel's appearances on *Wild Wild West*, there was a definite move away from the standard cowboy and war story. It's unlikely this was a calculated act on Jaeckel's part but merely a sign of the times and shifting interest. Audiences were ten solid years into TV westerns and the Vietnam War was escalating. They were looking for a different form of escapism.

Even though the *Time Tunnel* part wasn't much, Jaeckel did receive a bit of publicity in the form of a syndicated quote that was picked up by such newspapers as *The Ogden Standard*. Jaeckel addressed his numerous military roles with a bit of self-deprecating humor in the blurb. "I don't know how many TV shows or movies I've been in," he said. "And I don't know how many times I've been a member of the armed forces either. I've made enough landings and been shot up more times than is healthy. You'd think that with this kind of war record I'd get promoted or at least get an officer's rank. My chest isn't big enough to wear all the ribbons I'm entitled to. Anyway, I'm a non-commissioned officer in this show which isn't bad."

Jaeckel had settled firmly into his career as a character actor and family man. Despite the occasional bump in the road, his marriage had endured (nearly twenty years), and his boys were becoming men. Due to his favorable reputation, Jaeckel could work regularly on films and television in a variety of parts. He had grown comfortable with his lot in Hollywood, but if a prestige project were to elevate him into another level of professional and financial recognition, that would have been more than fine as well. He had just seen it happen with veteran character man Lee Marvin, who was collecting a Best Actor Oscar for his work on the comic western *Cat Ballou* (1965). The two now shared the same agent in Meyer Mishkin, who handled the careers of such fellow tough guy character leads as Charles Bronson, James Coburn, Claude Akins, L.Q. Jones, Strother Martin, Morgan Woodward, Jack Elam, R.G. Armstrong, Jim Davis, and William Smith. Although he was nearing his fortieth birthday, Jaeckel still retained his youthful vigor, infectious charisma, and beach boy good looks. He was about to enjoy his greatest commercial and critical success. It wasn't out of the realm of possibility that he could still headline films or TV.

✦ 6 ✦

Sailing Along

Jaeckel's friend Robert Aldrich was putting together a potential blockbuster in the form of *The Dirty Dozen* (1967), a World War II picture that would become the archetype for all the subsequent men-on-a-mission survival films. Lee Marvin headlines as the man handed the seemingly impossible assignment of melding together a ragtag group of military criminals for a dangerous mission. Among the dozen cast in the picture were Charles Bronson, Clint Walker, Telly Savalas, John Cassavettes, and professional football player Jim Brown. Superior officers would be played by old pros Robert Ryan, Ernest Borgnine, Robert Webber, Ralph Meeker, and George Kennedy. Despite his villainous pedigree, Jaeckel was offered the part of the spit and polish military policeman Sgt. Clyde Bowren, the hard-case who assists Marvin's Major John Reisman shape the men into a fighting unit. When pressed by Marvin at the outset for his honest opinion, Jaeckel confesses it's more likely the men would stab the major in the back at the first opportunity rather than successfully work together as a team expected to overtake a Brittany chateau full of Nazi officers prior to D-Day.

Ironically, with the promise of pardons for the survivors of the mission, the men do come together little by little. Early in the training a rebellious Cassavettes attempts to escape but is stopped by the formidable trio of Bronson, Walker, and Brown. As Marvin's chief enforcer, Jaeckel looks the other way when it is opportune. It becomes apparent the squad of accused killers has a few antiheroes that the audience can root for. They finally come together as a unit when they refuse to bathe and shave due to the condi-

Jaeckel as Sgt. Clyde Bowren in the hugely popular MGM World War II film *The Dirty Dozen* (1967).

tions of their training facility. Taking stock of this grungy line-up of characters, top-kick Jaeckel coins the name "The Dirty Dozen" to describe them.

After an entertaining sequence of war games against the men in the antagonistic Ryan's unit, Marvin's soldiers prove themselves worthy of dying in combat rather than the end of a rope. Interestingly, Jaeckel's grease gun–toting Bowren accompanies the dozen on their potential suicide mission out of loyalty to Marvin's Reisman. He is the major's protector to the end, both from Germans and potential Dirty Dozen turncoats. In the original E.M. Nathanson novel, the character of Bowren stows away on the plane prior to the mission, an important character-building moment that was cut from the film for time. The explosive climax at the chateau sees most of the dozen die for their Army's cause, with Bronson the only survivor amongst the convicts. Marvin and Jaeckel endure wounds in the battle but live. The film ends with the tough guy trio sharing a hospital room and a much-deserved laugh. Despite what ended up on the cutting room floor, Jaeckel creates great depth to his character in what could have been a throwaway part. It's a first-class performance that has stood the test of time and remains one of Jaeckel's signature roles.

The film was shot at MGM's London studios for the better part of six months, with Aldrich's normal efficiency slowed by bad weather and the unfamiliarity of working with an English crew. This necessitated football player Jim Brown to be issued a firm command to report to duty from the Cleveland Browns for their 1966 training camp. Brown opted to retire on the spot from football and become a movie star. Brown and some of the cast members took runs in Hyde Park or lifted weights with one another to stay in shape during the long days of filming. Health nut Jaeckel was no doubt in on some of these exercise sessions. Jaeckel had a close friend on the production in the form of supporting player Robert Phillips and also cemented his lifelong friendship with star Lee Marvin. Both were Meyer Mishkin clients. The cast joined together for excursions into 1960s mod London. Jaeckel would often recall it as one of his favorite films due to Aldrich, his co-stars, and the interesting location. Considering the lengthy shoot and the abundance of overtime, Jaeckel's final salary for the film was reported to be $200,000. It was the most he ever made working on a film, and that would include the next twenty-five years going forward.

Aldrich had some fun in the opening scenes at the expense of the brooding and taciturn Charles Bronson, a hard-muscled actor sensitive about his lack of height and tough guy screen image. When lining up the actors for the picture's role call scene, Aldrich initially placed the 5'8" Bronson between the massive frames of the 6'6" Clint Walker and 6'4" Donald Sutherland. Bronson took one look at the shoulder height of the men standing on either side of him and there was an instant verbal explosion of protest, to Aldrich's delight. According to Raymond Austin, who worked on the film as a stuntman, a similar ruse was concocted to tease Jaeckel, who took the ribbing altogether differently than the hot-tempered Bronson:

> Clint Walker who played Samson Posey, was 6'6" tall. Richard was not a tall man, I think about 5'9" or 5'10". We were filming at night at the MGM studios in Borhamwood, England. Aldrich was lining up a shot with Richard standing next to Clint Walker with other actors. Well, as you can imagine, everyone looked small when dwarfed by Clint Walker, but Richard really did look small! Well, stuntmen love a joke and Gerry Crampton, the stunt coordinator, was no exception. As stuntmen and stuntwomen, one of our most important roles is to double the stars of movies so they don't get hurt. To make this happen, we wear wigs to match the star's hair, along with the same clothes and match their height. It is not possible for us to shrink, but to get taller is very easy. We all carry in our bag of tricks lifts; these are pieces of cork shaped in a wedge that we slip into our shoes or boots that can lift you up to four inches. Now most of us are 5'11" to 6'2".

What happened was this: Richard had voiced to Crampton that he wasn't going to stand next to Walker any more as it made him look like a midget. So Crampton got all us stuntmen to put in our four-inch lifts and keep standing around Richard wherever we went. For a time Richard did not say a word but we could tell he felt very uncomfortable. But still would not say anything. Then it came to a meal break and we were all in line to eat. We had managed to get him in the center of I think six of us. He kept looking out of the corner of his eye at us. At that moment Clint Walker joined the line and stood next to one of the stunt guys who was 6'2" and now with the lift 6'6". Walker looked him up and down saying hurtfully, "I thought I was the tallest guy here." The stuntman gave him a "shush" but it was too late for the rest of us got the giggles and broke up. Richard caught on and laughed, saying, "I was worried my part had shrunk." The joke in the end was not driving Richard mad for the last four hours; it was that Clint was so hurt that he wasn't the tallest man on the unit![1]

Cast as a fellow military cop, Robert Phillips stuck closest to Jaeckel on the film, although he was also one of the few people who would willingly be around Jaeckel's former *When Hell Broke Loose* co-star Charles Bronson:

Charlie was Mr. Gloom. He had a cloud over his head walking around and he was just hoping it was going to rain on him all the time. I got along better than anybody with Charlie. I wouldn't take his bullshit. We never had words or anything. After a while, Charlie and I got along fine. He was a total bully, but he wouldn't hurt anybody. He wasn't that kind of a bully. He was a conversational bully. Jake and Charlie were always on each other's case; but not in a bad way. They were always chiding each other. They did a lot of that. Jake knew he was all bullshit. And Charlie was all bullshit. His bark was way, way worse than his bite.

I was the rookie on the show. The shoot itself was very interesting and London was part of that. London was an interesting town for someone who had never seen it before. Jake and I flew in together. I remember flying over Ireland on my birthday. We left New York at night. It was very, very exciting to me. Jake and the director of *The Dirty Dozen* Robert Aldrich were close friends. To give you an idea how close, when Aldrich got divorced he took residency and lived in Jaeckel's house. That's how close they were. Jake was very, very quirky. He didn't want to stand alongside anybody. He'd tell the director and they'd protect him. He wasn't short-short, but he was short. I'd say he was 5'7" and a half or 5'8".[2]

Critics tore the film apart for its violence and stance of opposition against the military, authority, and women. Audiences failed to heed the critical pans and flocked to *The Dirty Dozen*, making it one of the highest grossing films of the year. It subsequently became a television broadcast favorite and eventually appeared on many "Best of" lists. During its initial release, *Variety* singled Jaeckel out as "excellent," and termed it "one of Jaeckel's strongest screen roles in years." *The New York Times* wrote, "Charles Bronson, Richard Jaeckel, and Jim Brown stand out in the animalistic group." *The Los Angeles Times* opined, "Marvin's aides Richard Jaeckel and Ralph Meeker register sympathetically." *The Van Nuys Valley News* commented, "Solid performances by Savalas, Marvin, Bronson, Brown, Cassavettes, and Richard Jaeckel keep it going." *The Pittsburgh Press* added, "Charles Bronson, Jimmy Brown, Telly Savalas, Clint Walker, Richard Jaeckel and others acquit themselves commendably." *The Dallas Morning News* included Jaeckel among those offering "a general excellence in acting." *The Washington Post* found Jaeckel's performance "precise" and "the best part this actor has had in a decade." *The Oregonian* noted, "Richard Jaeckel as an MP sergeant is effective in a role in which he goes from a gruff, perfect NCO to a nice guy. It is not a character change, but a gradual revelation of character which he brings off well." In his book *The Films of Lee Marvin*, Robert J. Lentz wrote, "Perhaps the film's finest performance is given by Richard Jaeckel as Sergeant Bowren, the glue that holds the Dirty Dozen together.... Jaeckel is great in the small role, immaculate and shiny-faced, brimming with energy and enthusiasm under the most dogged of circumstances."

Jaeckel described his take on the character in the film's press material: "Sgt. Bowren is a professional M.P. He is tough—and the occasion demands it—but equally prepared to reward respect for authority. He is a good, honest soldier; first, last, and always." Jaeckel commented to reporter Marilyn Beck about the discipline required to work for Aldrich: "He would take no nonsense. When the bell rang, you did your job. If you didn't, you were on the way home." This was likely a reference to co-star Trini Lopez, who made too many demands on location and was sent packing; his character was simply written out of the climactic action by not surviving his parachute jump. Jaeckel told the *Fort Lauderdale News*, "I think I lasted as long as I did, almost to the end, because Bob Aldrich was a good friend of mine. He kept finding ways to get me in there as long as he could."

Given the length of shooting, Jaeckel formed several on-location friendships among the cast in addition to Aldrich, Marvin, Bronson, Phillips, and Jim Brown. On the DVD commentary for the film, actor Stuart Cooper, one of the back six of the dozen, referred to Jaeckel as "a sweetheart of a guy." Co-star Clint Walker recalled Jaeckel when interviewed for the book *White Hats and Silver Spurs*: "He's probably as nice a person as you ever hope to meet.... I'll tell you one thing. You'll never find a more professional actor. No sir! He was a no-nonsense actor. When he came, he was on time and was prepared. And the only job he ever did was a good one. He was a good actor."

When Jaeckel finally returned home from London, he tried to be more selective in choosing his next project. With his pockets temporarily full, there would be no more TV guest shots for the time being. Jaeckel and the other members of the cast attended a black tie formal premiere of the film in June of 1967. If Jaeckel was ever to become a star *The Dirty Dozen* might be the box office bonanza to push him there. It worked that way for young actors Jim Brown and Donald Sutherland and eventually character players Telly Savalas, George Kennedy, and Charles Bronson. Jaeckel told the *Oregonian*: "Man, we all knew this was going to hit big. When we finished, we all just waited for that to open, because we knew it was going to be a real monster."

His next film *The Devil's Brigade* (1968) is similar in nature to *The Dirty Dozen*. Jaeckel loses on-screen rank as he is cast as Pvt. Omar Greco in the Andrew V. McLaglen–directed World War II film, made on location in Italy and at Camp Williams in Lehi, Utah, in the spring of 1967. Key battle scenes were filmed atop Wasatch Mountain and in Corner Canyon in Utah. Concerning real-life specialized American and Canadian fighting units, it features another rugged cast: William Holden, Cliff Robertson, Vince Edwards, Dana Andrews, Andrew Prine, Claude Akins, Jeremy Slate, and Luke Askew. Jaeckel once again shaved his head

Jaeckel shaved his head once again to nab the part of soldier Omar Greco in the United Artists war film *The Devil's Brigade* (1968).

for his part as a circus acrobat, which helped him to stand out from the crowd. Greco is an escape artist and it is expected he will go over the wall at his leisure, but Jaeckel finds self-worth after beating the Canadian squad in a foot race and decides he wants to stick around to see the mission through. He has some nice scenes with fellow soldier Bill Fletcher, whom he befriends during the course of training.

One of the highlights is a large barroom brawl where the Americans and Canadians unite to fight off a group of lumberjacks. The extended melee ranks up there with the classic fights in *Dodge City* (1939), *McLintock!* (1963), and *The Great Race* (1965). Although Jaeckel was doubled by a stunt specialist for his acrobatic displays, he did nearly all of his own fight scene stunts and very effectively portrayed on-screen drunkenness. Incredibly, the entire brawl sequence was filmed in one marathon overnight sequence due to the limited availability of the location. During filming of the lengthy brawl, Jaeckel hung out on the set with professional football great Paul Hornung and boxer Don Fullmer, who were both working on the scene.

"That fight scene was courtesy of Hal Needham," recalls Ronnie Rondell. "He was the stunt coordinator. That was a good one and a lot of fun. I doubled Dick on *The Devil's Brigade*. They put a skullcap on me because he had his head completely shaved for it. I did a stunt in that for Dick where I take off and hit a trampoline and do a branny onto a guy. Then Dick jumps into the shot and throws a punch at the guy. They cut it so it looks like he did everything himself. Dick was good at doing fights, though. He'd go in and position himself for the cameras after I'd set it up. He was capable. Not a lot of actors are able to make it look really good."[3]

Strong friendships may form among character actors on extended location shoots, where men of similar background are thrust together in an intense working relationship. In this regard it is similar to the bonds that form among soldiers in the military or athletes on a sports team. Camaraderie grows between shared drinks and conversation over the weeks it takes to shoot a film. An informal fraternity of sorts exists between these actors, with friendships picking up and leaving off over a period of years the next time they work together. It is not uncommon for actors to claim a fellow thespian is a great friend even though they may not have seen one another for ten years or more.

The relationships formed on location during *The Devil's Brigade* are indicative of this phenomenon. From the location in Rome, Jaeckel and fellow Meyer Mishkin clients Claude Akins, Bill Fletcher, Tom Troupe, and Dave Pritchard sent their agent a photo of the group adorned in t-shirts reading "Meyer's Misfits." This was the first of three times that character actor Andrew Prine worked with Jaeckel and he was sufficiently moved to tell *Shock Cinema* that Jaeckel was "one of the best guys in the world." Jeremy Slate, who had played Jaeckel's brother on *Gunsmoke* a year earlier, admired Jaeckel's longevity in terms of both career and his physical appearance. "I thought he was never going to pass away," Slate told *Gunsmoke Chronicles*. "He looked the same way every time, through the years."

Director McLaglen told *Classic Images*, "Dick Jaeckel was an actor I used as much as I possibly could." So it is surprising that Jaeckel and Mishkin had to lobby for the role. Perhaps he had become over-identified with military credits dating back to *Guadalcanal Diary* nearly twenty-five years earlier. It had to be somewhat distracting for audiences to see the same blond-headed private looking as if he had stepped out of a time warp off the beaches of Guadalcanal and Iwo Jima. Prior to release, producer David L. Wolper edited out nearly twenty minutes of the picture over director McLaglen's objections, including some key moments of Jaeckel's part. Jaeckel told the *Oregonian*: "They didn't want me for *Devil's Brigade* and told me so. Well, my agent just gave them a picture of me with my head shaved for *Once Before I Die*, just a production still. I got the role just because of that picture. They cut out whole episodes of *The Devil's Brigade*, and I ended up in a few scenes in the beginning and was pretty much a face in the crowd for the rest of the movie."

Despite the editorial cuts, Jaeckel is actually a consistent and welcome presence throughout the film. He also comes off well in several action and fight sequences, especially the climactic battle atop a rugged mountain whose face he has just scaled to flank the Germans in a surprise attack. A running kick to the face of a German sentry is especially impressive and expertly timed. Many members of the cast are killed in the final battle with none being afforded a more memorable death scene than Jaeckel. Stepping in to save his buddy Fletcher, Jaeckel is battered by a hail of machine gun fire and is launched off a cliff in a spectacular fall performed by stuntman-circus aerialist Bill Couch. It's the top action moment in the film.

The Devil's Brigade is no *Dirty Dozen*, but it has its share of admirers and remains a welcome entertainment whenever it shows up on TV thanks to its quality action and strong, familiar cast. *Variety* wrote, "Richard Jaeckel is good as a sympathetic non-conformist," while the *Kossuth County Advance* noted that "Claude Akins and Richard Jaeckel do very well in roles that are well suited and familiar to them." The *San Diego Union* thought his role was "well-played" and the *Boston Record* praised his "colorful characterization." *The Hollywood Reporter* wrote, "Andrew Prine, Richard Jaeckel, Jean-Paul Vignon, Tom Troupe, Carroll O'Connor, Richard Dawson, and Patric Knowles are notably in brief roles, both those amplified cameo turns that were intended that way and secondary roles which emerged sketchy." The *Citizen News* declared the film, "highlights the talents of Vince Edwards, Richard Jaeckel, Jeremy Slate, Claude Akins, and Jack Watson." *The Van Nuys Valley News* at this point asked rhetorically, "What would a war picture be without Richard Jaeckel?"

In 1968 Jaeckel told the *Los Angeles Herald Examiner*, "I may look the same, but I'm not the kid with the big 'W' on his sweater any more…. People know who I am. They don't look at me with that what's-his-name look in their eyes. People stop me on the street and talk to me about my latest role…. Acting is like a seesaw. One minute you're down, the next you're up…. I travel all over the world. My bags are always packed, my passport ready. I can't think of any other profession I'd rather be in. I want to stay in it for a long time."

The times were changing around him but not Jaeckel. Miraculously he did still look like the same young fresh-faced U.S. Marine from *Sands of Iwo Jima*. When his shirt comes off in *The Devil's Brigade*, the well-shaped muscles are still there from his years of dedicated workouts. The anti–Vietnam War movement was in full swing with liberal factions taking on John Wayne's latest pro-military film *The Green Berets* (1968), which, surprisingly, Jaeckel didn't find a part in. Perhaps Jaeckel was career-savvy enough to realize it was okay to continue fighting World War II on screen but not Vietnam. Many actors in Hollywood were growing their hair long and hanging out on the Sunset Strip with hippies while delving into mind-altering hallucinogens. Not Jaeckel. His hair remained clipped short around his ears and high on his neck. He might have a beer or two after work with the stunt guys, but that was it for what he put into his body. Conservative Jaeckel was still making World War II action films and looking believable while doing so.

In 1968 Jaeckel was up for the second banana part of Danny "Danno" Williams on the long-running TV series *Hawaii Five-0*. He was turned down at the last minute as they decided to go with James MacArthur as Steve McGarrett's number one investigator. Jaeckel loved

Hawaii and really wanted the part, but it was not meant to be. It is likely Jaeckel's own tough-guy screen image was considered by the producers to be too competitive with star Jack Lord's iconic lead character rather than subservient to it. The series ran for twelve seasons and would have guaranteed him financial security and nice Hawaiian surf for a long time. However, it likely would have defined his career. Given his dislike of pomposity, he no doubt would have battled the inflated ego of series star Jack Lord the entire duration. Ironically, Jaeckel never even managed a guest shot on the series.

Jaeckel was also under consideration by director Sam Peckinpah to play the leading character of Dutch in the influential action film *The Wild Bunch* (1969). Jaeckel's friend Lee Marvin was originally lined up to star as Pike Bishop, but Marvin's agent Meyer Mishkin talked him into doing the musical western *Paint Your Wagon* (1969) instead as a change of pace. Advisors considered Peckinpah's film too similar in tone to Marvin's recent western *The Professionals* (1966). William Holden ended up starring in the classic western with Ernest Borgnine playing Dutch. The two actors are excellent, but one can't help but picture Marvin and Jaeckel being every bit as good under Peckinpah's muscular direction. For Jaeckel, the part could have been a career-changer. Jaeckel would later work for the director, essaying a small character part in the western *Pat Garrett and Billy the Kid* (1973).

Jaeckel did manage a lone TV guest assignment in November 1968 as a suspicious, calculating Czech consulate named Melchek who is apparently attempting to suppress the release of a book due to its anti-communist rhetoric on *The Name of the Game*. Utilizing a foreign accent, Jaeckel has several cat-and-mouse scenes with series star Gene Barry, who has been recruited to smuggle the book out of the country. The story's resolution provides an interesting twist. Filmed at Universal Studios, the episode "The White Birch" also features Boris Karloff, Roddy McDowall, Susan Oliver, and Pete Deuel. Curiously, Jaeckel is given co-star credit at the end rather than guest star credit in the opening titles. He is, however, the main guest star on the show and seen to advantage throughout in several scenes.

A 1968 guest shot such as this would typically have yielded a performer of Jaeckel's status a few thousand dollars during shooting, with that sum doubling on the episode's first broadcast rerun. However, Jaeckel was currently casting his eye toward features in hope of elevating his name and preventing overexposure. His villainous contemporaries such as Warren Oates and Bruce Dern were similarly attempting to move out of TV and do only features, although in Dern's case these films were of the exploitative drive-in variety. In his autobiography Dern recalled earning anywhere from $1,000 to $1,700 a week to star in low-budget quickies such as the motorcycle film *Cycle Savages* (1969). Bouncing between film and television could be a tricky balancing act for an actor attempting to upgrade both his pay and his status in the industry. Sometimes it depended on the challenge of the role when it came time to decide on doing episodic television or a B-film. Sometimes a man and his family simply needed to eat.

Jaeckel's *Dirty Dozen* co-star Charles Bronson had gone to Europe to star in Sergio Leone's *Once Upon a Time in the West* (1969) and the crime drama *Farewell, Friend* (1968) opposite Alain Delon. Around this time, veteran western heavy Lee Van Cleef went the same route to play opposite Clint Eastwood in Leone's *For a Few Dollars More* (1967) and *The Good, the Bad, and the Ugly* (1968). The foreign movies made Bronson and Van Cleef international stars and Jaeckel saw the value in seeking out other film markets where he could headline pictures instead of merely being categorized as a character player. However, whereas Bronson's foreign ventures were fairly serious-minded art, Jaeckel's journey to the Far East would be for a pair of schlockfests from the producers of Japanese monster movies. It's likely that Jaeckel was approached by Toho Studios due to his similarity to Nick Adams, Jaeckel's recently deceased friend who had headlined several films for the studio.

The Green Slime (originally titled *Battle Beyond the Stars*) oozed into U.S. theaters in the summer of 1969 after a run in its home country of Japan. Jaeckel, as space station commander Vince Elliot, is billed behind former *Wagon Train* TV star Robert Horton, although one could easily argue that audience sympathy falls in the heroic Jaeckel's court. From an actor's standpoint it's an interesting contrast of flawed heroes, one overly aggressive and the other overly passive. As played by a perfectly coifed Horton, Commander Rankin is an egotistical blowhard who takes over Jaeckel's leadership to destroy an asteroid heading toward Earth. He also attempts to steal Jaeckel's mini-skirted fiancée Luciana Paluzzi in the process. Jaeckel and his old rival clash at every opportunity, and Jaeckel builds up a realistic head of steam when he throws a much deserved punch. Horton is also the one directly responsible for haphazardly contaminating the ship with the mysterious substance that turns from a green gel into cyclopean four-foot killer energy rocks with tentacles.

Director Kinji Fukasahu, who did not speak English, presents a colorful, entertainingly

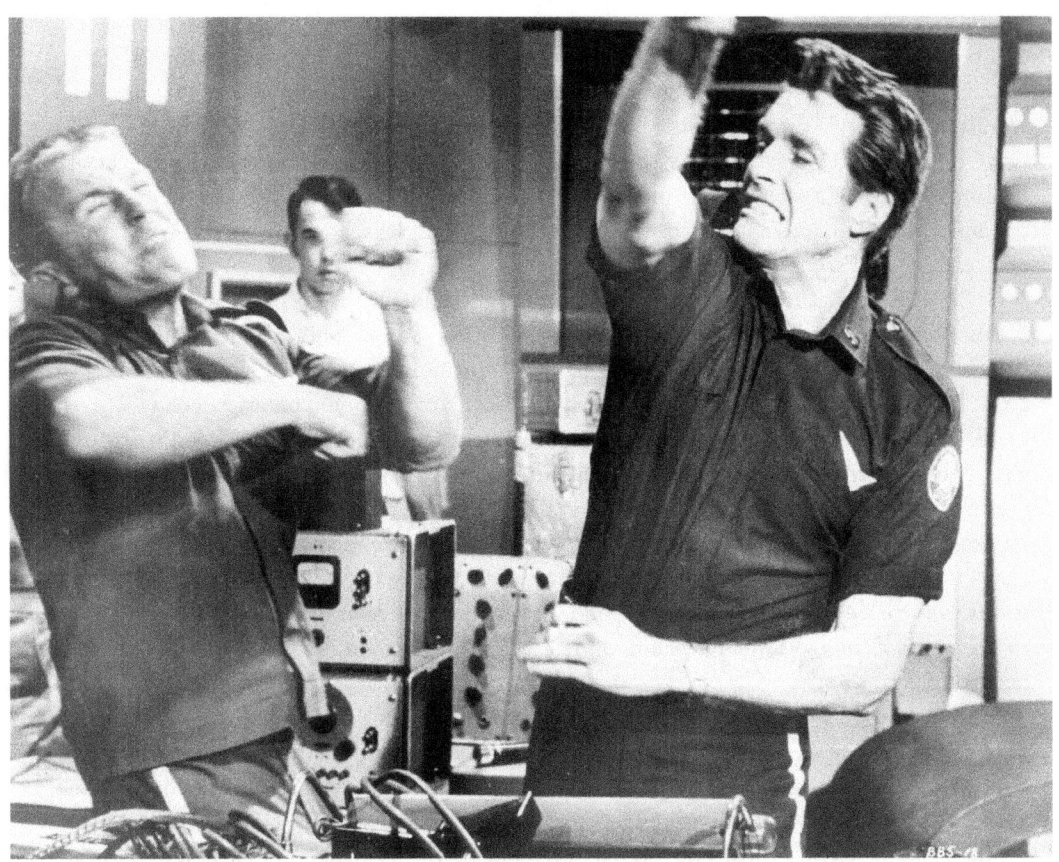

Jaeckel takes a screen punch from Robert Horton in the Japanese MGM sci-fi film *The Green Slime* (1968). Jaeckel enjoyed doing his own fight scenes.

goofy sci-fi film that sees Jaeckel and Horton play it straight to the best of their abilities, although there is every indication they knew they might be stuck in a monumental turkey. It was filmed at a time when audiences were blown away by the cinematic sci-fi presentation of Stanley Kubrick's *2001: A Space Odyssey* (1968); the cast had to be instantly aware that their costumes, sets, and dialogue were not in the same league. The green slime creatures were supposedly Japanese children in painfully obvious costumes and ultimately resembled something from a Saturday morning TV kid show. "To keep from laughing I kept biting the inside of my cheeks," Jaeckel told *The Washington Post*. The cheesiness of Jaeckel and Horton battling these absurd energy monsters with ray guns has led to the film's sustained cult status, as has the incredible fuzz tone guitar theme song that opens and closes the movie. All in all, it's a fun ninety minutes of escapism. In the film's climax, Jaeckel dies valiantly saving Horton, who gladly takes Paluzzi in his arms for the end credits.

The film received a major release and was reviewed by all the major trades, which couldn't have been thrilling for Jaeckel. Where were the abundant reviews for his stellar work in *Once Before I Die*? Few notices singled out the lead actors, with *Variety* finding "performances are routine" while *The New York Times* noted the "wooden acting." *The Hollywood Reporter* claimed, "The acting is stiff, the better not to snigger when delivering lines." *The Motion Picture Exhibitor* wrote, "Robert Horton and Richard Jaeckel are comic book heroes" while the *Oakland Tribune* termed them "plastic model actors." To be fair to the actors, their direction was coming to them in a different language. The Turner Classic Movies website notes, "Robert Horton and Richard Jaeckel deserve some kind of award for playing their roles absolutely straight without laughing."

Evidence of the continued interest in *The Green Slime* is apparent in the many reviews that can be found when surfing the web today. The *Film Fanatic* site writes, "To their credit, Jaeckel and Horton take their roles extremely seriously, never breaking concentration despite the fact that they're basically doing battle with walking Halloween costumes." The website *We Are Movie Geeks* adds, "Square-jawed Robert Horton delivers a comically wooden lead performance as the arrogant and condescending Rankin. As Elliott, Richard Jaeckel seems to have more fun with his role and makes a good space hero."

Despite any reservations about the quality of the production, Jaeckel remained a trooper. He took what direction was given to him and did his job with a smile on his face. When interviewed by the publication *G-Fan*, Luciana Paluzzi recalled Jaeckel as "adorable" and "nice." Co-star Robert Horton, once a few years ahead of Jaeckel at Hollywood High, told *Filmfax*: "Oh, he was a very nice guy. I'd known him for a long time. He was a very nice fella." Horton elaborated on Jaeckel in an interview with *G-Fan*: "I hadn't really known Richard Jaeckel, but I knew who Richard Jaeckel was. And we were both up for the same role in a film that he did called *Come Back, Little Sheba*. He was a bodybuilder, and he was not a very tall man, but he had a wonderful physique, and he was covered with muscles. And he was very, very nice, and we got along fine."

When questioned about the film, Horton termed the script "terrible." *Green Slime* co-writer Charles Sinclair had dashed the original screenplay off in two days at the producer's request, trying to play up the power struggle between the two leads. He had no inkling what the monsters would look like. Sinclair recalled for *Videoscope*, "It kind of looked like the actors directed themselves. They hammed it up pretty much.... The actors tended to overact all over the place. I think the best actor in the show was Richard Jaeckel." Jaeckel did try to make the best of the experience and his chance to take in the Japanese culture. "They weren't too bad," he told writer Dick Kleiner of his Japanese movie experience. "And they paid well."

Tom Korzeniowski was involved with Armed Forces Radio and worked as an extra on the film, as did many U.S. military personnel living in Japan. Korzeniowski recalls:

> On a whim I invited a group of actors with whom I was familiar because of our film dubbing experiences to come and eat with me. Jaeckel was standing nearby and heard my invitation, and asked if he could come along. He was most appreciative of being included.... My Japanese wife, Toshie, was up to the challenge of suddenly providing a meal for eight hungry actors, and in a few minutes we all sat down to eat.
> Richard Jaeckel was the perfect gentleman and complimented Toshie on her culinary skills. He was most gracious to me, and friendly. He was perfectly relaxed among us non-star extra types, and we had a wonderful conversation over lunch, acquainting him with the Japanese film industry as we knew it. I don't recall the specifics of the conversation, but he pitched in with a few Hollywood anecdotes too. Since then I've always felt a bond with this wonderful, easygoing, friendly and gracious man. I'm sorry that was our only encounter, for he was the kind of person one likes to have as a friend. I miss him since his passing.[4]

While making *The Green Slime* Jaeckel stayed at Tokyo's Palace Hotel, across from the Imperial Palace. In his free time he exercised with American gym owner Clark Hatch at his fitness center within the Azabu Towers. As was typical of weight trainers who began in the 1940s era, Jaeckel liked to train his entire body in a single workout rather than divide the exercise sessions up into different days for different individual body parts. A day or two of recovery would separate each weight training activity. Jaeckel favored his lower back with at least fifteen minutes of stretching, light deadlifts, and stationary bike work prior to engaging in a high-intensity weightlifting workout. An exercise session would incorporate both barbells and dumbbells and consist of varying renditions of standard exercises. Each individual exercise would be performed for three sets of ten repetitions with up to two minutes of rest between each set until the entire body had been covered. Jaeckel avoided squatting exercises that compromised his lower back. He rarely missed a workout and even into advancing age could routinely perform no less than fifteen strict chin-ups.[5]

Clark Hatch opened his groundbreaking Tokyo fitness center after being stationed in the area with the U.S. military. He eventually expanded into several other Asian countries as well as Hawaii and other American states. Hatch wrote in his book *Clark Hatch: Fitness Ambassador to Asia*:

> Dick Jaeckel frequently visited Asia for filming during which time he always stopped by my fitness centers for his daily exercise. We became very good friends and shared many workouts, interesting conversations, and meals together. He was like a brother and our own personal movie star who gave us an inside look at the movie business. At our centers he was well-liked by everyone he came into contact with and often joined us at our awards ceremonies and sports activities. He helped me in many ways and on numerous occasions would join me at the openings of my new fitness centers. This was always a hit because his fans and the press were impressed by his ever-youthful appearance and physique.
> Dick visited and exercised in my Tokyo, Hong Kong, Manila, Tucson, and Honolulu fitness centers. And all the staff and members have pleasant memories of him. I visited him in Los Angeles a number of times. We'd go to various gyms for our workouts. All the proprietors were proud to have him come. He was a good exercise ambassador. When we said farewell, and in our correspondence, we'd always say, "Until that time." We always looked forward to seeing each other again."

While overseas, Jaeckel took an interest in the physically demanding Japanese martial art Kendo ("the way of the sword"). The discipline utilized bamboo workout swords for both kata practice and one-on-one combat while wearing protective clothing and face mask. In the early 1960s Jaeckel's friend Nick Adams had studied Kenpo karate (an open-hand, self defense style) under Master Ed Parker and shared Jaeckel's fascination with the Japanese samurai

Jaeckel as Commander Vince Elliott in *The Green Slime* (1968). The films he made in Japan were silly but gave him the opportunity to play leading parts.

warrior. Jaeckel would become a dedicated Kendoka and practiced the educational sport regularly upon his return to the United States. During his Japan visit he was also exposed to sumo wrestling, judoka, and plenty of sushi and sake.

The *Green Slime* experience didn't dissuade Jaeckel from returning to Japan in the fall of 1968 to make another supremely silly cult sci-fi film. *Latitude Zero* (1969) features Jaeckel as Perry Lawton, the nominal hero exploring an underwater utopia. The Jules Verne–like fantasy is from director Ishiro Honda of the *Godzilla* films. Again the director did not speak English and used a translator to communicate with the U.S. actors Joseph Cotten, his wife Patricia Medina, Cesar Romero, and Linda Haynes, who in a *Shock Cinema* magazine interview recalled Jaeckel being "very nice." Co-produced by U.S. and Japanese interest, the movie ran into financial problems when the U.S. funding vanished. The American actors weren't sure if they were going to be paid or not during the two-month shoot, but professionalism ruled the day in a movie that features ridiculous giant bats, rodents, and a flying lion (all actors in sub-par costumes). The entire U.S. cast became quite sick during filming except for Jaeckel, no doubt due to his exercise regimen and healthy living habits.

Jaeckel approaches the crazy premise with straight-faced earnestness, even when he's asked to parade his forty-three-year-old physique around in a pair of swim trunks. Early in the film the console of a mini-sub catches fire, and Jaeckel takes his shirt off to smother it. Outside of that bit of beefcake exploitation, Jaeckel does the best he can to give his character a varied and basically likable personality. Jaeckel's inquisitive, sometimes cynical reporter at least comes off looking like a conventional hero and survives until the end credits. In sharp contrast, top-billed Cotten wears an odd assortment of outfits and scarfs while Romero goes over the top as the brain surgeon bad guy. Despite all the fine Hollywood films Jake made in his career, there are some who remember him as the star of these wacky Japanese sci-fi flicks. Nevertheless, Jaeckel was glad for the opportunity to be the hero for a change and never bad-mouthed these films to the press. Jaeckel's good friend Clark Hatch recalls, "I asked one of the movie friends in Japan why Dick was enjoying many invitations from producers in Asia. He replied that Dick was very dependable and always put in the hours and effort that exceeded their expectations. He did the same with his exercise."[6]

The film received no U.S. reviews at the time but has since been "discovered" on DVD and achieved cult status. Wayne Manor of the website *Spinning Image* writes perceptively on Jaeckel's involvement:

> Jaeckel might be considered a perennial second banana by some, and consequently, not getting the respect he deserves—as if high-profile stars would be where they are without supporting players. But one of Richard's outstanding qualities was his ability to play both sides of the good/evil coin with great conviction. Short, with a compact frame and boyish face, Richard could come off as the dependable industrious facilitator, just like he does in *Latitude Zero*. But by adding a trace of a smirk and some cockiness to his gait, Jaeckel became a jackal, the arrogant punk hiding behind a gun, a worm you'd give anything to see catch an uppercut square on the jaw. Many actors are able to constantly deliver as the saint or the sinner, but it takes a very special talent to be equally adept at both.

Jaeckel wasn't entirely done with his Asian film sojourn, traveling to the Philippines to appear in support of Barbara Bouchet, Mike Preston, and Michael Rennie in the espionage drama *The Surabaya Conspiracy* (1969). The film was also released under the titles *Gold Seekers* and *Stoney*. Jaeckel plays henchman Dirk. Apparently he agreed to make the minor film due to director Wray Davis having been a producer on *Once Before I Die*. Jaeckel's on-screen partner in crime Vance Skarstedt also worked on that film as a writer and associate producer. Friendship always went a long way with Jaeckel. When it involved a paycheck and an exotic location, it was all gravy.

Although given fourth billing in the film, Jaeckel is only in a handful of scenes and has very few lines before being blown away by a rifle at close range in a climactic double cross. It is likely Jaeckel was only brought in from Japan for a few days to add his name to the production to boost the film's chances in the marketplace. The picture would probably have benefitted greatly from giving Jaeckel the leading role that English actor Preston blandly essays, but in all likelihood Jaeckel's participation was an afterthought. The skimpy plot involving gold hidden under a swimming pool is nearly as flimsy as the beautiful Bouchet's revealing costumes. It is certainly nowhere near as infamous as Jaeckel's other Asian films. Long forgotten, it has subsequently resurfaced on DVD. It is worth a look only for the most die-hard Jaeckel fans.

Jaeckel was no doubt eager to get back on American soil for a good old-fashioned John Wayne western. In actuality *Chisum* (1970) was filmed in Durango, Mexico, by director Andrew V. McLaglen, but it is solid American cowboy entertainment. Jaeckel is in fine antagonistic form as fast gun Jess Evans, who pours lead into half a dozen men through the course of the story. He is recruited alongside hateful bounty hunter Christopher George by town boss Forrest Tucker and crooked sheriff Bruce Cabot to make things rough for cattleman Wayne and his partners Patric Knowles and Andrew Prine. Their range war is played out like a chess match. Ben Johnson is also featured in the strong cast as Wayne's right hand man, as is Glenn Corbett as Pat Garrett. Despite the multitude of characters, Jaeckel registers strongly with his tough guy dialogue and confident demeanor, and the film is a worthy addition to his western bad guy canon. There's a nice subplot involving tension between Jaeckel and former saddle partner Billy the Kid (Geoffrey Deuel), who guns Jaeckel down during a showdown in the action-packed climax. Looking up into the sky, a dying Jaeckel memorably recollects, "It ain't like old times, Billy."

As was typical of a John Wayne film, there was a tremendous amount of spirited drinking going on behind the scenes. The old guard of Wayne, Forrest Tucker, Bruce Cabot, and Ben Johnson broke out the hard stuff and challenged the new guys led by Jaeckel, Andrew Prine, Chris George, and Geoff Deuel to a drinking competition. The younger men did not fare well against the Hollywood heavyweights, who had been carrying on like this for decades on film sets.[7] In reality, at this point in his career Jaeckel fell somewhere in between the old and the new guard. This was a transition film for him where he became accepted by the older established stars as one of them despite his ever-youthful appearance. Twenty years elapsed between filming of *Sands of Iwo Jima* and *Chisum*. The two decades of hard living had not been kind to John Wayne or Forrest Tucker. They grew into crusty old men. Jaeckel, on the other hand, was still fit and bronzed with a full head of golden blond hair.

Veteran character actor Edward Faulkner had been a member of Wayne's stock company since *McLintock!* (1963). In *Chisum* he plays a storekeeper in the employ of bad guy Tucker. He recalls working with Jaeckel: "We often referred to him as 'The Golden Oldie' and it was a delight to be in a production with him. He contributed so much and was always cheerful and 'up' every day. He was some six years my senior but one of those individuals who always seemed to be the same age as you. An extremely talented actor and so comfortable to be in his presence."[8]

Jaeckel had previously worked with director McLaglen on TV's *Have Gun—Will Travel* and *Gunsmoke* as well as the motion picture *The Devil's Brigade*. They would team again years

Jaeckel as the villainous Jess Evans in the Warner Bros. western *Chisum* (1970).

later for the TV film *The Dirty Dozen: Next Mission* (1985). The son of Victor McLaglen, Andrew was an efficient director who set up action well with his stunt coordinator Hal Needham and helmed many of Wayne's films during this period. On the DVD commentary for *Chisum* McLaglen said, "Dick Jaeckel was another favorite of mine. Dick Jaeckel was always a good man to have on the set. He was always a fun-lover. One thing I remember is by the time they called lunch he was the first one in line.... He always looked years younger than his actual age."

The film's writer-producer A.J. Fenady has a similar memory of his experience with Jaeckel: "No matter how far away he was from where the lunch set-up was located on location, he invariably was the first in the chow line. How he got there I don't know. He ate plenty, but he exercised plenty. I don't think his waist ever expanded. His waist was always just about the same.... We had four stars from the *Sands of Iwo Jima*. Jake was very prominent in that in 1949. Exactly twenty years later we shot *Chisum* in 1969. The four stars were John Wayne, Forrest Tucker, John Agar, and Richard Jaeckel. We took a picture and replicated the four leads. Jake was the same size, same wardrobe, same size shirt—everything. His face was very unlined. Almost like at 17 on *Guadalcanal*. He was awfully, awfully good in *Chisum*."9

The critics agreed. *Variety*: "Christopher George and Richard Jaeckel are both convincing as gunmen." *The New York Times*: "Hardies Glenn Corbett, Ben Johnson, and Richard Jaeckel pitch in accordingly." *The San Diego Union*: "[Jaeckel and Christopher George] create villains of more than the usual one-dimension." The *Los Angeles Herald Examiner*: "Andrew Prine, Chris George, and Richard Jaeckel do well enough in standard roles." *The Oregonian*: "Richard Jaeckel and Chris George do fine small jobs as baddies so rotten you can't even like them."

Jaeckel was up for a role in the Jon Voight movie *The All-American Boy* and nearly took it instead of an on-again, off-again Paul Newman project that had been in discussion for over a year. The Voight boxing movie was made in 1970 but was not released until 1973 and quickly slipped from memory. The Newman project was *Sometimes a Great Notion* (1970), an adaptation of the famous Ken Kesey logging novel that many in Hollywood deemed un-filmable. Jaeckel became attached to the project when he was in Malibu visiting Arthur Loew with his family at the same time as Newman. Box office star Newman spent the day watching a relaxed Jaeckel interact with Loew's family and throw a football around. Newman began to see Jaeckel as the novel's character Joe Ben Stomper, an eternally upbeat Born Again Christian and dedicated family man. The studio wanted Newman's recent Oscar-winning *Cool Hand Luke* co-star George Kennedy to play his cousin Joe Ben in the film, but Newman was adamant that Jaeckel was the man for the job. In fact, he promised the role to Jaeckel on the Malibu sand. Newman liked seeing Jaeckel with the kids and thought it would present a side of the often mercurial actor seldom tapped into on screen. Jaeckel told *The Oregonian*, "It's kind of a novelty to play a family man, a nice guy who believes in God, loves his wife and kids. Usually I'm the grinning killer or some G.I. running through the jungle."

Kesey's book describes Joe Ben (Joby) as appearing much like Jaeckel, short and well-built. George Kennedy was 6'4" and dwarfed the 5'9" Newman. Jaeckel tended to think the fact that he possessed a lumberjack's muscles from his years of lifting weights helped him win the role, as did his swimming background and ability to hold his breath underwater during a crucial mouth-to-mouth resuscitation scene. Regarding Newman's promise, Jaeckel told Frank Gagnard of the *Times-Picayune*: "He said it has a good a scene as ever written for two guys—two straight guys, he made a point of that. At one point I heard the picture was going to be cancelled and I almost took another film. I didn't, though, because of Paul. Here was one guy who did what he said he was going to do instead of blowing smoke."

Jaeckel got the full story of Newman's going to bat for him with the studio executives and casting agents from mutual friend Annabel King. Jaeckel had endured twenty years of broken promises and false expectations within the industry. Newman sticking to his word moved Jaeckel unexpectedly. Jaeckel expounded on Newman for Joe Morella's biography *Paul and Joanne*: "I had chills running up and down, and I just broke into tears. It's not because I was going to get the job or not, but here was a guy who finally followed through and did what he said he was going to do.... That guy couldn't be any higher on my list."

Sometimes a Great Notion (aka *Never Give an Inch*) began filming in the summer of 1970 with Newman and Jaeckel joined by Henry Fonda, Lee Remick, and Michael Sarrazin as the stubborn, proud, independent Stamper family. Singer Linda Lawson was cast as Jaeckel's wife with Lee DeBroux, Sam Gilman, Cliff Potts, Jim Burk, and Roy Jenson rounding out the cast. Richard Colla was the original director, but he was replaced two weeks into the shoot after grumblings regarding intricate, time-consuming camera set-ups. Producer-star Newman assessed the footage shot thus far and opted to fire Colla and take over the production himself. It was a monumental task both directing and starring in the adaptation of an epic novel. For the most part Newman was successful, though the stress of the situation led him to recklessly turn to drinking to see him through the rough passages. There was another delay when Newman broke his ankle in an on-set motorcycle accident. Overall, though, it was a fun film to be a part of, largely due to the location.

Newman's harried state of mind and the combination of Jaeckel and a group of tough stuntmen on the set created a memorable experience that had the southern Oregon coast talking about the making of the film for decades. Newman had cases of his favorite Coors beer shipped to the location and open beer kegs on the set were commonplace throughout the course of filming. Vitamin B-12 shots were administered freely to anyone needing a pick-me-up or suffering from a hangover. One big set-piece in the film was a beach picnic that becomes a football game between the Stampers and the rival lumberjacks. This turns into a wild fistfight that spills into the ocean. Jaeckel was right in there with the stuntmen throughout the action. At the end of the scene, celebratory bottles of whiskey were passed around between the actors and the stunt guys. At one point Jaeckel was visited on the Oregon set by John Derek and his newest wife Linda Evans, who were on a camping trip up the coast. Newman's wife Joanne Woodward was there and celebrity friends such as Marlon Brando and Shirley MacLaine made brief stops to talk to Newman. Ken Kesey himself made an appearance. Outside of the firing of Colla, the film took on the atmosphere of one long Hollywood party.

During filming, Jaeckel, Henry Fonda, and screenwriter John Gay were flown to Portland on a private jet for a publicity opportunity. They attended the opening of a new high rise building and a performance by the Portland Opera Company. Adorned in tuxedos, the Hollywood trio were introduced to an appreciative audience by the state's governor, Tom McCall. Each made a short speech, although the champagne had been flowing throughout the evening. At some point Fonda had switched to bourbon. Gay remembered in his memoirs, "He was so swacked by then that Jake and I could hardly believe he was still vertical and moving. The next morning, we spoke to Fonda about his speech the night before. He didn't remember a word of it. Worse, he didn't even remember that he gave a speech."

The Newport and Toledo, Oregon, locals all took a liking to Jaeckel, who was warm and approachable with everyone. When he had free time he would rent a charter boat and go fish. Author Matt Love has written a book entitled *Sometimes a Great Movie* about the filming and the effect it had on the locals. Dick Wizner rented a boat to Jaeckel and recalled in Love's book: "Jaeckel went out several times. He was a nice, normal guy. We talked a lot and he told me about movies and I told him about fishing." Grad student Pam Bladine opined, "Richard

Jaeckel was the nicest guy in the world," and Mo's Annex waitress Cindy McEntee remembered him as "a super nice guy." Teenage extra Janna Farrington recalled, "Michael Sarrazin, Richard Jaeckel, Sam Gilman, and Henry Fonda treated everybody there as a colleague and friend. There was no difference between you and them. They would laugh and joke and talk and they'd try to get to know you."

Local logger Ron Bernard was cast in a running part in the film. He reminisced,

> He was quite a guy. I do recall the first day of filming that we all went out to the logging site. I rode out there with Paul Newman. We were standing around when I first saw Richard Jaeckel. The loggers here commonly wear hickory shirts. He was not a very tall guy, but he looked more like a logger than a logger does. I told him, "You look familiar." I thought maybe I had worked with him before. That's when he told me who he was.
>
> He was very approachable. A nice guy. He was the kind of guy who would say good morning to you. He never asked me about logging. They had technical guys for that on the picture and it wasn't my place to tell him. One time after I got to know him I asked him how he was able to be cast in so many motion pictures. He told me, "I'm very professional and very cooperative." And he was. He was a very nice guy. I really enjoyed working with him. I worked on *Sometimes a Great Notion* right up to the end. The last week of shooting we shot the fight on the beach, which was a lot of fun if you like rolling around in the surf and getting sand stuck everywhere. The whole movie was quite an experience.[10]

Local hair stylist Bonnie Stout was in her early thirties at the time and recently divorced. Her salon was in an annex across from the fishing charter office. During the course of the shoot the pretty blonde caught Jaeckel's eye and he began to initiate conversation. The two had a definite chemistry and both enjoyed the flirtatious repartee. Jaeckel was a married man, but location romances with locals are fairly commonplace for Hollywood crews and this was the free-wheeling 1970s. Stout's friends urged her to pursue Jaeckel. Stout was frank in her recollections for Love's book and recalled that although she and Jaeckel were both interested they never progressed beyond a few fondly remembered kisses at the wrap party:

> He was a wonderful man. He was a kind person and just pleasant to be around. I had a beauty shop on the waterfront where so many of them hung out. Part of the movie was filmed there. My beauty shop was part of a famous restaurant called Mo's, and Mo would throw parties for all of them. Richard Jaeckel was one of Mo's favorite characters. She really liked him as a person. It brings back such pleasant memories. He was such a charming man. He liked to hang out in my little beauty shop. He would sit in the dryer chairs and talk to all the ladies that would come in. He was really a pleasant, pleasant guy. As far as my knowing him, that book that Matt Love wrote is pretty much it. He was a happily married man at the time. So what happened between us was just very flirtatious. It was a flirting thing and a few stolen kisses, and that was it. But the friendship endured.[11]

The movie remains infamous for the scene in which Jaeckel is trapped beneath a log in the water while the tide is rising. It has been widely acknowledged as one of the big screen's most memorable death scenes. Veteran character actor Clu Gulager, who worked with Jaeckel during another memorable fatality on the TV western *The Tall Man*, recalls, "Dick's death scene in *Sometimes a Great Notion* underwater is by far the best death scene I've ever seen committed to film. Dick was so good in that, laughing as he drowned. Very tragic, very sad, and very powerful."[12] James Drury agrees: "I remember that wonderful scene he had when he was drowning and Paul Newman was trying to rescue him when the log is pinning him down. He was so optimistic Paul was going to get him out of there. That scene is seared in my memory. I can close my eyes and see it now.... I think that he stole the show. He was so bright and beautiful in that. I'll never forget him."[13]

Jaeckel winds up under a log in shallow water after a tree Newman is cutting splinters in the wrong direction. Assessing the situation, both Jaeckel and Newman downplay the severity of the accident. Newman tries to saw the log in two to extricate Jaeckel, but his chainsaw becomes waterlogged and he can't get it to restart. His effort to budge the great log is unsuccessful, but Jaeckel seems more concerned that his prized radio has stopped playing music. However, they both realize that the tide is rising and Jaeckel could soon go underwater. Jaeckel remains calm and jokes with Newman, confident that once the tide comes in the log will lift off of him. When that's not the case, the men's shared laughter turns into sudden desperation as Newman is forced to administer rescue breaths as Jaeckel slips under the surface. The situation deteriorates so quickly that Newman doesn't have time to look for anything for Jaeckel to breathe through. Newman continues attempting mouth-to-mouth resuscitation under the water, a scenario the two were joking old man Henry Fonda would have a fit seeing only minutes before. Jaeckel's last breath comes out in an underwater laugh. It's a near perfectly conceived handling of the ten-minute long scene which ends with the haunting image of Jaeckel's face underwater as Newman wails "Joby!" and the name echoes through the forest. Jaeckel felt that Newman as director "got the performance of my life out of me in that scene."

Regarding the mouth-to-mouth, Newman and Jaeckel couldn't stop laughing during the filming of the death scene, done on location at Yaquina Bay. An above-ground swimming pool

Jaeckel and Paul Newman in the famous drowning scene in Universal's *Sometimes a Great Notion* (1970). Jaeckel received an Oscar nomination for his performance.

about three feet deep was used for close-ups to provide cleaner water for the men. The scene was supervised by veteran Hollywood water specialist Fred Zendar. Jaeckel initially didn't think that audiences would believe the scenario, telling writer Ray Bennett that shooting the scene "took three days. We had wetsuits on under our clothes and because the river was dirty we shot the underwater scenes in a tank. We shot for eight hours each day and even though we had the wetsuits it was cold. But Newman brought in a case of Chivas Regal and after a couple of hours underwater, out came the whiskey. For three days we did that. It was cold, but I tell you man, we were feeling no pain."

That scene blew everyone away, and critics were unanimous in their praise of Jaeckel who was the heart and soul of the film. *Sometimes a Great Notion* premiered on New Year's Eve 1970, but didn't receive its full theatrical run until nearly a full year later, receiving very mixed reviews. It is remembered as a better film now than when it was released. *Time Magazine* said, "Richard Jaeckel is perfect" and *The Hollywood Reporter* noted the role was "well played by Richard Jaeckel." *The New York Times* called it a "lovely performance" while *Variety* mentioned that Jaeckel's death scene was "a perfect piece of filmmaking." *The Boston Globe* agreed, writing there was "a good characterization from Richard Jaeckel, who has an agonizing death scene." Noted film critic Leonard Maltin called Jaeckel's performance "outstanding." *The San Diego Union* wrote, "The film's best performance is given by Jaeckel, who does the most with the least. He is especially effective in a tragic scene in which Newman tries to save him. This also is Newman's best directed sequence." *The Times-Picayune* mentioned, "There are two unexpectedly fine performances by Michael Sarrazin and Richard Jaeckel. TV star Jaeckel will knock you out with his comic death scene." Roger Ebert of the *Chicago Sun Times* wrote, "Richard Jaeckel has a sort of sweet simplicity that seems out of place—until the scene where he dies. He dies in a way that is truly filled with grace and humor, and the scene is one of the several things in *Sometimes a Great Notion* that makes it worth seeing, even if its overall design is murky." The *Pittsburgh Press-Gazette* thought the film "will be remembered for an unusual, gripping death scene played by Richard Jaeckel, whose career it should revitalize." The *Schenectady Gazette* added, "Jaeckel makes a real and sympathetic character out of the assignment, adding more substance to the role than the book did and so adding more strength to the film."

Regarding all the positive notices, eternal team player Jaeckel told the *San Francisco Examiner and Chronicle*, "As an actor it's gratifying to be told you were great in one particular scene, but if one is going to be remembered at all, it is far better to be remembered as part of a very important picture where you were good throughout." He further commented on the value of his casting in the film to writer Dick Kleiner in a syndicated feature article: "I started as the apple-cheeked boy. Then for a while I was a tough kid. Then western bad man and then along came a career as a hoodlum. Then many films as a sergeant or corporal in the Army or the Marines. But there was never any dimension to any of them, until this one. This time I have a wife and children and a fully developed character. It's quite a thrill."

While waiting for the film's release, he still had to put food on the table. Jaeckel added a few more TV episodes to his expanding résumé, guest starring on the February 1971 segment of *The F.B.I.* entitled "Death Watch" as Sgt. Sam Ryker, a critically injured Marine in an episode dealing with extremists stealing military weaponry. The opening scene finds Jaeckel proposing to girlfriend Angel Tompkins, only to be attacked and knifed by what he terms "a couple of punks." The remainder of the episode finds Jaeckel fighting for his life in a hospital bed against a wound his doctor claims "would have killed anyone else." In addition to Jaeckel,

Glenn Corbett, Diane Keaton, Steve Sandor, and Bill Vint appeared. The Quinn Martin–produced Warner Bros. series starring Efrem Zimbalist, Jr., was in its sixth season of high-quality entertainment with storylines based on real FBI files. Jaeckel's longtime friend Paul Wurtzel served as the show's assistant director.

Jaeckel also guested on the October 1971 *O'Hara, United States Treasury* episode "Operation: Offset," acting opposite series star David Janssen. Jaeckel's *O'Hara* entry was paired by Universal Studios with another episode of the single-season series and the twofer was released to TV stations as the "movie" *Counterfeit Green* (1971). It's a passable entry, although Jaeckel's edgy muscle Barth is the same kind of role he was playing more than a decade earlier on shows such as *Tightrope*. He takes orders from main heavy Alex Dreier and reacts angrily when over-the-hill stripper Marilyn Maxwell calls him a psycho. In the climax a motorcycle-riding Jaeckel tries to clobber Janssen with a tire iron, only to crash into an opened car door in a parking garage. The most interesting thing about this assignment is the contrast between Jaeckel and the hard-living Janssen, who was four years younger than Jaeckel but looks some twenty years older. Janssen, star of TV's *The Fugitive*, was just 48 when he died after a heart attack in 1980.

In December of 1971 Jaeckel was back on the Paramount lot as the top guest star on the *Mission: Impossible* episode "Run for the Money." He played the smartly dressed syndicate gangster Edward Trask, trying to take over thoroughbred horse race betting action. Peter Graves and the IMF team go undercover to set up Jaeckel in pitting him against his acquaintance Herb Edelman for the purchase of a horse. Lynda Day George plays into Jaeckel's love for the ladies as she sets the trap. The conniving, threatening Jaeckel smells a rat but thinks he's outwitted the con, not counting on the retribution that is forthcoming from Edelman and his thug Charles Napier at the end of the episode. Jaeckel is entertaining throughout, although it's one of the lesser episodes of the classic show. *The Bridgeport Post* said, "Richard Jaeckel adds dash to the breezy little monster Casey (Lynda Day George) must butter up."

The Deadly Dream (1971) is an effective if barely remembered TV movie from Universal and director Alf Kjellin. It stars Lloyd Bridges as a genetic scientist whose terrifying dreams of a secret tribunal hunting him down begin to blur with reality. As characters intermingle between "dream life" and real life, Bridges begins to distrust even his wife Janet Leigh. The film manages to maintain a fair degree of suspense throughout as Bridges gradually loses his sanity. Jaeckel is cast as Delgreve, a bespectacled menace in a business suit who haunts Bridges' nightmares with calculated coolness. Solid performers Don Stroud, Leif Erickson, and Carl Betz round out the cast. *Variety* called the film "hokum" but did note, "Bridges and Richard Jaeckel had roles that permitted them to sustain believability longer than the others."

Even with his heroic sci-fi flicks and prominent roles in *The Dirty Dozen*, *The Devil's Brigade*, and *Sometimes a Great Notion*, Jaeckel remained aware that he constantly had to be working to maintain the homestead. He didn't have the luxury to casually pick and choose his parts, knowing that the next long dry spell could be around the bend. He'd take what work his agent landed, even if it was cookie-cutter TV shows. Jaeckel commented to *The Arizona Republic* on his multitude of villainous parts: "You take those roles because the man in the market still wants to be paid for groceries being purchased."

7

Riding the Wave

When the Oscars rolled around at the beginning of 1972, the positive notices for *Sometimes a Great Notion* compelled Universal Studios to push Jaeckel for an Academy Award nomination as Best Supporting Actor. Jaeckel was humbled by the gesture but chose not to toot his own horn. He'd seen backlash in the industry when friends such as Chill Wills and Nick Adams pursued the golden statue too aggressively for some tastes. Jaeckel told *The Arizona Republic*: "There's been talk that I might get a Supporting Actor nomination for the role. If I'm so fortunate, one thing I won't do—and I haven't done it up to now in the trades, either—I won't advertise looking for members of the Academy to vote for me. I just don't think it's right. I think an actor's performance should stand on its merits, not because one actor has more money to spend pushing for votes."

Jaeckel got the well-deserved nomination and a career revitalization. Also up for Best Supporting Actor were Ben Johnson and Jeff Bridges (both for *The Last Picture Show*), Leonard Frey (for *Fiddler on the Roof*), and Roy Scheider (for *The French Connection*). Bridges, Frey, and Scheider were all new film actors, and likely would be overlooked by the Academy this time out. Many considered the competition to be between Jaeckel and Ben Johnson, the much-beloved cowboy actor and former John Ford movie stuntman whom director Peter Bogdanovich recruited for the showy part of a weather-beaten Texan named Sam the Lion. The 44th Annual Academy Awards was staged on April 10, 1972, at the Dorothy Chandler Pavilion in Los Angeles with Richard Harris and Sally Kellerman presenting the statue. Jaeckel attended, handsomely attired in black tux and purple shirt.

As many felt was justified, both then and now, Ben Johnson ended up winning that year. Jaeckel's *Chisum* co-star was one of the few actors who could take the sentimental vote away from Jaeckel, even though he often claimed in interviews that all he ever did was play himself. Both men were extremely well-liked by their peers, and Jaeckel was happy to see the old rodeo hand honored with the Oscar. He was a most gracious loser. Ultimately, it would be the only nomination for both men. Jaeckel was simply overjoyed to be recognized and in the running for the award, telling the *Times-Picayune* the role was "the greatest thing that ever happened to me, period."

Jaeckel was well aware what the Oscar nomination could mean for his career in terms of work and quality of parts. He wouldn't have to do all the snarling TV villains, all of the second soldier on the left parts, or the silly Japanese sci-fi films. He was on the A-list in Hollywood for now and signed with the Herb Tobias Agency, talent rep for Johnson, Robert

Stack, Gene Barry, and Robert Young. The change in status was immediate and tangible. Top film scripts started coming his way. Jaeckel told the *Richmond Times Dispatch*, "Instead of telling me to meet the cast bus at the corner of Hollywood and Vine, they send cars to my house and pick me up."

More people were aware of his name and face than ever before. There was a better-than-average chance when he was out in public that he would no longer be mistaken for *Star Trek* TV star William Shatner or one of singer Bing Crosby's blond-haired sons. He was now Richard Jaeckel, the Academy Award nominee. Jaeckel's exercise buddy Clark Hatch recalls an amusing anecdote involving Jaeckel's familiar anonymity, writing, "I recall having lunch in L.A. with Dick and a customer came up and asked, 'Which of the Crosby boys are you?' Dick politely replied, 'Bing,' which got a big chuckle. He said that it was quite common for people to mistake him for other actors."[1]

Jaeckel never took offense at his lack of recognition by the general public. There was no bruised ego or anger displayed, merely graciousness at being recognized at all. He considered it a testament to how successful he was as a working character actor. He never enjoyed a higher standing with the studios as he did after the Oscar nomination. As would be expected, a flurry of scripts and offers came for Jaeckel to read and decide on. Jaeckel told the *Fort Lauderdale News*, "It broke the process and notion that I can do only one thing.... Each night I look up in the sky and say thank you."

The improved standing in Hollywood meant an increase in media coverage. Suddenly reporters were clamoring for access to Jaeckel, who while obliging remained reticent to share too much of his private life. He would volunteer he had been married to the same woman for twenty-five years and that they had two grown sons. He and Antoinette enjoyed Japanese food, and Jaeckel still loved the regular trips to the beach and exercise. He had only one suit jacket and was the owner of a German Shepard named Cruncher. "We're not part of the Hollywood social scene," Jaeckel told reporter Vernon Scott. "And we don't entertain much. We went through all that in the early going and I just found that we spent a lot of money doing absolutely nothing."

Jaeckel's sons Richard and Barry were now men. Richard Jr. finished up his collegiate studies at USC and occasionally worked behind the scenes as his dad's stand-in for camera set-ups. He's credited in the film *The Dark* (1979). Barry had finished attending Santa Monica Junior College and spent time as a caddy at the Riviera Country Club. The 1968 Southern California Amateur golf champion turned pro in 1971 and immediately went to Europe to compete. He won the 1972 Open de France before joining the PGA Tour in 1975. He would participate in 515 professional events between 1975 and 1995, winning the 1978 Tallahassee Open and logging two dozen top ten finishes. Barry came close to the big time on two occasions, finishing second at the Tournament Players Championship in 1981 after coming up short on a putt in a sudden death play-off with Raymond Floyd. He experienced a similar fate against Fred Couples at the 1983 Kemper Open. A win at either event would have given him a ten-year exemption for the big money finishes.

"Hollywood" Barry Jaeckel (as he was called by the press) was a popular golfer and traveled the world with his wife Evelyn, but he never became rich at his chosen profession. Like his dad, he made a living at it but was never able to sock away enough to retire in luxury. Although Jaeckel championed his son's accomplishments, he was somewhat reluctant to follow him around on tour, superstitiously fearing that he would jinx Barry's play. In 1999 Barry joined the Senior Tour. During the course of his career Barry often fielded questions about his father, always quick to point out his dad was an actor and not a star. "We've really grown close in the past three or four years," Barry told the *Hartford Courant* in 1976. "I've grown to understand his purposes, and he, mine. We've really got a great relationship."

Jaeckel himself was proud of being a husband and father to two fine young men, although he didn't mince words concerning the early 1950s period when he considered himself at fault for being overly self-involved and career-oriented. "I'm afraid I wasn't much of a father in the early years," Jaeckel told the *Boston Globe* in the early 1970s. "I've achieved a better balance recently. But of course both the boys are over twenty-one now, and they lead their own lives anyway."

By the time the Academy Awards were broadcast, Jaeckel had already completed a solid role opposite Burt Lancaster in Robert Aldrich's western *Ulzana's Raid* (1972). Concerning an ill-fated cavalry excursion into rugged Arizona territory in search of a renegade Apache and his marauding band, the film was extremely well-made and at times shockingly violent. Lancaster's veteran Indian scout was contrasted in the film with Bruce Davison's young, inexperienced officer from the academy back east. Jaeckel was the seen-it-all Sgt. Burns who followed orders to the letter even when it was against his own instinct for survival. The exciting climax finds both Jaeckel and Lancaster pinned down beneath a wagon under heavy rifle fire. Both die valiant but pointless deaths.

The violent Vietnam allegory was shot in Arizona's Coronado National Forest and Nogales along the Mexican border as well as the Valley of Fire outside of Las Vegas. A quiet and understated Jaeckel has solid moments, particularly with Davison when the two discuss Christianity and when Jaeckel loses one of his men needlessly due to a bad order. Jaeckel holds his own in his scenes with Lancaster, whose penchant for colorful teeth-baring histrionics is reeled in nicely by Aldrich's preference for world-weary wisdom and first-hand experience with death. The beard the perpetually youthful Jaeckel sports also hints at a man who has been aged by circumstances and too much Indian fighting. At a key moment he reveals that he has lost a child at the hands of the Apache, but he remains a professional soldier tuned to duty and not overcome by personal hatred.

Out of loyalty to Aldrich, Jaeckel took a substantial pay cut to work on the film. Aldrich's recent attempt at running his own film studio had met with financial failure and he needed the chance to prove himself once again. According to *The Films of Robert Aldrich*, Jaeckel told his friend, "Aldrich, anything you want, any time, whatever, let me know." Jaeckel was well aware of the quality

Jaeckel as a grizzled cavalry sergeant in Robert Aldrich's Universal western *Ulzana's Raid* (1972). Lensed in the deserts of Arizona and Nevada, the film was one of Jaeckel's toughest to make.

Aldrich was capable of putting on the screen. Studio pressure caused Aldrich and star Lancaster to clash, but Jaeckel told Lancaster biographer Gary Fishgall that both men were working toward making the film better. Despite the presence of Chuck Courtney on the film as Jaeckel's double, Jaeckel did the majority of his own hard riding. "It was a tough location," Jaeckel said. "Very tough."

Stuntman Neil Summers was hired on as one of the members of the cavalry and got to know Jaeckel. He remembers:

> Richard was a nice, nice guy. Everybody liked him. Claude Akins and Richard Jaeckel were the guys that everybody liked. Richard was a very friendly guy and a good actor. I worked with him on *Ulzana's Raid*, *Petrocelli*, *Gunsmoke*, and a few TV movies. The stunt guys didn't have a lot to do on *Ulzana* until the fight at the end. We mostly spent sixteen weeks riding behind Burt Lancaster until they cornered us in the canyon. It was a good film.[2]

Reviews for Jaeckel's performance were positive. *Films in Focus'* Andrew Sarris wrote, "Burt Lancaster gives the performance of his career as the world-weary scout, and Richard Jaeckel and Bruce Davison are right up there too…" *The Los Angeles Times* noted that Jaeckel was "fine as a sensible sergeant." *Variety* wrote, "Jorge Luke and Richard Jaeckel come off best in the film," while *The Boston Globe* noted, "Richard Jaeckel is good"; the *Pittsburgh Post* added, "Richard Jaeckel lends reality." The *Oregonian* found him "fine as the grizzled sergeant." Brian Garfield's book *Western Films: The Complete Guide* found Jaeckel to be "quite good." *The Hollywood Reporter* was turned off by the violence, labeling "the direction and performances in this grisly little film as merely heavy-handed." Jaeckel made a rare publicity appearance attending the Houston, Texas, premiere of *Ulzana's Raid*.

Although he probably didn't have to, Jaeckel fit in a couple of episodic TV guest shots. He participated in a one-scene cameo for the September 1972 *Emergency* episode "Kids," cast as a lawyer defending the parents of an injured child. Jaeckel nailed a scene with his old Universal pal Robert Fuller on the witness stand. It would be the only time the two actors would ever be seen together on film in a dramatic scene. "That was fun," Fuller recalls. "We had a great time. Jake played a prosecuting attorney and did an incredible job. I loved that."[3]

On the syndicated TV series *Insight*, Jaeckel and Arlene Golonka portray a mismatched couple in the comic episode "The System," directed by TV veteran Ralph Senensky. The show was filmed in black and white to match up with previous episodes when rerun. Jaeckel was so eager to be given a chance to play something light that he worked for scale. While one episode of *Insight* was rehearsing, another episode would be taping on the set. Both casts and crews would be treated to catered lunches. During one lunch break, a meeting was called between the two casts and it was suggested that all the actors should endorse their checks back to the production company for the sake of the show. Jaeckel found this suggestion especially humorous, revealing that his wife was already upset with him for accepting only scale to work on the show.

Senensky has an Internet blog where he writes in detail about the many productions he has worked on and answers questions from readers. He shares specific memories of working with Jaeckel on *Insight*: "This was the first time I worked with Richard Jaeckel, but since we were both contemporaries I had watched him grow up in front of the cameras…. At the age of forty-five he was well qualified to play working man Henry Burke. But could he play comedy? There was nothing in his filmography that answered that question. A few minutes into our first reading, and I had the answer. It was a great big YES, and most importantly he played comedy the way I wanted it played, totally real with a microscopic attention to detail."[4]

Jaeckel was back to more familiar territory on the October 1972 *Ironside* episode "The Countdown," playing a formidable bad guy should audiences forget that had always been his specialty. Jaeckel plays the paranoiac criminal, "Caesar" a crook who fastens an explosive belt around the waist of fellow guest Jackie Cooper and blackmails San Francisco police commissioner Raymond Burr into releasing a group of prisoners. By episode's end Jaeckel's plan unravels as he is done in by his own irrational fears of failure. "We have a very unpleasant thing in Hollywood called typecasting," Jaeckel told columnist Marilyn Beck at the time. "It's a result of laziness on the part of casting directors and producers who don't use their imaginations to picture an actor in something other than the roles he's played."

The television front had changed somewhat dramatically in recent years, with alternative programming cutting into the typical TV season to the point that the majority of shows now delivered far fewer episodes. A decade earlier a typical season consisted of up to 39 episodes. Now shows were delivering on average 24. As a result there was a great deal less work for many actors, especially those who went from show to show as guest stars to earn their living. In 1972 Jaeckel served on a special Screen Actors Guild council alongside Hollywood heavyweights Henry Fonda, Gregory Peck, Charlton Heston, Burt Lancaster, Glenn Ford, Clint Eastwood, Robert Stack, Ricardo Montalbon, Lloyd Bridges, Woody Strode, Craig Stevens, Raymond Burr, Agnes Moorehead, and Guild president John Gavin to address the problem. Media reports, without naming any names, mentioned the case of one familiar TV face who used to appear on as many as seven to eight different shows a TV season while earning $40,000 to $50,000 a year for his work. This particular actor was now appearing on approximately three shows a TV season and had even seen his established price recently drop to $3000 a guest shot due to the competition in place for the limited jobs. Among those mentioned as serving on the SAG council, Jaeckel seems to be the only one to fit this description.

There was a surefire way to remedy this financial problem. In addition to breaking out of the potential rut of typecasting, the lure of a steady, weekly paycheck became paramount in Jaeckel's mind, and he felt it might be best to strike while the iron was hot. He began to consider TV offers that might fill his pockets and further change his screen image with both casting directors and the public. One was a pilot film for a proposed action series entitled *Firehouse*, set in a New York City fire station and dealing with an arsonist torching tenement buildings. The 1972 production was based on the popular Dennis Smith novel *Report from Engine Company 82*. Jaeckel was cast in support of Vince Edwards and *Shaft* film star Richard Roundtree, with solid actors Val Avery, Andrew Duggan, and Paul LeMat also a part of the crew.

Jaeckel, as veteran firefighter Hank Myers, is forced to intercede between the two warring leads and their racial tensions. He is tough but fair, although he doesn't play favorites and doesn't make it easy on Roundtree even when Edwards is in the wrong. One memorable bit had Jaeckel and Avery forcing a barbell against Roundtree's throat to get an answer out of him as to why he let a young black arson suspect go free. It was a decently made TV movie that benefited primarily from its strong and diverse performances. However, *Firehouse* was put on the back burner as a more intriguing offer came Jaeckel's way.

The previous year, interesting young actor Robert Forster starred in the pilot film *Banyon* (1971) as a late 1930s private eye in the City of Angels. Veteran actor Darren McGavin played his contact with the police force, Pete Cordova. When the series sold, McGavin was unavailable and Jaeckel was approached to join the series as the similar Pete McNeil. Jaeckel loved the period setting and agreed to play the hard-nosed cop supporting Forster and actress Joan Blondell in the eventual series *Banyon* (1972–1973). The sometimes cynical character of McNeil was once Miles C. Banyon's partner on the squad, and the two would occasionally conflict with one another, creating some of the series' stronger moments. Overall the part was a good one and would be a further departure from Jaeckel's villainous image. In fact, it led to him being typed into a number of cop and authoritarian roles over the next twenty years.

Jaeckel as Lt. Pete McNeil in the short-lived Warner Bros. TV cop drama *Banyon* (1972). The 1930s period piece was a troubled production.

A great deal of the Warner Bros. series shot in the landmark Bradbury Building in downtown Los Angeles, noted for its skylight, birdcage elevators, patterned staircases, and wrought iron architecture. Miles Banyon drove a classic Packard Roadster. Jaeckel was excited about the prospects of the series and his role in it, telling *Variety*, "I feel we have a helluva premise and three good people going in." When questioned why a recently Oscar-nominated film actor would be so quick to join up with a TV show, a realistic Jaeckel answered, "An actor who says he doesn't want to do TV either has a lot of money or he's nuts."

A hit TV series that later went into syndication might guarantee Jaeckel's financial future and give him the freedom to pick and choose supporting parts in film with his new level of prestige. Unfortunately, *Banyon* met great resistance. Premiering in the fall of 1972, it was immediately set against tough competition in its Friday night time slot opposite the popular comedy *Love, American Style* and met with mixed reviews. The *Variety* review of the initial episode noted, "Support was good and in a compatible key to the lead, with Richard Jaeckel as the imitable police department counterpart." *The Los Angeles Times* wrote, "It would be nice to see more of Joan Blondell and Richard Jaeckel, two talented actors who had little to do in the initial episode." *TV Guide* said, "On the good side, there are two fine supporting actors. One is Richard Jaeckel, with his cocky, stocky portrayal of Lt. Pete McNeil. The other is Joan Blondell." The *Evening Independent* weighed in with, "The show has two solid performers in supporting roles—Joan Blondell as the hen mother to a brood of would-be secretaries, and underrated Richard Jaeckel as a Los Angeles police lieutenant one step behind Banyon every week. Jaeckel, particularly, is a good performer, and while he's not cast as a villain for a change, he's still underplayed and not given enough exposure."

Jaeckel's role would conceivably grow stronger as the series developed. However, there were a number of problems behind the scenes. Producer Ed Adamson, creator of the pilot film, considered the series his baby. It was prolific producer Quinn Martin though who sold the pilot to the networks a year after it aired and convinced them to let him take over. Relegated to a co-producing role, Adamson began fretting over his loss of control. Stressed to the brink of physical exhaustion, he had a massive heart attack and died at the age of 57, throwing the show into chaos. It was not an easy show to produce in the first place given the attention to period detail and the cost of ensuring that nothing anachronistic found its way onto the screen.

The show had yet to build an audience, in particular due to a network crackdown on the sort of action and violence that a tough private detective series such as *Banyon* nearly demanded. In regards to his character's handgun, "I'm not even sure it will work," Jaeckel told the *Chicago Tribune*. There had also been few chases or fistfights thus far. "If this keeps up, audiences will think we're pantywaists," Jaeckel lamented. There was talk of Richard Donner taking over the producing so the show could continue. However, NBC took stock of the series and pulled it from the airwaves in January 1973 after only fifteen episodes had aired. The seldom seen show has developed a loyal following among those who were fortunate enough to view it during its initial network run. Among the interesting guest stars were Pat O'Brien, Robert Webber, John Saxon, Bo Svenson, Jessica Walter, Teri Garr, Donna Mills, John Fiedler, Charles McGraw, Michael Delano, Dabney Coleman, Royal Dano, Jack Klugman, and Robert Phillips. *Banyon* director Ralph Senensky recalls:

> I wish I could tell you personal things about Richard while shooting *Banyon*, but the truth of the matter is that was a very difficult and not pleasant production. I just remember that he was always the total professional, was not given nearly enough to utilize his great talent. The same could be said about Joan Blondell, who was also a regular. Our major problem was that the creator of the series, Ed Adamson, resented the fact that ABC (sic) bought the series based on the movie-of-the-week he produced, and then put the series under the umbrella of Quinn Martin productions.... Everything was micromanaged and Ed resented that. That was unfortunate because they were doing a very fine job. Producing a [period] show with period costumes, hairdos, and those vehicles that always wanted to stall when they were required to move—it wasn't easy. I directed three of the first six and Quinn personally thanked me when I completed my commitment. Working with Richard on "The System" was far more fun. I recently ordered a DVD of his first film *Guadalcanal Diary*. He was a very young, totally untrained actor, and still came across with great empathy and sympathy. During his long career he developed immense skills, skills that I sometimes think are missing from today's performers.[5]

Choosing to do *Banyon* had likely kept Jake out of one or more potential film productions such as Aldrich's *Emperor of the North* (1973), John Milius' *Dillinger* (1973), and *The Train Robbers* (1973) with John Wayne. Now there were a couple of interesting offers on the table, including a small role in an adaptation of the John Steinbeck literary classic *The Red Pony* (1973). In *The Red Pony* Jaeckel appears as the character James Creighton for director Robert Totten, working with a star-studded cast that includes Henry Fonda, Maureen O'Hara, Jack Elam, Rance Howard, Roy Jenson, and Ben Johnson. As sometimes happens, Jaeckel's part was completely cut out of the abbreviated version that eventually aired on network TV although it did remain intact for the overseas theatrical release. The Universal film was nominated for an Emmy and won the Peabody Award for excellence. It's a noteworthy credit, but one that had no impact on Jaeckel's career. Regarding Fonda, Jaeckel told *Daredevils* magazine:

> I'm not attempting at all to be patronizing, but there has never been anybody who impressed me as much as Fonda. Not only as an actor, but also as a great human being. He was totally unaffected by this business. Fonda never looked as though he was acting, or even sounded like he was acting—he just did it. I recall him as being very democratic, a gentleman. On the other hand he never stood for any crap. You respected him. Acting with him was a delight. He would always give you time to prepare, be willing to work with you and give you encouragement.... I was very impressed when he came over to say hello to me on the first day of shooting. He remembered my name, my wife's name and asked about my kids. That made quite an impression on me. He was indeed a rare breed.

In early 1973 Jaeckel joined director Sam Peckinpah's troubled production *Pat Garrett and Billy the Kid* (1973) in Durango, Mexico. Jaeckel was cast as Sheriff Kip McKinney, a reluctant lawman recruited by Garrett (James Coburn) to help him close in on Billy the Kid (Kris Kristofferson) during the inevitable climax in Fort Sumner, New Mexico. In real life Thomas Christopher McKinney and Pat Garrett were both former outlaws who had become law officers. In the film, Jack Elam's character Alamosa Bill is similarly recruited. This blurring of identities and allegiances amongst friends was one of Peckinpah's attractions to the narrative. The conventional lines of black and white drawn between the heroes and the heavies had vanished over time, bringing an interesting dimension to the characters. In the film, a resistant Jaeckel senses the assignment is a death sentence, but agrees to go along when put on the spot for old favors owed. "I hope they spell my name right in the papers," he memorably sighs while downing multiple shots of whiskey.

Jaeckel was originally going to play the outlaw Black Harris with L.Q. Jones playing McKinney, but they ended up switching roles. It was Jaeckel who got saddled with McKinney's ill-chosen red wig. Outside of the occasions when he shaved his head, it marks one of the few instances where Jaeckel severely altered his appearance, somewhat unique for a character actor who would seem to be accustomed to the application of fake beards, putty noses, and differing hairstyles or color dyes. But then Jaeckel was a little different. He wasn't classically trained and he didn't recite Shakespeare in his spare time. He was, however, a smart man well-versed in camera technique with an uncanny ability to tap into varying facets of his own personality for the screen.

Jaeckel as Sheriff Kip McKinney in the MGM western *Pat Garrett and Billy the Kid* (1973). The dark wig was director Sam Peckinpah's decision.

The *Pat Garrett and Billy the Kid* shoot was notorious for studio meddling and Peckinpah's own runaway personal vices. Peckinpah's sometimes lyrical film was sabotaged at every opportunity by MGM head James Aubrey, whose interference exacerbated Peckinpah's already prodigious intake of alcohol and drugs. Many in the cast and crew became sick from Montezuma's Revenge or the dust that was stirred up by the production. It became a monumental task for the temperamental Peckinpah to realize his original vision given all the elements at play. At one point star James Coburn and Peckinpah were so drunk and sick that they didn't remember filming Jaeckel's big scene in the saloon where Coburn calls upon him. Jaeckel remembered it, as Peckinpah had fired off a gun beneath his chair during the scene to get a desired reaction. Peckinpah could be a brilliant but unconventional director, eliciting poetry from violence as only a mad genius could. In one memorable sequence he goaded the physically forceful character actor R.G. Armstrong into nearly tearing Kristofferson apart with his bare hands. Despite all the craziness, Peckinpah was very much an actor's director and his casts stood with him through thick and thin, even if they occasionally wanted to come to blows with him.

The critics were prepared to pounce on Peckinpah and his *Wild Bunch* reputation for filming screen violence in agonizing slow motion. When Aubrey and MGM took away Peckinpah's edit and rushed a truncated version into release, the critics trashed the film. Over the years various re-edits have been introduced, some attempting to put Peckinpah's original film back together. The result is a near masterpiece that has won a deserved cult following amongst Peckinpah devotees. Interestingly, there's not a whole lot to Jaeckel's extended cameo in any of the versions. This was the only time he was afforded the opportunity to work with the challenging, antagonistic former U.S. Marine Peckinpah.

In 1973 few critics mentioned Jaeckel at all, with *Variety* writing, "The editing, faulted by the director, conceals the post-production tinkering, but also reduces such players as Jason Robards, Richard Jaeckel, and Katy Jurado to walk-on status." *The Hollywood Reporter* called the performances of Jaeckel and the rest of the cast "uniformly excellent," as well as "vividly written and performed." *The Pittsburg Press*, however, noted, "Richard Jaeckel, Jason Robards, Jr., and Katy Jurado are squandered in bit parts which don't help bring the film to life," while *The Toledo Blade* opined, "Such stalwart character actors as Chill Wills, Jack Elam, and Richard Jaeckel are helpless against a weak and confusing script." *The San Francisco Chronicle* weighed in with, "Richard Jaeckel, Jason Robards, and Chill Wills are old pros in modest roles." Pauline Kael of *The New Yorker* called it "an amazing cast." Revisionists rightly realize that the presence of Jaeckel, L.Q. Jones, R.G. Armstrong, Jack Elam, Slim Pickens, John Davis Chandler, Dub Taylor, and Elisha Cook, Jr., among others seen in fleeting cameos or small character parts, bring a weightiness to the project that can't be measured in terms of screen time.

Jaeckel commented to the *Alton Telegraph* regarding the critical attacks on Peckinpah and his screen violence: "It's all a bunch of crap. Violence is nowhere near as bad as what they put in films these days. Violence is an essential part of action films. You have to have violence to carry the theme. If these wishy-washies who don't like violence don't like the movies, then let them stay home. All this nudity and sex crap serves no purpose. Nudity is not really important to any movie theme. The producers just use it to make money." Jaeckel further discussed the film with the *Fort Lauderdale News*: "It's not solely, completely violent. For instance, I worked the last third of the filming, about six weeks, and only two shots were fired.... When you're depicting a violent story you can't gloss over the violence itself."

When evaluating Peckinpah as a director, Jaeckel told the *Montreal Gazette*: "Every actor should have a chance to work with a director like him. In regard to actors, he's the best I've ever worked with. He had everyone's confidence. He knew what he wanted and he got it." Out of the fantastic group of character actors assembled for the film, none had worked with Peckinpah more than Jaeckel's contemporary L.Q. Jones. Peckinpah liked having Jones on his films because the latter didn't take guff and kept Peckinpah focused on the task at hand. His relationship with Peckinpah was sometimes strained, but he understood the complicated man at the helm better than most.

Jones commented on the making of *Pat Garrett and Billy the Kid* and Jaeckel:

> Richard did the part I was going to do, Sheriff McKinney, and I did Black Harris. Richard wasn't even going to be in the movie at one time. Sam wanted me to do Black, so we switched around. I wasn't particularly happy about it, except it's always fun to work. Richard did such a good job you can't get too pissed off. He did a different thing than I would have done and did it well. He did his job and never looked back. Richard was a nice person. He was warm to work with, very talented, very committed to doing what he did. It was always a pleasure to work with him.
>
> [Jaeckel's red wig] was Sam [Peckinpah's idea]. You never knew what he was going to do. He gets a hair, and when he does, God help you. You better learn to do what he wants you to do because he's a pain in the butt if you don't do the best you can do. But he used good people. People don't realize he was a better writer than he was a director. The thing that made his period pieces work so good was he was an absolute perfectionist about detail. Absolute. Richard sees that when he got out here. When Sam decides something, God help you. Sometimes he's right and sometimes he's wrong—like Richard's wig.... Richard carried his load, did what he had to do. Again you must take your hat off to what he was doing. It was sort of a thankless task in *Pat Garrett*. Everything was sort of a thankless task. Not a good picture, but there are brilliant moments in it.[6]

Actor Joseph Culliton had small parts in both *Pat Garrett* and the John Wayne film *Cahill—U.S. Marshal* (1973) which was filming on location in Durango at the same time. He recalls:

> I crossed paths with Richard Jaeckel on the set of *Pat Garrett and Billy the Kid* when I was 23 years old. We hung out together for three or four days. My brother Patrick had attended Loyola High School with one of Richard's sons. I told Mr. Jaeckel about that when we were introduced. That seemed to inspire a kind of fatherly–big brother attitude towards me on Richard's part. He'd join up with me first thing in the morning, and we'd stay together all day. We ate lunch together every day. And I remember one day, we both had eaten what we thought was very tender beef. After we'd finished we were informed that we'd eaten mule. We both got queasy but kept our food down. I remember those beautiful baby blue eyes of Richard's registering horror at the news that he'd dined on mule.
>
> But really what stays in my mind about Richard Jaeckel was what an old-fashioned man he was. The set of *Pat Garrett* was teeming with members of the counter-culture. Richard got along with everyone, but was a man apart. He was conservative in his manner, a real straight arrow. He reminded me of a cool and youthful Boy Scout leader, the kind who exemplified virtue and stood behind each and every kid in his troop. I was a naïve and idealistic young man, and I think that made us kindred spirits. Sam Peckinpah was late arriving on the set each day, and there was a lot of waiting around. But I never heard a word of complaint from Richard. Richard was a consummate professional and a superb actor. His attitude toward Sam was deeply and sincerely deferential. Richard honored Sam as a great filmmaker. And he also respected him as his director and as the man responsible for hiring him. I never saw any vestige of egotism in Richard Jaeckel. He had a charming way of speaking confidentially. He'd kind of sidle up facing forward and tilt his head in my direction. He'd then speak to me quietly and out of the corner of his mouth. It might have been a trait developed in his many years of being the kid on movie sets.[7]

Jaeckel did speak up one night in the local cantina, defending his hippie-like crew from teasing coming from the more old-fashioned John Wayne-Andrew McLaglen *Cahill* bunch. Jaeckel respected the hard work that men like long-haired musicians Kris Kristofferson, Bob Dylan, John Beck, and *Devil's Brigade* co-star Luke Askew were putting into the Peckinpah film and stood up for the counter-culture. Jaeckel's reputation was so strong that the Wayne group respected his opinion. It was a rare outburst coming from Jaeckel but one that he felt was justified on his part. Jaeckel explained to the *Boston Globe*: "The guys in the John Wayne movie ... used to get on us in the bar at night for being freaks. One night I lost my stack and told them they should act grown up, that we were all trying to get a job done.... I respect professionals. I like people who come prepared to do the job, get it done as quietly as possible, and act like adults."

The musicians and long hairs did provide some whimsy on the set. Jaeckel thought that

Rhodes Scholar–Air Force helicopter pilot Kristofferson was "an interesting guy." As for legendary lyricist Dylan, Jaeckel told the *Boston Globe*: "I found him polite, interested, a little distant. He seemed fascinated by the process of filmmaking. He sat and watched when he wasn't working, and at the end he said he'd like to form his own production company. I will admit he's a little strange. Sometimes you'd have to yell at him, 'Bob! Hey, Bob!' He'd drifted off somewhere. One time we waited all day to get a particular lighting effect. And just as we start the only take—the light wouldn't last long enough for two—two guys flash by in sweatshirts, jogging. It's Dylan and he didn't know what was up." Unconventional character actor Harry Dean Stanton was the other jogger, causing yet another memorable Peckinpah blow-up and a nearly $25,000 delay.

In promoting *Pat Garrett and Billy the Kid* for MGM, Jaeckel was interviewed for Boston TV station Channel 7 by reporter Garry Armstrong, a film buff with a great appreciation for Jaeckel's career. As was typical of Jaeckel's interaction with people, when the interview ended the two men carried on their conversation over drinks. Armstrong recalls:

> I spent a terrific afternoon with him in Boston while he was plugging *Pat Garrett and Billy the Kid*. Since I'm also a movie maven, I remember Jaeckel from his earliest roles. We had a great time with Jaeckel telling me lots of stories over cocktails after we had wrapped the TV interview. He was very proud of his son Barry.
>
> I don't remember the exact day but I do remember it was warm because we shot in shirt sleeves in the lobby of the TV station. I couldn't get a studio and was pressed to get the shoot done because "the suits" were not very impressed with Richard Jaeckel. James Coburn was the hot interview on the circuit as *Pat Garrett and Billy the Kid* was being pushed by publicists. Richard Jaeckel was very pleasant even before we rolled the camera. He asked what I did and I did a quick bio thing dating back to my radio days and shooting my own film at a previous TV station. He grinned and said it was good to be working with "a grunt." The rapport was established.
>
> I mentioned doing an interview with Gregory Peck about ten years earlier and how well we got along. Jaeckel segued right into working with Peck on one of his earliest films, *The Gunfighter*. As Jaeckel spoke I nodded for my cameraman to begin shooting. He smiled. He had been shooting since Jaeckel and I began swapping war stories. The interview flowed smoothly. It was more a conversation between friends than an interview promoting a film. We had gone more than ten minutes before I mentioned *Pat Garrett* and Jaeckel again smiled, saying that he forgot he was supposed to be promoting the film. He talked about working with the quirky Sam Peckinpah and scene stealers like Chill Wills. I asked about Bob Dylan. Jaeckel's smile grew bigger as he talked about the folk singer's kid-like behavior working with "movie stars." We wrapped the interview after about twenty minutes.
>
> I asked Jaeckel what was next on his schedule and he said he was free for the afternoon. I suggested a pub near the TV station might be fine for lunch. He quickly agreed. Drinks and meals ordered, Jaeckel began a long three-hour conversation touching on family, moviemaking, and the business of promoting movies. We found a common thread in our frustration with management—"the suits." I mentioned how I was always "the kid" at every stop in my career. He nodded and jumped in with stories about working with Richard Widmark, John Wayne, Karl Malden, and Richard Boone in some of his very early movies. He said they all treated him well but he was always called "the kid." Jaeckel broke into guffaws when I asked about working with character actors like Jack Elam, Lee Van Cleef, and Jack Lambert—all well-established screen villains. He said they were the easiest and nicest people to work "jobs" with in the business.
>
> Jaeckel slid into a brief note about his son Barry who was a rising [golf] player. I quoted some stats which prompted a very pleased smile and a final round of drinks. We finished off the afternoon with Richard Jaeckel picking up the tab, saying he *really* enjoyed the day and would check me out on the tube before leaving Boston. The next evening, just after our 6 p.m. news, I received a call. It was Richard Jaeckel who had caught me doing a news piece. "Good job, kid," he said. "Thanks, kid," I replied. We both laughed and wished each other well.[8]

The TV movie *Partners in Crime* aired in March 1973. It was actually a Universal pilot for an intended Lee Grant series. Jaeckel guest stars as Frank Jordan, an amnesiac ex-con who can't remember where the loot from a bank heist is hidden. Jaeckel does his usual rock solid job, although the television film was quickly forgotten by both the networks and the public. It has long been out of circulation and is now a rarity. *Variety* reviewed the Jack Smight–directed telefilm, writing, "Richard Jaeckel, Harry Guardino, Charles Drake, and Lorraine Gary were good."

His next film has had a more lasting impact, although Jaeckel's overall contribution to its reputation is merely as one member of a solid and interesting cast. John Flynn's *The Outfit* (1973) is an adaptation of a tough Donald Westlake story, top-lining Robert Duvall and Joe Don Baker as resourceful criminals attempting to collect money owed to them by syndicate boss Robert Ryan. Jaeckel shines in a small part as Chemey, an illicit auto dealer who can put a Porsche engine into a Volkswagen for a fast and stealthy getaway. Bill McKinney is Jaeckel's hot-headed brother and Sheree North his not-to-be-trusted sister-in-law, all living together in an isolated country home guarded by an attack dog. They are an interesting trio of characters as flirtatious floozy North plays the brothers against one another while entertaining their clientele. The scene turns memorably tense when North falsely says Baker attempted to rape her. Tough guy film favorites Timothy Carey, Tom Reese, and Roy Jenson also appear. Jaeckel's friend Ronnie Rondell ran the stunts.

Jaeckel's role was once again small enough and in such a large cast that his quiet cool barely received mention from the critics in the fall of 1973. Syndicated columnist James Bacon did note that Jaeckel was one of the cast members offering "standout bits," while *The Los Angeles Herald Examiner* mentioned Jaeckel "among the standout players with minimal screen time." *The New York Times* wrote, "Richard Jaeckel, Marie Windsor, Anita O'Day, Jane Greer, and Elisha Cook, among others, turn up in roles so small you might miss them without a scorecard." Roger Ebert of the *Chicago Sun Times* praised the supporting characters as "complex and real," and *The Hollywood Reporter* mentioned Jaeckel among "the assortment of fine actors who give it life and texture." *The Village Voice* commented on the personality cameos, saying, "Dropping Jaeckel so suddenly in the film after his stylish build-up of a smooth country boy may be the worst tactical error since J. Lee Thompson slaughtered Edward G. Robinson and Eli Wallach in *Mackenna's Gold*." Jaeckel, however, was proud to be part of such a strong cast.

As they had done earlier that year with *Pat Garrett and Billy the Kid*, MGM sent the always ready and reliable Jaeckel on the publicity trail with Joe Don Baker to promote the film. In two weeks they covered Denver,

Jaeckel as tough guy Chemey in MGM's *The Outfit* (1973).

St. Louis, Memphis, New Orleans, Miami, Toronto, Montreal, Boston, Washington, and New York. Jaeckel was paired with Baker to help the young actor along with the media and provide him a bedrock resource for anything out of the ordinary that might arise. Jaeckel enjoyed the trip but kept his priorities straight, telling the *Boston Globe*, "I can't do too much of this publicity traveling. I eat too much and drink too much and get out of shape."

While in Detroit, Jaeckel and Baker encountered *Windsor Star* writer Ray Bennett, who while doing an article on the rising Baker wrote, "Jaeckel, with thirty years in the business and no illusions, is a perfect mixture of charm and earthy conversation." Thirty-five years later Bennett was still writing fondly about meeting the "easygoing" Jaeckel and recalling how he and Baker kept soliciting old Hollywood set stories from Jaeckel during the younger actor's interview.

Both *Pat Garrett* and *The Outfit* have grown in cinematic stature over the years, but at the time neither was a hit nor did they provide Jaeckel with a showcase assignment. They were extended cameos that saw Jaeckel fitting expertly into large ensembles. Aldrich's *Ulzana's Raid* was too unsettling for most audiences of the day to digest. American audiences didn't even see him in *The Red Pony*, and the interesting noir TV series *Banyon* died a quick death. The stark reality was that none of Jaeckel's post–Oscar nomination decisions had panned out for him financially or in terms of career momentum. Jaeckel was again ready and willing to take what came his way.

It was back to Asia for a starring role as a hardboiled mercenary in Rolf Bayer's low-budget martial arts film *The Kill* (1973), shot in Hong Kong, the island of Cheung Chau, and Macao. Despite first billing, for Jaeckel the part was more a character lead than a traditional hero. Jaeckel's Ming is a tough, cynical womanizer looking out for number one. A former law enforcement officer, he has racked up significant gambling debts. Then his expertise comes in handy when a casino is robbed. The gambling boss offers to erase Jaeckel's markers and let him share in the recovery of the stolen money. Jaeckel finds the man responsible easily enough, Henry Duval, but then partners up with the criminal when he learns Duval has a big heroin heist on the horizon. The alliance is uneasy as Jaeckel is aware that Duval's last partner ended up dead. Jaeckel uses this knowledge to get Duval's girlfriend Judy Washington in his corner. The whole time, Jaeckel is keeping his former drug enforcement agent pal Bill Jervis aware of the situation.

The selling point of this colorful and decently plotted action picture is the nearly three-minute climactic fight scene between Jaeckel and a knife-wielding Duval on Cheung Chau's rocky shore. This is set up well by two earlier, abbreviated skirmishes between the men that saw Jaeckel taking his share of lumps from the martial arts expert. Jaeckel is wise to present his character as an underdog in the fights. Things look bad when his arm is sliced by Duval. However, Jaeckel rallies, using his strength to choke Duval out beneath the water. Given the constraints of the budget, Jaeckel carries the chop-socky film the best he can with his world-weary presence and engages in numerous karate battles. With the rising cinematic interest in martial arts, *The Kill* gave him an opportunity to display some of the self-defense techniques he had picked up during his earlier stays in Japan. He impressively does all of his own fighting and stunt work, including one extended backward fall on the beach.

The Kill (aka *The Heroin Syndicate* and *The Heroin Conspiracy*) was barely released but did eventually find shelf life as a VHS rental. The website *Mod Cinema* offers up a review: "It is nice to see Richard Jaeckel in a full-fledged leading role, even in a shabby internationally produced thriller like *The Kill*." Such pictures gave Jaeckel the chance to travel on someone else's dime and explore different cultures while filling in the sometimes long gaps between Hollywood films. There was a good chance that a movie like *The Kill* would only play in drive-ins or overseas. Films of this ilk might not have been the best career move but they were hard to turn down if the locale was interesting. It beat sitting at home waiting for a better offer that might not materialize. "He was always going on location to these weird places," friend Tim Lyon recalls.[9]

On the TV front, Jaeckel guest starred on episodes of the crime dramas *Shaft* and *The F.B.I.* Richard Roundtree went from the popular *Shaft* theatrical films to weekly television playing private detective John Shaft, but the series didn't catch on and disappeared after half a season. Jaeckel played vigilante cop Lew Turner in the October 1973 episode "The Enforcers," doing the bidding of lead heavy Robert Culp and retired judge Dean Jagger. As usually happened in these shows, Jaeckel died yet another violent death in the climax as he's thrown into a garbage disposal. He was the character Devlin in the "Selkirk's War" episode of *The F.B.I.* that aired in January of 1974, one of the final segments of the long-running series. The routine plot concerns a former Army major (Peter Haskell) breaking two military criminals (Jaeckel and Roger Robinson) out of the stockade for illicit duties. The return to episodic TV served to keep money in the bank and Jaeckel in the public eye, although it was an admission that his post–Oscar buzz was dying down.

Jaeckel returned to the Boston area for a celebrity softball game in connection with the George Peppard TV series *Banacek*. Jaeckel was presumably in line to film a guest shot on the show had his friend Peppard not opted to suddenly quit the highly regarded series in midstream. While in Boston, Jaeckel met up with his reporter friend Garry Armstrong, who recalls:

> We used to have a charity softball game on Boston Commons. It was the media all-stars versus George Peppard, the *Banacek* crew, and Playboy bunnies. Kegs of beer were set up for both benches. The drinking began before the game and never stopped. Before the first game, "the flacks" were introducing Peppard to media folks. At one point Jaeckel, who was a guest star on the *Banacek* series, pulled Peppard over and introduced me as his buddy, a "grunt" who knew his stuff. This was the holdover from our first meeting. Anyway, Peppard grinned broadly, shook hands and led us behind the bench where he had a carton of his private stock, "the good stuff." I don't remember much about that game. I do remember we did justice to that carton of the good stuff. The next day Peppard, who was notoriously difficult with the media, turned up for an interview I didn't even remember being scheduled. Richard Jaeckel was his driver.[10]

In the meantime, there was an interesting development. The controversial TV pilot *Firehouse* that Jaeckel had filmed in 1972 was picked up by ABC as a mid-season replacement series. That TV pilot's co-stars Vince Edwards and Richard Roundtree were not available at this late juncture, and the theme of racism would not be explored on a weekly basis. Edwards was replaced in the series lead by veteran actor James Drury, star of the long-running western *The Virginian*. The only actor from the pilot to actually be retained for the series was Jaeckel as veteran firefighter Hank Myers. It was a case of perfect casting and Jaeckel was happy to sign on, hoping that he might finally have a TV hit that would give him a sustainable income. Both he and Drury were initially hopeful the series could run five years or more.

The physically demanding show examined the everyday life of a fire department (Engine Company 23) more directly than the popular *Emergency*, which tended to focus on the paramedics at the station and the Rampart Hospital. However, the format for *Firehouse* was based on a scant thirty minutes rather than the network-nixed sixty. That was too short a time to

Bill Overton, James Drury, Brad David, Richard Jaeckel, and Michael Delano in the ABC-TV series *Firehouse* (1974). The failure of this series proved a turning point in Jaeckel's career.

do anything other than cram two fire calls into each plot in hopes of keeping the audience's attention riveted to the screen. The series was also relocated to Los Angeles, which further hindered its original gritty New York authenticity and made it nearly indistinguishable from *Emergency*. Finally, there were no significant guest stars hired to lure audiences in. The main actors involved soon realized there would be few close-ups and little shot at any character development during the show's abbreviated run. They'd mostly be running up stairs, chopping through doors, dragging heavy water hoses, and fighting fires. Jaeckel could see the writing on the wall and realized he was involved with another failed series. He took it for what it was worth though, a job he had been hired for that gave him six months of steady employment opposite an actor (Drury) he could call a friend. Upon the completion of some scenes, the two would bow to one another out of a mutual appreciation.

Critic William Sarmento of *The Lowell Sun* wrote, "It was so good to see James Drury in a series along with that fine actor Richard Jaeckel that I am almost tempted to say nice things about *Firehouse*, another new half-hour series. But I cannot." Cleveland Armory wrote in *TV Guide*, "The captain, Ryerson, is played by James Drury with his usual Gregory Peckiness. Under him is a second-in-command, Hank Myers, whose part has a little more scope but is still far from enough for an actor as good as Richard Jaeckel." The critical consensus seemed to match that of the public, and *Firehouse* was gone after only thirteen episodes. Having two cancelled TV series in two years had to have been a great disappointment to Jaeckel. It no doubt stirred up the character actor's sense of fear as to where the next job was coming from. The window of opportunity to pick and choose scripts in the wake of *Sometimes a Great Notion* had slid shut.

Although upset with the demise of the series, especially producer Charles Fries and the network's handling of the show, Drury enjoyed working with Jaeckel:

> I had always been a great admirer of him. And I enjoyed every minute I worked with him. He was a stalwart on that show. Unfortunately, it was not a very good show. We did not have very good scripts, and we had a lot of problems. It was a long walk on a short pier, but Jake was a stalwart throughout the whole thing. He was a man who was able to do anything. He had a great physical ability and was as handy as a pocket on a shirt. There was nothing anyone ever asked him to do that he couldn't do. I was very honored to work with him, and I wish I'd had a chance to work with him more.
>
> It is ingrained in my character to always be at war with the front office. I'm always fighting the producer and Jake would laugh at me. He'd say, "You're going to go up there and make all that noise and it's not going to change a goddamn thing." And he was right about it not changing anything. Not on that show. When I was doing *The Virginian* I was able to get things done, but you couldn't talk to Charles Fries. You might as well be talking to the wall. He didn't react to anything we wanted to do to improve the show. No reaction at all. I think they still show *Firehouse* in Europe or somewhere because every once in a while I get a little residual check for like $3.37 or something. It's such a bad show, it's hard to get anybody to watch it or anybody to pick it up. If you have a career in motion pictures, you're lucky if you get three or four things that are really good. *The Virginian* was a grand experience, and *Firehouse* was not a grand experience.
>
> But I wouldn't have missed working with Jaeckel for anything. He was a breath of fresh air. I just loved the guy. We had a friendship that lasted throughout our lives. I never saw much of him afterwards because I moved to Texas and he stayed in California. I sure did admire and appreciate him. He had a brand new little Volkswagen Bug he drove around. He bought that with his money from the show and he was thrilled with that car. It was funny to see him in that little car because even though he was short in stature he was bigger than life. Jaeckel filled the screen and filled your heart and mind when you saw him and here he was in this Volkswagen! He loved driving around in that little car, and he looked good in it.[11]

Actor-singer Michael Delano was cast in *Firehouse* as a younger, more handsome version of Val Avery's character Sonny Caputo. Delano says:

> I remember Jake well. A wonderful guy. I have fond memories of the Jake. He was a wonderful man. He was the consummate pro when it came to work, and he would always be ready to perform at any time. He was a practical joker. He'd do things when it was your close-up and he was off-camera. He'd do things to try to break you up. He used to get me all the time. He'd make me blow the scene and we'd have to shoot it again. Fortunately, the directors were all cool with it. They let him do what he wanted.
>
> That's the only thing we ever did together. I think I saw him once or twice after the series was done. I'm kind of lucky enough to be following in the same suit. Even into his older years he was still a pretty solid guy and in good health. I remember there'd be a couple of times we'd be doing something physical and he was a very solid man for his age. He kept himself in great shape. He was a prince of a man. Everybody would like to be like Jaeckel. As a professional actor and as a man. He was really something. He was someone to emulate. He was a wonderful guy and I miss him.[12]

Gone was the star treatment for headlining a network TV show. Gone was the small apartment that had been set up especially for Jaeckel at the studio. Gone was the weekly paycheck. Taking stock of his professional condition, Jaeckel commented to the *Charleston Gazette* about the track of his career. He could be an Oscar nominee one year, then a failed TV actor the next. That was the nature of the business. Jaeckel said, "I'm not going to hurt anyone out there. I'm not a great actor, but I'm a professional one. This business is a succession of cycles, and I depend on it for a living, since I don't have a line of laundromats on the side. I like it for its lack of monotony."

The *Firehouse* commitment kept Jaeckel from accepting the lead villain role in the pilot film for James Garner's highly successful TV series *The Rockford Files* (1974). Jaeckel's body-building pal William Smith ended up playing the show's muscular psychotic killer, a characterization that Garner told Johnny Carson on *The Tonight Show* helped sell the series. While that would have been a nice part for Jaeckel, there was a bigger film he lost out on during this period. Budgetary limitations prevented Robert Aldrich from casting Jaeckel and Ernest Borgnine in the box office hit *The Longest Yard* (1974) opposite Burt Reynolds. If Aldrich had his way, Jaeckel would have played the sadistic prison guard-football player that Ed Lauter eventually essayed.

Jaeckel's only 1974 theatrical release was *Chosen Survivors* (1974) for director Sutton Roley, made at Mexico City's Churubusco Studios in the early part of the previous year. It's a terrifying tale of nuclear disaster and a group of pre-determined citizens shuttled into an underground silo without their foreknowledge to sustain the race. Jaeckel is cast as Major Gordon Ellis, a military electronics expert sent underground to operate the hi-tech equipment. He is the only one in a cast that includes Alex Cord, Jackie Cooper, and Bradford Dillman given a moment to pine over lost loved ones. The nightmarish scenario sustains a fair amount of tension during the first half but devolves into a more conventional horror film as the group fights off vampire bats. Poor special effects severely hamper the film, although in Jaeckel's case it's a step up from his Japanese sci-fi when he fought men in obvious animal suits.

Co-star Bradford Dillman recalled the many problems encountered with the bats during the film's climax. In reality, the bats would not fly in the light and either remained on the floor or sought darkness by going up the pants legs of the actors. A number of remedies were unsuccessfully attempted. The final solution involved the actors pantomiming the attack in front of a processed image of the bats flying around the room in infrared light. Dillman found it ridiculous, claiming that only Jaeckel came across well in the battle as he threw fists into the air to ward off the imaginary bats. Dillman was highly complementary of Jaeckel in his autobiography, calling his colleague "a master" among character actors. He also revealed that a slightly mischievous Jaeckel snuck a little in-joke onto the screen for his fellow actors in the final scene.

Dillman expanded his thoughts on Jaeckel in a letter to the author, saying: "Dick Jaeckel was a beloved friend and terribly underrated actor. He had a marvelous sense of humor, as exhibited during the mass bat attack in *Chosen Survivors* when he got away with pantomiming masturbation. His children believed him to be a stern man and overly disciplinary. I, on the other hand, will have an abiding memory of the laughter we shared during ludicrous events like the bat attack. God bless him!"[13]

The New York Times called Jaeckel's performance "properly taut, if not memorable." *The Village Voice* wrote, "The two real talents in the film—Richard Jaeckel and the marvelous Diana Muldaur—are totally wasted." *Variety* said, "Performances, with possible exception of Jaeckel's, are stilted and often exceedingly mannered," while the *Los Angeles Times* wrote, "Such pros as Jackie Cooper, Richard Jaeckel, Bradford Dillman, and Diana Muldaur come on strong." *The Hollywood Reporter* added that Jaeckel and his veteran co-stars were "capable performers" under the tense direction of Roley.

Born Innocent (1974), a controversial, highly rated TV movie starring Linda Blair as an abused teenager, was shot in Albuquerque, New Mexico, by director Donald Wrye with Jaeckel playing the bad-dad character Mr. Parker. He doesn't appear until the forty-five–minute mark as Blair's controlling, violence-prone father, whose moods swing in a great arc. He seems decent enough at first, but that impression quickly changes. He drinks coffee from a cup with a smiley face on it but his disposition is anything but pleasant. Although he can tune his car to a tee, his home life is hopeless. Wife Kim Hunter turns a blind eye to Jaeckel's abusive nature, siding with him rather than her daughter. When Blair can't connect with this unfeeling parenting, she is placed in a juvenile detention center where she is assaulted with a broom handle by a bunch of girls. Jaeckel is in fine form, though the part no doubt put him back into the villainous ranks in the eyes of most casting directors.

Walt Disney aired the two-part TV movie *Adventure in Satan's Canyon* (1974) in November 1974. Jaeckel plays forest ranger Jack Ryan, who is injured in the wilderness and must rely on his kayak student David Alan Bailey's skill to save him. It's a wholesome show directed by William Beaudine, Jr., featuring Jaeckel's folksy narration and beautiful location filming in the Cascade Mountains of Oregon and Washington. Jaeckel gets to kayak on screen but is injured when he gets thumped in the back by a log in the water (perhaps a knowing nod to getting pinned in *Sometimes a Great Notion*). Jaeckel plays a solid good guy father figure, but the part didn't carry quite the emotional impact with audiences that his bad parent in *Born Innocent* did. Jaeckel's Hollywood High alum Larry Pennell appears in a supporting role as a plane pilot.

The 1974–1975 TV season saw Jaeckel appear on a number of episodic shows. The cult trucker series *Movin' On* gave Jaeckel the chance to play another flawed father figure. Jaeckel's driver Red Wallace is the loving single parent of teenager MacKenzie Phillips, but he's a poor role model for the girl. He is addicted to rolling dice in backroom gambling dens and is in hock to a loan shark who wants him to take part in illegal activity. Old pal Claude Akins can't get a straight answer out of either Jaeckel or his girl. His presence does help Jaeckel swear off gambling by the story's conclusion, but only after his daughter's lucky gambling streak pays off the debt. The hackneyed episode "Roadblock" aired in September 1974, chiefly benefitting from fine location work and the repartee between Akins and fellow lead Frank Converse.

The 1970s were rife with cop shows, and Jaeckel's stalwart, no-nonsense presence was a natural fit for a uniform or plainclothes tailored suit. Jaeckel portrayed Sgt. Wilson on the October 1974 "Fathers and Sons" episode of the superior show *Police Story*. (Creator Joseph Wambaugh's series featured rotating high-profile guest stars from week to week.) The plot sees Jaeckel utilize ethnic patrolman Tony Musante to find Serbian killer Ramon Bieri in the Los Angeles shipyards even as Musante's own immigrant dad Harold Gould emerges as a potential target. It's another good guy part on a high-quality TV show with Jaeckel appearing appropriately sympathetic and stern. It's surprising that Jaeckel wasn't called on to make multiple appearances as the character throughout the run of the show. The episode was directed by Gary Nelson.

Jaeckel could still be more than antagonistic on screen. On *Lucas Tanner* he was cast as tough high school coach Ed Scoley, butting heads with star David Hartman over a program that would allow uncoordinated students into a special gym class. If acting is all about sensory memory, Jaeckel had plenty of real coaching experience to draw from for his character. Veteran Leo Penn directed the episode "Winners and Losers" that aired in October of 1974. The December 1974 *Petrocelli* episode "Counterploy" saw Jaeckel cast as Sgt. Stanford, a close-minded policeman heading the investigation of a young cop accused of murder and clashing with Barry Newman's title lawyer in the process. The series was shot on location in Tucson, Arizona.

Truck drivers, cops, and coaches … none of them were much of a stretch for Jaeckel. It was only natural to find him playing a cowboy as well. His best appearance of the TV season came on the January 1975 *Gunsmoke* episode "Larkin" in which Jaeckel is cast as the title gunfighter Clay Larkin. It's one of Jaeckel's coolest characters, a dangerous man (thirty notches on his belt) that he humanizes throughout the course of the episode by talking wistfully of his lost loves. Captured by deputy Newley (Buck Taylor), the smooth-talking criminal is being brought to Dodge City but has a trio of scurrilous bounty hunters led by Anthony Caruso on his tail. Throughout their trek the cunning Jaeckel implores a wounded Taylor to free him to fight off the bad men. Taylor is resistant but ultimately has no choice as they hole up in Kathleen Cody's farmhouse. Jaeckel's Clay Larkin is quick and deadly. Even pushing 50, Jaeckel moves like a young man in the action scenes. The script by esteemed Western screenwriter Jim Byrnes was tailor-made for Jaeckel's strengths. Although the classic series was in its final season, it was still delivering quality entertainment and premium roles for its guest stars. *Gunsmoke* veteran Gunnar Hellstrom directed.

Byrnes also wrote *The Last Day* (1975), a deadly serious, well-received TV movie starring Robert Conrad as outlaw Bob Dalton and featuring a whiskered Jaeckel as his equally dangerous brother Grat. Richard Widmark co-stars as a former lawman reluctantly protecting his somewhat undeserving town in the Vincent McEveety–directed film about the western outlaws robbing two banks simultaneously in Coffeyville, Kansas. There are definite shades of *High Noon*, but with significant character development afforded the heavies. In the action-filled climax, Richard Widmark shoots Jaeckel down dead from his charging horse. Stuntman Louie Elias performed the saddle fall for Jaeckel. Others in the top-notch cast include Christopher Connelly, Tom Skerritt, Tim Matheson, Gene Evans, Morgan Woodward, Loretta Swit, Barbara Rush, Kathleen Cody, Logan Ramsey, Rex Holman, and Warren Vanders. Henry Morgan provides superb narration.

The Last Day is probably the best film veteran Paramount producer A.C. Lyles ever did. Grat Dalton is one of Jaeckel's toughest characters, given a memorably tense introduction at a card table when he catches Jon Locke cheating. Jaeckel is perfectly in line acting alongside fellow TV tough guy Robert Conrad as his sibling. Conrad liked to play up his two-fisted image for the public, but Jaeckel could match him pound for pound when it came to projecting an aura of danger on the screen without posturing. *The Los Angeles Times* wrote that Jaeckel's performance was "crisp and concise." Coupled with his recent *Gunsmoke* performance, this should have put Jaeckel up for more leading roles on television.

"He was a gentle, beautiful actor," director Vincent McEveety recalls. "A very good actor. He always deferred to somebody else on the set rather than himself. As a director, he was an actor who was very considerate and made my job a lot easier. He had a special quality when he walked around. He had a sense of humor. He had everything. He had everything that a young man should have. He was actually older than he looked, but he struck us all as being the most special man on the set. I share that because I can't say that about any other actor that I worked with. That's what he gave to me, and I tried to give to other people. But nobody gave it like Richard. He was very special."[14]

Veteran character player Morgan Woodward, who guest starred on *Gunsmoke* more than any other actor in history and made quite an impression as the eerily silent boss in *Cool Hand Luke*, portrays a steely lawman trying to intercept the Daltons before they hit Coffeyville. It was the first of two times he worked with Jaeckel. He says, "I wasn't social with Richard. I only knew him from the times that we worked together. I can say that he was very professional and highly believable in everything he did. He was a good actor.... It was a pleasure working with him."[15]

The Drowning Pool (1975) is a high-profile big screen misfire that still has a number of memorable moments of mood and execution. Jaeckel appears as the shady cop character Lt. Franks for director Stuart Rosenberg in this sequel to Paul Newman's detective thriller *Harper* (1966). Both films are based on Ross MacDonald's popular Archer character. Jaeckel aggressively harasses Newman from the moment he hits Louisiana, kept in check by the seemingly more level-headed superior officer Tony Franciosa. It turns out Jaeckel is not above taking cash as a trigger man for oil baron Murray Hamilton, leading to an especially tense scene where Newman turns the tables on Jaeckel. Newman puts two bullets in a gun and fires one shot near him for effect. He then sticks the barrel into Jaeckel's face and threatens to pull the trigger unless Jaeckel gives him information he wants. With each hesitation on Jaeckel's part, Newman clicks on an empty chamber. Jaeckel handles the scene of Russian roulette with realistic sweat-and-blood grimaces, throwing out the memorable line, "Sweet screaming Jesus!" as Newman pulls the trigger.

Jaeckel survives that encounter but isn't so fortunate later on. He is shot in the arm during a roadside shootout and is later besieged by Hamilton's pit bulls. In addition to the star power of Newman, the film boasts a solid cast including Joanne Woodward, Gail Strickland, Melanie Griffith, Linda Haynes, Paul Koslo, and Andrew Robinson. Reviews were mixed, and with scant promotional backing Jaeckel received surprisingly little mention. *Variety* tagged it "stylish, improbable, entertaining, superficial, well-cast, and totally synthetic." *The Los Angeles Times* noted, "Jaeckel is splendidly vicious," while *The Dallas Morning News* wrote, "Tony Franciosa, Coral Browne, and Richard Jaeckel are wasted under Stuart Rosenberg's shaky direction." The *Pittsburgh Post-Gazette* found the film "entertaining on its superficial level because it's played so competently by a dozen colorful performers." The *Evening Independent* found Jaeckel to be "impressive." But the good notices were too few and far between. Stills of Jaeckel do not even appear in the film's presskit.

As for the filming of the movie itself, it was a positive experience thanks to the large group of professionals assembled. Some initially prestigious films simply aren't able to make the grade from start to finish for whatever reason. *The Drowning Pool* is one of them. Jaeckel and Newman did have a good time together racing and chasing around the Lafayette, Louisiana, location, taking up where they left off from their professional friendship during the memorable making of *Sometimes a Great Notion* four years earlier. "It was fun, and it was reminiscent of an earlier association," Jaeckel told Joe Morella for the book *Paul and Joanne*. "And everybody else picked up on it, because I like to think that we still have great affection for each other."

Biographical film writer Joe Morella had the opportunity to meet Jaeckel on a couple of occasions. He recalls: "He was very proud that he was a working actor. We discussed the fact that although he never reached stardom he had a fine career. I interviewed him concerning *Sometimes a Great Notion*, which was his Academy Award–nominated performance. He was proud that he was a working actor and had supported himself and his family for all those years as an actor."[16]

Character actor Andrew Robinson made a great impact as the Scorpio Killer in his debut film *Dirty Harry* (1971) but by the time of *The Drowning Pool* he was still finding his way in the business after having been immediately typed as a heavy. He recalls: "I remember Richard with great affection. It's a cliché, but he was truly a considerate colleague and gentleman. He had a kind word for everyone and was always one of the first on the set to rehearse or shoot. I was also convinced that he had a painting of himself that he hung in his closet that grew old because he seemed to be immune to age. It was a thrill to work with him because he was one of the actors I grew up watching. I wish I had more specific memories, but I do have a strong memory of the man."[17]

Jaeckel is the special guest star in the feature film *Walking Tall, Part II* (1975), a sequel to the smash 1973 hit that starred Joe Don Baker. This time around 6'6" Bo Svenson takes over the lead role as real-life Southern sheriff Buford Pusser. Originally Pusser was screen-tested and was going to play himself in the second film, but he was killed in an auto wreck shortly prior to the start of filming. Jaeckel is cast as the character Stud Pardee, a grinning killer recruited by bad guys Luke Askew, Logan Ramsey, and John Davis Chandler for his stock car driving skills. Jaeckel loosens Svenson's front wheel before suckering him into a high-speed chase. Svenson survives; then takes his trademark oak club to Jaeckel's prized hot rod. Jaeckel's facial expressions at seeing his beloved Camaro demolished are priceless. It's the best scene in an otherwise routine action film. Jaeckel and star Svenson do a great deal of their own driving and did their own stunt work running away from an explosion. On location in Tennessee they worked out together at a local gym, with former judo champion Svenson recalling Jaeckel as "a super nice guy."[18]

Bo Svenson and Richard Jaeckel perform their own stunt work in AIP's *Part 2, Walking Tall* (1975).

Veteran character actor Bruce Glover played Deputy Grady Coker in both the Joe Don Baker and Bo Svenson *Walking Tall* films. He says,

> Richard Jaeckel was a nice guy with a strong presence. He was a manly guy. Very physical. You wouldn't want to get into a fistfight with him. I didn't know him that well, and we didn't get to talk that much; but he was quite a friendly gentleman. He was one of the bad guys in the film but a good guy; a pleasure to be around. *Walking Tall 2* was not a very good film compared with the first, so it was not a good opportunity for Richard or anyone else. But he was a pro, so he did what he could. I'm sorry we didn't work together on a better film, and I'm sorry Buford Pusser wasn't around. It would have been a good experience for Richard to meet him. I think they would have gotten along.[19]

Local actor Chris Ladd played an unbilled deputy in the film but was pleased to find that he and Jaeckel shared something in common. He relates,

> The main thing I remember about Richard is that he was different in person than the tough guy roles he always played. Down to earth, kind of quiet in a way. We became friends even though we did not have scenes together because I was a character actor and he was, and we both shared the same birthday, October 10. I remember him telling me when they wanted to test him for the part in *Guadalcanal Diary*, he really didn't want to do the test. He was working in the mail room at Fox and wanted to stay there. He really didn't see himself as an actor and enjoyed what he was doing. He was always kind to people and never forgot who you were. Never looked or acted like a big star actor, just one of the guys.[20]

The Earl Bellamy–directed rural actioner was attacked by the critics for its violence and low-level drive-in aspirations. The *St. Petersburg Times* claimed the film was "an embarrassment for all connected with it, including Richard Jaeckel who was so fine in *Sometimes a Great Notion*.... It is uncomfortable to see an actor of Jaeckel's talent in this sort of movie." Outside of that review, Jaeckel generally escaped unscathed from the critics' ire, as he should have. *Variety* wrote of the movie, "Richard Jaeckel is ... good here as a racing driver who fails to kill Pusser," while the *Los Angeles Times* added that he made "a good cameo." *The Los Angeles Herald Examiner* claimed, "The typecast supporting cast, which includes Luke Askew, Richard Jaeckel and Angel Tompkins as assorted baddies, plays along with the cartoon concept." *The San Diego Union* wrote, "Other than Jaeckel, usually good, the script gives the villains the worst of the dramatics."

And from there, Jaeckel caught the next wave of his career.

◆ 8 ◆

Choppy Surf

In late 1975 Jaeckel was on the Pittsburgh, California, location for *Bound for Glory* (1976), ostensibly to play a cameo role in the Hal Ashby film about singer Woody Guthrie taking on the Unions during the Great Depression. Jaeckel hung out on the set with star David Carradine, but when the two-and-a-half-hour film was released Jaeckel was nowhere to be found. It's likely his scene was cut. The same fate befell fellow character actor Read Morgan on the film. *Bound for Glory* was nominated for a Best Picture Oscar and numerous other awards. Jaeckel did not enjoy any of that glory.

There was another flurry of guest appearances on the 1975–1976 TV season. Jaeckel was cast as disgraced physician Cy Carter on the William Conrad detective series *Cannon*. Billed behind fellow guests David Birney and Don Gordon, Jaeckel plays a doctor with a drug problem. It's interesting to see the normally cool, military-erect Jaeckel sweaty and hunched over as he scratches at his arms in need of a fix. The role is a decided departure for Jaeckel that displays his range, but *Cannon* was little more than a routine detective drama from the Quinn Martin stable and Jaeckel's performance was hardly a showcase. His character is the victim of an overdose midway through the script. The Paul Stanley–directed episode entitled "Wrong Medicine" aired in September of 1975.

In the December 1975 *Ellery Queen* episode "The Adventure of the Blunt Instrument," Nick McVey (Jaeckel), a popular writer of tough guy fiction, loses a mystery writer's award to pompous Keene Curtis. When Curtis turns up dead, Jaeckel and others such as Dean Stockwell and Eva Gabor are suspects for star Jim Hutton to sift through. Playing a two-fisted Mickey Spillane—inspired writer, Jaeckel does his own snooping for the killer. *Ellery Queen* is a fondly remembered show, although it only lasted one season. *Joe Forrester* was a spin-off from *Police Story* that starred Lloyd Bridges as a veteran beat cop. Jaeckel played a by-the-book superior officer named Lt. Sullivan on the March 1976 episode "Pressure Point." The single season series has been out of circulation for years.

More readily accessible is Jaeckel's March 1976 guest appearance on the wholesome family show *Little House on the Prairie*. Jaeckel plays the character Murphy in "The Long Road Home." The episode was directed by series star Michael Landon, who took the helm when he thought an episode had something important to say. This episode dealt with racial prejudice. In the story, Jaeckel is hired to transport a wagon load of nitro with Landon and co-star Victor French. Jaeckel is paired with Lou Gossett and immediately voices his reluctance to be teamed with a man of color. However, he needs the money for his family and agrees to complete the dangerous ten-day journey for a hundred dollars. The episode is solid entertainment and a nice three-dimensional part for Jaeckel, who overcomes his bigotry by episode's end. He does a fine job balancing his character's faults and virtues so the audience can accept him as a good guy by the close of the story. *The Bridgeport Post* said, "The tension may be somewhat contrived but the interplay between Gossett and Jaeckel is valid and a good object lesson, especially for kids."

On the March 1976 *Baretta* episode "Aggie," Jaeckel is cast as the crooked narcotics officer Duncan who is seen killing his stripper girlfriend by a simple-minded waitress (Shelly Duvall). The girl is a friend of fellow cop Baretta (Robert Blake), so Jaeckel spends the bulk of the episode tying up loose ends. He comes on sweet and syrupy with Duvall until the inevitable shootout with Blake at the climax. Jaeckel is shot in the belly. As formula 1970s cop shows go, *Baretta* is memorable thanks largely to Blake's charisma and the Sammy Davis, Jr., theme song "Keep Your Eye on the Sparrow." Jaeckel and Blake were old friends from their time spent together in Germany on *Town Without Pity* (1961). Curiously, there is a quote from Blake on the Internet Movie Database coming from one of his many rambling interviews in which he says Jaeckel is the only guy he ever met who is "crazier than me." It's an odd statement coming from a man whose erratic behavior has been well-documented and resulted at times in outright blacklisting by the Hollywood establishment as he dealt with his myriad of psychological and substance abuse issues.

On March 27, 1976, Jaeckel narrated the Bicentennial Minute broadcast on national TV. In June 1976 he guest starred on the Jack Warden series *Jigsaw John* in the episode "Homicide 96403" as yet another lawman. Playing cops was Jaeckel's new calling and it kept the phone ringing periodically for his services. However, TV shows like the short-lived *Jigsaw John* were cast quickly, shot in a matter of days on a tight schedule, aired, and often never heard from again if they didn't pull immediate ratings.

With Hollywood's abandonment of the studio system and contract players, free agent Jaeckel took what work came his way. Outside of the quickly shot TV shows many of those projects were complete independent productions that may have promised only regional release or drive-in screen engagements. Work was work, but Jaeckel missed the good old days where a production was literally a production. He told the *Fort Lauderdale News*: "There was more charm and action when the studios ran the show. It was a motion picture business. Now, many of the executive types are efficiency experts."

Steven Spielberg's killer shark movie *Jaws* (1975) was big box office and the inevitable knock-offs began appearing within a year. Jaeckel was third billed above the title in the movie *Grizzly* (1976) as bear expert Arthur Scott. *Grizzly* (aka *Claws*) was made on location in Clayton, Georgia, for $750,000 by director William Girdler for Film Ventures International. Jaeckel was teamed with park ranger Christopher George and chopper pilot Andrew Prine as they attempt to bring down a giant man-killing grizzly bear. The stars were reportedly en route to the location before ever seeing a screenplay. The principals showed off their machismo, doing close quarter action with a live bear utilizing only an electric wire between them as protection. Behind the scenes the trained bear Teddy tore apart a dummy of Jaeckel to the point where it was unusable for the film. One of the film's best moments has Jaeckel attacked by the bear and buried alive. Jaeckel wakes up and slowly rises. As he takes in his surroundings and orients himself, he sees the bear is nearby watching him. Jaeckel lets out a deep sigh that says more than any words in his final screen moment.

Critics didn't think much of the film but it did fantastic theatrical business and reportedly made nearly forty million dollars. It remains a favorite with many fans who saw it when it was first released and remember the terrifying premise better than the occasionally sketchy execution and uneven supporting performances that surround the trio of professionals. Jaeckel plays his naturalist as a slightly off-kilter sort, interacting well with former *Chisum* co-stars George and Prine. Jaeckel prefers to capture the killer grizzly independently with a tranquilizer gun, riding through the forest on horseback clad in a bearskin while dragging bear bait behind him on a rope. It's an ill-fated decision.

Box Office Magazine wrote, "Christopher George, Andrew Prine, and Richard Jaeckel are excellent." The *Evening-Independent* said, "Despite the attendance of credible actors such as Christopher George, Andrew Prine, and Richard Jaeckel, *Grizzly* still comes off poorly." The *Sentinel and Enterprise* added, "The three people stars are outstanding, especially Richard Jaeckel who brings a lot of skill and experience to his role," while the *Syracuse Herald-Journal* called Jaeckel the film's "most appealing character." Less complimentary was *The Hollywood Reporter* review, which claimed Jaeckel, "merely rolls his blue eyes" in getting through the film. The *Observer-Reporter* wrote, "With the exception of Christopher George and Richard Jaeckel, the acting is uniformly atrocious." *The Washington Post* remarked, "Actors one expects in TV reruns—Christopher George, Richard Jaeckel—do what they can, but their function is like that of rats in a perfectly straight maze." The *Pittsburgh Post-Gazette* offered the most original take on the film: "The picture's strangest character is a naturalist who apparently lives in the park—played by Richard Jaeckel. The character is like an updated old man of the hills who knows everything about bears and other animals. At one point he is mistaken for the grizzly. So conditioned is this viewer to seeing Jaeckel as a villain that my first thoughts entertained the idea that Jaeckel might have been a mad killer in a bearskin."

Grizzly's young writer-producer David Sheldon recalls: "Richard Jaeckel was a joy to work with and a superb actor. I couldn't resist casting him, having seen television reruns of his early movies like *Come Back, Little Sheba*. And what a gentleman. He always addressed me as 'Sir' even though I was so young, producing one of my first films. I learned from him. I really didn't get to know him because it was a four-week shoot in the mountains where *Deliverance* had recently been filmed."[1]

"Working with him was wonderful," says leading lady Joan McCall on the film's DVD extra entitled *Jaws with Claws*. "He

Jaeckel as naturalist Arthur Scott in Film Venture International's *Grizzly* (1976). The low-budget film was a huge hit but unfortunately typed Jaeckel in B-films.

was professional and kind. He didn't try to hog the camera. He was a pro. He was really a nice man." The film's producer Harvey Flaxman agreed: "Richard Jaeckel was a very serious guy and a very special man…. We would all go out drinking afterwards—Christopher George and Andy and myself and some of the others. Richard Jaeckel would work out. He brought his weights with him and he would work out every day." Co-star Andrew Prine adds, "He always looked great. He was in great shape and just a terrific guy and had an incredible film history." Flaxman caps things off, saying, "We were very fortunate to have him as part of our team."

Jaeckel was elevated to a leading role in *Mako: The Jaws of Death* (1976). He plays shark-loving loner Sonny Stein for director William Grefe and spends a great deal of the film in the water. Jaeckel's character communicates telepathically with the sharks and hates others who exploit them. He will resort to violence to protect the creatures he loves. It was a challenge for Jaeckel to make the central character sympathetic, especially when he is shown killing three people in the very first scene. A ruddy-faced Jaeckel physically rose to the occasion as the anti-hero, swimming with real sharks and engaging in a martial arts fight with John Davis Chandler and Harold "Oddjob" Sakata of James Bond–*Goldfinger* fame. Director Grefe had filmed the shark scenes in the Bond film *Live and Let Die* (1973) and his footage here of real tiger sharks in the water with Jaeckel and the stuntmen is very good. The final reel finds Jaeckel shot down by the police and turned on by his own sharks after they detect the scent of his blood in the water.

The low-budget independent was filmed in the Miami Dade, Florida, area and in the Bahamas in September of 1975. In the wake of Steven Spielberg's *Jaws* (1975) the drive-in picture did decent business. At the time of its release it was reviewed by *The Village Voice* which called Jaeckel "modestly low-key" in his rare starring role. The *Boston Herald* termed him "an ageless, weather-beaten blond." Cleveland's *Plain Dealer* addressed his performance, writing, "Jaeckel does about as well as could be expected with an essentially nutty role that isn't supposed to be funny." The *Syracuse Herald-Journal* wrote, "A quietly restrained and compelling performance by Richard Jaeckel in the focal role almost deludes the viewer into declaring *Jaws of Death* a success." Retro Internet reviews have been complimentary to Jaeckel's performance and have sustained interest in the oceanic horror film. In the 1980s the USA Network's movie host Commander USA showed this film and created a humorous tribute to Richard Jaeckel during the broadcast.

Low-budget films like *Grizzly* and *Mako* gave Jaeckel an opportunity to explore interesting character traits on screen he didn't necessarily have in the majors. On the studio pictures it was all "hurry up and wait" with multiple conflicting powers sometimes dictating what got filmed. Jaeckel might spend a few months on a big film and end up in only a couple of scenes in the finished picture. On the low-budget quickies he worked around the clock for a week or two and could end up being called upon by a producer or director to dominate a film. He was hired specifically because of his name and reputation as a guy who could get it done. Low-budget directors, sometimes helming only their first or second film, typically gave him the freedom to do what he had done so well in the past. Still, Jaeckel never abused the privilege.

"Richard was one of my favorite actors," says *Mako*'s director William Grefe. "He came so prepared; never blew lines. He was fantastic. A super professional. I can't say enough nice things about him. I was his biggest fan. Over the years I worked with some real assholes and prima donnas, but not Richard. The guy was a super person. He was there to do his job and cooperate. A super nice guy."[2] Leading lady Jenifer Bishop, interviewed in the book *Wild*

Jaeckel fights professional wrestler Harold "Oddjob" Sakata in Cannon Film Distributors' *Mako, Jaws of Death* (1976). Jaeckel did his own stunts on the low-budget Florida film, including swimming with real tiger sharks.

Beyond Belief, concurred: "I worked with one of the all-time pros ever. Richard Jaeckel was a doll. Just a wonderful guy to work with. Just a wonderful man."

The first day of filming nearly turned into a nightmare for Grefe. An expensive Arriflex camera was broken and a camera boat got stuck on a sandbar, necessitating a quick switch of the shooting schedule. They hadn't planned on using Jaeckel for the first shot, but Grefe asked if his star could quickly get in wardrobe and salvage the lost time. Jaeckel said it was no problem and ran off. The first AD came in shortly after and presented Grefe with an even worse problem. In his haste to get back to the set, Jaeckel had fallen off a moving prop truck and split his head open. They had rushed him bleeding to the emergency ward. The day was turning into a total loss for Grefe, but within ninety minutes Jaeckel was back on the set claiming he was ready to go. Grefe was incredulous:

> He had six or seven stitches in the back of his head. He had been bleeding like a stuck pig. No actor would be expected to go back to work after that, but he insisted on it. He was so professional. He didn't miss a beat the whole picture, and he was in almost every scene. Richard just jumped right in and never missed a beat. I told him he didn't have to but he said, "Whenever I work in a movie, I say, 'Thank you dear Lord for letting me work today.'" And he never stopped working. He was in every war film and so many westerns. He made such an impression on me. I would have loved to work with him again. There were a couple of things, but it all depends on the casting and what he'd be right for. I wanted to use him in *Whiskey Mountain* but he was unavailable at the time.[3]

As for filming with the sharks, Big John McLaughlin, a legendary Florida diver who doubled for Lloyd Bridges on *Sea Hunt*, was in charge of the stunt work. Fellow stuntman Monty Cox remembers,

> I was going to go down to Miami and double Richard Jaeckel on *Mako* but Big John called me up and told me I could stay home. He said, "This guy is doing everything himself." Most guys don't have the balls to get into the water with the sharks. Jaeckel did. He was fearless. He was a man's man and what every man should be. He was a thinker. A very logical brain. If you explained something to him like John did, Jaeckel had a way of thinking in which he could evaluate it and he could do it. He was that way as an actor. He was real. He wasn't acting in a part. I've been doing this business for over 40 years and not many actors can make it real like that. You know they're acting. I think because of Richard's way of thinking, he could step in and become that person for the camera.[4]

Sticking around in Florida, Jaeckel headed the cast of the incredible cult film *The Amazing Mr. No Legs* (1977), directed by former *Creature from the Black Lagoon* stuntman Ricou Browning. Fellow pros Lloyd Bochner, John Agar, and Rance Howard also appear in the dated film which features a paraplegic martial artist hit man (Ted Vollrath) who has shotguns and Chinese throwing stars outfitted on his wheelchair. Plainclothes police detective Chuck Roberts (Jaeckel) is in charge of investigating the deaths related to a drug smuggling ring. The film features jaw-dropping tae kwon do action, much of it courtesy of the real-life double amputee Vollrath in his wheelchair. The fights are staged well enough, as is a climactic car chase with Jaeckel put together by Joie Chitwood's stunt team. Despite the low budget, Jaeckel delivers a typically professional performance in which his likable personality shines through as the good cop who looks out for his partner Ron Slinker.

Mr. No Legs was filmed in Tampa in 1975 as *Killers Die Hard*. Co-star Agar recalled for *Psychotronic Video* that his check for the film bounced and that he never was paid by the producer. The movie received a marginal release in Europe under the titles *Gun Fighter* and *Destructor* over the next few years but garnered its reputation with the advent of the Internet where it has received many reviews and positive word of mouth as something one has to see to believe. It is as evocative of 1970s low-budget action cinema as can be found. According to the website *Cult Movie Forums*, "The always watchable Richard Jaeckel is a decent lead."

The film's efficient director Ricou Browning recalls Jaeckel and his professional wrestling co-star Ron Slinker: "I sure enjoyed working with Richard Jaeckel on *The Amazing Mr. No Legs*. It was a very low-budget film. We shot it in 16mm then blew it up to 35. The actor playing the part of the other detective in the film was acting for the first time and was a friend of the producer of the film. Richard helped him with his acting, showing him all the ropes all the way through the film. I became a good friend of Richard. He was a great guy and we stayed in touch."[5]

In 1976 Jaeckel turned fifty but one would never know it judging by his ever-youthful appearance. His hair was still blond, and he looked at least a decade or so younger in his unlined face. When on location he kept himself fit with his traveling chin-up bar, pushups, knee bends, and handstand press-ups against a wall. If there was a local gym he found it. His muscled body would have been the envy of most professional athletes of the day as evidenced by his shirtless scenes in *Mako*. Perhaps a bit stockier, Jaeckel routinely rose at 5 a.m. for his workouts and trained regularly at the original Gold's Gym in California, the popular bodybuilding mecca. He still enjoyed a leisurely day at the beach and a run in the sand when his busy film and TV schedule permitted. He also participated in Celebrity Jog-A-Thon events for Holiday Health Spas. Brad Harris recalls:

Jaeckel and Ron Slinker are tough cops fighting a crime syndicate in Cinema Artists' *The Amazing Mr. No Legs* **(1977).**

> Richard and I worked out together at the old Gold's Gym. The originator of Gold's Gym was Joe Gold, and he was a tough old guy. All the bodybuilders who came to California would first go to Vince Gironda. They called him the Iron Guru, and he was out in the San Fernando Valley. But all these bodybuilders would eventually want to go down seaside and Muscle Beach. They migrated down to the beach area. Richard would come down and I lived right next to the beach where we hung out together. Then Joe Gold sold the rights to the gym and the rights to his name. Then came World Gym; so Joe Gold was actually the founder of Gold's Gym and World Gym.[6]

The biggest names in bodybuilding, such as Mr. Olympia Arnold Schwarzenegger and contest promoter/magazine publisher Joe Weider, knew Jaeckel. Multi-faceted bodybuilder Ric Drasin was a 1970s training partner of Schwarzenegger and had lengthy careers as both a professional wrestler and movie stuntman. A talented artist, he is best known for designing the iconic logos for both Gold's Gym and World Gym. He also trained with Jaeckel. He remembers: "After our workout at World Gym, Richard and I would sit out in the parking lot and get some sun and talk for an hour about all kinds of subjects. He was a great guy. I had minor surgery one time and he called my house and pretended to be Joe Weider. Did a pretty good job of convincing me too."[7]

Jaeckel also continued to solidify his reputation as a regular Joe who made an effort to be nice to everyone he encountered. He took his work seriously but not himself. *Santa Monica Daily Press* columnist Jack Neworth was working as messenger for a real estate office at the time and had a chance meeting with Jaeckel in the elevator of a Century City high-rise. A few months prior, Neworth had met Robert Redford and after some casual talk made the mistake of requesting an autograph for the ladies in his office. Redford did not sign autographs as a rule and his tone quickly changed when Neworth tried to coax it out of him. Redford asked Neworth if he was going to need to call Security. A dejected Neworth left the encounter with his tail between his legs and never mentioned to the girls in the office that he had met the golden boy movie star. So when Neworth recognized Jaeckel from *Sometimes a Great Notion*, he was initially apprehensive. Within the confines of the elevator he finally asked Jaeckel if he was an actor, and after a short dramatic pause, Jaeckel began to engage Neworth in conversation.

"He couldn't have been nicer," Neworth recalls, using the words "gracious" and "charming" to describe the very open Jaeckel. He also pegs him as "intellectually courteous" as they embarked on a fifteen-minute conversation about books, movies, writer Ken Kesey, actors Paul Newman and Henry Fonda, and director Robert Aldrich. Jaeckel told Neworth he was flattered at being recognized and actually followed Neworth to the underground parking garage. They continued talking even as Neworth got into his vehicle and rolled down his window in preparation to leave. "I thought I was going to have to call Security on him," Neworth jokes, remembering the encounter with great fondness.[8]

Although he seemed to be working regularly, Jaeckel was having a hard time getting back into better paying "A" projects. He no doubt would have loved to have been hired by Don Siegel as one of the gunmen facing down John Wayne in the Duke's swan song *The Shootist* (1976), but it was all a steady diet of B-pictures and formula TV shows. Two or three weeks work here and a week or so there. The two- to three-month duration-of-the-shoot jobs simply weren't being offered any longer. Emerging character actor Bill McKinney, who had played Jaeckel's brother in *The Outfit* and earlier scored as a deranged mountain man in *Deliverance* (1972), seemed to be the flavor of the moment and was getting the top parts that used to be earmarked for Jaeckel. It was McKinney getting gunned down by Wayne, McKinney playing a suspicious Army officer in the Charles Bronson western *Breakheart Pass* (1976), and McKinney going up against Clint Eastwood as a vicious Confederate red-leg in *The Outlaw Josey Wales* (1976). Meanwhile, Jaeckel was battling sharks and killer grizzlies in low-budget fare.

The 1976–1977 TV season once again saw a highly prolific Jaeckel. He appeared as the character Sheriff Matheson in the October 1976 *McCloud* episode "Bonnie and McCloud." The routine time-waster of a plot saw series star Dennis Weaver forced on the lam alongside guest Leigh Taylor-Young with bad guys Geoffrey Lewis and John Quade in hot pursuit. Jaeckel is a hardnosed cop under the false impression that Weaver has killed two of his deputies. Outside of the rare chance to see Jaeckel sporting a mustache, there's not a lot to recommend this episode.

On the abbreviated Ben Murphy sci-fi series *Gemini Man* Jaeckel was cast as Nik Radanski in the December 1976 episode "Support Your Local Police." Less than half of the eleven produced episodes about an intermittently invisible secret agent were aired in the United States, with Jaeckel's episode one of those that only saw the light of day on British TV. In the story Jaeckel's uniformed officer may be a sleeper Soviet agent, so Murphy goes undercover as the patrolman's partner. Top guest Jaeckel has a nice role and gets to display a wide range of emotions, but it's a silly show that died a quick ratings death.

Jaeckel once more ventured into the sci-fi genre for the equally short-lived TV series *The Fantastic Journey*. UFOs, aliens, time warps, and the Bermuda Triangle were all aspects of the haphazard hodgepodge that featured Jaeckel in the June 1977 episode "Innocent Prey." It was directed by Vincent McEveety, who considered Jaeckel a known and stable quality that could lend some sense of balance to the rest of the show's elements. Even that is a stretch as Jaeckel is asked to play the character York, a space criminal exhibiting advanced psychotic behavior who is freed when his transport ship crash lands in a utopian society immune to violence. Cheryl Ladd, Nicholas Hammond, and Gerald McRaney also appear as guests with a murderous Jaeckel zapping characters to death with a ray gun. In the climax he is incredibly reduced to his infant form. It's a strange fantasy series, and it is odd to see the normally grounded Jaeckel taking part in it.

Kingston: Confidential is a largely forgotten Raymond Burr series about a publishing magnate with a crimefighting sideline. It features Jaeckel as psychopathic Korean War veteran Miller White, who phones Burr to announce the military property targets he intends to destroy in the August 1977 episode "The Anonymous Hero." Burr himself directed the episode with his series underlings Pamela Hensley and Art Hindle handling the other acting chores. It was the last episode aired of the barely remembered series. Few of these fast-paced television shows provided Jaeckel with the optimum preparation time to enhance his performance. They all required him to basically hit the ground running with fresh script changes in hand. All in all, the 1976–1977 TV season was perhaps Jaeckel's most forgettable. Nevertheless, Jaeckel remained as professional as ever even when he was asked to take on the ridiculous or the mundane. He told *The TV Collector*,

> No matter what kind of film it is, whether it's about sharks or working with rubber monsters in Japan or fighting vampire bats in Mexico, which I've done, you've got to do it, and if you start laughing or thinking "This is crap, I wanna go home," then you shouldn't be in the business.... You have to put the ego away and stop thinking that you're gonna turn everything around. You're not the only one who can do it. You should always remember there's somebody that can do it better and probably cheaper than you're doing it, and not to get the idea that you're doing somebody a favor.

Jaeckel had a supporting role as frontier artist Ed Kern in the TV movie *Kit Carson and the Mountain Men*. A raspy-voiced Christopher Connelly starred as the title character and Gary Lockwood, Robert Reed, Dub Taylor, and Gregg Palmer were also in the cast of the entertaining Disney western. It aired in early 1977 as a two-part episode of *The Wonderful World of Disney* and has been out of circulation for years. It was directed by Jaeckel's familiar helmsman Vincent McEveety, who recalls that Jaeckel did "fine work."[9] Few of these quick assignments provided a needed boost to Jaeckel's career. Luckily, pal Robert Aldrich always looked for a part for Jaeckel when putting together a new project. Both had high hopes for their next collaboration.

Aldrich's *Twilight's Last Gleaming* (1977) is an ambitious, star-studded melodrama about a renegade general (Burt Lancaster) capturing a U.S. missile silo and threatening to launch on other countries unless secrets about the military's strategic policy in Vietnam are revealed. Aldrich employs multiple screen panels showing simultaneous action to develop great tension as Lancaster and fellow military criminals Paul Winfield, Burt Young, and William Smith infiltrate the base and take over the silo personnel led by Jaeckel and Morgan Paull. Jaeckel plays Captain Stanford Towne, who knows Lancaster personally and is able to engage in a philosophical discussion with him. When Jaeckel refuses to be an accomplice to Lancaster's crime, he is threatened with a screwdriver to the eye to force Paull to reveal crucial launch codes in one of the film's most memorable moments. General Richard Widmark and President Charles Durning enter desperate negotiations with Lancaster to prevent the threat of World War III. Lancaster's chief demand is the president himself as a hostage.

The superb technician Aldrich filmed in Munich, Germany, due to a lack of cooperation from the U.S. military but encountered few problems of note during production. Interviewed for *The Films of Robert Aldrich*, Jaeckel remembered that it was "a terrific film to be in ... the whole atmosphere was terrific." Jaeckel and Aldrich attended a sneak peek of the film in January 1977, staying at the Drake Hotel in Chicago for the premiere. Upon its release, Aldrich's film received mixed reviews, much of it due to the controversial subject matter and star Lancaster's known liberal leanings. Relegated down the cast list, Jaeckel received very little mention in the trades. It was somewhat taken for granted that Aldrich's cast of professionals such as Jaeckel, Melvyn Douglas, William Marshall, Leif Erickson, and Charles McGraw would turn in solid performances. It is one of the few films where Jaeckel can be heard using four-letter words. *The Hollywood Reporter* claimed, "The performances are all credible," specifically mentioning, "Richard Jaeckel and Morgan Paull are good as the hostages." *The Bakersfield Californian* found Jaeckel to be "impressive" while the *Pocono Record* mentioned Jaeckel among the "excellent performances." Nearly forty years later the movie still sparks heated debate and remains one to seek out.

Jaeckel's long-time friend William Smith, a former Air Force veteran and linguistic specialist for the CIA and the NSA, recalled that he and Jaeckel had a lot of fun in Germany. Since Jaeckel had worked with Lancaster before, the two Aldrich vets tended to team up in ribbing the 6'2", 210-pound Smith about his small part in the film and his minimal amount of dialogue. The ruggedly handsome Smith was in the midst of getting a major boost to his career for playing the menacing villain Falconetti on the TV mini-series *Rich Man, Poor Man* (1976), but at the time couldn't get into A-list films after having starred in a string of late 1960s low-budget motorcycle pics that typed him in the minds of casting directors. After Lancaster killed Smith on screen early in the picture, the star jokingly told Smith he did a good job on the film and that perhaps on their next project they'd even give him some lines.[10]

Day of the Animals (aka *Something Is Out There*) (1977) is a "nature run amok" tale from exploitation director William Girdler. A hiking expedition in California's High Sierras runs into a crazed and hyper-aggressive animal world: Above 5,000 feet elevation, the animals are being affected by solar radiation due to a depleted ozone layer courtesy of mankind's overuse of aerosol sprays. Girdler presents some interesting visuals of animals attacking a star-studded B-cast. The film headlines Christopher George and his real-life wife Lynda Day George and features Jaeckel in support as Professor Taylor MacGregor. Leslie Nielsen chews up the scenery as an antagonistic jerk who doffs his shirt and fights a bear, while Michael Ansara, Paul Mantee, Jon Cedar, Ruth Roman, and Andrew Stevens round out the cast. Andrew Prine was offered a role by Girdler but declined out of fear that too many B-level films would hurt his career.

Jaeckel wears heavy rimmed glasses and presents a book-smart character who turns analytical in attempting to decipher the reasons behind the animal behavior. Despite the character not being one of Jaeckel's conventional tough guys, it was a physically demanding role with lots of hiking at high elevations. In one scene Jaeckel fights off a mountain lion with a torch. Later, both he and Mantee are mauled to death by rampaging German Shepherds. Jaeckel has one subdued scene by a campfire with Lynda Day George, but mostly the part required an abundance of physical acting. Jaeckel did many of his own stunts working with the animals, but was doubled in the hairiest situations by animal handler-professional stuntman Monty Cox. Cox recalls,

> I had the pleasure of working with Richard Jaeckel on *Day of the Animals*. A great guy. He was the best. Can't say enough about him. As a guy, he was a man's man. There was no Hollywood about him. He was straight, up and down. I doubled him in that for the animal attacks, but he was fearless. I put him with the mountain lion and in the cabin with ten Shepherds. The only thing I did was take the bite from the attack dog because it can be dangerous if it switches its bite. Jaeckel would have done it, though, if I told him he could. He did anything and everything and he would have liked to have done it all. All you had to do was tell him how. He would stop and listen to what I told him, then he'd do it. He was a thinker with a man's brain. A very logical and fearless man.[11]

The movie received mixed reviews but, like Jaeckel's other ecological horror adventures from this era, now has a bit of a cult following by those who saw it when they were young. Upon its original release, *The San Diego Union* opined, "Christopher George and Richard Jaeckel, as a scientist on holiday, contribute effectively," while the *Syracuse Herald-Journal* wrote that Jaeckel and his fellow players "turn in respectable performances." *The Hollywood Reporter* added, "Jaeckel's role as a professor doesn't have the central importance it would have had in a '50s version; perhaps due to the growing wariness of science. Still, Jaeckel manages to be his

Jaeckel and Christopher George appeared in the physically demanding *Day of the Animals* (1977). The low-budget "nature run amok" film reinforced Jaeckel's image as a star of drive-in exploitation films.

engaging self while director William Girdler intelligently guides his cast through a wide emotional range as the suspense builds."

Despite the tough conditions and modest $1.2 million budget, the cast and crew got along quite well together during the shoot with Jaeckel a catalyst for the on-location humor. Director Girdler later got married at the Malibu beach house of Mantee and his actress wife Anne Newman. Guests included Jaeckel, Tony Curtis, and Michael Ansara. Girdler died in a helicopter crash in 1978 while scouting locations in the Philippines for a science fiction film entitled *The Overlords*. Jaeckel likely would have been offered a part in that film. On the special features section of the *Day of the Animals* DVD release, Jon Cedar recalls, "Richard Jaeckel was a real gentleman and a beautifully built guy. We used to exploit him to take his shirt off." Lynda Day George calls him "a very nice guy" and Paul Mantee said, "He was a most unique man." In fact, Jaeckel and Mantee would become very close friends through their remaining years.

The 6'2", 200-pound Mantee was a U.S. Navy vet, weight room devotee, and novelist. He had a notable lead in *Robinson Crusoe on Mars* (1964) but mostly worked as an imposing TV bad guy in show after show. In the book *Science Fiction and Fantasy Film Flashbacks*, Mantee stated, "One of the nicest things that happened on *Day of the Animals* was I fell in love with Richard Jaeckel, a marvelous man. We shot that about 130 miles east of San Francisco, at the foot of the Sierras, above Sonora in a place called Long Barn which is absolutely fabulous. Jake and I had a great relationship. Andrew Stevens, Dick Jaeckel, Michael Ansara, and I spent six weeks being children, eating and drinking too much, and having a wonderful time in that movie."

Actress-stuntwoman Susan Backlinie, best known as the initial shark victim in *Jaws* (1975), played one of the hikers in addition to doubling Lynda Day George and working as an animal handler on the film. She recalls: "Working with Richard Jaeckel on *Day of the Animals* was wonderful. I enjoy watching talented actors getting ready for and doing their scenes. There is so much to learn just by watching. He also had a great sense of humor. A couple of times he would stand just out of camera, but where we could see him, and he would try and make us crack up or laugh while we were filming. He was a very nice person."[12]

Jaeckel's fear of not having work manifested itself when he was dropped by his powerful talent agent. It seems inconceivable that an Oscar-nominated actor with a stellar reputation in the industry could be dumped, but that's show business. The biggest firms represent the biggest actors so they can sign the biggest deals. A journeyman character actor like Jaeckel was small potatoes in comparison. The mid–1970s was the midst of a change in the industry with a new generation of young casting directors taking over, many unacquainted with the work of the majority of Hollywood's veteran character players. Jaeckel was well aware of the humbling nature of the business. He had been forced to travel to the unemployment office more than once during his career, providing for his family's needs always paramount in his mind. Two weeks without work in Hollywood was a vacation. More than two weeks was unemployment.

The fact that Jaeckel remained so young-looking may have been working against him to a degree. Many of his contemporaries such as Warren Oates and Harry Dean Stanton had become weather-beaten souls whose rugged faces told stories of their own for the camera. Jaeckel still looked like the perennial boy next door, suggesting a more innocent and simpler time. It wasn't that he was any less of a talent, simply that he evoked a different era that didn't represent the cynical, jaded viewpoint of the post–Vietnam War Hollywood. Westerns and combat films, Jaeckel's stock in trade for decades, were both on the wane. "He was kind of down, believe it or not, in the business and wasn't getting work," friend Robert Phillips remembers. "He didn't have an agent. He got let loose by one of the big agencies."[13]

As a result, Jaeckel was forced to take whatever offers came his way, mostly more of the B-movie drive-in variety. *Speedtrap* (1977) is a car-crash picture featuring top-notch stunt work and little else. It's one of the films that helped put an end to Joe Don Baker's career as a leading man. Baker plays a private detective brought in on a police investigation of an auto theft ring, although his help appears to be more of a hindrance. Behind the wheel of a Dodge Charger he gets involved in several high speed chases himself and manages to personally cause the destruction of several police cruisers. Jaeckel is cast as Baker's grease monkey pal Billy and has a few brief scenes. The PG-rated film was intended to be rated R with more fistfights and gun battles. The studio ultimately decided to change the script and replace those violent scenes with more car chases to get the softer rating. It was shot in Phoenix, Arizona; it is interesting to see a number of locations and landmarks that changed with that city's rapid expansion in the ensuing years. TV veteran Earl Bellamy directed with Tyne Daly, Morgan Woodward, Timothy Carey, Lana Wood, and Robert Loggia co-starring. Screenwriter Henry C. Parke, who had a bit part in the film, remembers:

> Richard Jaeckel was one of the finest actors to grace the big screen and the small. Fred Mintz and I co-wrote *Speedtrap* when I was in my last year of NYU Film School. Two other writers subsequently worked on the script—badly—so Fred and I shared story credit. Fred was the producer who put the project together and I remember my thrill when he told me Richard Jaeckel was going to be in it. He'd absolutely broken my heart in *Sometimes a Great Notion* in that agonizing scene where Paul Newman can't save him from drowning.
>
> I was on the set for the final week of filming in Phoenix. I wish I could tell you I got to know Richard well, but I didn't. He was always very amiable, and we always exchanged friendly greetings, but I was a shy kid just out of college and not pushy enough. But I observed him at work. The thing that struck me was how nice he was to everyone—not just the other actors, not just the crew, but everyone around. One time he noticed that a short, elderly woman was watching a street scene being shot, and was craning her neck to see around the other watchers. He went past the Phoenix police who were keeping the crowds back, took her by the hand onto the set, and brought her around to meet Joe Don Baker, Tyne Daly, and director Earl Bellamy. Many other times, between takes, he was not in his trailer, but leaning against the saw-horse barricades, chatting with teenagers and everyone else.
>
> I was startled to see that this actor who usually played a tough guy was not the physically big man he portrayed, but just a little over five and a half feet. In *Speedtrap*, to avoid making the height difference between him and 6'1 1/2" Joe Don Baker too jarring, they did a couple of cute tricks at Richard's auto mechanic shop. Sometimes when Joe Don would come to see him, Richard would be standing behind a car he was working on, and you couldn't see that he was standing on a box. At other times he'd be under the car on a mechanic's dolly, so when he'd scoot out and sit up, Joe Don would be hunkering down, and again the disparity wouldn't be noticed.[14]

The *Quinlan Encyclopedia of Character Actors* list the 1977 B-action film *Assault on Paradise* (aka *Maniac* and *Ransom*) as a credit for Jaeckel. Starring Oliver Reed and Deborah Raffin, the movie was made in the Scottsdale, Arizona, area around the same time as *Speedtrap*. Jaeckel does not appear in the finished print so it's difficult to determine if he worked at all on the film. Vets such as John Ireland and Stuart Whitman do play small parts in the film. Arizona stuntman Rodd Wolff worked on *Speedtrap* with Jaeckel and was later in the transportation department as Jaeckel's driver on *Starman* (1984). A western film buff and horse fall specialist, Wolff remembers, "Richard Jaeckel was a really nice guy. He was good on a horse and did a lot of his own stunts."[15]

All the B-films may have been putting a damper on the memory of Jaeckel's Oscar nod, but it was work and kept him in the public eye. While their artistic merits can be debated, both *Grizzly* and *Day of the Animals* were big moneymakers. It is hard to pin the blame for Jaeckel's career direction on either his personal choices or the work of his agent. Jaeckel was a character actor and took what parts came his way, approaching each new job with the same sense of professionalism regardless if it was a big studio picture or an independently financed B-film. It's probably more a sign of the times that quality television shows such as *Gunsmoke* and *Police Story* were in the minority when it came to what was being put out on the airwaves. Jaeckel continued with a flurry of TV appearances.

Jaeckel's next TV guest shot was a controversial one. He appeared on the sitcom *Carter Country* as Victor French's fishing buddy Bill Peterson, a high school teacher and athletic coach who hides the secret of his homosexuality. Although leery about having once shared a sleeping bag with Jaeckel, French stands up for his friend's high character and teaching ability when the school tries to have him fired. The episode "Out of the Closet" aired in September 1977 and was directed by former actor Peter Baldwin. At the time Jaeckel's role was a potentially dangerous acting choice. Playing a gay character in the 1970s could label an actor and affect one's ability to find future work. A number of celebrities were still going to great lengths to keep their real alternative lifestyles away from the common households of America. For example, as of 1977 gay actor Rock Hudson remained a macho heterosexual in the eyes of the general public based upon his carefully sustained screen image.

It should be noted that some fifteen years after Jaeckel's death, scandalous books came out by Darwin Porter on the lives of Paul Newman and Steve McQueen, in which Porter alleges the deceased macho actors were bisexual and had affairs with practically everyone in Hollywood. Porter's books are heavy on racy dialogue and actions between the leading figures and offer little in the way of substantiation or documentation. In the Newman book Porter claims that Jaeckel was bisexual and had a decades-long affair with Newman. Porter also insinuates that Jaeckel had affairs with John Wayne, Burt Lancaster, Van Johnson, and anyone else who could further his career. Somehow these loose bios found their way onto the shelves of major book dealers. As a result of Porter's book, Jaeckel's name now tends to surface on Internet lists of bisexual actors.

Ultimately, the *Carter Country* part didn't seem to affect Jaeckel's ability to get work, although *The Los Angeles Times* gave him a rare negative review, complaining that the part was "played stiffly by Richard Jaeckel." He eventually signed with David Shapira & Associates, who would represent him for the remainder of his career. More barely remembered TV followed. There was the *Young Dan'l Boone* episode "The Plague" scheduled to air in October 1977 with Jaeckel as hard-headed settler Ed Harper, who kills a Cherokee Indian while his son fights an illness. A less-than-remorseful Jaeckel tries to stir up anti–Indian sentiment in his settlement, necessitating that Boone (Rick Moses) take his place for the Cherokee trial. The episode is most noteworthy for Jaeckel's donning of a dark wig beneath his colonial style hat. On *Big Hawaii* Jaeckel played an ailing rodeo champ named Cal Seward on the November 1977 episode "You Can't Lose 'Em All" opposite series star Cliff Potts. Jaeckel's conniving sidekick David Wayne attempts to drum up a contest between the two men and profit off the outcome.

Doing all these one-and-done shows was at times counterproductive. When they did not receive a second network airing, it meant that Jaeckel wasn't receiving a second healthy check for his work that he had become accustomed to over the years when the networks and sponsors were inclined to give a longer leash to struggling series. It became more difficult for

Jaeckel to plan ahead financially, knowing that residual money wasn't coming in. Although it may have seemed like Jaeckel's face was plastered all over television screens, it didn't necessarily mean that it was generating a great deal of income for him. Due to the complicated contracts in place during certain years, Jaeckel only received residuals on heavily syndicated TV shows such as *Perry Mason, Bonanza*, and the early *Gunsmoke* episodes up to the first six airings. After that he received nothing. Earning a decent living remained imperative.

An episode of *The Oregon Trail*, "The Scarlett Ribbon," has Jaeckel guest starring as the Army corporal Jess Smith alongside William Shatner, Donna Mills, and Bill Bixby, who also doubled as the show's director for this episode. The Rod Taylor western dealt with gunrunners supplying Indians with arms and co-starred rugged character actor Charles Napier as a tough trail scout. Shatner portrays Jaeckel's sergeant in a manner that is a bit out of sync in light of his over-familiarity to audiences as *Star Trek*'s Captain Kirk. Jaeckel's performance is far more grounded in the reality of the character. In a nice scene with an unjustly imprisoned Taylor, he explains his allegiance to his superior officer, a man who saved his life in combat. The episode aired in November 1977 immediately prior to the series being cancelled.

On the *Black Sheep Squadron* episode "The Iceman," Jaeckel was cast as Major John Duncan, taking over for Robert Conrad's Pappy Boyington when the World War II pilot is assigned a hero's post in Washington. Jaeckel's by-the-books Marine character is the night and day antithesis of Conrad and the episode concerns the ragtag squadron's period of adjustment to proper military protocol. Conrad eventually realizes at the conclusion that if he manipulates it so Jaeckel shoots down a Japanese ace known as the Iceman, it will be Jaeckel who gets the medals in Washington and Conrad can return to his men. Jaeckel plays the part with a stern but fair hand. Former Elvis bodyguard Red West played a mechanic while Jaeckel's long-time friend Chuck Courtney was the show's stunt coordinator. Series co-star Dana Elcar directed the episode, which aired in March 1978.

Jaeckel much preferred working on feature films to the quick pace of television, explaining to *Daredevils* magazine:

> On a feature there's much more time to rehearse, to get to know the other cast members and familiarize yourself with the props and location. In television, you hit the deck running! Rarely do you get the luxury to familiarize yourself with anyone. Usually, you get to the set and immediately have to do a love scene with an actress who is playing your wife or girlfriend. You barely know her from Adam, and of course vice versa. She might have eaten pizza for lunch and perhaps you've had chili, and mind you it's supposed to be a romantic setting and a serious love scene. There's only so much time and the director is expecting you to both play the scene as though you're both madly in love, but it just doesn't work. So what do you do? You just do it! Sure, it might not be the way you ideally would've liked the scene to play, and chances are you're not afforded a second or third take to smooth it out, but the director feels it's adequate. Time is money, so you do the best job you can and go on to the next shot. It's all part of being a professional.

Then again, the safety of the TV studio setting was sometimes preferable to the unknown of low-budget filmmaking. Not only were actors often not paid or forced to follow the money trail for the remainder of a lifetime in collecting portions of their due, they were sometimes put into situations that threatened their very lives. For Jaeckel, *Pacific Inferno* (originally *Ship of Sand*) (1978) was another journey to the Far East that proved to be an adventure. Cast opposite *Dirty Dozen* co-star Jim Brown, Jaeckel plays Robert "Dealer" Fletcher. The movie was filmed in Manila and Corregidor in the Philippines in late 1976 and early 1977. The director was Rolf Bayer, the man who had helmed Jaeckel's earlier picture *The Kill*. Timothy Brown of the Philadelphia Eagles professional football team and Filipino actor Vic Diaz co-starred.

The troubled low-budget action picture is set during World War II with captured U.S. Navy divers Brown and Jaeckel being forced by the Japanese to dive for a treasure of silver that General Douglas MacArthur has dumped in Manila Bay. Jaeckel was recruited by co-producer Jim Brown based upon their past friendship and the fact that Jaeckel could do his own diving and had previously made films in the Philippines. The experience was no doubt valuable as Brown quickly ran into financing problems and also a state of martial law in the Asian country. Brown's friends Richard Pryor, Don Cornelius, and Hugh Hefner came up with the needed money to keep the film going. The film's premise is interesting and the actors do their best, but the overall execution is uninspiring for an action film despite the scenic locale. It has since become a bargain bin DVD.

In an interview with *Sepia* magazine after the making of *Pacific Inferno*, neophyte producer Brown referred to Jaeckel as "my star" and praised him for seeing the film to its finish. Brown elaborated on Jaeckel, saying: "Of course he was in *The Dirty Dozen*. He had a fantastic part because he played the part of the officer who was in charge of us and he became sympathetic to the dozen and tried to help us and was very happy when we survived. He's a very good actor. He has helped me in many areas with my film. He took a lower salary and really participated. I have high regards for him."

Go West, Young Girl (1978) is a breezy TV movie pilot for a proposed western series that was to star Karen Valentine and Sandra Will. Jaeckel guest stars as James P. Stonehauser, a man suspected of being an older Billy the Kid. It is believed he went into hiding rather than being shot dead by Pat Garrett at Fort Sumner and now resides in Yuma Territorial Prison. Reporter Valentine wants to find him for the scoop. Stuart Whitman, John Quade, Cal Bellini, and Gregg Palmer also appear for director Alan J. Levi. It's a rather small guest star part for a whiskered Jaeckel, but it proves to be a tough physical assignment. A game Jaeckel can be seen digging a grave, sprinting across the screen, climbing a high ladder, and riding a horse across the Sonoran desert. The film was shot at Old Tucson Studios in Arizona and benefits greatly from the scenery. Location manager Jack N. Young had been a stuntman and worked with Jaeckel a number of times dating back to *3:10 to Yuma* where Jaeckel led the outlaw charge on horseback. Young calls Jaeckel "a great character actor and one of the good guys."[16]

Jaeckel appears in familiar western mode as the cavalry character Sgt. Lykes in the high-profile twenty-six–hour TV mini-series *Centennial* (1978). He had spent nearly thirty years in the saddle and culminates his cowboy career in excellent fashion. It was the end of an era and would be Jaeckel's last ride. His episode "The Wagon and the Elephant" was directed by Paul Krasny and concerned a family's journey on the Oregon Trail. It's a small character part featuring a nice scene with Gregory Harrison on the prairie where Jaeckel's veteran horse soldier speaks in metaphors about the land. Jaeckel also has a nice bit with Donald Pleasence, but much of his part becomes lost in the massive scope of the ambitious and well-regarded project that headlined Robert Conrad and Richard Chamberlain. Nevertheless, it's a quality show Jaeckel could be proud of. Many consider it one of the best mini-series of all time. Superior actors the likes of Andy Griffith, Brian Keith, Chad Everett, Robert Vaughn, David Janssen, Raymond Burr, Richard Crenna, Dennis Weaver, and Anthony Zerbe also appeared. The bulk of *Centennial* was filmed in Colorado, although some of Jaeckel's segment was filmed on location in Augusta, Kentucky, representing old St. Louis, Missouri.

Centennial producer-writer John Wilder recalls of Jaeckel: "He was aces. When I was a young actor, people in the industry would always say I reminded them of a young Richard

Jaeckel. I took that as a compliment, made it a point to be aware of his work, and we became acquainted in the 1960s while working out at the same gym (Bruce Connors) in Westwood. When I wrote and produced James Michener's *Centennial* for Universal and NBC in the late 1970s, I sent Dick off to join a great cast in Colorado. If I remember correctly he was in the chapter titled 'The Wagon and the Elephant,' maybe one or two others as well."[17]

The B-film *The Delta Fox* (1979) has Jaeckel special guest starring as Santana for the husband-and-wife directing team Ferd and Beverly Sebastian. The fast-paced film stars Richard Lynch, Priscilla Barnes, John Ireland, Julius Harris, and Stuart Whitman as the bad guy. It is an appealingly cast sleeper that features standout action sequences. Jaeckel's contribution is minimal. He has only a couple of scenes as anti-hero Lynch's reliable cohort, including a pier gunfight in which Jaeckel does his own stunt hanging halfway out of a moving sports car. The movie was filmed in southern Florida in 1977 with Jaeckel's primary wardrobe consisting of blue jeans and a jogging jacket. *Variety* praised the acting but overall found it to be "a dim action pic."

The Sebastians made their films efficiently with small crews, enabling them to afford veteran actors the caliber of Jaeckel, Ireland, and Whitman. Ferd Sebastian recalls working with Jaeckel, writing: "I remember Richard coming into casting for his part in *Delta Fox*. He came up to me, shook my hand, and said, 'Hi, Boss, whatever you want me to do I will do it.' That set the tone for the rest of the movie. Richard would say, 'Good morning or afternoon, Boss, what do you want me to do?' Then he would proceed to do it. We never got real close. He was just like a hammer. You wanted to drive a nail, you would call him and say, 'Go nail that scene,' and it was done."[18]

The 1979 sci-fi–horror hybrid *The Dark* (aka *The Mutilator*) gives Jaeckel a sizable co-lead opposite top-billed stars William Devane and Cathy Lee Crosby. He's cast as Dave Mooney, the seen-it-all veteran cop who is assigned to investigate a series of deaths in Santa Monica. Killings like this, he *hasn't* seen before: They're the work of a serial killer space alien who shoots laser beams from his eyes. Interestingly, Jaeckel is set up as both antagonist and protagonist in the film. He has a contentious history with ex-con writer Devane and plays those scenes tough, but he is also the main conduit for the audience regarding the search for the killer. Portions of the film are solidly enacted, although overall it's a disjointed effort that suffers from huge plot holes and scenes of red herrings that don't lead anywhere.

What eventually made it to the screen was far different from what was originally intended. Director John "Bud" Cardos replaced *Texas Chain Saw Massacre* director Tobe Hooper early in the troubled film's production with the goal to bring it in on time and on budget. Cardos, a stuntman by trade, was experienced in all facets of filmmaking including production manager, line producer, and second unit director. He knew how to get the most out of time and money. The producers were none other than Ed Montoro and Dick Clark of *American Bandstand* fame, who initiated the move toward the sci-fi elements during filming given the recent box office success of *Star Wars* (1977). "Sometimes when a new director takes over, talent is not too happy," Cardos reveals. "Bill Devane was a little upset, which lasted about a week. He wanted to work with Tobe. Cathy Lee Crosby was a princess. Keenan Wynn was fine. Richard Jaeckel was happiest of all. 'At least you're moving,' he said."[19]

Jaeckel and his cop partner Biff Elliot, who portrayed Mickey Spillane's Mike Hammer on the big screen in the early 1950s, are an inspired team. Jaeckel is particularly neat and hard-nosed, while Elliot is a wisecracking, jelly-donut eating slob who is always leaving a trail of crumbs. They have fun with the roles while managing to still play the premise straight. The action-heavy ending of the film after they battle the creature is bittersweet and Jaeckel's strongest moment, all done without a single line of dialogue. "A lot of that was not written in the script," Cardos says. "Richard, Biff, and I came up with it, the three of us. Like the donut sprinkles. That's stuff we'd play with during filming, a case of 'Let us do something here to add a little bit.'"

The Dark did decent box office business and Jaeckel generally escaped any ridicule despite the shots the critics took at the film. *Variety* noted, "Richard Jaeckel is terrific in a part that had no right to deserve him," while *The Los Angeles Times* said the cast "takes care of itself the best that it can," as it pointed out the "tiresome, tough dialogue" heard in Jaeckel and Devane's confrontations. *The Hollywood Reporter* had Jaeckel heading a "generally credible cast." Today the film enjoys a healthy presence on the Internet with the website *Cool Ass Cinema* writing, "Richard Jaeckel gives his all playing the frustrated cop on the case. He was one of the most dependable actors working in Hollywood and appeared in dozens of movies and television programs of various genres."

Cardos and Jaeckel hit it off as friends during the production. Cardos remembers, "He was a great guy to work with. Very personal, very professional. He had been in the business a long time. I loved him to death. We became close friends until he died. Lots of good memories. We threw quite a few parties, barbecue-type things in my backyard over the years. Keenan Wynn from *The Dark* would come to those too. Richard and I would go to lunch together once or twice a week. We'd go to Musso and Franks where he'd have a special seafood salad that they'd made him for something like forty straight years. He went up to my cabin in the Sierras a few times. I had a pilot's license and would fly us there. I wish I'd met Richard sooner because we did get along so great."

Quinlan's Character Actors lists George Lazenby, Nancy Kwan, Aldo Ray, and Jaeckel as appearing in the film *The Falcon's Ultimatum* (1979), a title for which little further information exists. It was a Harry Hope production that was announced in the trades in the spring of 1979 and was to be directed by Dan Seeger in Hong Kong, the Philippines, and Hawaii. Hope garnered some publicity for the would-be mystery thriller by offering a part to former U.S. President Richard M. Nixon. It was not uncommon for a film to be listed in the trades without ever going into production. Sometimes these productions begin filming and financing falls through prior to completion. A few films finish principal photography but are never released for varying reasons. They all become lost titles, attributed to the actors involved but never made available for viewing to the public. The disappearance of *Falcon's Ultimatum* is probably just as well given the fact that Hope's previous film was the abysmal martial arts pic *Death Dimension* (1978).

Far more intriguing for Jaeckel was the 1979 announcement in *Variety* that he had been signed to appear opposite Glenn Ford, Ernest Borgnine, Joe Don Baker, Jack Warden, Stacy Keach, Don Gordon, and William Watson in the Alcatraz prison escape drama *Six Against the Rock*. The film was based on the Clark Howard novel and was to be produced by Quinn Martin and directed by Richard Lang in the fall of 1979. However, competing Alcatraz dramas were in the mix in the form of the Clint Eastwood-Don Siegel film *Escape from Alcatraz* (1979) and the TV movie *Alcatraz: The Whole Shocking Story* (1980). Given the factors at play, Quinn Martin folded production on *Six Against the Rock*. It would eventually resurface as a TV movie in 1987 starring David Carradine and Jan-Michael Vincent.

Jaeckel's familiar visage reached a large audience in the TV film *Champions—A Love*

Story (1979). He is cast as Peter Scoggin, the father of figure skater Jimmy McNichol. Macho ice hockey coach Jaeckel thinks his son's new vocation is for sissies and pressures him accordingly. Still, it's not a standard heavy by any means but a layered, three-dimensional performance of a loving family man who simply doesn't understand his son's new devotion. The film, based on a true story, takes some poignant turns and allows Jaeckel to flourish dramatically. John A. Alonzo directed the well-received tearjerker, which aired in January 1979 and remains a favorite with audiences who caught it on its original broadcast.

Syndicated writer Jerry Buck noted, "Richard Jaeckel is Peter's father in what possibly may be the best role of his career." *The Seattle Daily Times* wrote, "Wonderful performances are contributed by Jennifer Warren and Richard Jaeckel as Peter's parents." *The Los Angeles Times* raved about the picture and Jaeckel's first-rate performance in particular: "It is Richard Jaeckel who owns every scene he is in. He achieves the portrait of an essentially old-fashioned man whose sensitivity and capacity to change seems a surprise even to him. It is arguably the finest performance in Jaeckel's long career."

The writer-producer of *Champions*, John Sacret Young, revealed to *The Los Angeles Times* how far Jaeckel had fallen in Hollywood's eyes since his Oscar nod. Although successful at the box office, movies like *Walking Tall 2*, *Grizzly*, *Mako: Jaws of Death*, and *Day of the Animals* had seen him become labeled as an exploitation actor. "We had to fight to get Richard Jaeckel," Young said. "It seems that everyone had seen the lousy movies that he had been in. I had seen him several years ago in *Sometimes a Great Notion* and he had a boyish quality that I liked."

A TV pilot film entitled *Salvage* (1979), about a wily junk antique expert who builds

Jaeckel, Jay Saunders, Andy Griffith, Trish Stewart, and Joel Higgins make up the cast of *Salvage One* (1979). The series is fondly remembered but not for its longevity.

his own spaceship and plans a launch to the moon to recover abandoned NASA equipment, was sold as a winter replacement series for the 1978–1979 season. Andy Griffith starred. Appealing co-stars Joel Higgins and Trish Stewart are on hand as a former astronaut and a fuel expert. On both the pilot and the subsequent series *Salvage 1*, Jaeckel was cast as Griffith's exasperated government foe Jack Klinger, who deep down inside is revealed to be a very good guy but must constantly investigate Griffith's many questionable dealings and excursions. On several occasions the F.B.I. agent's agreeable personality and depth of character seeps through as he is found secretly rooting for Griffith to pull off another one of his fantastic stunts. One storyline had Griffith transferring an iceberg to a drought-ravaged area. On some episodes Jaeckel was found working alongside Griffith for a common goal, although he was usually pressed into this service by circumstances. The role was old-hat for Jaeckel, but he was in typically fine form.

Variety wrote, "Much of the credit for its success within its own frame of reference comes from the likable work of Griffith, Higgins, and Stewart, plus Jacqueline Scott and Richard Jaeckel as an FBI man who snoops around with suspicions that they're up to something different than they actually planned." *The Los Angeles Times* found Jaeckel's Klinger to be "a character of outrageous camp, almost a parody of all the dumb cops Jaeckel has played in his career." The *Lakeland Ledger* also commented on Jaeckel: "He's made virtually an entire career out of playing tough bureaucrats, and his *Salvage 1* role fits handily into that category." *The Seattle Daily Times* noted, "Richard Jaeckel was entertaining as an F.B.I. agent who started out to sabotage the venture and ended up a flag-waving supporter." The *Oregonian* said that both Andy Griffith and Jaeckel "had seen better days."

Considering the talent involved in *Salvage 1* there was hope that this would be the series that would take off in the ratings and become a hit. Given Griffith's stellar reputation in the industry and his familiarity to viewers at home, there were early indications this would be the case. It had been five years since Jaeckel's last regular TV series and he always welcomed the promise of a steady paycheck. It was also nice to work from a home base and sleep in his own bed when he came home from the Burbank studio as opposed to a faraway location motel. Jaeckel told Vernon Scott, "I spent a lot of time in the Far East, Europe, and Mexico making movies. Doing a series keeps you locked in one place, which is fine with me."

The show was fun to film. In the book *Science Fiction TV Series*, producer Ralph Sariego said, "The cast was one of the most delightful groups of people that I've ever worked with" while frequent director Ron Satloff shared, "It was a good crew, with good actors and good producers." In a *Starlog* magazine interview, director Gene Nelson brought up Jaeckel specifically: "I loved Dick Jaeckel, who played the government agent, very similar to the one he did in *Starman*. He's good in those things, but he's a better actor than that."

Jaeckel liked working with Griffith but the ambitious series was probably better suited to the original TV movie format than a weekly recurring series. On-screen magic proved difficult to write for and produce, especially as eleven follow-up episodes were rushed onto the air after the pilot. Some of the plots left a lot to be desired. The actors were kept on hold throughout the summer of 1979 as the network debated whether or not to renew the series for another full season. At this point, Jaeckel moved on. The series finally went into production, but the plug was quickly pulled in the fall of 1979 after only a few episodes were in the can. In all, eighteen episodes outside of the pilot were made but only fourteen of them aired. The series has since developed somewhat of a cult following.

Jaeckel wasted little time getting back to work with a strong guest starring role on the November 1979 *Lou Grant* episode "Witness." Detective Dan Staley (Jaeckel) is assigned to protect Ed Asner's co-star Linda Kelsey when a threat is made against her life, but their personalities clash after Jaeckel makes a mildly chauvinistic assumption and she bristles at it. Throughout the rest of the episode he has fun pushing her buttons as they argue on a variety of topical issues while holed up together in protective custody. Eventually the two grow to like one another and Jaeckel does indeed save her life from a threat. *The Seattle Daily Times* noted, "Excellent work by Richard Jaeckel as a male chauvinistic policeman."

Jaeckel's next television appearances were not traditional network fare. He guest starred as Mark Marshall on the April 1980 episode "Princess" of the long-running syndicated show *Insight*. The story is about a teenage girl (Lenora May) adjusting to the divorce of her parents (Jaeckel and Corrine Michaels). Jaeckel had two TV movies air in early 1980. *The $5.20 an Hour Dream* (1980), a well-received knock-off of the Sally Field hit *Norma Rae* (1979), stars Linda Lavin as a divorced factory worker in Oregon City striving to get assigned to the male assembly line so she can earn an extra ninety cents an hour. Jaeckel is billed second in the Russ Mayberry–directed film as Albert Kleinschmidt. Character players Burton Gilliam and Robert Davi round out the cast.

The *Tyrone Daily Herald* nicely summarizes Jaeckel's participation, writing that Lavin "gets fine support from a cast headed by Richard Jaeckel as the line foreman whose sense of fair play makes him sympathetic to her plight. Jaeckel's performance, for those who remember him from his early World War II films, is a triumph of talent over typecasting." *Cue* opined, "Nicholas Pryor and Richard Jaeckel are excellent in supporting parts as her ex-husband and foreman, respectively." *TV Guide* remarked, "Good support from Nicholas Pryor and Richard Jaeckel makes the story palatable."

Reward (1980) is a routine TV movie that was intended as a pilot for a Michael Parks series that did not sell. Jaeckel is second billed as Captain Randolph, an antagonistic cop who trades punches with the iconoclastic Parks on the basketball court and at the bar. He mellows at episode's end after Parks brings in the murderer of fellow cop Andrew Robinson. As a by-the-book superior, Jaeckel would have been a constant presence on the show despite the fact that Parks was choosing to retire from the police force to become a private detective. Jaeckel and the always interesting Parks would have been quite a weekly match, but it was not meant to be. Director E.W. Swackhamer shot on location in San Francisco.

On the big screen Jaeckel's career continued to flounder. The Walt Disney film *Herbie Goes Bananas* (1980), third in a line of sequels to the popular smart car film *The Love Bug* (1968), is one of Jaeckel's silliest credits. He plays small plane pilot Shepard, in league with moronic bad guys John Vernon and Alex Rocco in trying to find the whereabouts of hidden gold but thwarted at every opportunity by the title Volkswagen and a small Mexican boy. The Vincent McEveety–directed picture gave Jaeckel a trip to Puerto Vallarta and involved him in slapstick antics such as slipping on banana peels and wearing a banana puree over his head. Eighth-billed Jaeckel does generate a laugh of absurdity during the picture's finale when Herbie demolishes his plane into sawed-off sections and he still tries to get it into the air while worrying about oil pressure. *The Boston Herald* wrote, "As the triumvirate of bad guys, scowling appropriately, Richard Jaeckel, Alex Rocco, and John Vernon do their jobs."

Jaeckel's next assignment carried serious clout, aligning him with the man who helmed *The Godfather* (1972) and *Apocalypse Now* (1979). The prestigious Francis Ford Coppola production *Hammett* (1982) began filming in 1980 on San Francisco locations. Acclaimed German director Wim Wenders handled an ambitious story about mystery writer Dashiell Hammett (Frederic Forrest) involved in a real Bay Area detective case in the late 1920s. Jaeckel was cast in a supporting role and filmed scenes at the House of Shields bar, sharing drinks with the locals over small talk between takes. *Hammett* became a troubled production when Coppola and Wenders began to clash with approximately eighty percent of the film completed. Filming was halted and Coppola ended up reshooting much of the story on Hollywood soundstages nearly a year later. Coppola scrapped a great deal of Wenders' original footage.

Jaeckel's entire part was cut out in the reshoot, as was that of actress Sylvia Miles. Co-star Brian Keith was unavailable at the later date and his part was recast with Peter Boyle assuming the role. Original leading lady Ronee Blakely divorced Wenders and her part was completely recast with leading man Forrest's then wife Marilu Henner. *Hammett* initially opened to mixed reviews, although it would later become regarded as an intriguing period piece of great interest. Jaeckel's early participation in the original shoot is not generally known. He was no doubt paid well enough for his initial work, although he would not be able to list working with Coppola and Wenders on his résumé or reap the eventual residuals generated by repeat television showings and videocassette sales.

In 1980 Jaeckel appeared in a Canadian-produced commercial for Midas Muffler with fellow character actor John Colicos. Jaeckel plays an Army general who has his Jeep brought into the shop for a quick repair. It's a humorous thirty-second spot as Jaeckel gives the muffler work a thorough inspection and emerges satisfied. After all his years in the movie military he had finally made top-rank courtesy of Midas Muffler. Film and television actors generally avoided becoming known as commercial hawkers during this period for fear it would cost them work in their preferred fields. However, heavily syndicated commercials could pay very well over a period of time. Fellow actors Lee Van Cleef, George Kennedy, and Jack Palance were also filming spots for Midas in this time frame.

In the *Greensboro Record*, Jaeckel's son Barry talked of parallels between his golf and his dad's acting career: "I like to think of him as sort of a top 60 actor. He makes a good living at it, but he's not a superstar. And he wouldn't want it any other way. Dad enjoys his private life too much. He wouldn't want people dictating to him what to do and when to do it. You have to give up a lot the way the business is today." Barry did confess to the *Spokane Daily Chronicle* that he had a personal fondness for his dad's most rugged portrayals. "Of all the roles he's played, I like the tough guy roles best. He's a great tough guy."

Jaeckel was one of the guests on the December 1980 *Charlie's Angels* episode "Island Angels." He receives top guest star billing but it's not much of a role in the campy series known for its overemphasis on form-fitting female outfits. Jaeckel is cast as Bud Fischer, a man visiting an exclusive swinger's club in Hawaii. The crime-fighting Angels are investigating the place; when Angel Tanya Roberts snaps his photo on the golf course he proves to be excessively camera-shy. The part afforded Jaeckel a free vacation to the islands he loved and an undemanding time in the sun. While working on *Charlie's Angels* he befriended production coordinator Nancy Ellen Barr. It was a thrilling moment for Barr, who'd had a schoolgirl crush on Jaeckel for a long time. "I called him Richard," she says. "Because that's how he introduced himself to me. His good friends like Robert Fuller and Chuck Courtney called him Jake. I first met him on *Charlie's Angels* when the show went to Hawaii. *Charlie's Angels* was a difficult show to do. I went to the airport to see them off. He and I sat and chatted for quite a while.

Richard wanted me to go to Hawaii. I could have, but I didn't. I should have. I adored him. I didn't know anybody that didn't like him. A nicer man you could not meet."[20]

An actors' strike kept Jaeckel from filming anything new during the late summer of 1980. The Screen Actors Guild was negotiating residual rights for the burgeoning videocassette and pay cable industry. In the fall Jaeckel was at MGM for ...*All the Marbles* (aka *The California Dolls*) (1981), a crowd-pleasing female wrestling film from director Robert Aldrich featuring Peter Falk as the manager of Laurene Landon and Vicki Frederick. Jaeckel has a supporting role as Bill Dudley, the crooked ref in charge of the big match during the film's finale who tries his best to swing the odds in favor of the other tag team. It was a very physical performance with Jaeckel repeatedly up and down on the mat and in the middle of the action pulling the competitors off one another. Despite the brevity of the part, *The New York Times* regarded Jaeckel's role as a "funny cameo." *The Hollywood Reporter* found, "One hates Jaeckel the moment he steps into the ring." Most reviews made no mention at all of Jaeckel.

There is a bit part actor in the film named Jon Garrison Clark that had previously worked on *The Dark* and struck up a strong friendship with Jaeckel. His daughter Melody Faith Clark remembers:

> Richard Jaeckel was a great guy. I met and saw him several times. I think he and my dad met on a film set and became buddies. I know my dad dragged me into doing a tiny role on ...*All the Marbles* because he was friends with Richard. Richard was a star in that film and we were very small parts. But my dad was

Jaeckel, Vicki Frederick, Ursaline Bryant-King, and Laurene Landon do their own ring action in MGM's wrestling drama *All the Marbles* (1981). Jaeckel's roles were growing smaller, even in his friend Robert Aldrich's films.

never one of those who defined his friendships or worth by the largeness of his acting roles. He was friends with a good handful of stars, both actors and musicians. To these guys, they all considered themselves working actors and musicians, not necessarily stars, and actors who had yet to be on the map were their colleagues, which is a healthy attitude. It is about the art, and they appreciated that art. They went to theater in the little venues in town to support their other acting buddies as well. I remember going with them to a play. I think it was a version of *Moby Dick*! If you can imagine that in play form. All I can remember is a guy who looked like a sea captain and ocean wave sounds in the play and that the venue was small.

I seem to remember that Richard and my dad took Kendo workout classes together and rode horses as well. My dad took me along sometimes when they went out to dinner. Richard was a great and funny friendly guy, and I had a good time with him and my dad. Though sometimes they went out to what I considered crazy food like soul food restaurants. Pickled pigs feet was not my thing then or now. I also got dragged to a few samurai films, and as a kid, after seeing just one of those films, I never wanted to go again. All that decapitation and all was *not* for me! But since they did that Kendo stuff together, they liked going to those films. I know they discussed doing something like producing a film and were working on something very part time. Out of that came a script my dad wrote titled *Retribution, C.O.D.* Some name, huh? Anyway, life got in the way and they didn't end up having the time to do anything with it.... My father passed away of an accidental overdose of a muscle relaxant in 1982, way before Richard passed away. Richard attended my dad's funeral at Church on the Way in Van Nuys. I appreciated that so much. I saw Richard a few times after that but life took us in different directions and we kind of lost touch. It was my dad's friendship, but I appreciate the love and concern Richard had for our family.[21]

...*All the Marbles* would be the last film Jaeckel's friend Robert Aldrich would ever make. After serving as the president of the Directors Guild in the late 1970s, the iconoclastic filmmaker created several enemies within the studio system. The grand critical and commercial failure of his film *The Choirboys* (1977) was a tremendous blow to his Hollywood clout. When his movies stopped making money, he stopped getting hired to make them. Jaeckel continued to spend time visiting his friend's office and home, where they discussed potential projects, sports, and politics. At one point Aldrich was attached as the director for the Charles Bronson–Lee Marvin adventure film *Death Hunt* (1981). At that time it was known by the title *Arctic Rampage*. Had Aldrich directed that film rather than Peter Hunt, it's quite probable that Jaeckel would have played a supporting role.

Physically Aldrich had always been on the heavy side and in 1983 required surgeries to remove both his gall bladder and his spleen. Complications led to his kidneys shutting down. Aldrich hated kidney dialysis machines and the idea that he would be forever dependent on them. Coming to grips with his mortality, he demanded to be allowed to go home and die on his own terms. Jaeckel was one of those at his bedside in the final days. Legend has it that Jaeckel asked his friend if there was any last thing he could do for him. Aldrich's reply was to find him a good script. Robert Aldrich died on December 5, 1983, at the age of 65.

The lives and careers of Jaeckel's other prime benefactors Don Siegel and Sam Peckinpah were also coming to a close. Hence, Jaeckel's chances to be cast in further films by these once top-of-the-line auteurs became nil. Hollywood quickly forgets and the entire film business seemed to be in transition in the 1980s. Drive-ins and grindhouses were going out of business and mall cineplexes were sprouting up around the country. Movies increasingly needed to appeal to the teenage demographic and the MTV generation. Commercialism did away with the intimate theatrical drama and the quick assembly line of television became the only outlet for many established actors. By the end of the decade, even TV would soon move away from the expensive hour action drama to more cost-controlled sitcoms and reality television. Good actors such as Jaeckel were often left out in the cold and scrambling for work if they hadn't made wise investments over the years or built up a comfortable nest egg.

Fortunately for Jaeckel, there was more in the way of TV work during this period. His most memorable credit during these years was the shocking two-part *Little House on the Prairie* episode "Sylvia" airing in February of 1981. Jaeckel appears as Walnut Grove blacksmith Irv Hartwig, rapist of fourteen-year-old Sylvia (Olivia Barash). He commits the assault wearing a blank white clown mask that proved extremely scary for the many youngsters who watched the show. Throughout the episode Jaeckel comes across as caring and concerned, a wolf in sheep's clothing. It was a risky, top-notch part that Jaeckel nailed. Three decades later *Little House* watchers still recall the power of the character and the performance. Series star Michael Landon directed the episode with great sensitivity for the subject matter. On her website, Olivia Barash commented: "That particular cast of actors was amazing to work with. From Matthew Laborteaux to Royal Dano, who played my abusive father, to Richard Jaeckel who played the rapist. All highly professional veterans and genuinely good people."

Jaeckel was not afraid to push the envelope and accept challenging material, even though these tricky roles could have an immediate negative effect on his career. He had played a rapist in *Town Without Pity* and the gay teacher on *Carter Country*. Now he was being seen on screen as a sexual deviant preying on an innocent girl in a wholesome family-oriented show. There had to be some second-guessing going on in Jaeckel's camp. These roles are somewhat surprising given his predilection for never rocking the boat. Then again, he rarely said no when work was offered. He would gladly accept any part and play the role to the best of his ability. It should be noted that in retrospect the gay teacher and the child rapist are barely if ever mentioned nowadays in connection with Jaeckel. He is remembered as a screen soldier, cowboy, cop, or forceful tough-talking villain. However, at the time Jaeckel had to be wondering what direction his career was heading in. On a personal note, Jaeckel's mother Millicent died in December of 1981.

There was more TV roles, none of it particularly impactful. Jaeckel filmed an unsold Paramount TV pilot entitled *Hot W.A.C.S.* (aka *Soldier Girls*), playing the sexist Major Phillip Seabrook. The thirty-minute pilot aired June 1, 1981, with Julie Payne headlining. The February 1982 *King's Crossing* episode "Home Front" cast Jaeckel as Josh McCall opposite series star Bradford Dillman. In the *Cassie & Company* episode "Friend in Need" (July 1982), Jaeckel was cast as Captain Rowan, the former police mentor of Angie Dickinson's private eye; he's now embroiled in a messy death involving the husband of his mistress. It was broadcast after the series had been cancelled and the network was merely looking for summer filler to air. At least it was a role with a little meat to it.

McClain's Law reunited Jaeckel with his old surfing pal James Arness in a modern cop series set in the California harbor town of San Pedro. Jaeckel is cast as Josh Lawford, the owner of a marine supply store who decides to take the law into his own hands after his shop is robbed by young punks Joe Pantoliano and James Russo. Jaeckel buys a .357 Magnum and learns how to use it, but also has to deal with the gravity of taking a life when the criminals return. Veteran cop Arness helps guide him. Vigilantism was a popular subject at the time given the success of Charles Bronson in *Death Wish* (1974) and Jaeckel rises to the acting challenge. It's a good role and even affords Jaeckel a romantic subplot with actress Shelia Larken. He is believable throughout. The episode "What Patric Doesn't Know" aired in February of 1982. Despite the presence of fan favorite Arness, the show was not renewed for a second season.

Some of Jaeckel's past projects were still getting spotty regional theatrical release. Jaeckel had filmed the $800,000 independent film *Cold River* (1982) in October of 1978 in the

Adirondacks and Saranac Lake in New York State. The solid family drama concerning a young sister and brother (Suzanne Weber and Pat Petersen) lost in the wilderness was based on William Judson's novel and directed by Fred G. Sullivan. Jaeckel receives special billing for his appearance as the children's likable father Mike Allison, a mountain guide who sets out to take his kids on an instructional canoe and camping trip. Jaeckel suffers a fatal heart attack while rowing the boat and the children are left to brave the wilderness on their own. In full family man mode, Jaeckel is very good in his brief part. Leonard Maltin opined, "Jaeckel is wasted," but *Variety* called him "excellent" and "one of Hollywood's most underrated actors."

Blood Song (aka *Dream Slayer*) (1982) from director Alan J. Levi was a different story. It was a low-budget, mostly ridiculous psychological horror film attempting to cash in on the hot slasher genre. Singing star Frankie Avalon is an odd casting choice as the flute-playing killer, stalking teenager Donna Wilkes because she received his blood after a transfusion. Jaeckel is far more plausible as Wilkes' abusive, alcoholic father Frank Hauser. He does a good job with what he is given; commanding the screen as he rants and raves about his daughter's perceived promiscuity. The volatile Jaeckel steps up to confront an axe-wielding Avalon in a violent fight where Jaeckel is repeatedly hacked but still manages to knock Avalon around. It is by far the bloodiest of Jaeckel's many screen deaths. Shot in Coos Bay and North Bend, Oregon, *Blood Song* was a film that Jaeckel did not particularly enjoy making due to its subject matter.

While in Oregon, Jaeckel drove over to the seaside town of Newport and Mo's Annex to surprise Bonnie Stout, his hair stylist friend from the making of *Sometimes a Great Notion* over a decade earlier. She was told there was someone at the salon who needed their hair cut but she had no idea it was Jaeckel. It was a great surprise to find Jaeckel sitting in her chair with a big smile when she arrived. They embraced, shared a kiss, and went to lunch to catch up on old times. There was no attempt to follow up on their missed-out-on romance. It was merely an opportunity for them both to recall with great fondness the memorable summer of 1970 when the Oregon locals blended so well with the Hollywood stars. Stout says:

> It's beautiful here in Newport. It's so friendly. That's one of the things that they all loved about Newport was how friendly and open everyone was. It wasn't just because they were movie stars. People here are like that all the time. It was a magical time for everyone. When he came back many years later he looked me up and wanted his hair cut again. He was making a film in Coos Bay. I said, "Maybe I could drive down to Coos Bay and watch you guys work." He said, "I wish you wouldn't. I'm not very happy that I chose to work on this film. I'm not happy with it at all." He seemed very disgusted with whatever it was. It was something that he wasn't pleased that he agreed to do.... He didn't age, and he didn't change in appearance at all. That was one of the first things Mo said to him. "Oh, my God! How come you look so young?" Richard just laughed and said he didn't realize he looked so young. It was an exciting and interesting time in my life, and all I can say is that he was a wonderful friend and a wonderful person.[22]

Paramount's *Airplane II: The Sequel* (1982) from director Ken Finkleman recycles many of the jokes from the 1980 original hit *Airplane!* and parades a large cast of familiar faces such as Rip Torn, John Vernon, John Dehner, Chad Everett, Kent McCord, and Raymond Burr spoofing their strait-laced images. Lloyd Bridges and Peter Graves return from the first film, effectively joined by Chuck Connors and William Shatner as they try to rescue a space shuttle dangerously hurtling toward the sun with a crazed bomber (Sonny Bono) on board. Their only hope is Robert Hays, the confidence-shaken pilot from the first film. In regard to their destination and the extenuating circumstances, space traffic controller Jaeckel memorably intones, "They're screwed."

He is far down the cast list with twenty-third billing as the nameless "Controller #2," although Bridges calls him Stinson at one point. It's an odd assignment for a one-time Oscar nominee. Jaeckel is given a few humorous bits but the part is hardly worthy of his talents or his reputation. It's almost as if he was hired for the film to be on retainer in case military presence Shatner suddenly opted not to make fun of the years that he spent commanding the *Enterprise* on TV's *Star Trek*. One could see Jaeckel being an optimum second choice to step in and play a space commander, particularly Shatner whom he had repeatedly been mistaken for on the street. As it turns out, Jaeckel plays Controller #2. He does it well and he does it nearly anonymously. When it was over, Jaeckel simply moved on to his next job.

There was one missed opportunity during this period in the form of a key role in the action film *First Blood* (1982) starring Sylvester Stallone as Vietnam vet John Rambo. Lee Marvin had originally been approached to appear opposite Stallone as the highly trained soldier's Special Forces mentor but turned the role down after reading the script. Kirk Douglas was eventually signed for the part of Colonel Sam Trautman, the man who comes to a Pacific Northwest town that is waging a personal war against Stallone to warn the sheriff Brian Dennehy what he has gotten himself into. Both Marvin and Douglas were high-powered names who could bring gravitas to the movie. However, due to creative differences with Stallone and director Ted Kotcheff, Douglas left the picture at the start of filming. An immediate replacement was needed for Douglas, and actor Richard Crenna stepped in at a moment's notice, making Trautman the signature role of his career. No doubt Jaeckel would also have made an excellent choice to play the experienced military hard-case, but he was either working on something else or not approached at all. Jaeckel explained the process of landing a career-defining role to syndicated writer Pat Hilton: "The reason you have it could be luck, could be timing, could be a million different things besides talent. It doesn't mean you're the only one who can do the job. It only means you have it."

Jaeckel continued taking what offers came his way as a TV guest on formula shows. Each guest shot would be filmed at a fast pace in no more than a single week, leaving long gaps between jobs. On the January 1983 episode of the light detective series *Matt Houston*, "Rock and a Hard Place," Jaeckel played shady boxing promoter Kip Williams, investigated by star Lee Horsley as a murder suspect. The series was enjoyable, the part undemanding. Later that month he was on the campy *Fantasy Island* episode "Operation Manhunt" in which fellow guest Ben Murphy attempts to rescue government double agent Kodiak (Jaeckel) from a fortress-like prison. The once popular Ricardo Montalban series often teetered on the edge of outright silliness, but offered employment to a wide variety of weekly guest stars. As always, Jaeckel was grateful for the opportunity to work. "I don't go along with the old-timers who say the business is going to the dogs," Jaeckel told *The Washington Post*. "There are changes and you've got to adjust to them, but if you keep plugging away, you'll get the opportunities.... I can't complain. I've managed to adjust to changes in the business and keep on acting and surviving. I've had my share of good breaks."

In 1983 Jaeckel journeyed to the Bahamas to be the guest of his friend Robert Fuller for an episode of Fuller's syndicated television series *Fishing Fever*. Each episode featured a fishing or diving excursion with Fuller and one of his Hollywood pals such as Doug McClure, Jock Mahoney, or Ron Ely. "We had a marvelous time," Fuller says. "We had ten days on that in the Bahamas to scuba dive and deep sea fish. Jake was fearless. I don't know that he had done scuba that much before but he didn't hesitate. He went right down to 50 to 60 feet. It was a lot of fun."[23]

Fuller and Jaeckel began working on putting together a film of their own, *Prisoners of the Sea*. "We came up with a great story," Fuller says. "John Champion, my producer from *Laramie*, wrote it. Everything was going our way and we were going to film in the Bahamas. We even had the cast set—Jock Mahoney, Bill Smith, and Aldo Ray were going to be in it. A beauty queen was tested for the female lead. It would have been an independent—a movie for TV with a budget of around three million. In the end the producer failed to come up with the money and we didn't get to make it."

Coming hot on the heels of the big screen success of the military comedies *Private Benjamin* (1980) and *Stripes* (1981), the Army sitcom *At Ease* was given the network green light in early 1983 by ABC. Never mind that *M*A*S*H* had been mining this vein for the better part of a decade, *At Ease* attempted to be sillier and more of a throwback to the shenanigans seen on Phil Silvers' *Sgt. Bilko* series from the late 1950s. David Naughton and comedian Jimmie Walker were cast as con artists with Jaeckel given the part of their beleaguered straight man Major Hawkins. Roger Bowen, George Wyner, Josh Mostel, John Vargas, and Jourdan Fremin rounded out the cast. Jaeckel had been looking to do a comedy for at least the past decade, telling the *Montreal Gazette*, "It's something I've never done, though some of the films seemed that way."

George Wyner, Richard Jaeckel, Jimmie Walker, and Steve Nevil in the short-lived ABC-TV series *At Ease* (1983). Jaeckel was cast as the bellicose Major Hawkins.

Jaeckel's Hawkins was an intense, often chauvinistic gung ho man of action lost during peace time while dealing with the shady maneuverings of his administrative unit recruits at Camp Tar Creek. Physical humor was derived from Jaeckel smashing through locked doors, running an obstacle course, performing late-night calisthenics, golfing in a hurricane, and becoming stone-faced on pain medication after breaking an ankle jumping from a plane. Jaeckel had fun with some fanciful wordplay on the need to adapt to adapting in the new Army, but for the most part *At Ease* was a misfire complete with annoying laugh track. None of the characters resembled real people that the audience could identify with. The Aaron Spelling–produced show premiered as a replacement series in the spring of 1983 and was off the air for good by mid–July after only fourteen episodes.

Reviews for *At Ease* were not very kind although Jaeckel generally escaped unscathed from a critical blasting as the rules- and regulations-barking major. Although the episodes have never been released to home video, they have surfaced on the Internet. Cleveland's *Plain Dealer* noted that Jaeckel "stole the premiere as a super macho major, who imagines he's still in a commando outfit rather than one dedicated to computer technology." *Variety* claimed that Jaeckel was "trapped in this fiasco." *TV Guide* commented, "Jaeckel as Hawkins gets a good line now and then, as when he barks, 'Wars will always be fought by men with bombs, guns, and bayonets, the way civilized people have been doing it for centuries.' But I have never thought of Jaeckel as a comedian, and now I'm pretty sure I'm not going to."

Regarding his decision to once again tread the waters of a weekly series, Jaeckel commented to the *Aiken Standard*: "I'm sometimes asked why do I do a television series. To me, that's a stupid question. You can say that you enjoy eating or that you enjoy working. But what an actor most enjoys is a successful TV series. In my opinion it's a gamble worth taking.... I've been in this business forty years. I consider myself fortunate coming in at the tail end of the feature business. I got a taste of the glamour. It's not all gone today, but you have to hunt for it."

Character actor George Wyner enjoyed the experience of working closely with Jaeckel and remembers:

> One of the nice things about working in this business when you're younger is the established people you get to work with. It's like, "This is great. Look who I'm working with today." Richard was famous for, among other things, never aging and being the eternal boy soldier in World War II movies. We had a young company on that show, and Richard was the seasoned veteran. I think he was a little out of his element in some ways. It was a silly sitcom show and I think it surprised him that they even wanted him for it. But Richard's straight-ahead delivery without trying to be funny was perfect and actually very funny. That's why he was a perfect choice for that. He and I were kind of foils for each other. We got to do a fair amount together which was fun. He and James Garner were alike in many ways. Garner was beloved by the crews he worked with because of how he treated everybody.
>
> When you get on set they have breakfast for you or you can put in an order. In our case you could also order lunch. At some point during the run we got word that they were not going to be providing lunch any more. It wasn't a big deal. We were regulars on a series and could all afford lunch, but it was a bit of an indication to us, a crack in the armor. I'll never forget what Richard did about it because he liked having his lunch delivered to the set. The next day we gave our breakfast order and when it came Richard called me over. He lifted the lid to his breakfast box and inside was roast chicken. Richard had ordered lunch for breakfast. That's how he got around the "no free lunch" rule. He had this big smile on his face because he obviously cared more about lunch than breakfast. He was going to get his free lunch by simply ordering it for breakfast. I remember how clever I thought that was and the smile on his face. He had that boyish face still and a little boy look about him like he pulled something off on his parents. It was a small victory, but he enjoyed that he had outsmarted these producers. He stashed it away and when the time came he had it for lunch. He was the only one they actually kept providing lunch for although they never knew it. It encapsuled Richard, the veteran who knew how to get around it. He enjoyed the little gamesmanship of it

all. It was kind of adorable. You don't think of adorable when you think of Richard, but that was a very cute little moment. He was a good man and I have good memories.[24]

Nancy Ellen Barr, whom Jaeckel met on *Charlie's Angels*, worked on the TV series *At Ease* and had a production office at Warner Bros. During this period she was also a part of putting together the casting for Jaeckel and Robert Fuller's would-be film *Prisoners of the Sea*. She began to see Jaeckel at the studio on a regular basis and he always made time to shoot the breeze and see how her day was going. Barr recalls of Jaeckel: "He would stop by all the time and chat. He was such a nice, sweet man."[25]

Jaeckel's perennial good nature masked the disappointment that no doubt existed in regard to the trajectory of his career. He knew the business well, how an actor could be up one minute and down the next. It had been over ten years since he was riding high with his Oscar nomination, and there had been many professional disappointments since. He couldn't get a TV series to stick, literally enduring four half-season failures in that time. The episodic TV he did do now was little more than time-filling fluff. Still, he remained consistent in his acting approach even if the quality of the parts he took had become wildly inconsistent. Some of it was no doubt the result of poor choices, some of it was his only choice. He had never been opposed to taking small parts in big movies, but now it seemed he was being offered too many small parts in small movies. Some of his better work was unaired and gathering dust, offering little chance for an immediate change.

The Awakening of Candra (1983) is one such case. A frank and absorbing TV movie from director Paul Wendkos, it stars Blanche Baker and Cliff DeYoung as her brainwashing kidnapper. Jaeckel is featured as small town sheriff Robert Harrison, assigned to investigate the apparent accidental shooting of the girl's husband by DeYoung. It's a story Baker backs, sort of. Although billed third, Jaeckel is essentially the male lead and carries the story as the sympathetic cop whose gut instinct leads him to reopen the closed case and bring in psychiatrist friend Jeffrey Tambor to help. It was filmed in Kern River, California, in 1981 but initially shelved due to its sometimes brutal depiction of the girl's abuse. Jaeckel did fine work as the driven and concerned lawman, but the film found no audience.

Local actor Dan Moberly had a small part and his interaction with Jaeckel is a fine example of the consideration Jaeckel showed for his co-workers.

> I will never forget the first time I met Richard. I had a location call time of 0700 a.m. in Kernville, California, a small town located near Lake Isabella in Kern County. It was a beautiful crisp summer morning. After meeting up with the property master, they sent me to check in with wardrobe, and established a check-in time with makeup. Catering was serving breakfast so I went for a cup of coffee and sat down at a row of tables and looked over the shot-list for the day. A gentleman walked up to the table wearing a light windbreaker and holding a cup of coffee and asked if he could join me at the table. I responded back to him as I stood up and shook his hand that he offered out to me. At this time I knew this man looked familiar to me but didn't know who he was or his purpose in being on location.
>
> I recall that he was short in stature. I had noticed as we sat there that he was wearing shoes that had thicker soles than you would normally see. Richard was very friendly and interested in me and engaged me in conversation, asking what my job was on location. While we sat and talked for a while, he finally said, "Should we grab some breakfast?" He went to the buffet line loaded with hot food, grabbed some scrambled eggs, potatoes, some mixed fruit, and a slice of toast. We both went right back and sat down. At this point I still did not know who I was sitting with eating breakfast! I soon realized that I had breakfast with one of the principal actors working on this movie location.

Local actor Dan Moberly had a small part and his interaction with Jaeckel is a fine example of the consideration Jaeckel showed for his co-workers. There was no one on a film set too big or too small for Jaeckel. Moberly remembers:

My role for the day was to portray a Canby County sheriff's deputy. As it turned out I ended up working three days with Richard on various locations north of the lake and up in the high forest area of the Kern River. He was the chief of police, in which case I actually had several shots with him. I even had him riding shotgun in a half day worth of shooting us coming up in a sheriff car in which I drove us into the shot as we were called out to investigate the shooting. I remember Richard Jaeckel as a very talented character actor and a fantastic man.[26]

Jaeckel made two very minor films during this period, one of which he top-lined. *The Fix* (aka *The Agitators*) (1984) was filmed in Wilmington, North Carolina, in the summer of 1983 by director Will Zens. Jaeckel stars as federal agent Charles Dale, trying to take down drug smugglers led by veteran tough guy actors Vince Edwards, Robert Tessier, and Charles Dierkop. It's a low-budget, amateurish quickie that's buoyed by Jaeckel's professionalism and little else. Former swimming champion Edwards' career had taken a long and dramatic slide since his heyday of popularity as the TV doctor Ben Casey in the early 1960s. Edwards' chief obstacle thwarting his career was a well-publicized obsession with gambling at the horse track that became all-consuming and earned him a bad reputation and several ex-wives. Despite Jaeckel's long-standing good reputation in Hollywood, he and Edwards both found themselves starring side by side in this direct-to-video release.

Even when he was stuck in a film beneath his talents, Jaeckel maintained his personal code of professionalism and his forever friendly demeanor on location. He fit in well with fellow character actors such as Dierkop from TV's *Police Woman*. Dierkop recalls, "He was a great man to work with, always seemed to have a smile on his face and talk a lot about his son who played professional golf. He was very proud of him."[27]

Killing Machine (aka *Goma 2*) (1984) is a low-budget international action feature filmed in Spain and Mexico by director Jose Antonio de la Loma. Jaeckel is cast as Martin, henchman to main heavy Lee Van Cleef. Jaeckel does some evil deeds and for his trouble is beaten up by former hit man hero George "Jorge" Rivero, torched, then blown up in a car to ensure he's dead as payback for Rivero's wife's murder. Although he's special billed, it's a rather thankless part for Jaeckel. Margaux Hemingway, Ana Obregon, Willie Aames, and Aldo Sambrell also starred. The violent movie eventually surfaced on video on a cassette hosted by the buxom Sybil Danning. Regarding the overall quality of his many films, Jaeckel told the *Register Star*, "I could sure tell you the good ones real quick."

The 1983–1984 television season saw Jaeckel doing his due diligence. He appeared on two courtroom episodes of the top-rated nighttime soap opera *Dallas* playing the professionally manipulative prosecuting attorney Percy Meredith. Both appearances saw him performing expertly with Charles Aidman as the judge and Glenn Corbett as series regular Steve Kanaly's defense attorney. Jaeckel got to grill both Patrick Duffy and Charlene Tilton on the witness stand in a controversial euthanasia case. His episodes "Ray's Trial" and "The Oil Baron's Ball" aired in November 1983. "I knew him from Gold's Gym and we had a lot of mutual friends," *Dallas* director Michael Preece recalls.

> He was friends with a lot of stuntmen. He lived in the Palisades and I used to see him over there. I was not a close friend but I knew him well. He was a terrific guy. He came to a few parties at my home and we used to have lunch together with Brad Harris at a place called Patrick's Roadhouse on the Pacific Highway. One time all he had was fruit, and I remember thinking that was how he stayed in such good shape. He ate very well. He liked to drink a little but didn't overdo it. He was always hard as a rock. He had an overly firm handshake and would always squeeze your bicep when greeting. We used to go down near the

old Muscle Beach on the outside equipment and do dips and chins. He'd say that was all you needed to do to stay in shape was dips and chins. For him and his frame, it worked.

I only worked with him that one time on *Dallas*. The producer Lenny Katzman was a friend of his as well and suggested Jaeckel, and I agreed he'd be perfect for the part. He had a lot of dialogue on that show playing an attorney. It was kind of a different role for him in a suit and tie. He always looked great. He'd be forty years old and still playing privates in war films and look the part. If you look at his films, he never had long stretches of dialogue. Everything was a little shorter. I knew him well enough that before we shot, he came up to me and said, "Can you help me?" He was having problems with all the words and asked if I could break it up. We did it a little bit at a time and he was perfect. As an actor he was very professional. Always on time. Socially, if you were going to meet him for lunch, he was there when he said he would be. I think he was a devoted father and very proud of Barry's golf accomplishments. It would be hard to ever say anything bad about him. He was a good guy and it seemed like he knew everybody.[28]

On a January 1984 episode of *The Love Boat*, "Bet On," Jaeckel is Frank Bannon, a shady gambler in Monte Carlo who drags his sister (Celeste Holm) and an innocent new bride (Leah Ayres) into his world of debt. Jaeckel gets to play several facets to his character, but it is nonetheless extremely odd seeing him on the kitschy show. The premise of the short-lived series *Masquerade* presented espionage agent Rod Taylor recruiting everyday citizens for undercover assignments around the globe with Chuck Courtney coordinating the action. The April 1984 episode "Spanish Gambit" takes place in Barcelona, Spain, and guest stars Jaeckel as Tucker, Taylor's competitive peer. The two old pros engage in entertaining repartee, and Jaeckel gets the opportunity to kick in doors and forward roll into rooms with his gun drawn.

Jaeckel as no-nonsense government agent George Fox in Columbia's *Starman* (1984). The popular sci-fi film gave Jaeckel's career a needed boost.

Jaeckel looks sharp in his sport jacket and tie and in some scenes even dons military fatigues. However, hardly anyone tuned in. It was another show that aired and quickly disappeared.

After a string of low-budget run-of-the-mill films, bit part cameos, undistinguished TV guest shots, and short-lived series, Jaeckel was in need of something high-profile for the sake of his career. He got that role in John Carpenter's *Starman* (1984) playing National Security agent George Fox, the tenacious bureaucrat ruthlessly hunting down Karen Allen and the title alien in human form (played by Jeff Bridges). The gentle sci-fi film was a sleeper hit that connected with audiences and garnered Bridges an Oscar nomination. Jaeckel received his greatest level of exposure in a number of years, playing a part that seemed like Jack Klinger's nastier brother from *Salvage 1*. Jaeckel ratcheted up the on-screen meanness a notch, dead-set on dissecting the alien whether it comes in peace or not. His character is driven and unsympathetic, and he doesn't try to humanize it. Throughout the film, Bridges' alien grows more human than Jaeckel. At one point when arguing with scientist Charles Martin Smith, Jaeckel utters the immortal and oft-quoted line, "I'll have you eviscerated."

Critics responded in mixed fashion to Jaeckel's character and performance with *Variety* noting, "Jaeckel, as the head heavy, is so one-dimensional and simplistic as to deny the immediacy and urgency of the hunt." *The New York Times* labeled the subplot "somewhat gratuitous" but found that Jaeckel and Charles Martin Smith "bring conviction to their roles." *The Morning Call* gave props to Jaeckel and Smith for their "fine supporting acting." The *Oregonian* had problems with the way Jaeckel's part was written but noted, "Jaeckel at least does a good job playing the jerk," while the *Deseret News* called him "the epitome of the evil government agent." The *Williamson Daily News* added, "Richard Jaeckel, best known for his numerous roles as arrogant bad guys, finds himself cast in the same type here. In fact, Jaeckel may be at his most despicable in this film." *L.A. Weekly* wrote, "Everyone involved with this film has done their best work ever. More than fine are Charles Martin Smith and Richard Jaeckel as the good and bad government agents whose adversarial positions give the film much of its dramatic thrust." *The Dispatch* echoed those comments, saying that Jaeckel and Smith gave "good supporting performances." The *Herald-Journal* was more direct in its praise of Jaeckel: "Richard Jaeckel effectively portrays the role of Fox, a hard-nosed, by-the-book government agent."

Director Carpenter talked to *Starlog* magazine regarding Jaeckel, saying, "I'm a longtime fan of him. Richard is a really good actor, a lot of fun to work with. He has a real presence on the screen." Character actor David Wells was working on one of his first films and was cast as Jaeckel's assistant in *Starman*. He recalls that on the set, Jaeckel was "a total gentleman. I was new to Hollywood and I remember how he treated the crew and the director, Mr. Carpenter, by always saying, 'Yes, sir.' Just old school film etiquette. Taught me a lot about working on a big time movie set."[29]

Jaeckel didn't sit on his laurels. On episodic television he guest starred as murderous corporate heavy Joe Stanton on the action series *Cover Up* in the January 1985 episode "Murder Offshore." A bespectacled Jaeckel wears a suit and tie and spends the episode instructing underling Jesse Vint to recover a disc with a valuable oil drilling geological survey for the Gulf of Mexico. His plans fall apart due to the heroics of undercover fashion model-espionage agents Jennifer O'Neill and Anthony Hamilton. The globe-hopping series lasted only one season. It's known now only for the on-set death of the show's original male lead Jon-Erik Hexum when he recklessly shot himself with a blank load from a firearm.

Typical of a fast-paced TV production, Jaeckel was in and out and done in a matter of days. Fellow character actor Jesse Vint is best known for starring in the independent drive-in hit *Macon County Line* (1974) and performing bits in films such as *Little Big Man* (1970) and *Chinatown* (1974). He comments on his brief working relationship with Jaeckel: "I didn't know him well at all. When working on *Cover Up* we barely talked. He was a man to himself, without being aloof. He was highly professional, listening and responding to the director's wishes with an absolute respect for the storyteller. He would always say, 'Yes sir.' 'No sir.' 'Thank you, sir.' That's all I remember."[30]

The Dirty Dozen enjoyed sustained success since its original 1967 release and had become regarded as a classic. Inexplicably, there was a clamor to revisit the surviving characters and the basic format of their World War II exploits. Lee Marvin was approached with a hefty monetary offer to reprise his role as Major Reisman for a quick telefilm. Marvin's career had endured many bumps over the past decade and with a little arm-twisting he was persuaded to sign on for the money. His only further request according to the *Syracuse Herald-Journal* was, "Get Jaeckel. I need my sergeant."

With Marvin aboard, Jaeckel and Ernest Borgnine were also asked to reprise their original roles. As character actors they had less artistic control in turning down the promise of a paycheck. "Where's my helmet?" Jaeckel asked, ready once again to go into battle with his old pal. Unfortunately, the hard-living Marvin had aged significantly during the nearly eighteen years between the original and its sequel, a time period which represented only eighteen months between the narrative of the films. Even the ever ageless Jaeckel would have a difficult time pulling off that miracle of contrivance. Still, Jaeckel stuck up for the casting of Marvin in the action film, telling the *Syracuse Herald-Journal*, "I don't know any young guys who'd have the juice to keep up with him."

Jaeckel revisits the role of Sgt. Clyde Bowren in the NBC telemovie *The Dirty Dozen: Next Mission* (1985). Despite eighteen years between films, his soldier uniform still fit.

The TV movie *The Dirty Dozen: The Next Mission* (1985) was filmed over six weeks in a cold and rainy England by Andrew V. McLaglen in late 1984. The basic format of the original is reprised as Marvin's Reisman and Jaeckel's Bowren recruit a new dirty dozen consisting of Ken Wahl, Larry Wilcox, Gavin O'Herlihy, Sonny Landham et al. Incredibly, dialogue passages from the original were lifted word for word. It had to be odd for Jaeckel and Marvin to be revisiting these characters and their interaction in such a manner. Nevertheless, Jaeckel was very pleased to be working once again with Marvin. He told *Daredevils* magazine: "When I was asked to do this sequel, I felt happiness and a great sense of appreciation for Bob Aldrich, who cast me in the original.

It's been terrific working with Lee again, and I've known Andy McLaglen a good many years. I worked for him in *The Devil's Brigade*."

In 1970 Marvin abruptly ended a relationship with girlfriend Michelle Triola and married a former childhood sweetheart. Marvin and his new wife Pamela soon moved away from Malibu and settled in Tucson, Arizona. In her memoirs, Pamela Marvin recounts her own sentimental feelings upon eventually meeting Jaeckel. She writes a passage about World War II, saying: "In the movies the bad guys were all 'Japs' or 'Krauts.' The good guys were John Wayne and our own wonderfully handsome, boyish and blond Richard Jaeckel. When I met Richard Jaeckel many years later, I felt an immediate rush of warmth, familiarity, and love for him and the time we had 'gone through' together: me as a teenager sitting on a stiff wooden chair, eyes glued to the screen watching him crawl through the mud on Guadalcanal."

The critical reception for *Next Mission* was decidedly lukewarm, although *Variety* wrote, "Ernest Borgnine and Richard Jaeckel repeat their roles from the original picture and do well this time around." Jaeckel did enjoy some much-needed publicity for the *Dirty Dozen* reunion and discussed the notion of typecasting when interviewed by the *Syracuse Herald-Journal*. "It's been around as long as you and I," he said. "But I don't buy the guy who says, 'I don't do crap. I only do Hamlet.' There's nothing wrong with having the car come to take you to the studio. It doesn't make you a lesser person. My boys are both over 30 and I must have done something right. They both want to be around me. I'm not an S.O.B. all the time."

The boost in exposure segued nicely into the part Jaeckel had been waiting for when another potential TV show based on a literary property appeared on the horizon. Jaeckel was cast as a police superior named Lt. Martin Quirk in the pilot film for *Spenser: For Hire* (1985). Produced by John Wilder and directed by Lee Katzin, the high-quality series opener starred Robert Urich as writer Robert B. Parker's much-beloved boxer turned cerebral Boston sleuth, who is as quick to quote Wordsworth as he is to punch out a bad guy. Spenser is a man of honor committed to his school guidance counselor girlfriend Susan (Barbara Stock) but is tough enough to stand up to local enforcer Hawk (Avery Brooks), a fascinating character who makes threats through a charismatic smile. The two men respect one another and often end up working as allies even when plot machinations send them in opposing directions. Hawk would eventually warrant his own spin-off series *A Man Called Hawk* and deservedly so. Spenser also enjoys a healthy friendship with Jaeckel's cop character—until bodies start piling up or he ruffles too many influential feathers. At that point Jaeckel can turn as hard-nosed as ever—though the camera often lingers on him after Urich has gone to reveal the beginnings of a smile on the tough cop's face.

To say that Jaeckel had played this kind of role before would be redundant. He got the part precisely because he had played it so many times and always done it well. Audience recognition goes a long way when a TV show is broadcast into a family's home and by this point of his career Jaeckel was an "old friend" to many a TV demographic. The producers (led by *Centennial* alum John Wilder) hired him for his work ethic and reputation and Jaeckel delivered. He was able to flesh the character out a bit over time and give him a background beyond the standard police chief role. War veteran Marty Quirk was married with two grown daughters, although one later story arc explored him having an extramarital affair. His wife was played in two episodes by Oscar nominee Shirley Knight. Quirk was also a fan of the Boston Red Sox baseball team, loyal to his friend Spenser, and always suspicious of the activities of Hawk. Jaeckel made Quirk as interesting and three-dimensional as this type of role gets.

Series writer-producer-director Wilder recalls casting Jaeckel on *Spenser*:

> When I was at Warner Bros. and put *Spenser: For Hire* on ABC, he was the only person I considered for the part of Lt. Quirk. He wasn't physically what Bob Parker had written in his novels, but Bob loved Dick in the part. I especially loved directing him in the first episode after the two-hour pilot; we had a good time, shared a lot of laughs and got some good dramatic scenes together. He had a real presence on screen because he was a real person. His acting was natural, truthful, and always effective.... What I knew of him I truly liked. He was a guy's guy, modest and self-effacing, as professional as they come and as personable.[31]

Critics agreed, with *TV Guide* writing, "The inevitable police lieutenant with whom a private eye must maintain a love-hate relationship is played by the fine character actor Richard Jaeckel, who to our knowledge has never given less than a first-rate performance, no matter the role he is given." *Newsweek* concurred: "Adding weight to Robert Urich in the lead part are the ever-excellent Richard Jaeckel and Avery Brooks as Hawk." *The New York Times* called Jaeckel's character "well-conceived."

Taking into account the built-in audience from Parker's books, the absorbing series was an easy sell to the network. Real Boston area locations kept everything looking fresh and different from anything else on the air. It appeared Jaeckel might have finally found the TV vehicle he'd been searching for. Despite being shuffled around on the schedule, *Spenser* pulled modest Nielsen ratings, garnered decent reviews, and seemed to be resonating with viewers. Jaeckel commented on his lack of television luck to the *Boston Herald*: "I've done about three or four of them. They all went belly up after about episode fifteen.... I think [*Spenser*] has unlimited potential if they use all the possibilities of the story. The story is the whole thing, with all due respect to the actors."

Co-star Ron McLarty played a cop in Jaeckel's department named Sgt. Frank Belson—a character somewhat similar to the humorous Biff Elliot in *The Dark* with his messy donut-eating. "We kind of play the comedy relief, you might say," Jaeckel related to the *Herald*. "We enjoy it. Hopefully, though, we will be a little more important to the series this year. When you have four or five principles, the top three are usually in it most of the time, as it should be. As numbers four and five, we are in and out. Then somewhere along the line we are given a show where we are featured. At those times you get to do a little bit more."

When Jaeckel worked on the pilot in the snowy spring of 1985, he stayed at the Fox and Hounds hotel in Boston. When the series began, he was stationed across the river at the Charles Hotel. As was typical of Jaeckel's friendly demeanor he easily made acquaintances in his new digs. A few months later he surprised the Fox and Hounds restaurant staff by dropping in to say hello and catch up. He ultimately lived in Cambridge, Massachusetts, for nine months while shooting the show's debut season. Wife Antoinette would visit him. "She likes it very much," Jaeckel told the *Boston Herald*. "Sometimes I'll rent a car and drive to Gloucester or see the mansions in Newport. I take a lot of walks along the Charles River."

At times shooting on location could be strenuous, but all involved felt the quality of the show was worth it. Jaeckel even did print and media publicity for the series, making a rare TV interview appearance on ABC's *Good Morning, America* in July of 1985. The *Spenser* cast became fairly tight-knit, buoyed by the presence of the likable leading man Robert Urich. In that sense, Jaeckel fit right in. Veteran supporting actor and writer Ron McLarty recalls, "Richard was the most complete and generous person I have ever worked with. He was probably the most giving actor I have ever played opposite. He was one of a kind and writing this reminds me of just how very much I miss him."[32]

Jaeckel and Ron McLarty are bundled up for the Warner Bros. TV series *Spenser: For Hire* (1985–1987). The popular series filmed on location in Boston, Massachusetts.

Jaeckel certainly realized the expectations and had no problem meeting them. He told reporter Marilyn Beck the secret of his success as a character actor: "We were taught to be there ahead of the star, on camera, ready to go, not to make the star wait. Little things like that: being on time, being in the right costume." He had never formally studied acting but explained, "I used to watch and listen a lot. Whatever I use came from some pretty good people. No sense in taking anything from the bums.... In the niche I'm in, I can gain a few pounds, lose a few teeth and a few hairs—it's not going to make that much difference. I'm not up for a beauty contest. I'm happy. Just as long as the phone keeps ringing."

Hollywood reporter Pat Hilton got an interview along the same lines, with Jaeckel reiterating his pride in being a working character actor and a survivor of the filmmaking trenches: "I've gotten used to it, and I'm very proud of it. Every big star who has any longevity will be the first to admit that character actors, co-stars—whatever you want to call us—are very much responsible for them being in the position they are.... It doesn't mean I can sit down and phone it in. I still have to maintain whatever professional reputation I have, which I'm very proud of. I'm not necessarily interested in what people think of me on a social basis, but I guard my professional reputation."

With *Spenser: For Hire* enjoying audience and critical accolades in its first season, Jaeckel saw the release of another theatrical feature at the beginning of the year. *Black Moon Rising* (1986) is a sleek and fun action flick that benefits from top stunt sequences and an engaging

Tommy Lee Jones in the lead as a professional thief. Jones has swiped a valuable cassette tape for a government shadow agency. But he has to stash the cassette in the Black Moon, a cutting edge designer car, to keep it from thugs led by Lee Ving. Before he can recover the tape, the one-of-a-kind vehicle is stolen by a sophisticated car theft ring led by Robert Vaughn. Jaeckel is seen in support as Earl Windom, designer of the speedy eco-friendly car. Jaeckel joins with Jones to steal the vehicle back from an impregnable high-rise office building with the aid of Linda Hamilton, who stole the Black Moon in the first place.

Director Harley Cokliss directed the entertainingly preposterous film from an old John Carpenter script and keeps the pace moving with thrilling car chases and brutal fight scenes. Dan Shor and William Sanderson appear in support as Jaeckel's cohorts, although we learn little about their characters—or Jaeckel's, for that matter. Even when one of his pals bites the dust, there's no time to mourn the loss. It was a physical role for the fourth-billed Jaeckel involving running, climbing, and maneuvering through narrow passageways. He gets short-changed in the end, receiving his precious Black Moon in less than pristine condition.

Punk rock singer Lee Ving from the group Fear was a real-life friend of Jaeckel's from World Gym, where they would see one another with regularity. Ving recalled Jaeckel and his joy of having a job when interviewed by *Shock Cinema*: "I was complaining about something, and I turned to Richard and said, 'What do you think?' And he said, 'Man, I'm just happy to be here.' I thought to myself, 'Oh, man, I wish I had said that.' My hats off to you, Richard, wherever you are, bless you man."

Character actor Dan Shor also has fond memories of Jaeckel:

> What a warm and delicious man Richard Jaeckel was. He was so kind and funny and self-effacing during our shoot of *Black Moon Rising*. Bill Sanderson, Jaeckel and I spent a lot of time together and I was proud to work with him. He was a family man who considered show business to be merely his business. He was a consummate professional who went to work, enjoyed his castmates, savored the work, yet placed far more importance on what occurred after the work. So many actors consider their work some sort of sacred sacrifice, or their existential *raison d'etre*. But Dick was an old school, long-time pro, who had the old-fashioned American work ethic. He took pride in always knowing his lines, never missing his mark, and simply being kind and considerate to his fellow company members. He approached his career as if he were a lunch-pail worker, equal to any other craftsman on the set, be they actor, camera operator, best boy, or p.a.
>
> As an actor he didn't think of himself as anything special, merely a pro. But he was dedicated to being a kind, generous, caring gentleman who, through his absolute commitment, always managed to elevate the atmosphere around him. This very quality was the essence of his magic. This was the quality that made his fellow cast-mates celebrate his greatness. You could feel his kindness through the screen and that kindness is what we colleagues and audiences will always remember.[33]

Critical reaction was mixed, with most reviewers enjoying Jones as the leading man. *The New York Times* wrote, "Supporting cast are good, but not in the same league." The *Los Angeles Times* said that Jaeckel and the rest of the cast gave "canny, almost stylized, minimalist performances," while *The Washingtonian* opined, "A promising cast including Tommy Lee Jones, Lee Ving, Robert Vaughn, and Richard Jaeckel threaten to turn this routine action movie into something more satisfying." The *Sun-Sentinel* noted, "The venerable Richard Jaeckel is low-key," while *People Magazine* said, "Richard Jaeckel effects an air of nerdy determination as the ex–NASA scientist who designed the experimental car." The science fiction magazine *Cinefantastique* called the film "first-rate [with] a talented cast of yeoman character actors."

All in all, *Black Moon Rising* was a fairly solid big screen credit coming in the wake of the success of *Starman*. However, once he became firmly entrenched in his regular gig on *Spenser*,

Jaeckel had nothing to follow it up with on the big screen. Had *Spenser* been shot in Hollywood, Jaeckel's down-time would have allowed him to chase other film work. In New England there was nothing else to do except try to stay warm and hope they needed him in the next episode. There were also changes afoot in the format of the show, including a new leading lady for Urich and the absence of Jaeckel's producer friend John Wilder. *The New York Times* in their review of the series' follow-up year commented, "For whatever artistic or budgetary reasons, this year's scripts have reduced just about everybody to walk-on status. Such regular characters as Richard Jaeckel and Ron McLarty keep popping into weekly episodes as if they are being paid by the hour, and overtime is out of the question." Jaeckel filmed two full seasons of *Spenser*, but by the end of the second he was feeling the strong pull of the California sun.

♦ 9 ♦

Back to the Beach

Despite mixed feelings, Jaeckel left *Spenser* in the beginning of the third season after tiring of being away from his wife and his sunny California home. There were also new grandkids in the fold, courtesy of son Richard and his wife Laura. The *Spenser* exit was bittersweet. He did leave on good terms with the show's new producers, his character enduring a heart attack and forced retirement. Future guest shots on the series were left open. The constant ice, snow, and slush of the East Coast bothered his bones and an increasingly balky lower back. The always athletic Jaeckel hated the stiffening up that age and cold weather brought on. His body was beginning to feel the many years of pumping iron, getting on and off horses, and being pounded by heavy ocean waves. It seemed that some of his old stuntman pals who had spent their careers falling off horses, wrecking cars, and spending hours in the studio saloons were getting around without as much pain and difficulty as he now was. Jaeckel no doubt convinced himself that it was the cold weather bothering him and that a return to the golden state would remedy his aches and pains.

Jaeckel loved exercising in the fresh ocean air at World Gym's outside deck in Marina Del Rey. He had been a California beach boy for as long as anyone in the industry could remember. His favorite vacation destination was Hawaii, which he tried to visit at least once a year to surf, swim, and tan. In his travels he always tried to go where the sun shone brightest. His career in the Merchant Marine saw him tour the Pacific extensively, and both his films and recreation often exposed him to the salty sea air. Professionally his movie work took him several times to the Western Hemisphere in the Philippines and Japan. His many cowboy roles had him squinting into the sun on Hollywood back lots or rugged locations such as Arizona, California, or Mexico deserts. The fair-haired Jaeckel was seldom without a golden tan.

Jaeckel was now 60. Not a real concern for someone who took such good care of themselves physically but nonetheless an age where a man becomes more aware of his own mortality. Another good friend had recently passed on, Lee Marvin. The former Marine had pushed his body hard over the years with his heavy drinking and smoking; in many ways he was the antithesis of Jaeckel. The prematurely gray Marvin always looked several years older than he actually was. Marvin never fully recovered from complications following intestinal surgery and died of a heart attack in the hospital near his Tucson, Arizona, home. He was only 63.

In the fall of 1987 Jaeckel was quick to land work in Hollywood, beginning with a solid TV guest spot on the October *Murder She Wrote* episode "The Way to Dusty Death." Jaeckel portrayed Dr. Leon Chatsworth, who helps Angela Lansbury's Jessica Fletcher prove that

Cornel Wilde's death is murder rather than an accident. The Sunday evening staple *Murder She Wrote* was considered a prestigious TV guest appearance for Jaeckel, who shared several one-on-one scenes with the star. Actors enjoyed working on this show because it paid top dollar to its guests and offered them the opportunity to work alongside the esteemed Miss Lansbury as she solved her well-written and produced mysteries. Coincidentally, *Spenser: For Hire* had been moved to Sunday nights to go up against Lansbury's series.

Jaeckel also lined up another regular job, something that might have been in the making even before he left *Spenser*. This job locale was more to his liking, as the TV pilot *Supercarrier* (1988) cast him as a lifelong Navy man aboard the fictional aircraft carrier U.S.S. *Georgetown*. Banking on the big screen popularity of *Top Gun* (1986), the military show was an easy sell to the network and seemed to have potential. Jaeckel received special billing playing Master Chief Sam Rivers in support of Paul Gleason, Robert Hooks, Ken Olandt, and Cec Verrell.

The original 90-minute ABC pilot was shot on the U.S.S. *John F. Kennedy* off the coast of Norfolk, Virginia, in the fall of 1987. It's serviceable as pilots go, introducing the characters and the premise. The veteran performers tend to come off far better than the younger ones as written, with Jaeckel once again appearing comfortable in uniform and flight jacket. He describes himself to his men as their "gruff uncle" but the niceties of his personality far outweigh his crusty exterior. He's more apt to make them his special hangover cure than bark orders at them. It was a role that was intended to develop as the show played out, with *Variety* claiming that in the pilot, Jaeckel "doesn't have much to do."

Supercarrier went into production as a replacement series for the winter 1988 schedule with Dale Dye taking over for Paul Gleason as the ship's captain. The show had barely set sail when the Navy suddenly withdrew support for the series after unhappiness with some of the storylines. They felt certain aspects of Navy life were being presented in an unfavorable light. Losing the ability to shoot aboard a real aircraft carrier, the show scrambled about to film scenes on ships harbored in Long Beach, California. The initial promise of a small screen *Top Gun* quickly evaporated with the production turmoil. Most notable among the smattering of guest stars was Jaeckel's old friend William Smith, portraying a Russian submarine commander in the episode "Common Ground." Only six episodes were aired outside of the pilot, and Jaeckel was forced to add another television failure to his résumé.

Supercarrier did give him the opportunity to work with career Marine Dale Dye, who was just starting as an actor in Hollywood after a featured role in Oliver Stone's *Platoon* (1986). Dye had hoped to find work

Jaeckel was back in uniform as Master Chief Sam Rivers for the ABC-TV U.S. Navy drama *Supercarrier* (1988).

as a technical advisor in the industry and improve upon the way Hollywood portrayed the military but was quickly thrust into on-screen roles because he so looked the part. He had a special interest in Jaeckel's career given the actor's extensive war film credits dating all the way back to *Guadalcanal Diary, Battleground,* and *Sands of Iwo Jima.* Dye shares his memories of meeting Jaeckel in the following letter:

> Over the years on a lot of movie and TV projects, I've been privileged to work with a bunch of distinguished and talented people, but none of them remain as rock solid in my memory as Richard Jaeckel. He wasn't imposing, brash, colorful, or bubbling over with obvious talent, but he was ... well, Dick Jaeckel was familiar. There was an odd familiar feeling on the day in 1988 when he first shook my hand and introduced himself on the set of a short-lived TV series called *Supercarrier.* It was as if I was meeting a storied uncle or cousin that I'd heard about for years but somehow never got around to meeting in person. Having seen his work in so many films and not wanting to appear star-struck—although I most definitely was—I simply mumbled something about what a great privilege it was to meet him. "Let me know if I can help," he said. "I know this whole deal can be a little intimidating." And then he walked off to the craft service table leaving me to wonder why he would know that I was in my first featured role as a recurring character on a TV show. A producer later told me in private that Jaeckel had asked about me and seemed tickled to learn that I was a twenty-year U.S. Marine just breaking into the acting dodge.
>
> Without making an issue out of it, he would often join me at lunch or during down times between setups and gradually we began to share stories about military life. He seemed to have a warm place in his heart for people in uniform and we were both playing military roles. As usual, he was the crusty, old—no, wait that word should never be used to describe Dick Jaeckel—make it crusty and world-wise chief petty officer on an aircraft carrier commanded by my character. "I never made chief," he told me one day, "but I damn sure met a bunch of them ... mostly after I'd done something stupid." It was difficult to get him to tell a war story although he had served in the Navy during the last two years of World War II and for two years after the war ended. Mostly he'd just start a story and then end up ribbing me about being a Marine. "Marines are a different breed of cat," he said during one lunch break as he tucked into a corned beef sandwich. "I never did understand you guys."
>
> Richard Jaeckel may not have understood Marines but he knew enough about them to play one realistically and touchingly in a string of military-themed movies. He told me fascinating stories about working with John Wayne on *Sands of Iwo Jima* and related some of his adventures making *Guadalcanal Diary.* He was full of stories like that but it was always a chore to pry them out of him. He was self-effacing and modest about his show biz career; saying about all he got out of it was a lot of fun and a bad back. One of the most memorable times on set with Dick Jaeckel was the day veteran character actor Mako showed up to play a guest starring role on our series. They apparently knew each other from several other projects and often huddled off set for friendly conversations. I blatantly eavesdropped and was treated to hours of the funniest and most insightful stories about old Hollywood that can be imagined. It was like listening to a couple of vaudevillians dropping names and dimes on some of Hollywood's legends.[1]

At this point in Jaeckel's career, his reputation no doubt preceded him. He was in the running for every venerable cop and military commander in current development. It would seem he would have the ability to pick and choose his parts and their quality at his discretion, having fostered positive relationships at every stop along the way. Perhaps a heavy hitter such as Paul Newman would once again come through with a choice role harkening back to Jaeckel's showcase in *Sometimes a Great Notion.* Everywhere he went, Jaeckel generated admiration amongst cast and crew.

He took on a familiar supporting part in *Ghettoblaster* (1989). The *Death Wish* knock-off about a street gang terrorizing a Los Angeles neighborhood starred familiar TV actor Richard Hatch as a war veteran who takes on the gangs with martial arts and a variety of trickery. Third-billed Jaeckel is seen as ineffectual plainclothes cop Mike Henry, who is powerless to get convictions against the gang members and can only suggest to Hatch early on that he move somewhere else. The film initially shows some energy and stylistic editing but is quickly weighed down by its lack of production value and stereotypical storyline and characters. Veteran actors R.G. Armstrong, Rose Marie, and Harry Caesar are also in the cast. The film's director Alan L. Stewart remembers:

> It was a great pleasure to work with Dick Jaeckel. He was the most prepared and professional actor I ever worked with, and a true gentleman. I was so happy to have the chance to meet him and express my great admiration for his performance in *Sometimes a Great Notion*. I play golf with Jim Brown, who of course worked with Dick in *The Dirty Dozen*, and he also speaks very highly of him and remembers him fondly…. He asked to be called by Dick on the set as I recall, rather than Richard. I'm not sure if that is what his friends called him. He seemed to have some difficulty walking over uneven surfaces, as though he had a hip problem. I didn't ask him about it, but my DP and I were impressed with how he always hit his marks and never complained or asked for special treatment, though it was apparent he was in some discomfort. He was just the very definition of a trouper.[2]

A great deal of cost-cutting production began in Canada around this time and Jaeckel was quick to accept a film offer there. Unfortunately the financing fell through and filming was halted. The film was never completed. One untapped financial outlet for Jaeckel was personal appearances and he was signed to be one of the guest stars for Starline Celebrity Tours, meeting and greeting tourists aboard the *Queen Mary* docked in Long Beach Harbor. Tour guide Clive Roberts remembered Jaeckel in the pages of *Movie Memories*:

> I first met Richard Jaeckel in the lobby of the Hollywood Roosevelt Hotel during one of our tours. He was on his own at the time so I went over and introduced myself and he invited me to sit down and chat with him. An hour later we were still there chatting about his films and the people he had worked with. I remarked how little he had changed over the years since I first saw him in *The Gunfighter* with Gregory Peck. He told me he was still busy working and had just been making a film in Canada but unfortunately the money ran out so they had to close the production down! We also discussed one of his more important films *The Dirty Dozen* and he said how lucky he'd been to work with such a distinguished cast.… Some months later after our meeting I met him again on a Starline Celebrity Event on the *Queen Mary*. He was delighted to see me—and we had several photos taken together—which was nice.

In 1989 Jaeckel's former *Sands of Iwo Jima* co-star William Joseph Murphy died in Sacramento at the age of 68. Nothing had been heard of Murphy, who initially showed so much promise, for several years in Hollywood circles. After nearly a decade without a speaking part of note, Murphy showed up on location in Arizona in the late 1960s where old acquaintances Elvis Presley and Robert Mitchum gave him some extra work on the films *Charro* (1969) and *Young Billy Young* (1969). He also did a couple of *Gunsmoke* episodes during this period before drifting away from the business. Muscle Beach regular Read Morgan remembers Murphy got "a little crazy" and stopped getting work.[3] Hollywood could be like that. Personalities came and went with great regularity. Few had the steady career endurance of a Richard Jaeckel.

Jaeckel's lifelong standing as a dedicated beach boy and his past history as a Santa Monica lifeguard led to his employment in a new TV movie. Jaeckel initially appeared on the popular series *Baywatch* in the 1989 pilot film "Panic at Malibu Pier" as the supporting character Al Gibson, an aging lifeguard told by new head of the outfit David Hasselhoff that because of his advanced years he faces mandatory retirement. This does not sit well with Al, who proves his usefulness in the climax by saving a large number of people in the water. But Al perishes as a result of his heroism. The closing of the pilot film sees Hasselhoff and the other lifeguards hold a memorial for him at sea. The *Baywatch* pilot was created by producer-director Gregory J. Bonann, a real Los Angeles County lifeguard.

Sometimes things have a way of coming around, especially when they involve good deeds and richness of character. Bonann happened to have a history with Jaeckel. He writes:

> Mr. Jaeckel was much more than an actor I cast on *Baywatch*. He was my little league coach, father to classmates of mine in first, second, and third grade, and one of the most fantastic athletes I had ever seen in person as a child. I had no idea that he was an actor until I was at least 12 to 13 years old and saw him in *Devil's Brigade* and *Dirty Dozen*—that is when it really hit me that this man was not only the dad of my two buddies—who could play ball better than any other dads, but also had something special going on outside of being Barry and Richard's father. Over the years we became friendly at church at St. Martins of Tours on Sunset Boulevard and on the little league field, and even though I lost touch with his sons when I switched to public school and they stayed in private school, I was forever hooked on Richard as one of my favorite actors of all time. My parents then added to the legend of Richard Jaeckel and introduced me to *Sometimes a Great Notion* and many of his other films. I was a young teenager still.
>
> After many, many years passed, his name came up on a casting list for our backdoor pilot movie-series and I went nuts. I could not believe that we might be able to get R.J. on *Baywatch*. And so I did whatever it took to get him! We became good friends again and giggled about those days when he would kick the football over the fence and out of sight at Barrington Park where his sons and I played together.... We cast him as the heroic mentor to our leading man David Hasselhoff (Mitch Buchanon). I directed all of his action and water work myself and we developed a fantastic relationship as actor-director. I remembered, all too well, what an incredible athlete he was so I benefitted on camera by letting him do what he wanted to do—much of the athletic work that the scenes required—no stunt man, no photo double.... He was just awesome.
>
> That mentor role required that he die heroically saving Mitch Buchanon's son Hobie in one of the final scenes of the movie, and I had no idea that after we did that, and after the movie aired, that his character would measure as the most likable character in the whole movie! The audience wanted to see him on the soon-to-be series more than any other character in the pilot movie, including the lead characters Hasselhoff, Parker Stevenson, etc. When we told the network NBC that we wanted to have him back on the series they said, "You can't do that, he is dead! You killed him in the pilot!" NBC never really understood the power of the individual actor over the character he plays. They were a bunch of people who took their own creative business way too seriously over their real business–entertainment. So for that first season on NBC we were not allowed to have R.J. on the show.[4]

The pilot sold as a network series and aired during the 1989–1990 season without any further involvement from Jaeckel. The series was heavy on showing its athletic cast in shorts, tank tops, and swimsuits, but didn't offer a great deal in the way of weighty dramatic content. It was light entertainment and aimed to be little more. The network decided to cancel the series. At this point David Hasselhoff discovered the show was especially popular in foreign markets, where he had a ready audience for his musical recording career and publicity appearances for his previous TV series *Knight Rider*. As co-producer and star he managed to find parties interested in *Baywatch* as a syndicated effort, and the show took on a slightly revamped format the following year.

In the meantime, Jaeckel supported karate star Chuck Norris in the feature film *Delta Force 2—The Colombian Connection* (1990), a sequel to the 1986 original that had co-starred Lee Marvin with Norris. Jaeckel is cast as DEA agent John Page. Chuck's brother Aaron Norris directed the film, which was shot in the Philippines. Some work was done in Tennessee, with both locations standing in for the jungles of the fictional South American country San Carlos. Jaeckel appears at the beginning of the film in Rio de Janeiro where three DEA agents are murdered by drug lord Billy Drago. After Jaeckel recruits Chuck Norris and his Delta Force commandos to thwart Drago, Jaeckel is captured by the villain and held in a mountain compound. At the film's climax he is rescued by Norris and fights Drago's men alongside the hero.

The film is decent in the action department but unremarkable overall. Despite its fairly wide theatrical release, a new generation of film critics barely mentioned Jaeckel's venerable presence or steely contribution. Unfortunately, the film is best known for a tragedy that occurred during filming in the Philippines: A helicopter crashed, killing five crew members and injuring character actor John P. Ryan. Sixty-three-year-old Jaeckel did lots of running for the film, although his increasing arthritic problems left him in a great deal of physical pain. He was doubled in the heavier action scenes by stuntman Dick Warlock, but could very well have been in the helicopter with Ryan when it crashed.

"I felt so bad for Richard as he was really having trouble getting around at that point," says Warlock, best known for regularly doubling Kurt Russell and memorably portraying the shape Michael Myers in the horror genre favorite *Halloween II* (1981). "He was one of the gutsiest guys I have ever known. He was so fortunate not to have been in that chopper when it went down. I was supposed to be in it but the director talked John Ryan into getting in it for this one shot. The chopper wasn't supposed to lift off except for perhaps two feet, but we know what happened. I wish that I had met Richard earlier in my career. I so badly wanted to do westerns since that's where my heart is and was."[5]

The direct-to-video market was in full swing by the late 1980s with dozens of low-budget films going straight to video in a flurry. Most of these movies featured a few recognizable names to aid foreign sales and lend overall credibility to otherwise bottom-of-the-barrel productions. The actors were generally paid their traditional rate but often worked on these films for only a matter of days. Occasionally there was a gem. Such was the case with the martial arts film *King of the Kickboxers* (1990) starring Loren Avedon as an undercover cop who works with Interpol to bring down a snuff film racket in Thailand. There was plenty of cheesiness in the plot, but the film was highlighted by fantastic fight sequences between Avedon and Billy Blanks as the main bad guy. These mind-boggling kickfests created a cult reputation for the Lucas Lowe film.

Jaeckel appears as Captain O'Day, the beleaguered police official who assigns Avedon to work with Interpol agent Don Stroud in Thailand. Interestingly, Jaeckel and Avedon shot their main two-man scene largely independent of one another. Despite the unconventional nature of the filming, screen veterans Jaeckel and Stroud are credible in their few brief scenes. Jaeckel and the charismatic Stroud had something in common in real life in their love for surfing. Stroud was raised in Hawaii, and in the early 1960s was the fourth-ranked surfer in the world. He entered the business as a stunt double for Troy Donahue on the TV series *Hawaiian Eye*. Jaeckel did get to take a brief trip to Thailand courtesy of the film. The online site *Comeuppance Reviews* notes, "Richard Jaeckel plays the classic 'yelling police captain' with aplomb."

Unfortunately, Jaeckel's decreased mobility made it extremely difficult for him to get acting work at this point. Some references attach him to the TV movie *Summer Dreams: The Story of the Beach Boys* (1990) in the part of Murry Wilson, the demanding father of the originators of the popular 1960s surf band, but Jaeckel did not work on the film; Arlen Dean Snyder played the part. Jaeckel's potential roles became limited, and many productions were hesitant to hire him due to insurance concerns as his discomfort had become so noticeable. No one was quite sure what was going on with him physically. Jaeckel was under the impression it was severe rheumatoid arthritis. James Coburn had recently been nearly crippled by a similar diagnosis, but eventually managed to overcome his malady and work again. Jaeckel sought treatment at the renowned Soft Tissue Center in Los Angeles, a rehabilitation center for elite athletes recovering from injury. Jaeckel gave it his best shot, but there had to be a lot of disappointment when going on auditions and interviews.

There were few new film or TV appearances for Jaeckel throughout the remainder of

1990 and into 1991. Given his extensive career body of work, one might think that he was easing into an early retirement to rest his overworked body while living off his SAG pension and residuals. He did appear as a guest star on the Vietnam War drama *China Beach*, playing the crippled father of actor Jeff Kober in the June 1991 episode "Quest." The episode's storyline involved Kober's return to the States after his time in Vietnam. Jaeckel's casting as "Dad" Winslow was prophetic as his mobility was now so severely hindered that he could only land a part that called for an on-screen handicap. Playing the victim of a stroke, Jaeckel has not a single line of dialogue. He relies on his eyes to do all of his acting in his scenes with Kober and Dana Delany and the effect is both haunting and heartbreaking. The show's producer John Sacret Young directed.

At this point Greg Bonann and David Hasselhoff's new version of *Baywatch* was ready to go before the cameras. Among the cast changes was the return of Jaeckel as the new character Lt. Ben Edwards, a man who differed from the previous character Al Gibson only in the fact that one was alive and one was dead. There would be no talk of Edwards and retirement. When setting up casting for the new series, Bonann's first phone call went out to Jaeckel to gauge his interest in returning to the show. Jaeckel answered in the affirmative. "I was over the moon to think that our syndicated *Baywatch* would start off with R.J. in the main title," Bonann says. "That would make the show, in my opinion, automatically better than the version that NBC cancelled…. And it did."[6] But there was a surprise in store for Bonann.

> What I was not ready for was the deterioration of his physical health over the two years since I had last seen him. He was carrying a cane when we met at a restaurant (which he had carefully chosen beforehand and arrived early so I would not be able to see him arrive or exit). His son, still a friend after almost thirty years, had called me and warned me of his physical limitations…. What no one could tell me though was how impressive he still was as a man and as an actor! He was sharp as a tack and emotionally he still wanted to contribute to something, be a part of something, and act—what he knew best. I only learned later that others in the business were unwilling to cast him because of his seemingly physical limitations or were worried about insurance, etc. I agreed to cast him on the spot and lunch was fantastic. I worked around his physical limitations as gracefully and respectfully as possible—as if he was my own father.

The new series began to air in the fall of 1991 with the two-part episode "Nightmare Bay." Fellow screen veteran actor Monte Markham also joined the cast as Captain Dan Thorpe, yet another senior member of the lifeguard staff. When Markham left the show after a season, Jaeckel's character was elevated to the status of captain. The new version of the show became a worldwide phenomenon, launching the careers of buxom beauties Pamela Anderson, Erika Eleniak, Nicole Eggert, Yasmine Bleeth, and Carmen Electra. Critics had a field day ripping the series apart. In regard to the two-part premiere, *Variety* said, "The most painful moments come from the accomplished Monte Markham and Richard Jaeckel, who are forced to contend with the cast's two worst-written roles as the team's grizzled veterans." *The Hollywood Reporter* was a little kinder: "Markham and Jaeckel provide romantic appeal for the geriatric crowd."

The negative reviews didn't matter to viewers who embraced the show. For Jaeckel it was regular work, and he was much beloved on the set. Cast members who were not working would still show up on the set or the beach to watch Jaeckel work. His body was really giving him trouble though, particularly his right hip. On screen his character used a cane and many of his scenes were filmed with him in a more accommodating seated position. Most episodes only featured a relatively short segment with Jaeckel, and by the third season (1992–1993) Jaeckel only appeared in a half dozen shows. His best moment on the series came in the February 1992 episode "Sea of Flames" where he rekindles a long-ago beach romance with an

Despite great physical pain, Jaeckel kept himself in shape for his role as senior lifeguard Ben Edwards on the hit TV series *Baywatch* (1991-1994). John Allen Nelson (left) co-starred.

aging Hollywood starlet played by Constance Towers. If anything on *Baywatch* could be described as touching, the way this nostalgic episode was handled would be it.

Actress Alexandra Paul arrived in Jaeckel's final *Baywatch* season and portrayed Stephanie Holden, the most level-headed and brainy of the show's beautiful female lifeguards. She says of Jaeckel: "I remember that he was a very nice man, but that he was in a lot of pain in his last year so it was not easy for him to get around. Because of that he was not in the show as much so I did not get to know him very well at all. Plus I was slightly intimidated by him, as he was a much respected actor with a long career and it was my first season on *Baywatch*."[7]

Stuntman Dick Warlock recalls:

I remember Richard fondly. I didn't get to know him until late in his life. My son Billy played Eddie on *Baywatch*. Since Billy was one of the main characters and I knew the stunt coordinator too, it was a natural for me to come in to double Richard in the pilot for the series. We did that in Hawaii. I spent a week on Oahu and had a ball. Richard's role required him to drown in a boat accident. When the pilot sold and they started the series, for some unexplained reason after he had died in the pilot, Richard was hired back as one of the main characters. So be it. Later on I was called in to double him again to do a rescue jump from the pier where this drowning sequence was to take place. Yes another drowning, but this time it wasn't him.[8]

In late 1992 Jaeckel was honored with a Golden Boot Award at the tenth annual cowboy ceremony. The Golden Boot was an event begun in the early 1980s by character actor Pat Buttram to pay tribute to those within the film industry who had made a significant contribution to the western genre. The celebration was also an opportunity for the remaining Hollywood cowboys of film and TV to get together to reminisce about the good old days. Fellow honorees the year Jaeckel received his award include actors Ronald Reagan, Tom Selleck, Katy Jurado, Ann Miller, Rand Brooks, Pierce Lyden, Sheb Wooley, and Tim Holt, stunt performers Montie Montana, Alice Springsteen, and Henry Wills, producers Arthur Gardner, Jules V. Levy, and A.C. Lyles, and directors Arnold Laven and John Sturges. Jaeckel's award was presented by his friend A.J. Fenady.

Many attending the awards that year were shocked to see how much Jaeckel had physically changed in only a few years. Jaeckel, the man Hollywood claimed never aged, was now walking with a cane and showing his sixty-five years. He was graying at the temples and his face was finally showing the signs of age that he had so long evaded. Jaeckel graciously accepted the Golden Boot Award, although it had to be a bittersweet moment as he realized his present condition would prevent him from ever saddling up for another great western. "Jake was a proud man," Fenady wrote in *Wildest Westerns*. "He didn't want his old friends to see and remember him like that."

Jaeckel was no longer able to work out at the gym with his accustomed intensity, causing him to begin to lose the eye-popping muscles once so prominent in his arms and shoulders. However, he still went to the gym regularly to share in the camaraderie among his brothers of iron. Sometimes he could be seen seated in a wheelchair still pumping away at the iron. *Spenser: For Hire* producer John Wilder writes, "The last time I saw him was at Gold's Gym in Venice. His health was in decline and he was walking with canes. I remember him saying he didn't 'work out' any more, he 'exercised,' but I loved that he was in the gym because training had been such a big part of his life and I remember how strong he was as a young man."[9]

Jaeckel has a small but important role in the direct-to-video action film *Martial Outlaw* (1993). He plays Mr. White, a former cop who is the father of the film's opposing law enforcement leads Jeff Wincott and Gary Hudson. The performances, karate action, and drama in this Kurt Anderson–directed film is as well-done as the genre gets, but Jaeckel's presence is minimal and his deteriorating physical condition is distracting. The father character is an arthritic man who walks gingerly and stooped with the aid of a cane. He kills his pain with glass after glass of bourbon, but anyone familiar with Jaeckel will realize that the part is fit to the actor rather than the actor to the part. He does add depth to the character when it's revealed that his drinking is in actuality an attempt to drown the sorrow of knowing his son Hudson is a dirty cop. Jaeckel is in four scenes and appears to be in a great deal of discomfort throughout. It is sad and unfortunate that an ailing Jaeckel still felt he had to work at this point in his career given his many years in front of the camera, but work he did.

By 1993 it became apparent that continuing on *Baywatch* would be next to impossible for Jaeckel. It was simply too painful for him to get around without drawing attention to himself and his condition. He was given a send-off episode in "The Red Knights," the beginning of season four that aired in January of 1994. The plotline involves a gathering of old lifeguards that forces Jaeckel's Ben Edwards character to confront his injury. Hasselhoff reveals that Edwards permanently damaged his hip while hang-gliding over the ocean. Spotting a surfer in trouble, he jumped over thirty feet into the water to save the man, destroying his own hip in the process. By episode's end Jaeckel has one last heroic moment when he rescues a young boy after a boat crashes into the pier. The flashback photos of a young Jaeckel used for this episode were actually photos of Tim Lyon's surfer son Andy. In real life Andy Lyon named his own son Jake.

When Jaeckel left *Baywatch*, the show honored him with a pair of bronzed shorts and an open invitation to return when he felt better. After all his TV misses over the years, Jaeckel finally found himself a hit series with global appeal. He went out on top. Gregory Bonann sums up Jaeckel's *Baywatch* experience: "We had many great episodes together over the years, including his last as an actor, and I considered myself very lucky to work with him and direct him. He was a very special man and just writing this brings a tear to my eye."[10]

10

The Sun Sets

Details on Jaeckel's life at this point become sketchy due to his private nature, but it appears that the physically ailing actor was beset with a number of tough breaks. His wife Antoinette's health had deteriorated over the past few years and she was diagnosed with severe depression and the onset of Alzheimer's Disease. No doubt the early warning signs were part of the reason that Jaeckel had opted to leave the safety and success he had finally found on *Spenser*. Jaeckel held true to his core values and principles and remained committed to the woman he married and loved. However, it is apparent that Jaeckel's earnings were flowing out the door faster than he could bring them in and now he could no longer work due to his physical pain. This was something Jaeckel opted to keep a private matter.

There was more bad news. Jaeckel's painful rheumatoid arthritis was in reality the early stages of skin cancer that was metastasizing into his bones. It is with great irony that the sunshine that Jaeckel coveted and the beach lifestyle that he promoted was likely the cause of his body's destruction. A chief suspect would be the bad sunburn he received during the making of *Once Before I Die* in the Philippines. There is also the chance that the many lotions and skin care products he applied as a young man might have been a contributing factor. Studies on that front have been inconclusive. A more likely culprit was simply his genetic background.

Actor-stuntman Budd Albright, a former employee of Vic Tanny's health club, recalls Jaeckel from the beach and the gym, saying: "Richard Jaeckel was a great guy, always smiling, in a good mood. He was a Muscle Beach guy. He was always very tan—blue eyes and blond hair. From 1956 to 1962 the beach guys used baby oil mixed with iodine. Bad choice. A number of them later died of skin cancer, as did Richard Jaeckel. Most of those guys were dark-skinned and fared better—mostly Italian, Greek, some Jewish."[1]

Jaeckel was in so much pain he was no longer able to care for Antoinette at home. His attorney Gerald Margolis later told *The Globe*, "He just couldn't look after her, but they loved each other very much." Antoinette was committed to the Wilshire Retirement Center in Canoga Park, which specialized in Alzheimer care. Medical bills for the couple mounted and Jaeckel had nothing left and no means to earn new income, save for sporadic residuals that were dwindling in at varying and sometimes trivial amounts. Sons Richard, Jr., and Barry were unable to provide a financial solution for their parents. Earlier that year Jaeckel had been forced to file for bankruptcy with debts exceeding $1.7 million. The Brentwood home was lost, as were many of their prized possessions and cherished heirlooms. It was an extremely stressful situation that affected Jaeckel's own ability to fight off the cancer invading his body.

No doubt his great pride was shattered at the situation. He had worked fifty high-profile years in Hollywood and now had nothing to his name. Jaeckel was in a great deal of physical pain and tried to get into the Motion Picture Home in Woodland Hills where the motto was "We take care of our own." Despite his six decades of film and television contributions, he was denied due to the extenuating financial circumstances. When influential star Gregory Peck learned of the Motion Picture Home's denial, he went to bat for Jaeckel, writing a heartfelt letter that implored them to accept his former *Gunfighter* co-star. Peck's campaign worked and Jaeckel was accepted into the home in 1994. Still, it was not an easy road for Jaeckel by any means. At least he was now able to get the medical care he needed within the quiet seclusion of the Home's private bungalows.

Jaeckel's friend Nancy Ellen Barr hadn't seen him for a few years, encountering her own misdiagnosed health problems since the time they worked together on the TV series *At Ease*. She was initially thought to be suffering from multiple sclerosis and was in a great deal of pain herself, forced to travel via wheelchair. Paying a visit to the Motion Picture Home, she was dismayed to see a vehicle pull in before hers and take the handicap space. Initially angry, she was surprised to the point of elation when she saw who emerged from the passenger seat. It was Jaeckel.

> I saw him from the back. I didn't recognize him until he turned around. At first I thought it was a woman. His hair was long and he had aged. He had just been accepted into the Home. He was so excited he had got into the Home. We hugged and he kissed me. The friendship was always there. I never stopped adoring him. We talked and it was the last time I saw him. He just disappeared. He was fortunate to get in. It was extremely expensive, but he went there for free. All the money he had was gone. He had told me he had rheumatoid arthritis and was in a lot of pain. I didn't know about the melanoma. I tried so hard to reach him at the Motion Picture Home, but he wasn't taking visitors. I know Bob Fuller tried too, but Richard wanted to be left alone. He was a very private person. He was such a sweet, wonderful man. I am delighted to have been able to call him a friend. And he was that.[2]

The National Enquirer broke the news of Jaeckel's entry into the Actor's Home and were granted an interview by Jaeckel in which he said, "There's an end for all of us—and if this is it, then that's the way it is. I know people are pulling for me to beat this thing. But let them just have a glass at the bar for me and let it go at that." Daughter-in-law Evelyn told the *Enquirer*, "He has melanoma which has gone into the bones. He didn't know what his illness was until recently—He told everyone that he had an arthritic problem because that was what he understood at the time."

"My wife can't take care of me any more," Jaeckel said to the *Enquirer*, keeping her problems from the public. "So I moved in here three months ago. I've done my last show on *Baywatch*—they couldn't keep writing about the world's oldest lifeguard who can only walk with a cane.... I've put in fifty years in movies and my wife and I have traveled all over the world. I've been very lucky." *Baywatch* co-producer Craig Kwasizur held out hope Jaeckel could beat the cancer: "We've been keeping his role open in the hope that he'll be able to come back and join the show."

Jaeckel spent the next three years quietly and nobly fighting his private battle with the cancer. Very few were allowed access. Jaeckel didn't take many calls, and while he read the letters sent to him he didn't respond to them. Long-time friend Robert Fuller recalls, "He didn't want to see anybody. That hurt me a little bit.... I wanted to see him. I would have been out there every day to see him if they'd let me. At the same time, I never saw him sick. In my mind I see Dick Jaeckel, always young and smiling. I like that image. I miss him. He was a good pal."[3]

Fuller eventually relocated to Texas. Tough guy actor William Smith, a close friend of Jaeckel's from the Muscle Beach days, won out in seeing Jaeckel through persistence. He made it a point to physically go to the Motion Picture Home and visit weekly over Jaeckel's last year. They would reminisce about the good old days of fun in the sun and tossing around iron in the gym. Smith recalled that Jaeckel was a great guy and one of his best friends in the business.[4]

Stuntman Dick Warlock says: "By this time in Richard's life he was having trouble getting around. He spent some of his last days where I last visited him in the Motion Picture Hospital in Woodland Hills, California. He was the kind of man I wish I could have been as an actor. Rough and tumble little guy. Spunky and tough but very kind to me for the short time I spent with him. He was a joy to watch on the big screen. I miss him."[5]

"I actually saw him a lot in his last days," stuntman Ronnie Rondell reveals, "because my father had been in the film business and was in the Motion Picture Home in Woodland Hills at the same time. Every time I'd go to see my dad, I'd stop and see Dick and we'd B.S. about the old days. I was amazed that he ended up in there because he'd taken such good care of himself over the years. He always looked so young. I remember the last time I saw him. He was sitting in a wheelchair out on the patio in the garden. He had his head back and he was sunning, just like he did all those years on the beach! I patted him on the arm and he looked up at me. We talked, and it wasn't much longer after that before he was gone."[6]

Jaeckel wasn't the only fit, good-looking actor whose health had taken a surprising nosedive during this period. His friend Michael Landon passed away suddenly from pancreatic cancer in 1991 at the age of 54. George Peppard, the handsome blond former Marine who became a 1960s movie star, succumbed to lung cancer in 1994 at 65. Doug McClure, another golden Hollywood beach boy and pal of Jaeckel's, battled lung cancer as well. The diagnosis came as a great surprise given his age and vigor. Like Jaeckel, the handsome and likable McClure tended to light up any room he entered with his friendly smile and energetic presence, constantly promoting the California surfing and gym lifestyle to the masses as the healthiest in existence. McClure succumbed to the cancer in his lungs in February 1995. He was only 59. Landon, Peppard, and McClure had all been heavy drinkers and smokers at varying times throughout their lives. Jaeckel had merely spent too much time in the sun.

Surprisingly, a job offer came Jaeckel's way. Director Joe Dante was making the kids movie *Small Soldiers* (1998) starring animated toy action figures. As an in-joke he wanted to have cast veterans of *The Dirty Dozen* provide voices for the toys. Ernest Borgnine, Jim Brown, George Kennedy, and Clint Walker all agreed and there was hope that Jaeckel would be able to voice the character of communications expert Link Static. That ultimately didn't happen, and Bruce Dern ended up playing the part. Jaeckel's last credit would remain *Baywatch*.

After fighting the cancer in his bones for more than three agonizing years, Jaeckel died on Saturday night, June 14, 1997, in Woodland Hills, California, with son Barry and daughter-in-law Evelyn at his bedside. "He missed acting and was in great pain," Evelyn said at the time in an article for *The Globe*. "It was a relief when he passed away, because he didn't have to suffer any more." Motion Picture and Television Home spokesperson Carol Pfannkuche and nursing supervisor Ann Walsh didn't release a cause of death out of respect for the family, but Jaeckel's State of California death certificate lists a six-year struggle with multiple myeloma and a contributing cause of renal failure. Fellow actors Brian Keith, Robert Mitchum, and Jimmy Stewart all died within two weeks of one another, somewhat eclipsing write-ups on

Jaeckel although his obituary ran in all the major news outlets. Even in death, Jaeckel was relegated to being an underappreciated supporting player.

The New York Times called him "a durable movie tough guy" and "a familiar face to generations of film and television fans." Film critic Rex Reed wrote a remembrance of Jaeckel in the *New York Observer*, saying, "A great loss for the screen was the marvelous, underrated Richard Jaeckel, the angel-faced kid in so many action films who finally proved himself an artist of wide and challenging emotional substance when he got an Oscar nomination in 1972 for stealing scenes from Henry Fonda and Paul Newman in *Sometimes a Great Notion*." According to the film magazine *Wildest Westerns*, "He was strong and athletic, and made a marvelous villain and action hero in noteworthy westerns." *Daily Breeze* columnist John Bogert wrote a personal remembrance of Jaeckel, declaring him "the subtle glue of filmdom." Bogert concluded by writing that Jaeckel was "[a] damn good actor in the worst of his roles. He was also this really nice guy.... Through it all he was a working man, something I could understand, a straight-talking, arm-grabbing memorable guy."

"He was a California surfer," director William Grefe recalls. "But he was fair-haired. He got melanoma and didn't get it taken care of in time. It was tragic the way he died."[7] Fellow Florida director Ricou Browning opines, "His death was a great loss."[8] *Spenser: For Hire* producer John Wilder says, "I hated learning of his passing and will always remember him fondly."[9] Bud Cardos concurs: "I felt a great loss of his friendship when he passed away so early in life. He was a wonderful man."[10] "I hope he's in Heaven," director and friend Vincent McEveety adds. "I'm sure he is, and hopefully we'll all see him one day. He was very special."[11] A.J. Fenady remembers: "Near the end he worked in a series my brother did [*Baywatch*] and at that time he suffered quite extensively from an arthritic condition. He walked with a cane, and he spent his last days at the Motion Picture Home. When he died they had a memorial service there for him in the auditorium and it was packed. I was there and spoke some words about my friend Richard Jaeckel."[12]

"I lost track of him," Malibu surfing pal Walter Hoffman says. "I heard he fell down off a ladder. We tried to get in touch with him in the Valley, but nobody could see him.... Might have been pride."[13] Muscle Beach friend Read Morgan recalls, "I thought he developed some sort of a back injury. Skin cancer makes sense. He was very fair-haired and spent a lot of time in the sun. He did everything right with diet and exercise and didn't have any bad habits that I knew of. He never seemed to age and was the perennial juvenile in Hollywood for a long time. Maybe the only mistake he ever made was he spent too much time in the sun. You can't do anything about bad luck."[14] Long-time pal Robert Phillips says, "He died at the Motion Picture Home. I had went out to see him several times. I was the only one he was talking to. He was having some marital problems.... His end days were not too happy."[15] Former workout buddy Dick Tyler recalls, "It was easy to like Dick so his passing hurts all who knew him. There will never be another Jake—the mold was broken long ago."[16] "He was a great guy," stuntman Monty Cox says. "A physical guy. I'm that way too. They can tell you to stay out of the sun, but I'm sure Jaeckel lived his life his way and did what he loved. He had his time and now he's gone. Nobody gets out of here alive."[17]

"We miss him," gym entrepreneur Clark Hatch writes of himself and his fitness clientele from around the globe.[18] Longtime Malibu pal Tim Lyon says of Jaeckel, "He was the best guy in the world. He and I were really close. We shared a lot of time together. I talked to him on the phone not more than two weeks before he checked out. I asked if I could bring something out to him but he said, 'No, I look shitty and I don't want anybody to see me. I'm not feeling too hot.' That was my last contact with him."[19] Friend and workout partner Brad Harris says, "I was very, very sad to lose him. When he got ill we were pretty much buddies, you know. Then he went out to the hospital way out in the Valley. I spoke to him a couple of times on the phone. He didn't want me to come out. He was a very proud guy, a proud and tough guy, and he just didn't want me to see him like that. I don't blame him. I vote for that also. Whenever I go down seaside where we used to hang out, Richard always comes into my memory bank."[20]

James Drury also thinks of Jaeckel nearly every day:

> There's a scene in *Sometimes a Great Notion* that is seared in my memory. At one point in that, he was such a happy man he'd wake up in the morning and look out at whatever was going on and he'd say, "Bless this day." When I think of Jaeckel, I think of that. I bless each day I can get up and be vertical and look up and see the sky and breathe in and out. I think of Jake each morning when I do that. It's pretty dear to me, and he's pretty dear to me. He's with me every day in one way or another first thing in the morning when I get up. There's no other actor who I have that kind of connection with. To see that close-up in my mind and to see that wonderful line of life expressed in just those three words, that's a tribute to what a great actor he was. He was underused and underappreciated, but every time he got a chance to do anything, he shone like a beacon.[21]

A memorial service was held for Jaeckel at the Louis B. Mayer Theatre at the Motion Picture TV Fund Campus. He was cremated and his ashes were scattered in the Pacific Ocean three miles off of the coast of Newport Beach. At some point he undoubtedly rode one final wave into shore. In the end he became one with the sea that he loved. It's a fitting place of rest for the surf-loving mariner. The ocean steadily pounds away just like Jaeckel did in the tough town of Hollywood for fifty-plus years. Jaeckel once offered up the secret to his sustained success in a syndicated newspaper blurb: "You show up on time and don't let them call you more than once. Know what you're supposed to do and do it." It was all that simple to him and he made that personal philosophy work like a charm.

Audiences and co-workers remember Jaeckel's smiling image with great fondness. This is how he appeared in *Sometimes a Great Notion* (1970).

Close friend Robert Phillips echoes those words, recalling Jaeckel was more apt to roll with the punches in order to be the one left standing when the dust cleared. Phillips sums up the easygoing Jaeckel by saying, "He was different than me. He wasn't going to rock the boat. He could be described as a guy who never rocked the boat. That's not me. I rock the boat all the time. But I always admired Jake, and I always respected him. But he didn't rock the boat, ever. Sometimes he'd prod me to rock the boat..."[22]

Although Jaeckel's last years were painful and ultimately cut short, he had lived a full life of interesting adventure and travel. His friendships and accomplishments were many and the lives he had touched were countless. With an Oscar nomination to his name, he had the respect of his peers and was one of only a small percentage of actors to earn a handsome living at the profession. He had performed with and been requested by some of the biggest stars and directors in the history of the movies. He had a fifty-year marriage in a business notorious for short liaisons. He raised two sons into full-grown, college-educated men. Jaeckel proudly served his country during the war and sailed the great oceans of the world. He pushed and pulled at tons of iron to perfect his body while maintaining and radiating a youthful vigor, promoting health and fitness everywhere he went. He rode the best waves on the sandiest beaches and had a kind word and a smile for everyone. Most importantly, he was a professional and a man of character. A class act, he will forever be missed.

Filmography

Guadalcanal Diary (1943) as Johnny "Chicken" Anderson
Wing and a Prayer (1944) as Beezy Bessemer
Jungle Patrol (1948) as Lt. Dick Carter
City Across the River (1949) as Bull
Battleground (1949) as Bettis
Sands of Iwo Jima (1949) as Pfc. Frank Flynn
The Gunfighter (1950) as Eddie
Wyoming Mail (1950) as Nate
Fighting Coast Guard (1951) as Tony Jessup
The Sea Hornet (1951) as Johnny Radford
Cave of Outlaws (1951) (recycled footage from *Wyoming Mail* only)
My Son John (1952) as Chuck Jefferson
Hoodlum Empire (1952) as Ted Dawson
Come Back, Little Sheba (1952) as Turk Fisher
Big Leaguer (1953) as Bobby Bronson
Sea of Lost Ships (1953) as Ensign H.G. "Hap" O'Malley
The Shanghai Story (1954) as Knuckles Greer
The Violent Men (1955) as Wade Matlock
Apache Ambush (1955) as Lee Parker
Attack! (1956) as Pvt. Snowden
Ain't No Time for Glory (TV) (1957) as Sgt. Lou Mertz
3:10 to Yuma (1957) as Charlie Prince
Cowboy (1958) as Paul Curtis
The Lineup (1958) as Sandy McLain
The Naked and the Dead (1958) as Gallagher
The Gun Runners (1958) as Buzurki
When Hell Broke Loose (1958) as Karl
Platinum High School (1960) as Hack Marlow
The Gallant Hours (1960) as Lt. Commander Roy Webb
Flaming Star (1960) as Angus Pierce
Town Without Pity (1961) as Corporal Birdwell "Birdie" Scott
The Young and the Brave (1963) as Corporal John Estway
4 for Texas (1963) as Pete Mancini
Nightmare in the Sun (1965) as the motorcyclist
Town Tamer (1965) as Johnny Honsinger
Once Before I Die (1965) as Lt. Custer
The Dirty Dozen (1967) as Sgt. Clyde Bowren
The Devil's Brigade (1968) as Pvt. Omar Greco
The Green Slime (1968) as Commander Vince Elliott
Latitude Zero (1969) as Perry Lawton
Stoney (aka *The Surabaya Conspiracy*) (1969) as Dirk
Chisum (1970) as Jess Evans
Sometimes a Great Notion (1970) as Joe Ben Stamper
Deadly Dream (TV) (1971) as Delgreve
Counterfeit Green (TV) (1971) as Barth
Ulzana's Raid (1972) as Sgt. Burns
Firehouse (TV) (1973) as Hank Myers
The Red Pony (1973) as James Creighton
Partners in Crime (TV) (1973) as Frank Jordan
Pat Garrett and Billy the Kid (1973) as Sheriff Kip McKinney
The Outfit (1973) as Kimmie Chemey
The Kill (1973) as Ming
Chosen Survivors (1974) as Major Gordon Ellis
Born Innocent (TV) (1974) as Mr. Parker
Adventures in Satan's Canyon (TV) (1974) as Jack Ryan
The Last Day (TV) (1975) as Grat Dalton
The Drowning Pool (1975) as Franks
Part Two—Walking Tall (1975) as Stud Pardee
Grizzly (1976) as Scott
Mako: The Jaws of Death (1976) as Sonny Stein
Bound for Glory (1976) (scenes deleted)

The Amazing Mr. No Legs (1977) as Chuck
Kit Carson and the Mountain Men (TV) (1977) as Ed Kern
Twilight's Last Gleaming (1977) as Captain Stanford Towne
Day of the Animals (1977) as Professor Taylor McGregor
Speedtrap (1977) as Billy
Pacific Inferno (1978) as Robert "Dealer" Fletcher
Delta Fox (1978) as Santana
Go West, Young Girl (TV) (1978) as Billy
Centennial (TV) (1978) as Sgt. Lykes
Champions: A Love Story (TV) (1979)
Salvage (TV) (1979) as Jack Klinger
The Dark (1979) as Detective Dave Mooney
The Falcon's Ultimatum (1979)
The $5.20 an Hour Dream (TV) (1980) as Albert Kleinschmidt
Reward (TV) (1980) as Capt. Randolph
Herbie Goes Bananas (1980) as Shepard
…All the Marbles (1981) as Bill Dudley
Cold River (1982) as Mike Allison
Airplane II: The Sequel (1982) as Controller #2
Blood Song (1982) as Frank Hauser
Hammett (1982) (scenes deleted)
The Awakening of Candra (TV) (1983) as Robert Harrison
Killing Machine (1984) as Martin
The Fix (1984) as Charles Dale
Starman (1984) as George Fox
The Dirty Dozen: Next Mission (TV) (1985) as Sgt. Clyde Bowren
Spenser: For Hire (TV) (1985) as Lt. Martin Quirk
Black Moon Rising (1986) as Earl Windom
Supercarrier: Deadly Enemies (TV) (1988) as Master Chief Sam Rivers
Ghetto Blaster (1989) as Mike Henry
Baywatch: Panic at Malibu Pier (1989) (TV) as Al Gibson
Delta Force 2: The Colombian Connection (1990) as DEA Agent John Page
The King of the Kickboxers (1990) as Capt. O'Day
Martial Outlaw (1993) as Mr. White

Television Shows

The Bigelow Theatre "TKO" (10–29–1951)
Front Page Detective "The Perfect Secretary" (1952)
Four Star Playhouse "The Squeeze" (10–1–1953)
Stories of the Century "Billy the Kid" (1–30–1954)
The U.S. Steel Hour "The Last Notch" (3–30–1954)
Public Defender "The Prizefighter Story" (4–8–1954)
Public Defender "The Last Appeal" (8–30–1954)
Goodyear Playhouse "Big Man on Campus" (9–12–1954)
The Elgin Hour "Floodtide" (10–5–1954)
The Ford Television Theatre "Daughter of Mine" (10–7–1954)
Kraft Theatre "Papa Was a Sport" (10–13–1954)
California (TV Special) (10–16–1954)
The Millionaire "The Nancy Marlborough Story" (3–9–1955)
The Bob Cummings Show "Advice to the Lovelorn" (4–24–1955)
Producer's Showcase "The Petrified Forest" (10–30–1955)
Matinee Theatre "For These Services" (12–7–1955)
Jane Wyman Presents the Fireside Theatre "Big Joe's Comin' Home" (12–27–1955)
They Seek Adventure (2–1956)
Front Row Center "Dinner Date" (3–18–1956)
Matinee Theatre "Night Must Fall" (5–4–1956)
Climax "To Scream at Midnight" (6–14–1956)
Wire Service "Nameless" (10–4–1956)
West Point "Honor Code" (10–26–1956)
The 20th Century–Fox Hour "Smoke Jumpers" (11–14–1956)
Schlitz Playhouse "Tower Room 14-A" (1–11–1957)
Matinee Theatre "The Brat's House" (2–11–1957)
West Point "The Command" (2–22–1957)
Navy Log "War of the Whaleboats" (3–13–1957)
Crossroads "Paratroop Padre" (3–29–1957)
Crossroads "The Light" (4–5–1957)
Matinee Theatre "Aftermath" (5–20–1957)
Panic "Mayday" (6–11–1957)
Playhouse 90 "Ain't No Time for Glory" (6–20–1957)
Matinee Theatre "The Awakening" (8–27–1957)
The Silent Service "The Starfish Came Home" (10–25–1957)
Man Without a Gun "The Seven Killers" (11–8–1957)
The Gray Ghost "The Hero" (1958)

Alcoa Theatre "The Days of November" (2-24-1958)
Panic "Flight" (aka "Parachute Jump") (6-8-1958)
The Millionaire "The Betty Hawley Story" (9-3-1958)
The Silent Service "The Swordfish Story" (10-3-1958)
Cimarron City "The Blood Line" (12-13-1958)
Behind Closed Doors "Message from Hardenburg" (1-8¬-1959)
The Texan "The Man Behind the Star" (2-9-1959)
Trackdown "The Protector" (4-1-1959)
Naked City "Baker's Dozen" (4-14-1959)
Alcoa Theatre "Ten Miles to Doomsday" (4-20-1959)
Tightrope "The Cracking Point" (10-6-1959)
Zane Grey Theater "The Man in the Middle" (2-11-1960)
The Rebel "The Rattler" (3-13-1960)
Tales of Wells Fargo "The Kinfolk" (9-26-1960)
77 Sunset Strip "The Office Caper" (10-7-1960)
The Rebel "Run, Killer, Run" (10-30-1960)
The Untouchables "The Otto Frick Story" (12-22-1960)
The Tall Man "The Grudge Fight" (1-21-1961)
Lawman "Blue Boss and Willie Shay" (3-12-1961)
Alfred Hitchcock Presents "Incident in a Small Jail" (3-21-1961)
Wagon Train "The Chalice" (5-24-1961)
Frontier Circus (series regular) (1961–1962) as Tony Gentry
The Mighty O (unsold 1955 pilot) (8-21-1962)
Have Gun—Will Travel "The Predators" (11-3-1962)
The Alfred Hitchcock Hour "Forecast: Low Clouds and Coastal Fog" (1-18-1963)
Wagon Train "The Lily Legend Story" (2-13-1963)
The Dakotas "Fargo" (2-25-1963)
Gunsmoke "Two of a Kind" (3-16-1963)
Perry Mason "The Case of the Lover's Leap" (4-4-1963)
The Alfred Hitchcock Hour "Death of a Cop" (5-24-1963)
Combat "Gideon's Army" (12-31-1963)
Temple Houston "The Case for William Gotch" (2-6-1964)
The Virginian "A Matter of Destiny" (2-19-1964)
The Outer Limits "Specimen: Unknown" (2-24-1964)
The New Phil Silvers Show "Keep Cool" (4-4-1964)
Suspense "The Leader" (6-3-1964)
Bonanza "Between Heaven and Earth" (11-15-1964)
The Alfred Hitchcock Hour "Off Season" (5-10-1965)
CBS Vacation Playhouse "Luke and the Tenderfoot" (8-13-1965)
Perry Mason "The Case of the Bogus Buccaneers" (1-9-1966)
Gunsmoke "The Raid" (1-22, 1-29-1966)
The Wild Wild West "The Night of the Grand Emir" (1-28-1966)
The Time Tunnel "The Ghost of Nero" (1-20-1967)
The Wild Wild West "The Night of the Cadre" (3-24-1967)
Bonanza "Night of Reckoning" (10-15-1967)
The Name of the Game "The White Birch" (11-29-1968)
The F.B.I. "Death Watch" (2-14-1971)
O'Hara, U.S. Treasury "Operation: Offset" (10-22-1971)
Mission: Impossible "Run for the Money" (12-11-1971)
Insight "The System" (4-18-1972)
Emergency "Kids" (9-23-1972)
Ironside "The Countdown" (11-23-1972)
Banyon (series regular) (1972–1973) as Lt. Pete McNeil
Shaft "The Enforcers" (10-9-1973)
The F.B.I. "Selkirk's War" (1-27-1974)
Firehouse (series regular) (1974) as Hank Myers
Movin' On "Roadblock" (9-19-1974)
Police Story "Fathers and Sons" (10-1-1974)
Lucas Tanner "Winners and Losers" (10-9-1974)
Petrocelli "Counterploy" (12-4-1974)
Gunsmoke "Larkin" (1-20-1975)
Cannon "The Wrong Medicine" (9-24-1975)
Ellery Queen "The Adventure of the Blunt Instrument" (12-18-1975)
Little House "Long Road Home" (3-3-1976)
Joe Forrester "Pressure Point" (3-22-1976)
Baretta "Aggie" (3-24-1976)
Jigsaw John "Homicide 96403" (6-14-1976)
McCloud "Bonnie and McCloud" (10-24-1976)

Gemini Man "Suspect Your Local Police" (12–1976) (unaired in U.S.)
The Fantastic Journey "The Innocent Prey" (6–16–1977)
Kingston: Confidential "Anonymous Hero" (8–10–1977)
Carter Country "Out of the Closet" (9–29–1977)
Young Dan'l Boone "The Plague" (10–1977) (unaired in U.S.)
The Oregon Trail "The Scarlett Ribbon" (11–1977) (unaired in U.S.)
Big Hawaii "You Can't Lose 'Em All" (11–30–1977)
Black Sheep Squadron "The Iceman" (3–8–1978)
Salvage 1 (series regular) (1979) as Jack Klinger
Lou Grant "Witness" (11–12–1979)
Insight "Princess" (4–4–1980)
Charlie's Angels "Island Angels" (12–14–1980)
Little House on the Prairie "Sylvia" (2–9 & 2–16–1981)
Hot W.A.C.S. (pilot) (6–1–1981)
McClain's Law "What Patric Doesn't Know" (2–5–1982)
King's Crossing "The Home Front" (2–27–1982)
Cassie & Co. "Friend in Need" (7–6–1982)
Matt Houston "Rock and a Hard Place" (1–2–1983)
Fantasy Island "Operation Breakout" (1–15–1983)
At Ease (series regular) (1983) as Major Hawkins
Dallas "Ray's Trial" (11–11–1983)
Dallas "The Oil Baron's Ball" (11–18–1983)
The Love Boat "Bet on It" (1–14–1984)
Masquerade "Spanish Gambit" (4–20–1984)
Cover Up "Murder Offshore" (1–12–1985)
Spenser: For Hire (series regular) (1985–1987) as Lt. Martin Quirk
Murder She Wrote "The Way to Dusty Death" (10–25–1987)
Supercarrier (series regular) (1988) as Master Chief Sam Rivers
China Beach "Quest" (6–25–1991)
Baywatch (series regular) (1991–1994) as Captain Ben Edwards

Chapter Notes

Introduction
1. L.Q. Jones (phone conversation, January 2014).

Chapter 1
1. Paul Wurtzel (phone conversation, July 2013).
2. Stuart Whitman (phone conversation, November 2014).

Chapter 2
1. William Phipps (phone conversation, August 2014).
2. Tim Lyon (phone conversation, April 2014).
3. Dick Tyler (e-mail correspondence, January 2014).
4. Barbara Bond (e-mail correspondence, July 2013).
5. Walter Hoffman (phone conversation, March 2014).
6. Tim Lyon (phone conversation, April 2014).
7. Cal Porter (written correspondence, October 2014).
8. Clark Hatch (e-mail correspondence, March 2014).
9. Tim Lyon (phone conversation, April 2014).
10. Tim Lyon (phone conversation, April 2014).
11. Leonard Gumley (phone conversation, September 2014).
12. Clark Hatch (e-mail correspondence, March 2014).
13. Robert Fuller (phone conversation, January 2014).

Chapter 3
1. Tim Lyon (phone conversation, April 2014).
2. Tim Lyon (phone conversation, April 2014).
3. William Phipps (phone conversation, August 2014).
4. Tim Lyon (phone conversation, April 2014).
5. Brett Halsey (e-mail correspondence, October 2014).
6. L.Q. Jones (phone conversation, January 2014).

Chapter 4
1. Stuart Whitman (phone conversation, November 2014).
2. Brad Harris (phone conversation, January 2014).
3. L.Q. Jones (phone conversation, January 2014).
4. L.Q. Jones (phone conversation, January 2014).
5. Robert Phillips (phone conversation, January 2014).
6. Tim Lyon (phone conversation, April 2014).
7. L.Q. Jones (phone conversation, January 2014).
8. Raymond Austin (e-mail correspondence, January 2014).
9. A.J. Fenady (phone conversation, January 2014).
10. Clu Gulager (phone conversation, February 2014).

Chapter 5
1. James McMullan (e-mail correspondence, October 2014).
2. Robert Fuller (phone conversation, January 2014).
3. Ronnie Rondell (phone conversation, October 2014).
4. Denny Miller (personal meeting, March 2009).
5. Ronnie Rondell (phone conversation, October 2014).
6. Read Morgan (phone conversation, March 2014).
7. Tim Lyon (phone conversation, April 2014).
8. James Drury (phone conversation, March 2014).
9. Clark Hatch (e-mail correspondence, March 2014).
10. James Drury (phone conversation, March 2014).
11. Read Morgan (phone conversation, March 2014).
12. Vincent McEveety (phone conversation, May 2014).

Chapter 6
1. Raymond Austin (e-mail correspondence, January 2014).
2. Robert Phillips (phone conversation, January 2014).
3. Ronnie Rondell (phone conversation, October 2014).
4. Tom Korzeniowski (e-mail correspondence, September 2013).
5. Clark Hatch (e-mail correspondence, March 2014).
6. Clark Hatch (e-mail correspondence, March 2014).
7. Garry Armstrong (e-mail correspondence, March 2014).
8. Edward Faulkner (e-mail correspondence, April 2014).
9. A.J. Fenady (phone conversation, January 2014).
10. Ron Bernard (phone conversation, June 2014).
11. Bonnie Stout (phone conversation, June 2014).
12. Clu Gulager (phone conversation, February 2014).
13. James Drury (phone conversation, March 2014).

Chapter 7
1. Clark Hatch (e-mail correspondence, March 2014).

2. Neil Summers (personal meeting, October 2014).
3. Robert Fuller (phone conversation, January 2014).
4. Ralph Senensky (electronic correspondence, April 2014).
5. Ralph Senensky (electronic correspondence, April 2014).
6. L.Q. Jones (phone conversation, January 2014).
7. Joseph Culliton (e-mail correspondence, July 2013).
8. Garry Armstrong (e-mail correspondence, March 2014).
9. Tim Lyon (phone conversation, April 2014).
10. Garry Armstrong (e-mail correspondence, March 2014).
11. James Drury (phone conversation, March 2014).
12. Michael Delano (phone conversation, May 2014).
13. Bradford Dillman (written correspondence, January 2014).
14. Vincent McEveety (phone conversation, May 2014).
15. Morgan Woodward (phone conversation, November 2014).
16. Joe Morella (e-mail correspondence, October 2014).
17. Andrew Robinson (e-mail correspondence, February 2014).
18. Bo Svenson (e-mail correspondence, July 2013).
19. Bruce Glover (phone conversation, February 2014).
20. Chris Ladd (e-mail correspondence, November 2014).

Chapter 8

1. David Sheldon (e-mail correspondence, February 2014).
2. William Grefe (phone conversation, January 2014).
3. William Grefe (phone conversation, January 2014).
4. Monty Cox (phone conversation, November 2014).
5. Ricou Browning (e-mail correspondence, February 2014).
6. Brad Harris (phone conversation, January 2014).
7. Ric Drasin (e-mail correspondence, September 2014).
8. Jack Neworth (phone conversation, February 2014).
9. Vincent McEveety (phone conversation, May 2014).
10. William Smith (personal meeting, July 1997).
11. Monty Cox (e-mail correspondence, November 2014).
12. Susan Backlinie (written correspondence, March 2014).
13. Robert Phillips (phone conversation, January 2014).
14. Henry C. Parke (e-mail correspondence, October 2014).
15. Rodd Wolff (personal meeting, August 2013).
16. Jack Young (e-mail correspondence, June 2013).
17. John Wilder (e-mail correspondence, April 2014).
18. Ferd Sebastian (written correspondence, February 2014).
19. Bud Cardos (phone conversation, April 2014).
20. Nancy Barr Ellen (phone conversation, July 2013).
21. Melody Clark Faith (e-mail correspondence, March 2014).
22. Bonnie Stout (phone conversation, June 2014).
23. Robert Fuller (phone conversation, January 2014).
24. George Wyner (phone conversation, August 2014).
25. Nancy Barr Ellen (phone conversation, July 2013).
26. Dan Moberly (e-mail correspondence, July 2014).
27. Charles Dierkop (written correspondence, June 2014).
28. Michael Preece (phone conversation, June 2014).
29. David Wells (e-mail correspondence, May 2014).
30. Jesse Vint (e-mail correspondence, May 2014).
31. John Wilder (e-mail correspondence, April 2014).
32. Ron McLarty (e-mail correspondence, August 2013).
33. Dan Shor (e-mail correspondence, April 2014).

Chapter 9

1. Dale Dye (e-mail correspondence, April 2014).
2. Alan L. Stewart (e-mail correspondence, March 2014).
3. Read Morgan (phone conversation, March 2014).
4. Gregory J. Bonann (e-mail correspondence, April 2014).
5. Dick Warlock (e-mail correspondence, July 2013).
6. Gregory J. Bonann (e-mail correspondence, April 2014).
7. Alexandra Paul (written correspondence, February 2014).
8. Dick Warlock (e-mail correspondence, July 2013).
9. John Wilder (e-mail correspondence, April 2014).
10. Gregory J. Bonann (e-mail correspondence, April 2014).

Chapter 10

1. Budd Albright (e-mail correspondence, May 2013).
2. Nancy Barr Ellen (phone conversation, July 2014).
3. Robert Fuller (phone conversation, January 2014).
4. William Smith (personal meeting, July 1997).
5. Dick Warlock (e-mail correspondence, July 2013).
6. Ronnie Rondell (phone conversation, October 2014).
7. William Grefe (phone conversation, January 2014).
8. Ricou Browning (e-mail correspondence, February 2014).
9. John Wilder (e-mail correspondence, April 2014).
10. Bud Cardos (phone conversation, April 2014).
11. Vincent McEveety (phone conversation, May 2014).
12. A.J. Fenady (phone conversation, January 2014).
13. Walter Hoffman (phone conversation, March 2014).
14. Read Morgan (phone conversation, March 2014).
15. Robert Phillips (phone conversation, January 2014).
16. Dick Tyler (e-mail correspondence, January 2014).
17. Monty Cox (phone conversation, November 2014).
18. Clark Hatch (e-mail correspondence, March 2014).
19. Tim Lyon (phone conversation, April 2014).
20. Brad Harris (phone conversation, January 2014).
21. James Drury (phone conversation, March 2014).
22. Robert Phillips (phone conversation, January 2014).

Bibliography

"After All Those Roles, Actor Finally Promoted to Sergeant." *The Ogden Standard.* January 22, 1967.
"After 28 Years Richard Jaeckel Is Star." *Salt Lake Tribune.* January 22, 1972.
Albert, Stephen W., and Diane Albert. "Our Guest Today: Richard Jaeckel." *TV Collector.* Oct/Nov. 1985.
Albright, Brian. "As Slime Goes By: Screenwriter Charles Sinclair." *Videoscope.* Spring 2011, #78.
Albright, Brian. *Regional Horror Films, 1958–1990.* Jefferson, NC: McFarland, 2012.
Albright, Brian. *Wild Beyond Belief!* Jefferson, NC: McFarland, 2008.
Aldrich, Robert, Edwin T. Arnold and Eugene L. Miller. *Robert Aldrich: Interviews.* Jackson: University Press of Mississippi, 2004.
Anderson, Nancy. "Drury Warmed Up for Role." *Scottsdale Daily Progress.* April 12, 1974.
Anderson, Penny P. "His Face Looks a Little Familiar." *Richmond Times Dispatch.* March 27, 1974.
Armstrong, Stephen. "Andrew V. McLaglen Looks Back." *Classic Images.* April 2009.
Arness, James, and James E. Wise, Jr. *James Arness: An Autobiography.* Jefferson, NC: McFarland, 2001.
Arnold, Edward T., and Eugene L. Miller, Jr. *The Films and Career of Robert Aldrich.* Knoxville: University of Tennessee, 1986.
Arnold, Gary. "Plugging Away." *The Washington Post.* May 18, 1973.
Ashe, Isobel. "Television's *Frontier Circus* Offers Something for Everyone." *The Reading Eagle.* November 19, 1961.
Barnhart, Tony. "Different Strokes." *Greensboro Record.* April 4, 1981.
Baskette, Kirtley. "Everything's Jake." *Modern Screen.* April 1945.
Beck, Marilyn. "Actor Survives 43 Years in Hollywood." *Santa Fe New Mexican.* July 6, 1986.
Beck, Marilyn. "Hollywood Close-Up." *Milwaukee Journal.* January 6, 1972.
Behrman, S.N. "Mr. Jaeckel and a Few Hides." *New Yorker.* April 9, 1932.
Blevins, Winfred. "The Third Guy on the Left: Jaeckel Gets that Bigger Role." *Los Angeles Herald Examiner.* February 12, 1972.
Bogert, John. "Nobody Can Say Actor Richard Jaeckel Wasn't Somebody." *Daily Breeze.* June 19, 1997.
Buck, Jerry. "Jaeckel Goes from Mail Room to Battlefield in New 'At Ease.'" *Aiken Standard.* April 29, 1983.
Canfield, Own. "Jaeckel's No Actor When It Comes to Golf." *Hartford Courant.* August 22, 1976.
Cangey, R.M. *Inside the Wild Wild West.* Self-published, 1996.
Condon, George E. "Jaeckel Just Might Hide Four-Legged Leotards." *Plain-Dealer.* August 26, 1961.
Cook, Ben. "Jaeckel Likes Casting as Heel." *San Mateo Times.* May 3, 1952.
Coons, Robbin. "The Reluctant Actor." *Motion Picture.* July 1947.
Curtis, Tony, and Barry Paris. *Tony Curtis: The Autobiography.* New York: William Morrow, 1993.
Deere, Dorothy. "Everything's Jaeckel." *Photoplay.* July 1944.
Dern, Bruce, and Christopher Fryer. *Things I've Said, But Probably Shouldn't Have: An Unrepentant Memoir.* Hoboken, NJ: John Wiley & Sons, 2007.
"Dig Film Tough: 'I've Reformed.'" *Salt Lake Tribune.* September 25, 1961.
Dillman, Bradford. *Are You Anybody? An Actor's Life.* Santa Barbara, CA: Fithian Press, 1997.
Dixon, Wheeler W., and Reginald LeBorg. *The Films of Reginald LeBorg: Interviews, Essays, and Filmography.* Metuchen, NJ: Scarecrow, 1992.
Dudley, Fredda. "Right Guy." *Movieland.* March 1945.
Dudley, Fredda. "The Tired Admiral." *Photoplay.* November 1944.
Erickson, Hal. *Syndicated Television: The First Forty Years, 1947–1987.* Jefferson, NC: McFarland, 1989.
Eyman, Scott. *John Wayne: The Life and Legend.* New York: Simon & Schuster, 2014.
Eyres, Allen. "The Private War of Robert Aldrich." *Films and Filming.* #13, 1967.
Fagen, Herb. *White Hats and Silver Spurs: Interviews with 24 Stars of Film and Television Westerns of the Thirties through the Sixties.* Jefferson, NC: McFarland, 1996.
Finn, Gerry. "What's in a Name?" *Springfield Union.* August 21, 1976.
Fishgall, Gary. *Against Type: The Biography of Burt Lancaster.* New York: Scribner, 1995.

Gagnard, Frank. "Still in Shape." *Times Picayune*. May 11, 1973.

Gaucher, Claire. "Two Boys Named Richard." *Motion Picture and Television Magazine*. April 1953.

Gay, John, and Jennifer Gay Summers. *Any Way I Can: 50 Years in Show Business*. BearManor Media, 2008.

Glines, Carol. "Lonely Last Days of Richard Jaeckel." *The Globe*. July 1, 1997.

Greenland, David R. *The Gunsmoke Chronicles: A New History of Television's Greatest Western*. Albany, GA: BearManor Media, 2013.

Greenletter, Horace. "Actor to Gamble on One Assignment." *Los Angeles Daily News*. November 24, 1952.

Hardy, Phil. *The Western*. New York: William Morrow, 1983.

Henry, William. "Richard Jaeckel Lives Movies." *Boston Globe*. June 3, 1973.

Hilton, Pat. "Jaeckel Takes Pride in Solid Reputation." *Victoria Advocate*. June 29, 1986.

Homenick, Brett. "Cult Classic Commander: G-Fan Interviews Robert Horton." *G-Fan*. #86. Winter 2008.

Homenick, Brett. "Lucianna Paluzzi Discusses *The Green Slime*." *G-Fan*. #81. Fall 2007.

Hughes, Mike. "Marvin, Borgnine March into 'Dirty Dozen' Sequel." *Register Star*. February 2, 1985.

"Jaeckel Gains Spotlight." *Spokane Daily Chronicle*. March 21, 1981.

"Jaeckel Peps Up Show's Pace." *Charleston Gazette*. January 19, 1974.

"Jaeckel's Dilemma." *Los Angeles Herald Examiner*. January 13, 1968.

"Jake Comes Home." *Movie Star Parade*. April 1947.

Jankiewicz, Pat. "Dancing Around Triskelion." *Starlog* 1992.

Johnson, Erskine. "In Hollywood." *Kingsport Times*. July 17, 1953.

Johnson, Erskine. "In Hollywood." *The Long Beach Independent*. April 20, 1953.

Karr, Jeanne. "Jake of the Maritimes." *Modern Screen*. October 1944.

Kaufman, Dave. "Jaeckel expounds on *Banyon*." *Variety*. June 1, 1972.

Kleiner, Dick. "Richard Jaeckel: Up from Obscurity." *Abilene Reporter*. February 11, 1972.

Lanken, Dane. "Jaeckel: Support for the Movies." *Montreal Gazette*. May 16, 1973.

Lawrence, Marc. *Long Time No See: Confessions of a Hollywood Gangster*. Palm Springs, CA: Ursus Press, 1991.

Lentz, Robert J. *The Films of Lee Marvin*. Jefferson, NC: McFarland, 2000.

Lewis, Grover. "The Battle Cry of Aldo Ray." *Movieline*. January 1, 1991.

Lockwood, Gary. *2001 Memories: An Actor's Odyssey*. Boca Raton, FL: Cowboy Press, 2001.

"Lonely Last Days of Richard Jaeckel." *National Enquirer*. June 1997.

Love, Matt. *Sometimes a Great Movie*. South Beach, OR: Nestucca Press, 2012.

Mahan, Bill. "Takes Acting in His Stride." *Winnipeg Free Press*. June 14, 1975.

Mahar, Ted. "Family Man Role Novelty to Heavy." *Oregonian*. July 27, 1970.

Maltin, Leonard. *Leonard Maltin's Movie Encyclopedia*. New York: Dutton, 1994.

Maltin, Leonard. *Leonard Maltin's 2014 Movie Guide*. New York: Signet, 2013.

Martin, John Bartlow. "Television USA." *Saturday Evening Post*. November 1961.

Marvin, Pamela. *Lee: A Romance*. London: Faber & Faber, 1997.

Mason, Todd. "Richard Jaeckel Survived Through Bad Pictures." *San Francisco Examiner and Chronicle*. February 6, 1972.

Moore, Terry. *The Beauty and the Billionaire*. New York: Pocket, 1984.

Mosby, Aline. "Young Actor Returns to Wife, Finds Security, Solidarity." *Deseret News*. February 1, 1956.

"Mrs. Jaeckel Wins Divorce." *Los Angeles Herald Examiner*. February 4, 1953.

Murray, Jim. "A Different Handicap." *The Los Angeles Times*. May 19, 1978.

Oviatt, Ray. "Circus Gives Jaeckel New Role." *The Toledo Blade*. August 28, 1961.

Peary, Danny. *Guide for the Film Fanatic*. New York: Simon & Schuster, 1986.

Pezman, Steve. "Hobie's Story: Chapter from His Early Years." *Surfer's Journal*. August 2009.

Radosta, John. "Jaeckel Gets Day Off." *The New York Times*. March 23, 1981.

"Richard Jaeckel Promotes Two Films." *Times Daily*. May 20, 1973.

"Richard Jaeckel, 70, Tough Guy in Movies Career Spanned 'Dirty Dozen' to 'Baywatch.'" *South Florida Sun-Sentinel*. June 17, 1997.

Richards, Allen Grant. "Jaeckel Thrives in 'Spenser' Role." *Boston Herald*. November 9, 1986.

Roberts, Clive. "Meeting Some of Hollywood's Character Performers." *Hollywood Movie Memories*.

Roosevelt, Edith. "Solid Film Hit Needed by Jaeckel." *Los Angeles Daily News*. March 1, 1952.

Rubin, Steven Jay. *Combat Films: American Realism, 1945–2010*. Jefferson, NC: McFarland, 2011.

Rude, Jeff. "Journeyman Barry Jaeckel." *Golf Week*. May 6, 2011.

Ryfle, Steve. "More Than Just a Pretty Face: An Interview with Actress Linda Haynes." *Shock Cinema*. #36, 2009.

Sarmento, William E. "Richard Jaeckel's Long Career Reaches New High." *Lowell Sun*. July 22, 1973.

Schow, David. *The Outer Limits: The Official Companion*. New York: Ace Science Fiction, 1986.

Scott, Vernon. "Actors Form Posse to Fight Work Cuts." *Schenectady Gazette*. July 26, 1972.

Scott, Vernon. "Character Actor Richard Jaeckel Homebody, Not Filmland Swinger." *Simpson's Leader*. November 27, 1972.

Scott, Vernon. "His Face Is More Familiar Than His Name." *Hutchinson News*. April 28, 1979.

Simeone, Linda. "The Dirty Deeds of Richard Jaeckel." *Daredevils*. May 1985.

South, John, and Ed Susman. "*Baywatch* Star Richard Jaeckel Dying of Cancer." *National Enquirer*. 1994.

Squire, Nancy Winslow. "Chicken Jake." *Modern Screen*. July 1944.

Strassberg, Phil. "Jaeckel Won't Buy His Oscar." *The Arizona Republic*. March 1, 1972.

Swires, Steve. "John Carpenter on *Starman*." *Starlog*. #92. March 1985.
Taylor, Nora E. "Western Gunslinger Quiet, Polite in Boston." *Christian Science Monitor*. May 25, 1973.
"Terry Catches On." *Screenland Plus*. January 1953.
Thompson, Doug. "Violence Doesn't Bug Him." *Alton Telegraph*. May 19, 1973.
Twomey, Alfred E., and Arthur F. McClure. *The Versatiles*. New York: A.S. Barnes, 1969.
Vadeboncoeur, Jane E. "Marvin, Jaeckel Reprise 'Dirty Dozen' Roles." *Syracuse Herald-Journal*. January 31, 1985.
"*Wagon Train* with Elephants." *TV Times*. April 28, 1962.
"War Film Actor Is Seaman Now." *Times-Picayune*. January 23, 1945.
Wiedrich, Bob. "Tower Ticker." *Chicago Tribune*. October 12, 1972.
"Wife Sues for Divorce." *Los Angeles Herald Express*. January 8, 1953.
Wilson, Maggie. "Mailman Becomes Star Actor." *The Arizona Republic*. February 6, 1954.
Witbeck, Charles. "Star Burns with Enthusiasm in New Firehouse Program." *The Bridgeport Post*. January 17, 1974.
Young, A.S. Doc. "How Jim Brown Beats the Hollywood System." *Sepia*. February 1978.
Zink, Jack. "Movie Longevity Can't Bog Down Jaeckel." *Fort Lauderdale News*. May 20, 1973.

Websites

Ancestry.com: www.ancestry.com (newspaper archive)
A/V Forum: www.avforum.com (film reviews)
Bonanza: Scenery of the Pondarosa: www.ponderosascenery.com (*Bonanza* website)
Comeuppance Reviews: www.comeuppancereviews.com (film reviews)
Cool Ass Cinema: www.coolasscinema.com (film reviews)
Cult Movie Forum: www.cultmovieforum.com (film reviews)
Film Fanatic: www.filmfanatic.org (film reviews)
Find a Grave: www.findagrave.com (Richard Jaeckel Memorial)
Genealogy Bank: www.genealogybank.com (newspaper archive)
Google News: www.news.google.com (newspaper archive)
IMDB: www.imdb.com (movie database)
ModCinema: www.modcinema.com (film reviews)
Newspaper Archive: www.newspaperarchive.com (newspaper archives)
Ralph's Cinema Trek: www.senensky.com (director Ralph Senensky's television blog)
Ray Bennett's the Cliff Edge: www.thecliffedge.com (Ray Bennett website)
Screen Actors Guild: www.sagaftra.com (Screen Actors Guild website)
The Spinning Image: www.thespinningimage.co.uk (film reviews)
TCM: www.tcm.com (Turner Classic Movies database)
U.S. Merchant Marines: www.usmm.org (merchant marine website)
We Are Movie Geeks: www.wearemoviegeeks.com (film reviews)
Wikipedia: www.wikipedia.org (general info)

Index

Numbers in **_bold italics_** indicate pages with photographs.

Aames, Willie 159
ABC 42, 113, 120, 156, 164, 169
Academy Awards 107, 108, 109
Academy Players Directory 44–45
actor's strike 64, 65, 151
Adams, Julie 76
Adams, Nick 53, 63, 66, 94, 96, 107
Adamson, Ed 112–113
Addy, Wesley 77
Adirondacks 154
Adler, Luther 32
Adler Elevator Shoes 78
Adventure in Satan's Canyon (1974) 124, 185
Adventures of Kit Carson 47
Agar, John 25, 77, 101, 134
agelessness 4, 66, 85, 99, 101, 106, 127, 134, 140, 154, 157, 160, 162, 170, 171, 176, 180
agents 27, 37, 42, 47, 67, 86, 88, 91, 107, 140, 141, 142
The Agitators 159
Agua Dulce 74
Ahn, Philip 39
Aidman, Charles 159
Ain't No Time for Glory (1957) 54–55, 185
Airplane! (1980) 154
Airplane II: The Sequel (1982) 154–155, 186
Akins, Claude 63, 70, 86, 90, 91, 92, 110, 124
Alabama Hills 43
Alaska 16
Albert, Eddie 48–49, 59, 70
Albertson, Jack 81
Albertson Ranch 48
Albright, Budd 178
Albright, Lola 48
Albuquerque, New Mexico 123
Alcaide, Chris 70

Alcatraz: The Whole Shocking Story (1980) 146
Alcoa Theatre 56, 61, 187
Aldrich, Robert 3, 38, 42, 48–49, 69, 77, 78, 87, 88, 89, 90, 109, 110, 113, 119, 123, 136, 137, 138, 151, 152, 162
Alfred Hitchcock Hour 75, 76, 84, 187
Alfred Hitchcock Presents 67–68, 187
The All-American Boy (1973) 101
All Quiet on the Western Front 26
All the Marbles (1981) 151, 152, 186
Allen, Corey 61
Allen, Irwin 86
Allen, Karen 161
Alonzo, John A. 147
Alper, Murray 13
Alter, Hobie 20
Alzheimer's Disease 178
Amazing Mr. No Legs (1977) 134, 135, 186
The Amboy Dukes 22
Ameche, Don 13
American Bandstand 145
American Eagle 39
American Federation of Radio Artists 14
Anderson, John 70, 84
Anderson, Kurt 176
Anderson, Pamela 174
Andes, Keith 61
Andress, Ursula 39, 77, 78, 81, 82
Andrew Furuseth School of Seamanship 15
Andrews, Dana 13, 81, 82, 90
An Annapolis Story (1955) 57
Ansara, Michael 138, 140
Apache Ambush (1955) 47, 185
Apocalypse Now (1979) 149
appearance 4, 18, 33, 37, 39, 54,

60, 66, 74, 86, 91, 92, 95, 96, 99, 101, 132, 134, 140, 154, 159, 160, 161, 165
Archer, John 10
Arctic Rampage 152
Ardennes Forest 23
Arlen, Richard 77, 81
arm-wrestling 80–81
Armory, Cleveland 121
Armstrong, Garry 117, 120
Armstrong, R.G. 70, 84, 86, 115, 171
Arness, James 19–20, 23, 29, 75, 85, 153
arthritis 168, 173, 174, 178, 179, 181
Arthur, Indus 84
Arthur, Robert 27
Ashby, Hal 129
Ashe, Isobel 72
Askew, Luke 90, 116, 127, 128
Asner, Ed 149
Assault on Paradise (1977) 141
At Ease 156–158, 179, 188
athletics 6, 7, 8, 18, 46, 171
Attack! (1955) 48–49, 58, 185
Aubrey, James 114, 115
August, Adelle 47
Augusta, Kentucky 144
Austin, Raymond 65–66, 88–89
Autry, Gene 40
Avalon, Frankie 80, 154
Avedon, Loren 173
Avery, Val 111, 122
The Awakening of Candra (1983) 158, 186
Ayres, Leah 160
Azabu Towers 96

Bacall, Lauren 45
back/hip injury 19, 168, 170, 171, 173, 174, 181
Back Stage Bar 85

195

Backlinie, Susan 140
Bacon, Irving 13
Bacon, James 118
Baer, John 32
Bahamas 132, 155, 156
Bailey, David Alan 124
Baker, Blanche 158
Baker, Joe Don 118, 119, 127, 128, 141, 146
Balboa, California 59
Baldwin, Peter 80, 142
Banacek 120
Bancroft Junior High 6
bankruptcy 178
Banyon 111–113, 119, 187
Barash, Olivia 153
Barcelona, Spain 160
Barcroft, Roy 32
Baretta 130, 187
Barnes, Priscilla 145
Barnes, Rayford 76
Baron Leone 19
Barr, Nancy Ellen 4, 150–151, 158
Barrington Park 172
Barry, Don "Red" 81
Barry, Gene 55, 93, 108
Barrymore, John Drew 55
baseball 38–39, 46, 172
Batanides, Arthur 80
Battle Beyond the Stars 94
Battle Cry (1955) 57, 59
Battleground (1949) 23–24, 27, 170, 179, 185
Bavaria, Germany 69
Bayer, Ralf 119, 143
Baylor, Hal 26, 55
Baywatch 3, 171–172, 176–177, 179, 180, 181, 188
Baywatch: Panic at Malibu Pier (1989) 186
beach activities 8, 19, 20–21, 38, 79, 80, 101, 108, 134, 171
The Beach Boys 80, 173
Beatty, Ned 68
Beaudine, William, Jr. 124
Beck, John 116
Beck, Marilyn 90, 111, 165
Begley, Ed 29
Behind Closed Doors 61, 187
Bel Air, California 60, 78
Bellamy, Earl 128, 141
Bellini, Cal 144
Bendix, William 9, 10, **11**, 77
Benedict, Richard 22, 23
Bennett, Bruce 55
Bennett, Ray 57, 105, 119
Benny, Jack 40
Berlinger, Warren 63
Bernard, Ron 103
Best, James 57, 58, 79
Bettger, Lyle 81, 82
Betz, Carl 106
Beverly Hills Hotel 7, 11

Bicentennial Minute 130
Bickford, Charles 13
Bieri, Ramon 124
Big Hawaii 142, 188
Big Leaguer (1953) 38–39, 48, 185
The Big Trail (1930) 25
Bigelow Theatre 32, 186
Billy the Kid 29, 40, 53, 67, 99, 114, 144
Bireley's Orange Juice 10
Birney, David 129
bisexuality rumors 142
Bishop, Jenifer 132–133
Bishop, Joey 57
Bissell, Whit 29, 39, 48
Bixby, Bill 143
Black Moon Rising (1986) 165–166, 186
Black Sheep Squadron 143, 188
Black Star 64
Bladine, Pam 102–103
Blair, Janet 45
Blair, Linda 123–124
Blake, Robert 62, **68**, 69, 130
Blakely, Ronee 150
Blanks, Billy 173
Bleeth, Yasmine 174
Bloch, Robert 84
Blocker, Dan 86
Blondell, Joan 112, 113
Blood Song (1982) 154, 186
The Bob Cummings Show 48, 186
Bochner, Lloyd 134
bodybuilding 18–19, 33, 47, 54, 75, 95, 123, 134–135
Boetticher, Budd 40
Bogart, Humphrey 37, 45–46, 59, 64, 76
Bogdanovich, Peter 107
Bogert, John 181
Bonanza 70, 73, 80–81, 86, 143, 187
Bond, Barbara 20
Bonnan, Gregory J. 171, 172, 174, 177
Bono, Sonny 154
Boone, Richard 74, 117
boot camp 9, 15, 24, 26, 57
Booth, Shirley 32–35, **33**, 38
Borgnine, Ernest 61, 87, 93, 123, 146, 162, 163, 180
Borhamwood, England 88
Born Innocent (1974) 123–124, 185
Boston, Massachusetts 117, 119, 120, 163, 164
Botany Bay (1953) 37
Bouchet, Barbara 98, 99
Bound for Glory (1976) 129, 185
Bowen, Roger 156
Bowers, William 21
boxing 7, 12, 32, 40, 48, 101, 155
Boy Scouts of America 6, 12, 116

Boyd, William 40
Boyle, Peter 150
Bradbury Building 112
Bradford, Lane 70
Brady, Scott 32
Brand, Neville 69, 80
Brando, Marlon 64, 69, 102
Breakheart Pass (1976) 136
The Breaking Point (1950) 59
Brennan, Walter 39
Brentwood, California 46, 178
Brentwood Playhouse 84
Brian, David 74, 75
Bridges, Jeff 107, 161
Bridges, Lloyd 51, 106, 111, 129, 134, 154, 155
Brodie, Steve 30, 39
Bronson, Charles 60–61, 64, 75, 77, 86, 87, 88, 89, 90, 93, 136, 152, 153
Brooklyn, New York 22
Brooks, Avery 163, 164
Brooks, Norman 48
Brooks, Rand 176
Brown, James 26, 27, 31, 39
Brown, Jim 87, 88, 89, 90, 143, 144, 171, 180
Brown, Peter 75
Brown, Timothy 143
Browne, Coral 126
Browning, Ricou 134, 181
Bruce Connors Physical Services Gym 18, 19, 145
Bryant-King, Ursaline **151**
Brynner, Yul 64
Buchanan, Edgar 61
Buck, Jerry 147
Buono, Victor 77
Burk, Jim 102
Burr, Raymond 76, 84, 111, 137, 144, 154
Burrhead 19
Buttons, Red 70
Buttram, Pat 175
Byrd, Ralph 10
Byrnes, Edd "Kookie" 66
Byrnes, Jim 125

Cabot, Bruce 81, 82, 99
Cady, Jerry 8
Caesar, Harry 171
Cagney, James 10, 37, 64, 76
Cahill—U.S. Marshal (1973) 116
Calabasas, California 81
Calhoun, Rory 53, 62, 77
California 40, 186
The California Dolls 151
Cambridge, Massachusetts 164
Cameron, Rod 31
Camp Pendleton 9, 25, 26
Camp Williams 90
Campbell, William 38, 57, 58
Canby County, California 159

Index

cancer 4, 178, 181
"Cane and a High Starched Collar" 65
Cangey, Dick 85
Caniff, Milton 32
Cannon 129, 187
Cannon Film Distributors 133
Canoga Park, California 178
Cardos, John "Bud" 145, 146, 181
Carey, Harry, Jr. 70
Carey, Phil 81
Carey, Timothy 118, 141
Carpenter, Carleton 61
Carpenter, John 161, 166
Carr, Paul 76
Carradine, David 129, 146
Carradine, John 40
cars 10, 17, 19, 41, 122
Carson, Johnny 123
Carter Country 142, 153, 188
Carthay Circle Theater 45
Caruso, Anthony 125
Cascade Mountains 124
Cassavettes, John 87, 89
Cassell, Wally 26, 27
Cassie & Company 153, 188
casting directors 6, 36, 42, 56, 62, 73, 124, 138, 140
Cat Ballou (1965) 86
Catalina Island 9, 15, 16, 63
Cave of Outlaws (1951) 29, 185
CBS 48, 61, 73
Cedar, Jon 138, 140
Celebrity Jog-A-Thon 134
Centennial (1978) 144–145, 163, 186
Central Park, New York 41
Century City, California 136
Chamberlain, George Agnew 17
Chamberlain, Richard 144
Champion, John 156
Champions: A Love Story (1979) 146–147, 186
Chandler, Jeff 37
Chandler, John Davis 84, 115, 127, 132
Chaney, Lon 8
Chaney, Lon, Jr. 68, 81
Chapman, Lonny 32
character actors 1, 44–45, 65, 69, 76, 86, 91, 140, 165
Charles Hotel 164
Charles River 164
Charlie's Angels 150–151, 158, 188
Charro (1969) 171
Cheung Chau 119
Cheyenne 63
Chicago, Illinois 7, 138
China Beach 174, 188
Chinatown (1974) 162
Chisum (1970) 99–101, 107, 131, 185
Chitwood, Joie 134

The Choirboys (1977) 152
Chosen Survivors (1974) 123, 185
Church on the Way 152
Churubusco Studios 123
Cimarron City 61, 187
Cimarron Strip 12
Cinderella (1950) 43
Cinema Artists 135
The Cisco Kid 40
City Across the River (1949) 22–23, 185
Clark, Dick 145
Clark, Jon Garrison 151–152
Clark-Curzon, Melody 151–152
Claws 130
Clayton, Georgia 130
Climax! 50, 186
coaching 17, 46, 124, 172
Coburn, James 64, 86, 114, 117, 173
Cody, Kathleen 125
Coe, Peter 27
Cohn, Harry 59
Cokliss, Harley 166
Cold River (1982) 153–154, 186
Coleman, Dabney 80, 113
Coleman, Nancy 45
Colla, Richard 102
Columbia Pictures 39, 43, 47, 50–51, 55, 59, 160
The Comancheros (1961) 12
Combat 78–79, 86, 187
Come Back, Little Sheba (1952) 3, 9, 18, 32–35, 36, 37, 38, 40, 41, 64, 69, 95, 131, 185
Commander USA 132
Condon, George E. 72
Connelly, Christopher 80, 125, 137
Connors, Chuck 63, 154
Connors, Mike 60, 63
Conrad, Michael 84
Conrad, Robert 85, 125, 143, 144
Conrad, William 129
Conte, Richard 10
controversial roles 69, 81, 120, 123, 142, 153
Converse, Frank 124
Coogan, Jackie 20
Cook, Ben 34
Cook, Elisha Jr., 63, 115, 118
Cool Hand Luke (1967) 101, 125
Cooper, Jackie 111, 123
Cooper, Stuart 90
Coos Bay, Oregon 154
cop roles 112, 124, 130, 148, 163
Coppola, Francis Ford 149, 150
Corbett, Glenn 99, 101, 106, 159
Corby, Ellen 31
Cord, Alex 123
Corey, Jeff 22
Cornelius, Don 144
Corner Canyon, Utah 90

Coronado National Forest 109
Corregidor 143
Corrigan, Ray "Crash" 47
Costello, Ward 64
The Cottage 80
Cotton, Joseph 98
Couch, Bill 92
Counterfeit Green (1971) 106, 185
Couples, Fred 108
Courtland, Jerome 23
Courtney, Chuck 56, 73, 85, 110, 143, 150, 160
Cover Up 161, 162, 188
Cowboy (1958) 55–56, 185
Cox, Monty 134, 139, 181
Craig, Yvonne 85
Crain, Jeanne 17
Crampton, Gerry 88–89
Crane, Kenneth G. 60
Crane, Stephen 30
Crawford, Broderick 42
Creature from the Black Lagoon (1954) 121
Crenna, Richard 144, 155
Crosby, Bing 108
Crosby, Cathy Lee 145
Crosland, Alan, Jr. 71
Crossroads 56, 186
Culliton, Joseph 116
Culliton, Patrick 116
Culp, Robert 62, 120
cult films 95, 98, 115, 134, 139
Cummings, Bob 45, 48
Curtis, Keene 129
Curtis, Tony 22–23, 37, 140
Cycle Savages (1969) 93

The Dakotas 74. 187
Dale, Dick 80
Dali, Salvador 54
Dallas 159–160, 188
Dallas, Texas 52
Daly, Tyne 141
Daniels, Lisa 61
Danning, Sybil 159
Dano, Royal 113, 153
Dante, Joe 180
Danton, Ray 79
The Dark (1979) 108, 143–146, 151, 164, 186
Dark, Christopher 63
Darro, Frankie 29
Darwell, Jane 41
Da Silva, Howard 29
Davalos, Dick 54
Daves, Delmer 51, 55, 80
Davi, Robert 149
David, Brad **121**
David Shapira & Associates 142
Davies, Marion 6
Davis, Glenn 34
Davis, Jim 31, 40, 84, 86
Davis, Sammy, Jr. 67, 70, 81, 130

Davis, Wray 98
Davison, Bruce 109, 110
Dawson, Richard 92
Day, Doris 40
Day of the Animals (1977) 138–140, 142, 147, 186
The Deadly Dream (1971) 106, 185
Dean, James 32
De Arakel, Zane W. 7
Death Dimension (1978) 146
Death Hunt (1981) 152
death scenes 13, 29, 30, 43–44, 47, 51, 61, 62, 63, 66, 67, 68, 79, 82, 84, 92, 95, 99, 103–105, 109, 120, 125, 126, 130, 132, 138, 154, 159
Death Takes a Holiday (1934) 21
Death Wish (1974) 153, 170
DeBroux, Lee 102
Dehner, John 154
De La Loma, Jose Antonio 159
Delano, Michael 113, *121*, 122
Delany, Dana 174
Deliverance (1972) 131, 136
Delon, Alain 93
Del Rio, Dolores 65
Delta Force 2—The Colombian Connection (1990) 172–173, 186
The Delta Fox (1979) 145, 186
Dennehy, Brian 155
Dennis, Nick 78
Denver, Colorado 51, 118–119
Derek, Bo 39
Derek, John 39, 70, 72, 81, 82–83, 102
Dern, Bruce 80, 93, 180
Desilu 62, 67
The Desperate Hours 45–46
Destructor 134
Detroit, Michigan 119
Deuel, Geoffrey 99
Deuel, Pete 93
Devane, William 145
The Devil's Brigade (1968) 90–92, 99, 106, 116, 123, 172, 185
Deyoung, Cliff 158
Diaz, Vic 143
Dickinson, Angie 153
Dierkop, Charles 159
Diesel, Vin 84
diet 8, 12, 19, 66, 96, 98, 101, 108, 116, 119, 146, 152, 157, 158, 159, 170, 181
Dillinger (1973) 113
Dillman, Bradford 123, 153
The Dirty Dozen (1967) 3, 60, 61, 65, 66, 87–90, 92, 93, 106, 143, 144, 162, 172, 180, 185
The Dirty Dozen: Next Mission (1985) 100, 162, 186
Dirty Harry (1971) 126

Dodge City (1939) 91
dogs 6, 108
Doheney 20
Donahue, Troy 173
Donlevy, Brian 30, 31, 32, 62
The Donna Reed Show 73
Donner, Richard 113
Donovan 19
Dorothy Chandler Pavilion 107
Douglas, Kirk 37, 69, 155
Douglas, Melvyn 138
Drago, Billy 172
Dragon Seed (1944) 13
Dragoon, Arizona 51
Drake, Charles 118
Drake Hotel 138
Drasin, Ric 135
Dream Slayer 154
Dreier, Alex 106
drinking 15, 41, 42, 73, 80, 85, 91, 92, 99, 105, 116, 117, 119, 120, 150, 159
drive-in movies 3, 64, 93, 120, 128, 130, 132, 139, 141, 152
The Drowning Pool (1975) 126–127, 185
drowning scene 103–104
Drury, James 79, 82–83, 103, 120, *121*, 182
Duffy, Patrick 159
Duggan, Andrew 111
DuMont Network 32
The Dungeon 54
DuPont, Ricky 81
Durango, Mexico 99, 114, 116
Durning, Charles 138
Duryea, Dan 45, 63, 64
Duryea, Peter 80
Duval, Henry 119
Duvall, Robert 81, 118
Duvall, Shelly 130
Dwan, Allan 25, 26, 74
Dye, Dale 27, 169, 170
Dylan, Bob 116, 117

Eastwood, Clint 70, 93, 111, 136, 146
Ebert, Roger 105, 118
Ebsen, Buddy 48–49
Edelman, Herb 106
Eden, Barbara 65
Edwards, Blake 42, 45
Edwards, Vince 32, 53, 54, 90, 92, 111, 120, 159
Egan, Richard 29
Eggert, Nicole 174
Ekberg, Anita 77
El Paso, Texas 55
Elam, Jack 59, 69, 74, 75, 77, 79, 86, 113, 114, 115, 117
Elcar, Dana 143
Electra, Carmen 174
Eleniak, Erika 174

The Elgin Hour 42, 45, 186
Elias, Louie 125
Ellery Queen 129. 187
Elliott, Biff 145–146, 164
Ely, Ron 82, 83, 155
Emergency 35, 110, 120, 121, 187
Emperor of the North (1973) 113
England 17, 88, 162
Erickson, Leif 106, 118
Escape from Alcatraz (1979) 146
Evans, Gene 29, 125
Evans, Linda 39, 102
Everett, Chad 74, 144, 154
exercise regimen 7, 8, 18, 33, 46, 60, 66, 92, 96, 98, 101, 108, 132, 134, 160, 168, 176, 181

Fairbanks, Jerry 32
The Falcon's Ultimatum (1979) 146, 186
Falk, Peter 151
fan club 13
fan magazines 13, 17, 18, 37, 41
The Fantastic Journey 137, 188
Fantasy Island 155, 188
Farewell, Friend (1968) 93
Farr, Jamie 48
Farrington, Jenna 103
The Fastest Gun Alive (1956) 42
fatherhood 17, 46–47, 108–109
Faulkner, Edward 99
The FBI 105–106, 120, 187
fear 166
fearlessness 134, 139, 155
Fenady, Andrew J. (A.J.) 66, 101, 176, 181
Fernandez, Peter 22, 23
Fiddler on the Roof (1971) 107
Fiedler, John 67–68, 113
Field, Sally 149
fight scenes 22, 25, 26, 32, 42, 50, 54, 55, 58, 60, 63, 66, 74, 75, 77, 78, 84, 85, 90, 91, 94, 102, 103, 105, 119, 132, 149, 154, 159
Fighting Coast Guard (1951) 30–32, 185
Film Ventures International 130, 131
financial struggles 17–18, 73, 83, 94, 106, 111, 122, 136, 140, 142–143, 152, 178
Finkelman, Kevin 154
Finnigan, Joe 72
Firecreek (1967) 85
Firehouse 79, 120–123, 187
Firehouse (1973) 111, 185
Fireside Theatre *see Jane Wyman Presents the Fireside Theatre*
First Blood (1982) 155
Fishgall, Gary 110
fishing 102, 155
Fishing Fever 155
fistfights 6, 16, 41

The $5.20 an Hour Dream (1980) 149, 186
The Fix (1984) 159, 186
Flaming Lance 64
Flaming Star (1960) 64–65, 185
Flaxman, Harvey 132
Flaxman, Vicki 80
Fletcher, Bill 91, 92
Flight see Panic
Floyd, Raymond 108
Flynn, Errol 8
Flynn, John 118
Fonda, Henry 45, 85, 102, 103, 104, 111, 113, 136, 181
football 6, 17, 25, 32, 101, 102, 172
For a Few Dollars More (1967) 93
Ford, Glenn 3, 42, 43, 51–52, 55, 56, 111, 146
Ford, John 25, 107
Ford, Ross 21
The Ford Television Theatre 42, 45, 186
Forrest, Frederic 150
Forrest, Steve 65
Forster, Robert 111
Fortier, Robert 41
Foster, Ben 51
Foster, Preston 9, 10
4 for Texas (1963) 61, 77–78, 185
Four Star Playhouse 41, 42, 186
Four Star Television 62
Fowley, Douglas 23
Fox and Hounds Hotel 164
Foy, Brian 8, 9, 13
Fragile Fox 48
Franciosa, Tony 126
Francis M. Smith 17
Francks, Don 85
Frank Cooper Association 67
Frankenheimer, John 50
Franz, Arthur 21, 26, 27
Frederick, Vicki *151*
Fremin, Jourdan 156
French, Victor 129, 142
The French Connection (1971) 107
Frey, Leonard 107
Friedkin, William 84
Fries, Charles 122
Front Page Detective 32, 186
Front Row Center 42, 45, 186
Frontier Circus 70–73, 80, 82, 187
frugality 6, 10, 41, 108, 157
The Fugitive 106
Fukasahu, Kenji 94
Fuller, Robert 4, 34–35, 73, 75, 110, 150, 155, 158, 179, 180
Fullmer, Don 91
Fulton, Rad 69
Funicello, Annette 80

Gabor, Eva 129
Gagnard, Frank 101
Gaines, Red 20, 22, 53
The Gallant Hours (1960) 64, 185
The Gang's All Here (1943) 10
Gardner, Arthur 176
Garfield, Brian 110
Garfield, John 59
Gargan, William 45
Garner, Don 48
Garner, James 41, 50–51, 70, 123, 157
Garnett, Tay 71
Garr, Teri 113
Gary, Lorraine 118
Gavin, John 84, 111
Gay, John 102
Gemini Man 136, 188
General Foods 60
George, Christopher 99, 101, 130, 131, 138, *139*
George, Lynda Day 106, 138, 139, 140
U.S.S. Georgetown 169
Ghetto Blaster (1989) 170–171, 186
G.I. Joe 22
Gidget 80
Gilliam, Burton 149
Gilman, Sam 103
Girard, Bill 13
Girdler, William 130, 138, 140
Gironda, Vince 135
Gish, Dorothy 45
Gist, Robert 57, 58
Gleason, Paul 169
Glover, Bruce 128
Go West, Young Girl (1978) 144, 186
The Godfather (1972) 149
Godfrey, Arthur 77
Godzilla 98
Gold, Joe 54, 135
The Gold Seekers (1969) 98
Golden Boot Awards 175–176
The Golden Oldie 99
Goldfinger (1964) 132
Gold's Gym 134, 135, 159, 176
golf 46–47, 78, 150, 159, 160
Golonka, Arlene 110
Goma 2 (1984) 159
Good Morning, America 164
The Good, the Bad, and the Ugly (1968) 93
Goodyear Playhouse 41, 186
Gordon, Bruce 66
Gordon, Don 85, 129, 146
Gordon, Leo 63
Gorgeous George 19
Gorilla Park 19
Gossett, Lou 129, 130
Gould, Harold 124
Grable, Betty 12
Grant, Lee 117
Graves, Peter 79, 106, 154
Gray, Lorna 31

The Gray Ghost 56, 186
The Great Escape (1963) 77
The Great Race (1965) 91
The Green Berets (1968) 59, 92
The Green Slime (1968) 94–98, 185
Greene, Clarence 60
Greene-Rouse 60
Greer, Jane 118
Grefe, William 132, 133, 181
Gregory, Paul 57
Griffith, Andy 144, *147*, 148
Griffith, James 39, 47
Griffith, Melanie 126
Grigg, Ricky 80
Grizzly (1976) 130–132, 142, 147, 185
Grossman, Milton 37
Grossman, Ted 30
Gruber, Frank 81
Guadalcanal Diary (1943) 3, 8, 9, 11, 12, 14, 18, 25, 32, 34, 35, 66, 91, 101, 113, 128, 170, 185
Guardino, Harry 118
Gulager, Clu 67, 74, 103
Gumley, Leonard 26, 27
Gun Fighter 134
The Gun Runners (1958) 59–60, 63, 185
The Gunfighter (1950) 3, 27–28, 35, 43, 82, 117, 171, 179, 185
Gunsmoke 19, 74, 75, 84–85, 91, 99, 110, 125, 142, 143, 171, 187
Guthrie, Woody 129

H. Jaeckel and Sons, Incorporated 5
Haade, William 31
Haas, Charles 63
Hal Roach Studios 48
Hale, Alan, Jr. 28, 48, 70
Hale, Jean 79
Hale, Nancy 41
Halloween II (1981) 173
Halsey, Brett 45
Hamilton, Anthony 161
Hamilton, Linda 166
Hamilton, Murray 126
Hammerhead 19
Hammett (1982) 150, 186
Hammett, Dashiell 150
Hammond, Nicholas 137
Hardwicke, Sir Cedric 13
Harper (1966) 126
Harris, Brad 54, 134–135, 181
Harris, Frank 55
Harris, Julius 145
Harris, Richard 107
Harrison, Gregory 144
Harrison's Landing 20
Hartman, David 124
Hartman, Paul 45
Harvey, Don 47

Index

Harvey School 45
Haskell, Jimmie 81
Haskell, Peter 120
Hasselhoff, David 171, 172, 174
Hatch, Clark 21, 33, 81, 96, 98, 108, 181
Hatch, Richard 170
Hatfield, Hurd 13
Hathaway, Henry 13
Have Gun—Will Travel 73–74, 99, 187
Hawaii 16, 20, 92, 93, 96, 146, 150, 158, 168, 173, 175
Hawaii 5-0 92
Hawaiian Eye 173
Hawks, Howard 62
Hayden, Sterling 37
Hayes, Helen 32, 38
Hayes, Joseph 45
Haynes, Linda 98, 126
Hays, Robert 154
Hays, Ron 86
Heflin, Van 32, 51
Hefner, Hugh 144
height 3, 7, 15, 37, 39, 50–51, 63, 78, 89, 95, 101, 122, 141, 158
Helfer, Ralph 73
Hell Is for Heroes (1962) 73
Hell's Kitchen, New York 41
Hellstrom, Gunnar 125
Hemingway, Ernest 59
Hemingway, Margaux 159
Hendrix, Wanda 39
Hensley, Pamela 137
Henner, Marilu 150
Herb Tobias Agency 107
Herbie Goes Bananas (1980) 149, 186
Here's Hollywood 72
The Heroin Conspiracy 119
The Heroin Syndicate 119
Heston, Charlton 37, 111
Hexum, Jon-Erik 161
Heyes, Douglas 55
Hickman, Dwayne 48
Higgins, Joel *147*, 148
Higgins, Michael 75
High Noon (1952) 125
Hilton, Pat 155, 165
Hindle, Art 137
Hitchcock, Alfred 67–68
Hodiak, John 23
Hoffman, Flippy 20
Hoffman, Herman 61
Hoffman, Walter 4, 20, 181
Holden, James 27
Holden, William 90, 93
Holiday Health Spas 134
Hollywood Athletic Club 8, 25
Hollywood Boulevard 19, 53
Hollywood High 7, 8, 12, 15, 66, 124
Hollywood Roosevelt Hotel 171

Holm, Celeste 160
Holman, Rex 75, 125
Holt, Tim 176
Homeier, Skip 28
Honda, Ishiro 98
Hong Kong 96, 119, 146
Honolulu, Hawaii 96
Hoodlum Empire (1952) 32, 185
Hooks, Robert 169
Hooper, Tobe 145
Hope, Harry 146
Hopper, Hedda 32
Hornung, Paul 91
horseback riding 29, 30, 41, 73, 110, 131, 141, 144, 152, 168
Horsley, Lee 155
Horton, Robert 32, *94*, 95
Horvath, Charles 64
Hot W.A.C.S. 153, 188
House of Shields 150
Houston, Texas 110
Howard, Clark 146
Howard, Rance 113, 134
Hoy, Robert 65
Hudson, Gary 176
Hudson, Rock 37, 142
Hughes, Howard 34
Hughes, Whitey 85
Hunt, Peter 152
Hunter, Jeffrey 79, 84
Hunter, Kim 124
Hunter, Tab 32
Huston, John 30
Hutton, Jim 129
Hyde Park 88

Imperial Palace 96
Inge, William 32
Insight 110, 149, 187, 188
Ireland, John 141, 145
Ironside 111, 187
Irving, Richard 67
Italy 17, 90, 91
Iverson Ranch 47

Jackson, Sherry 66
Jaeckel, Adelbert 7
Jaeckel, Antoniette (Toni) 17, 19, 22, 37, 38, 39, 46–47, 108, 110, 164, 178
Jaeckel, Barry 17, 19, 46, 72, 73, 78, 108–109, 117, 150, 159, 160, 172, 178, 180
Jaeckel, Dorothy Hanley 5, 19
Jaeckel, Evelyn 108, 179, 180
Jaeckel, H. Francis 5
Jaeckel, Hazel 11
Jaeckel, Hugo 5, 6
Jaeckel, Laura 168
Jaeckel, Millicent Hanley 5, 6, 9, 11, 12, 13, 17, 53
Jaeckel, Richard, Jr. 17, 19, 22, 46–47, 71, 108, 172, 178

Jaeckel, Richard, Sr. 5, 6, 7, 9, 41, 46
Jaeckel, Walter 5, 7
Jaeckel Building 5
Jaeckel Furs 5
Jagger, Dean 32, 45, 120
Jailhouse Rock (1957) 53, 65
Jane Eyre (1943) 10
Jane Wyman Presents The Fireside Theatre 42, 45, 186
Janis, Conrad 17
Janssen, David 106, 144
Japan 94–99, 119, 168
Jaws (1975) 130, 132, 140
Jaws with Claws 131
Jenson, Roy 65, 102, 113, 118
Jervis, Bill 119
Jigsaw John 130, 187
jobs 6, 7, 8, 10, 15
Joe Forrester 129, 187
U.S.S. *John F. Kennedy* 169
Johnson, Ben 84, 99, 101, 107, 113
Johnson, Erskine 18, 34, 39, 40
Johnson, Russell 80
Johnson, Van 13, 23, 142
Jones, Dickie 23, 26
Jones, Henry 51
Jones, L.Q. 3, 51, 57–59, 65, 84, 86, 114, 115–116
Jones, Tommy Lee 166
Jory, Victor 75
judo 30, 98
Jungle Patrol (1948) 21–22, 185
Jurado, Katy 115, 176

Kael, Pauline 58
Kanaly, Steve 159
Kane, Joseph 30, 31, 32, 39
Karloff, Boris 93
Karnes, Bob 17
Katzin, Lee 163
Katzman, Lenny 160
Kaufman, Albert 80
Kaufmann, Christine 69
Keach, Stacy 146
Keaton, Diane 106
Keith, Brian 42, 43, 70, 144, 150, 180
Keith, Robert 56
Kellerman, Sally 107
Kelley, Barry 39
Kelley, DeForest 81
Kelly, Jack 50
Kelly, Paul 40
Kelsey, Linda 149
Kemper Open 108
Kendo 96, 98, 152
Kennedy, Douglas 39
Kennedy, George 87, 90, 101, 150, 180
Kenpo 96
Kern River 158, 159
Kernville, California 158

Index

Kerouac, Jack 41
Kesey, Ken 101, 102, 136
Key West, Florida 59
Keymas, George 47
The Kill (1973) 119–120, 143, 185
The Killers (1964) 74
Killers Die Hard 134
Killing Machine (1984) 159, 186
Kincaid, Clarence L. 37
King, Annabel 101
King, Henry 17, 27, 28, 33
The King of the Kickboxers (1990) 173, 186
King Surf 74, 78
King's Crossing 153, 188
Kingston: Confidential 137, 188
Kirkland, Jack 41
Kit Carson and the Mountain Men (1977) 137, 186
Kjellin, Alf 106
Kleiner, Dick 64, 77, 96, 105
Klugman, Jack 45, 113
Knight, Shirley 163
Knight Rider 172
Knowles, Patric 92, 99
Knox, Mickey 21, 22, **23**
Kober, Jeff 174
Kohner, Frederick 20
Korzeniowski, Tom 96
Korzeniowski, Toshi 96
Koslo, Paul 126
Kotcheff, Ted 155
Kozsewski, Irwin "Zabo" 54
Kraft Theatre 42, 186
Krasny, Paul 144
Kratzenstein, Elly 5
Kristofferson, Kris 114, 115, 116, 117
Krumpler's 19
Kubrick, Stanley 95
Kurosawa, Akira 64
Kwan, Nancy 146
Kwasizur, Craig 179

Laborteaux, Matthew 153
Ladd, Alan 37, 38
Ladd, Cheryl 137
Ladd, Chris 128
Lafayette, Louisiana 126
Laguna Beach, California 20
La Jolla, California 19, 20
LaLanne, Jack 4, 18
Lambert, Jack 70, 77, 117
Lancaster, Burt 3, 32, 33, 34, **35**, 109, 110, 111, 137, 138, 142
Landham, Sonny 162
Landon, Laurene **151**
Landon, Michael 62, 70, 80–81, 129, 153, 180
Lang, Richard 146
Lansbury, Angela 168, 169
Laramie 35, 73, 155
Larken, Shelia 153

Las Vegas, Nevada 85, 109
Lasswell, Mary 41
The Last Day (1975) 125, 185
The Last Picture Show (1971) 107
The Last Sunset (1961) 69
La Starza, Roland 80
Latitude Zero (1969) 98, 185
Lauter, Ed 123
Lauter, Harry 21
Laven, Arnold 176
Lavin, Linda 149
Lawman 67, 187
Lawrence, Marc 81
Lawson, Linda 102
lawsuit 10–11
Lazenby, George 146
Leachman, Cloris 70
leading roles 37, 39, 40, 69, 70, 72, 74, 76, 94–95, 97, 98, 119, 132, 134, 145, 158, 159
LeBell, Gene 78
LeBorg, Reginald 29
Lehi, Utah 90
Leigh, Janet 106
LeMat, Paul 111
Lemmon, Jack 55, 56
Lentz, Robert J. 49, 89
Leonard, Elmore 51
Leone, Sergio 93
LeRoy, Mervyn 13
Levi, Alan J. 144, 154
Levy, Jules V. 176
Lewis, Geoffrey 136
Leyte 16
liability insurance 173, 174
lifeguarding 8, 25, 35, 171, 179
Linder, Milton 37
The Lineup (1958) 56–57, 58, 59, 185
Little Big Man (1970) 162
Little Caesar (1930) 38
Little House on the Prairie 129–130, 153, 187, 188
Little League 46, 172
Live and Let Die (1973) 132
live TV 41–42, 45
Lloyd, Frank 39
Lloyd, Harold, Jr. 63
Lloyd, Norman 68
Locke, Jon 125
Lockwood, Gary 84, 85, 137
Loew, Arthur 80, 101
Loftin, Carey 65–66
Loggia, Robert 141
London, Jack 16
London, England 88, 89, 90
Lone Pine, California 43
The Lone Ranger 40
Long, Richard 7
Long Barn, California 140
Long Beach, California 5, 169, 171
Long Island, New York 5
The Longest Yard (1974) 123

Lopez, Trini 90
Lord, Jack 93
The Lotion King 12
Lou Grant 149, 188
Louis B. Mayer Theatre 182
Love, Matt 102
Love, American Style 112
The Love Boat 160, 188
The Love Bug (1968) 149
love scenes 34, 35, 143
Love That Bob 48
Lowe, Edmund 32
Lowe, Lucas 173
Loyola High 47, 116
Lucas Tanner 124, 187
Lugosi, Bela 8
Luke, Jorge 110
Luke and the Tenderfoot 61, 187
Lux Radio Theatre 14
Lyden, Pierce 176
Lyles, A.C. 76, 77, 81, 82, 125, 176
Lynch, Richard 145
Lynn, Diana 49
Lyon, Andy 176
Lyon, Francis D. 77
Lyon, Tim 4, 19, 20, 22, 25, 37, 41, 44–45, 61, 78, 80, 120, 176, 181–182

Macao 119
MacArthur, James 92
MacDonald, Ross 126
MacKenna's Gold (1969) 118
MacLaine, Shirley 102
MacLane, Barton 39, 81
Macon County Line (1974) 162
The Magnificent Seven (1960) 64, 77
Mahoney, Jock 4, 73, 82, 83, 155, 156
Mailer, Norman 57
Major Dundee (1965) 84
The Making of Sands of Iwo Jima 26
Mako 170
Mako: The Jaws of Death (1976) 132–134, 147, 185
Malden, Karl 28, 117
Malibu, California 9, 20, 60, 61, 80, 101, 140, 163, 181
Maltin, Leonard 26, 27, 28, 69, 105, 154
A Man Called Hawk 163
Man Without a Gun 55, 186
Maniac 141
Manila 143
Mann, Daniel 33, 35
Manor, Wayne 98
Mantee, Paul 138, 140
Mara, Adele 31
Marches, John 22
Margie (1946) 17, 28, 33
Margolis, Gerald 178

Marie, Rose 171
Marina Del Rey, California 168
The Mark (1961) 12
Markham, Monte 174
marriage 17, 37–38, 39, 46, 86, 108, 109, 178
Marshall, E.G. 69
Marshall, William 138
martial arts 96, 97–98, 119, 132, 134
Martial Outlaw (1990) 176, 186
Martin, Dean 62, 77, 78
Martin, Dewey 23, 32, 49
Martin, Quinn 106, 112, 113, 129, 146
Martin, Strother 55, 86
Martinson, Leslie H. 79
Marvin, Lee 3, 41, 45, 48–49, 60–61, 63, 65, 73, 74, 80, 86, 87, 89, 90, 93, 152, 155, 162, 163, 168, 172
Marvin, Pamela 163
*M*A*S*H** (1970) 156
Masquerade 160–161, 188
Massey, Raymond 57, 59
Mate, Rudolph 42, 63
Matheson, Tim 125
Matinee Theatre 42, 49, 186
Matt Houston 155, 188
Maud, Texas 41
Maverick 50, 70
Maxwell, Marilyn 106
May, Lenora 149
Mayberry, Russ 149
Mazurki, Mike 63, 77, 78
MCA 77
McCall, Joan 131–132
McCall, Tom 102
McCallister, Lon 17
McCarey, Leo 32
McClain's Law 153, 188
McCloud 136, 186
McClure, Doug 79, 80, 155, 180
McCord, Kent 154
McCroskey, John 15
McDowall, Roddy 93
McEntee, Cindy 103
McEveety, Bernard 66
McEveety, Vincent 85, 125, 137, 149, 181
McGavin, Darren 111
McGrath, Frank 73, 74
McGraw, Charles 113, 138
McHugh, Matt 13
McIntire, John 65
McKinney, Bill 118, 136
McLaglen, Andrew V. 74, 75, 90, 91, 99–101, 116, 162, 163
McLaglen, Victor 45, 100
McLarty, Ron 164, *165*, 167
McLaughlin, Big John 134
McLintock! (1963) 90, 99
McMullan, James 72

McNally, Stephen 22, *29*, 80
McNichol, Jimmy 147
McQueen, Steve 64, 69, 70, 73, 142
McRaney, Gerald 137
McVeigh, Eve 86
Medina, Patricia 98
Meeker, Ralph 87, 89
Melbourne, Florida 38
Memphis, Tennessee 119
Men in War (1957) 59
Merchant Marine 12, 15–17, 168
Merlin, Jan 76
Metty, Russell 29
Mexico City, Mexico 123
Meyer's Misfits 91
MGM 13, 23, 24, 30, 38, 53, 54, 63, 79, 87, 88, 94, 114, 115, 117, 118, 151
Miami, Florida 119, 132, 134
Michaels, Corrine 149
Michener, James 148
Midas Muffler 150
The Mighty O 48, 187
Mike Hammer 145
Miles, Sylvia 150
Miles, Vera 70
Milestone, Lewis 62
military roles 11, 25, 27, 86, 91–92, 105, 140
Miller, Ann 176
Miller, Kristine 21
Miller, Denny 74
The Millionaire 48, 61, 186, 187
Mills, Donna 113, 143
Mills, Mort 55
Milner, Martin 26, 30, 32
Mintz, Fred 141
Mishkin, Meyer 86, 88, 91, 93
Mission—Impossible 106, 187
Mr. Muscle Beach 47
Mitchell, Gordon 54
Mitchell, Millard 28
Mitchum, Robert 53, 77, 171, 180
Moberly, Dan 158–159
Moby Dick 152
Mohr, Hal 22
Monroe, Tom 48
Montalbon, Ricardo 23, 111, 155
Montana, Montie 116
Montgomery, Elizabeth 72
Montgomery, George 61
Montgomery, Robert 49, 64
Montoro, Ed 145
Montoya, Alex 47
Montreal, Quebec, Canada 119
Moore, Helen 62
Moore, Terry 32, *33*, 34, *35*, 63, 64, 81
Moorehead, Agnes 111
Morella, Joe 102, 126
Morgan, Henry 125
Morgan, Read 54, 75–76, 84, 129, 181

Mormactern 15–16, 43
Morrow, Jeff 42
Morrow, Vic 79
Mo's Annex 103, 154
Mosby, Aline 38, 46
Moses, Rick 142
Mostel, Josh 156
Motion Picture Home 179, 180, 181
Movin' On 124, 187
Muldaur, Diana 123
Muller, Eddie 56
Munich, Germany 138
Murder She Wrote 168–169, 188
Murphy, Audie 30, 32, 37, 39, 59
Murphy, Ben 136, 155
Murphy, George 23
Murphy, William "Billy" 19, 20, 21–22, 23, 25, *26*, 27, 30, *31*, 32, 37, 41, 53, 54, 171
Musante, Tony 124
Muscle Beach 18–19, 47, 54, 75, 135, 160, 171, 178, 180, 181
Museum of Television and Radio 45
Musso and Franks 146
The Mutilator 145
My Reminisces 55
My Son John (1952) 32, 185

Naish, J. Carroll 61
The Naked and the Dead (1958) 57–59, 185
Naked City 62, 66, 187
The Name of the Game 93, 187
Napier, Charles 106, 143
Nathanson, E.M. 88
Naughton, David 156
Navy Log 54, 186
NBC 113, 145, 172, 174
Neary, Thomas 7
Needham, Hal 74, 75, 91, 100
Nelson, Dennis 47
Nelson, Ed 66
Nelson, Gary 124, 148
Nelson, John Allen **175**
Nelson, Ricky 62
Never Give an Inch (1970)
Nevil, Steve 156
New Orleans, Louisiana 17, 119, 126
The New Phil Silvers Show 78, 80, 187
New York Athletic Club 7, 41
New York City 22, 41, 62, 75, 89, 111, 119, 121
Newman, Anne 140
Newman, Barry 124
Newman, Joe 21
Newman, Paul 44, 45, 69, 101–102, 103, **104**, 136, 141, 142, 170, 181
Neworth, Jack 136

Newport, Oregon 101, 102, 154
Newport Beach, California 59, 182
Nichols, Barbara 58
nicknames 6, 12, 99
Nielsen, Leslie 138
Night Must Fall 49
Nightmare in the Sun (1965) 81, 185
Nixon, Richard M. 146
No Toys for Christmas 82
No Warning see *Panic*
Nogales, Arizona 109
Nolan, Lloyd 9, 10, 84
Noonan, Tom 21, 23
Norfolk, Virginia 169
Norma Rae (1979) 149
Norris, Aaron 172
Norris, Chuck 172
North, Sheree 118
North Bend, Oregon 154
Notre Dame Victory 17
nudity 82, 115

Oahu, Hawaii 175
Oates, Warren 84, 93, 140
Oblath's 66
Obregon, Ana 159
O'Brian, Hugh 30
O'Brien, Edmund 39
O'Brien, Margaret 45
O'Brien, Pat 45, 81, 84, 113
Oceanside, California 9
O'Connor, Carroll 92
O'Day, Anita 118
Ogilvie, Joe 73
O'Hara, Maureen 113
O'Hara, United States Treasury 106, 187
O'Herlihy, Gavin 162
Okinawa 17
Olandt, Ken 169
Old Tucson Studios 51, 144
Oliver, Susan 74, 93
O'Malley, J. Pat 70
On the Road 41
Once Before I Die (1965) 82–84, 92, 95, 98, 178, 185
Once Upon a Time in the West (1969) 93
O'Neill, Jennifer 161
Open de France 108
The Oregon Trail 143, 188
O'Sullivan, Maureen 45
Oswald, Gerd 80
The Outer Limits 78, 79–80, 187
The Outfit (1973) 118, 119, 136, 185
The Outlaw Josey Wales (1976) 136
The Overlords 140
Overton, Bill **121**
Ozzie and Harriet 62, 73

Pacific Coast Highway 10, 159
Pacific Inferno (1978) 143–144, 186
Pacific Palisades 17, 46, 159
Paint Your Wagon (1969) 93
Palace Hotel 96
Palance, Jack 42, 48–49, 80, 150
Palisades High 47
Palladium 17
Palmer, Gregg 137, 144
Paluzzi, Luciana 94, 95
Panama 57, 59
Panic! 55, 56, 186, 187
Pantoliano, Joe 153
Paramount Pictures 32, 36, 38, 54, 66, 76, 81, 106, 125, 153, 154
Paris, Jerry 57, 58
Paris, France 5
Parke, Henry C. 141
Parker, Earl 79
Parker, Ed 96
Parker, Jean 28
Parker, Robert B. 163, 164
Parks, Michael 149
Parsons, Louella 6, 8
Partners in Crime (1973) 117–118, 185
Pat Garrett and Billy the Kid (1973) 93, 113–117, 118, 119, 185
Patrick's Roadhouse 159
Paul, Alexandra 175
Paull, Morgan 137, 138
Payne, Julie 153
Peary, Danny 83
Peck, Gregory 27, 28, 35, 43, 62, 111, 117, 121, 171, 179
Peckinpah, Sam 84, 93, 114, 115, 116, 117, 152
Pedersen, Eric 30
Pendleton, Chuck 54
Penn, Leo 24
Pennell, Larry 7, 124
Peppard, George 62, 69, 120, 180
Perry Mason 74, 76, 84, 143, 187
Peters, Erika 67
Petersen, Pat 154
The Petrified Forest 45, 186
Petrocelli 110, 124, 187
Peyser, John 67
Pfannkuche, Carol 180
Philippines 82–84, 98–99, 140, 143, 144, 146, 168, 172, 178
Phillips, Mackenzie 124
Phillips, Robert 4, 59–60, 63, 85, 88, 89, 113, 140–141, 181, 182
Phipps, William 16, 42–43
Phoenix, Arizona 41, 141
physical limitations 174, 176, 178
Picerni, Paul 39
Pickens, Slim 84, 115
Pickford, Mary 6

The Picture of Dorian Gray 3, 66, 127
Pinson, Allen 30, 83
Pirosh, Robert 23
Pittsburgh, California 129
Platinum High School (1960) 63–64, 185
Platoon (1986) 169
Playhouse 90 42, 54, 186
Pleasence, Donald 144
Poggiali, Chris 4
Police Story 124, 129, 142, 186
Police Woman 159
Pollack, Sydney 71
Pork Chop Hill (1959) 62
Porter, Cal 20–21
Porter, Darwin 142
Portland, Oregon 102
potential roles 13, 17, 27, 30, 32, 37, 50, 52, 62, 64, 69, 73, 74, 80, 84, 92–93, 101, 113, 123, 129, 140, 146, 150, 152, 155, 156
Potts, Cliff 102, 142
Powell, Dick 42, 63
Preece, Michael 159–160
Presley, Elvis 53, 64–65, 171
Preston, Mike 98, 99
Prine, Andrew 90, 91, 92, 99, 101, 130, 131, 138
Prisoners of the Sea 156, 158
Pritchard, Dave 91
Private Benjamin (1980) 156
private nature 66, 108, 150, 178, 179
Producer's Showcase 42, 45, 186
professionalism 25, 28, 29, 33–34, 36, 38, 44, 75, 76, 77, 90, 98, 103, 113, 116, 122, 126, 128, 131, 132, 133, 137, 142, 143, 145, 146, 159, 160, 161, 162, 163, 164, 165, 166, 171, 182, 183
The Professionals (1966) 93
promotional appearances 31, 47, 50–51, 70, 96, 102, 110, 118–119, 120, 134, 138, 171
Pryor, Nicholas 149
Pryor, Richard 144
Public Defender 40, 186
Puerto Vallarta, Mexico 149
Pusser, Buford 127, 128
Pyle, Denver 79

Quade, John 136, 144
Queen Mary 171
Quinn, Anthony 10, **11**

Raffin, Deborah 141
Rainey, Ford 65
Ralston, Vera 32
Ramsen, Al 22, 23
Ramsey, Logan 125, 127
The Range Rider 40
Ransom 141

Rathbone, Basil 74
Rawhide 70
Ray, Aldo 57, 58, 59, 70, 81, 83, 146, 156
Raynor, Grace 62
Reagan, Ronald 73, 176
Reason, Rex 55
The Rebel 63, 66, 187
The Red Badge of Courage (1951) 30
The Red Pony (1973) 113, 119, 185
Red Skies of Montana (1952) 45
Redford, Robert 44, 69, 136
Redwing, Rodd 44
Reed, Oliver 141
Reed, Rex 181
Reed, Robert 137
Reese, Tom 65, 118
Reinhardt, Gottfred 69
Remick, Lee 102
Renegade Roundup 47
Rennie, Michael 63, 98
Reno, Nevada 70
Rensing, Violet 60
Report from Engine Company 82 111
Republic Pictures 25, 30, 31, 32, 39, 49, 61
residual payments 65, 84, 93, 122, 143, 150, 151, 174, 178
Retribution, C.O.D. 152
Revue 67, 68, 70, 71
Reward (1980) 149, 186
Reynolds, Burt 123
Reynolds, Gene 21
Rich Man, Poor Man 138
Richards, Jay 12, 47
Richards, Jeff 38, 61
Riemers, Charlie 80
The Rifleman 63
Rincon 20
Rio Bravo (1959) 62
Rio de Janeiro 17, 172
Rip Goes to War 13
Ritter, Tex 47
Ritter, Thelma 22
Rivero, George "Jorge" 159
Riviera Country Club 78, 108
RKO 34, 48, 57
Robards, Jason 115
Roberts, Clive 171
Roberts, Roy 10, 29, 39
Roberts, Tanya 150
Robertson, Cliff 57, 59, 90
Robertson, Dale 65
Robinson, Andrew 126–127, 149
Robinson, Chris 75
Robinson, Edward G. 38, 39, 42, 43, 118
Robinson, Roger 120
Robinson Crusoe on Mars (1964) 140
The Rockford Files 123

Rocco, Alex 149
Roddenberry, Gene 80
Rogers, Roy 40
Roley, Sutton 123
Roman, Ruth 39, 138
Rome, Italy 91
Romero, Cesar 98
Rondell, Ronnie 74, 75, 91, 118, 180
Rooney, Mickey 63, 70
Rosalie Stewart Agency 27
Rosenberg, Stuart 126
Ross, Leo 10, 15
Rothaker, Watterson R. 17
Roundtree, Richard 111, 120
Rudolph, Oscar 55
Rush, Barbara 70, 125
Ruskin, Joseph 62
Russell, John 30, 32
Russell, Kurt 173
Russo, James 153
Ryan, John P. 173
Ryan, Robert 87, 88, 118

sailing 46, 75
St. Cyr, Lilli 58
St. Louis, Missouri 119
St. Martin of Tours Catholic School 46, 172
Saipan 16
Sakata, Harold "Oddjob" 132, *133*
Salt Break 20
Salvage (1979) 147–148, 186
Salvage 1 66, 147, 161, 188
Sambrell, Aldo 159
samurai warrior 96, 98, 152
San Diego, California 9, 31, 64
San Francisco, California 15–16, 22, 45, 111, 140, 149, 150
San Onofre Beach 19, 20
San Onofre Surf Club 19
San Pedro, California 153
San Rosarito Beach 20
Sanderson, William 166
Sandor, Steve 106
Sands of Iwo Jima (1949) 3, 20, 25–27, **26**, 36, 53, 74, 92, 99, 101, 170, 171, 185
Santa Barbara, California 20
Santa Fe, New Mexico 55
Santa Monica, California 8, 20–21, 46, 145, 171
Santa Monica Boulevard 18
Santa Monica Junior College 108
Saranac Lake, New York 154
Sariego, Ralph 148
Sarmento, William 121
Sarrazin, Michael 102, 103, 105
Sarris, Andrew 110
Satloff, Ron 148
Saunders, Jay *147*
Saunders, Russ 54
Savalas, Telly 87, 89, 90

Saxon, John 113
Schaefer, Natalie 45
Scheider, Roy 107
Schlitz Playhouse 42, 186
Schow, David J. 79, 80
Schwab's 18
Schwarzenegger, Arnold 54, 135
Schweiber, Lew 8
Scott, Jacqueline 148
Scott, Vernon 108, 148
Screen Actors Guild 18, 64, 111, 151, 174
screen tests 9, 34, 57
scuba diving 74, 155–156
Scudda Hoo! Scudda Hay! 17
The Sea Hornet (1951) 31–32, 185
Sea Hunt 51, 134
Sea of Lost Ships (1953) 39, 40, 70, 185
Seaman's Union 15
Sears, Fred F. 47
Seattle, Washington 45
Sebastian, Beverly 145
Sebastian, Ferd 145
Seeger, Dan 146
Segal, Alex 42
Seiler, Lewis 10
Selander, Lesley 81
Selleck, Tom 176
Seltzer, Frank 21
Senensky, Ralph 110, 113
sense of humor 9, 36, 42, 65, 77, 86, 89, 104, 108, 110, 122, 123, 125, 135, 140, 156
Sgt. Bilko 80, 156
Serling, Rod 84
Seven Arts 59
Seven Samurai (1954) 64
77 Sunset Strip 65, 187
Shaft (1971) 111
Shaft (TV) 120, 187
Shane (1953) 42
Shane, Maxwell 22
The Shanghai Story (1954) 39–40, 185
Sharpe, Dave 29
Shatner, William 108, 143, 154, 155
shaved head 82, 90–91, 92
Sheffield, Johnny 20
Sheldon, David 131
Shelley, Joshua 22, 23
Ship of Sand 143
The Shootist (1976) 136
Shor, Dan 166
Shulman, Irving 22
Siegel, Don 3, 56, 57, 59, 60, 64, 65, 73, 74, 136, 146, 152
The Silent Service 54, 186, 187
Silvers, Phil 80, 156
Silvestre, Armando 29
Simpson, Mickey 55
Sinatra, Frank 77, 78
Sinclair, Charles 95

Index

Sip 'n' Surf 20, 38
Six Against the Rock 146
Skarstedt, Vince 98
Skerritt, Tom 125
skin care products 12, 178
skin diving 16, 19, 20, 46, 75, 144
Slate, Jeremy 76, 84, 85, 90, 91, 92
Slinker, Ron 134, **135**
Small Soldiers (1998) 180
Smight, Jack 118
smile 3, 8, 72, 73
Smith, Alexis 29
Smith, Charles Martin 161
Smith, Dennis 111
Smith, John 61
Smith, Tom 12
Smith, William 4, 54, 86, 123, 137, 138, 156, 169, 180
Smithers, William 48
Smoke Jumpers 45, 186
smoking 11, 30
Snyder, Arlen Dean 173
Soft Tissue Center 173
Soldier Girls 153
Sombrero Playhouse 41
Something Is Out There 138
Sometimes a Great Notion (1970) 3, 101–105, 106, 107, 122, 124, 126, 128, 136, 141, 147, 154, 170, 171, 172, 181, 182, 185
Sondock, Mal **68**, 69
The Song of Bernadette (1943) 10
Sonora, California 140
Speedtrap (1977) 141, 186
Spelling, Aaron 157
Spenser: For Hire 3, 66, 163–165, 167, 168, 169, 176, 181, 188
Spenser: For Hire (1985) 186
Spielberg, Stephen 130, 132
Spillane, Mickey 129, 145
Springsteen, Alice 176
Springsteen, R.G. 62
squib shots 82
Stack, Robert 67, 107–108, 111
Stader, Paul 30
stage productions 41, 45–46, 84
Stagecoach (1939) 25
Stahl, Doug 12
Stallone, Sylvester 155
Standard Oil 17
Stander, Lionel 10
Stanley, Paul 129
Stanton, Harry Dean 117, 140
Stanwyck, Barbara 42, 43
Star Trek 80, 108, 143, 155
Star Wars (1977) 145
Starline Celebrity Tours 171
Starman (1984) 141, 148, 160, 161, 186
Starr, Eve 42
Stearns Hotel 7
Steele, Bob 81
Stefano, Joseph 79

Steinbeck, John 113
Stevens, Andrew 138, 140
Stevens, Craig 48, 111
Stevens, Inger 75
Stevens, Leslie 79
Stevens, Stella 70
Stevens Cup Wrestling Trophy 7
Stevenson, Adlai 60
Stevenson, Parker 172
Stewart, Alan L. 171
Stewart, James 85, 180
Stewart, Trish **147**, 148
Stock, Barbara 163
Stockwell, Dean 129
Stone, Oliver 169
Stoney (1969) 98, 185
Stories of the Century 40, 186
The Story of G.I. Joe (1945) 22
Stout, Bonnie 103, 154
Strauss, Robert 48–49
Strength & Health 47
Strickland, Gail 126
Stripes (1981) 156
Strode, Woody 111
Stroud, Don 106, 173
studio contracts 10, 12, 13, 36, 38
Studio 57 see *Jane Wyman Presents the Fireside Theatre*
stuntmen 18, 20–21, 30, 43, 51, 54, 65–66, 73, 85, 92, 102, 110, 159, 168
stunts 51, 78, 91, 119, 127, 130, 133, 139, 141, 145, 172
Sturges, John 64, 176
Suds in Your Eye 41
Sullivan, Barry 54–55
Sullivan, Fred G. 154
Summer Dreams: The Story of the Beach Boys (1990) 173
Summers, Neil 110
Sunset Boulevard 8, 12, 172
Sunset Strip 6, 92
Supercarrier 169–170, 188
Supercarrier: Deadly Enemies (1988) 186
The Surabaya Conspiracy (1969) 98–99
surfing 16, 19–20, 74, 75, 79, 80, 93, 168, 173, 180, 181, 182
Suspense 74, 187
Sutherland, Donald 88, 90
Sutton, Frank **68**, 69
Svenson, Bo 113, **127**, 128
Swackhammer, E.W. 149
Swanson, Gloria 6
Swenson, Karl 65
Sweeney, Joe 45
swimming 7, 16, 46, 73, 101, 132, 172
Swit, Loretta 125

Tail of the Cock 38
Tales of Wells Fargo 65, 187

The Tall Man 67, 103, 187
Tallahassee Open 108
Tambor, Jeffrey 158
Tampa, Florida 134
Tanny, Armand 54, 75
Tanny, Vic 18
Taylor, Buck 125
Taylor, Don 23
Taylor, Dub 115, 137
Taylor, Rod 50, 62, 143, 160
Taylor-Young, Leigh 136
Tea for Three 5
Teal, Ray 47
Temple Houston 78, 79, 187
Tennessee 128, 172
Terry and the Pirates 32
Tessier, Robert 159
The Texan 61–62, 187
The Texas Chainsaw Massacre (1974) 145
Thailand 173
They Seek Adventure 49, 186
thievery 66
Thirty Seconds Over Tokyo (1944) 13
Thomas, Bob 18
Thompson, J. Lee 118
Thompson, Marshall 23, 49
Thorson, Russell 62
The Three Stooges 77
3:10 to Yuma (1957) 3, 50, 51–52, 55, 58, 64, 82, 144, 185
3:10 to Yuma (2007) 51
Thunder in the East (1952) 37
Tightrope 60, 63, 66, 106, 187
Tijuana, Mexico 17, 20
Till the End of Time (1946) 22
Tilton, Charlene 159
The Time Tunnel 86, 187
To Have and Have Not (1944) 59
To Hell and Back (1955) 30
Toho Studios 94
Toledo, Oregon 102
Toluca Lakes, California 73
Tompkins, Angel 105, 128
The Tonight Show 123
Top Gun (1986) 169
Torn, Rip 70, 154
Toronto, Ontario, Canada 119
Torpedo Squadron 8 13
Torrey, Roger 81
Totten, Robert 113
Tournament Players Championship 108
Towers, Constance 175
Town Tamer (1965) 81–82, 185
Town Without Pity (1961) 3, 68, 69, 80, 130, 153, 185
Trackdown 62, 187
The Train Robbers (1973) 113
Tregaskis, Richard 8
Tremayne, Les 64
Trent, Buzzy 80

Trevor, Claire 32
Triola, Michelle 162
Trouble at Sixteen 64
Troupe, Tom 91, 92
Trowbridge, Charles 13
Tucker, Forrest 25, 27, 30, **31**, 32, 99, 101
Tucson, Arizona 96, 124, 163, 168
Tully, Tom 39
Turich, Felipe **29**
Turner, Lana 18
TV commercial 150
TV Guide 72
TV pilots 48, 49, 61, 74, 111, 117, 123, 144, 148, 149, 153, 164, 169, 171, 172
Twelve O'Clock High (1949) 27
20th Century Fox 8, 10–14, 17, 18, 21, 27, 55, 65
20th Century Fox Hour 42, 45, 186
Twilight's Last Gleaming (1977) 137–138, 186
Twitty, Conway 63
2001: A Space Odyssey (1968) 95
Tyler, Dick 19, 181
typecasting 48, 111, 112, 130, 131, 138, 163, 170

UCLA 46, 74
Ulzana's Raid (1972) 109–110, 119, 185
Unemployment Office 73, 140
United Artists 68, 90
U.S. Coast Guard 15, 30, 39, 48
U.S. Marine Corps 25, 170
U.S. Navy 12, 15, 16, 31, 43, 169, 170
Universal 22, 28–29, 30, 37, 48, 70, 71, 72, 73, 74, 75, 79, 93, 104, 106, 107, 109, 110, 113, 117, 145
The Untouchables 67, 187
Urich, Robert 163, 164, 167
The U.S. Steel Hour 42, 186
USA Network 132
USC 21, 108

Vacation Playhouse 61
Vadis, Dan 54
Valentine, Karen 144
Valley of Fire, Nevada 109
Van Nuys, California 152
Van Cleef, Lee 93, 117, 150, 159
Vanders, Warren 125
Vargas, John 156
Vasquez Rocks 74, 80, 85
Vaughn, Robert 64, 144, 166
Venice Beach, California 176
Ventura County, California 76
Verne, Jules 98
Vernon, John 149, 154
Verrell, Cec 169

Vic Tanny's Health Club 178
Vignon, Jean-Paul 92
villains 22, 42, 43, 51, 55, 62, 63, 72, 93, 99, 105, 106, 112, 124, 131
Vincent, Jan-Michael 146
Ving, Lee 68, 166
Vint, Bill 106
Vint, Jesse 161, 162
violence 82, 115
The Violent Men (1955) 42–43, 47, 51, 53, 64, 82, 185
The Virginian 78, 79, 120, 122, 187
Vitaphone 49
Vogel, Virgil W. 68
Voight, Jon 101
volleyball 20–21, 54
Vollrath, Ted 134

wages 9, 13, 38, 55, 59, 65, 70, 76, 81, 82, 86, 88, 93, 96, 109, 110, 111, 144
Wagon Train 35, 68, 70, 72, 73, 74, 94, 187
Wahl, Ken 162
Waikiki, Hawaii 16
Walker, Clint 63, 87, 88–89, 90, 180
Walker, Jimmie 156
Walker, Robert 32
Walking Tall Part II (1975) 127, 128, 147, 185
Wallach, Eli 56, 118
Walsh, Ann 180
Walsh, Raoul 57–59, 80
Walt Disney 124, 137, 149
Walter, Jessica 113
Wambaugh, Joseph 124
Wanted—Dead or Alive 70
war films 48, 170
Warden, Jack 41, 45, 67, 80, 130, 146
Warlock, Billy 175
Warlock, Dick 173, 175, 180
Warner Bros. 50, 58, 66, 74, 79, 100, 106, 112, 158, 164, 165
Warren, Jennifer 147
Wasatch Mountain 90
Washington, Judy 119
Washington, D.C. 39, 119
Watson, Jack 92
Watson, Minor 32
Watson, William 146
Way, Guy 56
Wayne, David 142
Wayne, John 3, 8, 12, 25–26, 27, 36, 53, 59, 62–63, 92, 99, 100, 101, 113, 116, 117, 136, 142, 163, 170
Weaver, Dennis 64, 136, 144
Webb, Richard 26, 27
Webber, Robert 41, 80, 87, 113

Weber, Suzanne 154
Weider, Joe 135
weightlifting 18, 33, 53–54, 60, 73, 96, 101, 132, 168, 180
Weissmuller, Johnny 8
Wellman, William 23
Wells, David 161
Wenders, Wim 150
Wendkos, Paul 158
Wessel, Dick 48
West, Red 143
West of Tomorrow 21
West Point 54, 186
Westcott, Helen 28
Westerfield, James 42
westerns 30, 73, 99, 105, 140, 144, 168, 175–176
Westlake, Donald 118
Westwood, California 19, 145
When Hell Broke Loose (1958) 60, 89, 185
Whiskey Mountain (1977) 133
White Plains, New York 5
Whitman, Stuart 7, 12–13, 50, 53, 62, 141, 144, 145
Whitmore, James 23
Widmark, Richard 50, 117, 125, 138
Wiener, Dick 102
Wiesbaden, Germany 5
Wilcox, Larry 162
The Wild Bunch (1969) 93, 115
The Wild Wild West 85, 187
Wilde, Cornel 169
Wilde, Oscar 66
Wilder, John 144, 163, 164, 167, 176, 181
Wilke, Bob 70
Wilkes, Donna 154
Will, Sandra 144
Williams, Bill 47
Williams, Les 20
Williams, Van 80
Williams College 5
Wills, Chill 31, 70, 72, 107, 115, 117
Wills, Henry 176
Wilmington, North Carolina 159
Wilshire Retirement Center 178
Wilson, Terry 73
Wincott, Jeff 176
Windansea 20
Windsor, Marie 118
Winfield, Paul 137
Wing and a Prayer (1944) 13, 185
Wire Service 186
Withers, Grant 31, 32
Witherspoon, Cora 41
Witney, William 40, 71
The Wizard of Oz (1939) 8
Wolf Creek 17
Wolff, Rodd 141
Wolper, David L. 91

The Wonderful World of Disney 137
Wong, Sam 6
Wood, Lana 141
Wooden, John 46
Woodland Hills, California 179, 180
Woods, Tiger 73
Woodward, Joanne 102, 126
Woodward, Morgan 86, 125–126, 141
Wooley, Sheb 176
work ethic 6, 10, 22, 76, 163, 166
World Gym 135, 166, 168
World War II service 15–17
Wrye, Donald 123
Wurtzel, Paul 9, 106
Wurtzel, Sol 9
Wyner, George 156, 157–158
Wynn, Keenan 81, 145, 146
Wyoming Mail (1950) 29, 185

Yaquina Bay, Oregon 104
Yates, Herbert 32
YMCA 6, 7, 41
York, Dick 55
U.S.S. *Yorktown* 13
Young, Burt 137
Young, Jack N. 144
Young, James 32
Young, John Sacret 147, 174
Young, Robert 108
The Young and the Brave (1963) 76–77, 185
Young Billy Young (1969) 171
Young Dan'l Boone 142
The Young Philadelphians (1959) 64

Zane Grey Theater 63, 187
Zendar, Fred 30, 105
Zens, Will 159
Zerbe, Anthony 144
Zimbalist, Efrem, Jr. 66, 106
Ziv 61

www.ingramcontent.com/pod-product-compliance
Lightning Source LLC
Chambersburg PA
CBHW081557300426
44116CB00015B/2913